THE
VERY RICH BOOK

Jacqueline Thompson

THE
VERY RICH BOOK

America's Supermillionaires and

Their Money—Where They Got It,

How They Spend It

by
Jacqueline Thompson

WILLIAM MORROW AND COMPANY, INC.
New York   1981

Library of Congress Cataloging in Publication Data

Thompson, Jacqueline.
   The very rich book.

   Bibliography: p.
   1. Millionaires—United States—Biography.
I. Title.
HG172.A2T48   973′.09′92 [B]   80-21618
ISBN 0-688-00072-X

Printed in the United States of America

First Edition

1 2 3 4 5 6 7 8 9 10

BOOK DESIGN BY MICHAEL MAUCERI

*   *   *

The author would like to express her gratitude for permission to reprint passages from the following books and magazine articles:

The Rich and the Super-Rich, Copyright © 1968 by Ferdinand Lundberg, published by arrangement with Lyle Stuart, Inc., Secaucus, N.J.

The Protestant Establishment, by E. Digby Baltzell. Copyright © 1964 by E. Digby Baltzell. Quoted with permission of Random House, New York.

The Higher Circles, by G. William Dumhoff. Copyright © 1970 by G. William Dumhoff. Quoted with permission of Random House, New York.

The Money Motive, by Thomas Wiseman. Copyright © 1974 by Thomas Wiseman. Quoted with permission of Random House, New York.

Excerpt from "How to Tell Old Money From New Money," by Lewis H. Lapham; WRAPAROUND section, *Harper's* magazine, November 1973. Also, excerpt from WRAPAROUND, "Liberty, Fraternity, etc." by Gerald

*To William—my harshest critic,
my biggest supporter, and my best friend.*

CONTENTS

CONTENTS

Who is the rich man?
He who is satisfied with what he has.
—T<small>ALMUD</small>

INTRODUCTION

Money is power. Money is security. Money is freedom.

"Money is like a sixth sense—and you can't make use of the other five without it," according to Somerset Maugham.

That's the positive side of the golden coin. Those taking the negative view maintain that money in great quantity corrupts, isolates, and saddens. As Stewart Alsop put it, "Having that invisible dollar sign hovering over his head tends to hedge a Very Rich man off from his fellows as divinity doth hedge a king."

The wealthy Americans—by "wealthy" I mean those worth at least $50 million—profiled in this book are as confused about money and its value as the rest of us. Their opinions about money range from very enthusiastic (particularly if they've made it themselves) to obsessively guilt-ridden (if they've inherited it).

To a "self-made man," money is a gauge of how well he's played "the game." Entrepreneurs keep score by comparing the size of their pile with that of the next guy. In contrast, an heir or heiress often views his or her inherited fortune as a symbol of inferiority, a gnawing reminder that daddy or granddaddy was the dynamo. What have they achieved by comparison?

In reality, the super-rich undergo the best and the worst of all possible worlds. While they encounter life's usual milestones—births, deaths, marriages—they bear some additional millstones as well. Burglars, kidnappers, extortionists, fortune hunters, greedy relatives and, of course, the Internal Revenue Service are the burden of their lot, not to mention those interminable jokes propagated by the media which stereotype all rich people as ruthless moneygrubbers (dishonest, of course), vacant playboys, senile eccentrics, social-climbing *nouveaux riches*, superficial culture vultures, domineering tightwads, or antisocial tax evaders.

Maybe the first Henry Ford, the auto tycoon, gave the most accurate description of the experience of being rich. Asked to pinpoint money's major drawback, he paused and said, "For me it was the day Mrs. Ford quit cooking."

WHO THEY ARE

I

THE TEN RICHEST AMERICANS
AND HOW THEY GOT THAT WAY

Benjamin Franklin got it right when he said nothing is more certain than death and taxes—certain to dissipate a family fortune, that is. The proof lies in the most current list of the United States' ten wealthiest citizens. With the deaths of such supermillionaires as J. Paul Getty, H. L. Hunt, John D. MacArthur, and Howard Hughes, a new hand has been dealt in the nation's plutocratic poker game, and some relatively unknown people now comprise the winners' circle.

You may be surprised to learn that, with the exception of a Mellon heir, the descendants of America's entrenched financial dynasties—the du Ponts, Rockefellers, Fords, and others—are now relegated to the sidelines. This is not to say that these scions, acting collectively, don't continue to exert a powerful influence over our economic affairs. Indeed, many wealthy families retain a financial alliance—if not an emotional one—for just this reason. But as individual fortune-holders, heirs and heiresses are generally out of the Top Ten list and make weak contenders in the money game. And those inheritors who foolishly take their money and run often live to regret it.

A *caveat* is in order. In today's world, the super-rich—at least most of them—do not flaunt their pile as did tycoons of old. To the contrary, many are downright incommunicado and it's likely the U.S. Internal Revenue Service doesn't even have a complete picture of who owns how much in America.

Net Worth Figures Aren't Worth Very Much

These estimates of net worth came from a variety of public sources —magazine and newspaper articles, SEC registration statements, annual reports, and the like. Occasionally, a persistent financial journalist has gotten a top wealth-holder to state his worth,[1] usually in weak moments when ego gratification triumphed over good sense and the admonitions of his tax attorney. But, keep in mind, even these financial confessions are "guesstimates."

A truly wealthy person's monetary worth is always a matter of conjecture. Not even the accountant who handles a rich person's affairs can guarantee a totally accurate figure. Why? It's impossible to place a precise dollar value on certain kinds of assets, the kinds most wealthy folk have in abundance. How, for example, would you assign a monetary value to 500,000 acres of prime ranch land (that may well contain undeveloped oil deposits to complicate matters further) until that turf is actually put up for sale to the highest bidder? Or how would you evaluate 1 million shares of the XYZ Company until the day the securities actually change owners? You can't. The fabulously wealthy Texas oil wildcatter H. L. Hunt spoke for all modern Midases when he quipped, "If I knew what I was worth, I wouldn't be worth very much."

In 1979, the U.S. Trust Co., which manages some $6 billion in personal assets of the country's richest families, released a marketing study which estimated that about 520,000 Americans—or one quarter of 1 percent—had achieved millionaire status. U.S. Trust admitted, however, that its estimate was based on a theoretical computer model and that neither it nor the IRS could pinpoint the number exactly. An IRS spokesman concurred: "A head count has never been done. There's no way to do that."

So, as they say down on Wall Street, my information is believed to be reliable, but I cannot vouch for its total accuracy or completeness. However, one thing is ironclad: everybody profiled in the following list and throughout this book is very, very rich—at least $50 million worth.

The Ten Richest Americans in Profile

Who are our ten richest citizens? For the most part, they're men who got ahead with the help of inherited grubstakes. Demographically, they're a mixed bag. More than half are Protestant; three are Jewish. Three are public-school dropouts and two had some college education. Another five actually graduated; one holds an MBA degree, and another two master's degrees in engineering. In most cases, wealth did not come to them early in their careers. The majority are over sixty-five and still married to their first wife. Except for Charles Koch, all have children to carry on the family's lordly financial traditions.

How do they spend their money? Modestly. Most live as typical senior corporate executives—which the majority are—in large homes and apartments in affluent neighborhoods: urban, suburban, and rural. Not surprisingly, the exceptions are two of the heritage-bound heirs on the list. Paul Mellon and Michel Fribourg have adopted aristocratic life-styles in the European manner, maintaining numerous residences and following the expected pursuits of their class: art collecting, hoarding fine wines, thoroughbred breeding, yachting, and hobnobbing with their society-set peers at charity balls.

When it comes to charity, educational causes—followed closely by medical research—are the most popular with the Top Ten. Other philanthropies that claim one or more of their loyalties are fine-arts institutions, Jewish organizations, fundamentalist religious groups, and both left- and right-wing political causes. But more on the generosity—or lack thereof—of the super-rich in later chapters.

Now, the moguls:

Daniel K. Ludwig, eighty-four, New York and The Bahamas: $2–3 billion

Daniel Ludwig, one of the world's richest men, is credited with pioneering the buy-now-pay-later plan in shipbuilding. His destiny was fixed at an early age when, as a nine-year-old in South Haven, Michigan, he bought a sunken boat for $75, repaired it, and char-

Daniel K. Ludwig (left) chats with composer Leonard Bernstein at the 1980 Princeton University commencement. Both received honorary degrees. KATZ/GAMMA/LIAISON (1980)

tered it for twice the price. The same basic method made him perhaps the world's largest fleet owner (National Bulk Carriers) by age forty.

Today, this very private mogul does a land-office business in other industries ranging from savings and loans to real estate and natural resources. His current undertaking is his most ambitious and risky: developing 500,000 acres—almost the size of the state

of Connecticut—of dense Brazilian jungle. To reports that Ludwig has finally overextended himself, the elusive billionaire makes no reply. An associate, Luis Antonio Oliveira, claims Ludwig's latest gamble should not be viewed in strictly monetary terms: "Mr. Ludwig is nearing the end of his life, and he is now more interested in undertaking something of great socioeconomic significance than in earning quick profits."

To friends and business associates, Ludwig is accessible, but he prefers to remain faceless to the general public. He hasn't granted a press interview since 1931, nor does he allow himself to be photographed if he can humanly prevent it. Twice divorced, he lives alone in a Fifth Avenue penthouse and usually walks to work in midtown Manhattan. He frequents the usual haunts of Gotham's affluent, often lunching at "21" or the Warwick Hotel. He has no hobbies to distract him from his work.

He is mute on the subject of possible heirs, although *Time* magazine reports a daughter by his first marriage. He is also said to have a stepson by his second marriage. But all he will say is that he wants his estate to go toward cancer research.

In January 1978, his nonpublicized existence was shattered when the loquacious insurance billionaire John D. MacArthur died and journalists spotlighted Ludwig as his successor to the title "richest American." Not long thereafter, Ludwig's gravely ill and purportedly destitute first wife slapped him with a $10-million damage suit. She claimed he tricked her into signing a small-potatoes support agreement in 1939 and throughout the years had concealed his actual net worth from her. Ludwig denies deserting her in her hour of need.

Forrest E. Mars, Sr., seventy-seven, Las Vegas: $800 million–$1 billion

Frank Mars, Forrest's father and the rugged founder of the family candy empire, was determined that the old chestnut, "Shirt sleeves to shirt sleeves in three generations," would not apply to his progeny. Thus, in 1932, he gave his only son Forrest, a newly minted industrial engineer from Yale, a check for $50,000, the foreign rights to Milky Way and several other candy trademarks, and an edict: "Go to some other country and start your own business. This company isn't big enough for both of us."

Forrest—as feisty and autocratic as his father—did just that. Mars, Ltd., was soon among the leading candy firms in England.

Mars Inc. officials are so tight-lipped that they won't even discuss whether the mammoth candy company's longtime ruler, Forrest E. Mars, Sr., is dead or alive. He's alive, but refuses to talk to reporters or have his picture taken. The last photo of him—wearing a riding habit and astride a gray hunting horse—appeared in FORTUNE *magazine in May 1967. That photo has been "lost."* JACQUELINE THOMPSON

Petfoods, Ltd. and M & M, Ltd. followed, proving once and for all that Forrest was a canny entrepreneur capable of presiding over his father's enormously successful Mars, Inc. But after his father's death, his stepmother and her family took control; it wasn't until 1964 that Forrest finally came into his birthright and achieved firm control of one of the nation's largest and most secretive closely held corporations.

Today, virtually all the company's stock is owned by Mars, Sr.; his two sons, Forrest E. Mars, Jr., and John Mars; several other family members; and the tax-exempt Mars Foundation. Until recently, Mars commuted from "Marland," his 615-acre estate in The Plains, Virginia, to his office at corporate headquarters in McLean each day to oversee the company's far-flung operations. Today, he lives in seclusion in Las Vegas, ignoring those who refer to him as "the Howard Hughes of the candy business." His mission there is to build a Nevada plant that will process high-quality, elegantly boxed chocolates for, perhaps, $30 a pound. Nevada was chosen as the site because that state, unlike most others, allows candy to have alcohol in the tradition of premium European candy.

Mars' two sons, also Yale alumni, are presently sharing the presidency of the company, although "the old man is still in control in spirit and by telephone," according to one former Mars executive. Current Mars executives are forbidden to speak to the press—and they don't if they value their jobs.

Paul Mellon, seventy-four, Upperville, Va.: $500 million–$1 billion

Early in his life, Paul Mellon renounced the moneygrubbing creed of his father, U.S. Treasury Secretary Andrew Mellon. Educated at Choate, Yale, and Cambridge, Mellon put in three years at the family bank in Pittsburgh but soon realized that spending the family fortune was more his style than adding to it.

Since then, Mellon, a third-generation heir, has devoted himself to aesthetic and charitable pursuits, operating out of one of his five homes in Virginia, Washington, D.C., New York, Cape Cod, and Antigua. Mellon maintains that "giving large sums of money away is a soul-searching problem because you can cause as much damage with it as you may do good." To date, his personal benefactions include a $50+ million art gallery-study center at Yale and money to advance women's vocational interests at five colleges. He is also a prime mover in Washington's National Gallery of Art, which his father founded; and various Mellon family foundations. All told, Mellon has given away works of art —and paid for the buildings to house them—at a cost of more than $200 million. *Time* magazine claims "no other living American has committed himself to art patronage on this scale."

But Mellon's life also has its quiet, contemplative moments. Mellon, who once said, "What this country needs is a good five-cent reverie," lives the genteel life of an English country squire most of the year on "Rokeby Farm," his rural 4,000-acre estate in the foothills of the Blue Ridge Mountains of northern Virginia. There he devotes himself to the care and breeding of his thoroughbreds, winners of such prestigious races as the 1964 Belmont Stakes and 1971 Epsom Derby; fox hunting; and the reading of the rare books he collects. Meanwhile, his second and current wife, "Bunny," a Listerine heiress, keeps busy with her hobbies: interior decorating and horticulture.

Mellon's life may be placid now, but the image has been marred by a few ripples throughout the years. His first wife, Mary Conover Brown Mellon, died suddenly in 1946 of an asthmatic attack brought on by a particularly fatiguing hunt. His daughter from that marriage, Catherine, was once married to John Warner, now Elizabeth Taylor's spouse. His son Timothy is an urban planner and amateur pilot. Both stand to inherit the bulk of Mellon's personal fortune, although some consideration will probably be given his stepchildren by his second marriage, Bunny's son and daughter by her previous marriage.

Paul Mellon relaxes in a gallery at the Yale Center for British Art, one of his many benefactions to his alma mater. In toto, he has given Yale University well over $50 million. KEN LAFFAL/NYT PICTURES (1980)

Leonard Stern (age thirty-five when this photo was taken) poses at pool-side in his ultramodern summer home in Atlantic Beach, Long Island.
MICHAEL EVANS/NYT PICTURES (1973)

Leonard Stern, forty-three, New York: $500–700 million

Wunderkind Leonard Stern may well be the only American to have made $700 million by age thirty-five. On the other hand, he didn't exactly emerge from a pile of rags and skyrocket to riches all by himself. His uncle and his father, Max, both immigrants from the Hartz Mountain region of Germany, founded the family pet food and accessory enterprise—the Hartz Mountain Corporation—which Leonard now heads. But without the rescue efforts of precocious whiz-kid Leonard, the two senior Sterns might have run the company into the ground.

After earning a night-school MBA cum laude from New York University, Leonard entered the business at age twenty-one, turned the company around, and in 1972 took it public, a move which made him an instant paper multimillionaire (he owns 70 percent of the stock). Later, when the stock dipped, he bought out his public shareholders for a mere $70 million in cold cash, or $14 a share. It was a major coup since the stock went on the market for $22.75 a share in 1972. At one point the stock sold for as high as $39.75 a share. When it nosed-dived to $7.75 just before Stern made his tender offer, some dissident stockholders got suspicious and tried to block the sale with no success.

Stern has made an inordinate number of enemies on his way up. *Forbes* magazine said, "There's at least as much Jimmy Hoffa in Leonard Stern as there is Horatio Alger. Nearly everything he does is surrounded by controversy and leaves behind a tangle of accusations and lawsuits." Recently, a major lawsuit was brought by the A. H. Robins Co., makers of the Sergeant's line of pet supplies. The antitrust suit alleged that Stern's strong-arm tactics against competitors would make a two-bit gangster blush. Before all the lurid details came out in a courtroom, Stern settled for $42.5 million. It was one of a number of out-of-court settlements which cost Hartz Mountain millions in late 1979.

The ruthless Mr. Stern is a workaholic first and foremost, and secondarily a wealthy man. Although Hartz's corporate headquarters is in Harrison, New Jersey, Stern prefers to live in New York City and reverse commute. He and his family reside in a large Fifth Avenue co-op and spend their summers in a rambling house on Long Island with periodic jaunts to their apartment in the Virgin Islands in between. Although gerbils and flea collars are the mainstays of his empire, Stern owns no breeding farms, horses, or the like. He claims he finds the degree of his wealth "unbelievable, ungraspable" and shuns publicity as "more trouble than it's worth." However, he couldn't escape some press notice several years ago when he became one of N.Y.U.'s youngest trustees.

Today, Stern is embarked on another project which promises to swell his fortune even more. Through some felicitous real-estate deals in the 1960s, he got ownership of more than 1,000 acres of prime New Jersey land, of which a 700-acre plot is just minutes away from Manhattan. He is developing this land under the banner of Hartz Mountain Industries and estimates its worth should be nearly $350 million upon completion.

Charles G. Koch, forty-five, Wichita: $500–700 million

Charles Koch (pronounced "coke") is the president of a company that may well be the most profitable private business in the U.S. (If Koch Industries were publicly held, its $6+ billion in sales would place it about number forty on the *FORTUNE 500* list.) But the extent of Koch Industries' earnings is a closely guarded family secret. Charles and his younger twin brothers, who also work for the company, have followed their late father's lead when it comes to publicity: They shun it.

Fred C. Koch, the family patriarch, was a Texas farmboy who worked his way through Massachusetts Institute of Technology— where Charles and his brothers also trained—and, in the 1920s, he developed a thermal cracking process for refining oil. When the major American oil companies refused to give the Rock Island Oil & Refining Co. (the company's original name) their business, Fred Koch got his big break by selling to the Russians. Eventually, he built fifteen refineries there, although he spent much of his life fighting Communism at home as a zealous supporter of the John Birch Society.

When the old man died on a duck-hunting trip in 1967, one of Charles' first acts was changing the company name. "We used to get calls in the middle of the night asking when the next train leaves. I decided we had an identity problem." His next move was to diversify beyond the oil business (exploration, transportation, refining, marketing, and trading) into such fields as the manu-

Charles G. Koch submitted to having this photo taken—something he seldom does—in 1979 to promote a new business lobby he is spearheading called the Council for a Competitive Economy. The council's mission is to convince businessmen, legislators, and consumers that it is in the

United States' best interests to eliminate all government controls and sub-sidies. The result, Koch believes, will be an America "rejuvenated by the spirit of competition." WICHITA EAGLE & BEACON (1979)

facture of chemicals, fiber-glass products, pollution-control systems, venture-capital programs, and even cattle raising.

Koch remained single until well into his thirties, living modestly in a local high-rise apartment house. Today, he and his wife Elizabeth live more conspicuously in a $2-million home on eighty acres within the Wichita city limits. Koch still spends much of his leisure time reading tomes that support his conservative, laissez-faire economic beliefs.

"Government intervention just hinders the market's ability to satisfy the needs of individuals and is directed instead toward solving the political desires of politicians," he maintains. "Before a coercive solution to any problem is tried there should be at least an attempt to find a voluntary solution." Politically, he categorizes himself as "a libertarian like Jefferson or Thoreau." (Koch reportedly has donated $10–15 million to the Libertarian Party since 1976. His brother, David Koch, was the Libertarians' vice presidential candidate in 1980.)

Koch is also an active sportsman. He's an expert marksman, a skier, and, by all accounts, a championship-quality tennis player. His favorite outdoor activity remains white-water kayaking in the Rockies, because, he says, "It's terrifying."

Michel Fribourg, sixty-eight, New York: $400+ million

Michel Fribourg is the fifth generation to direct the family commodities business and the first to do so in the United States. Belgian Jews, the Fribourg clan fled Europe in 1940 just ahead of Hitler's advancing army and set up the privately held Continental Grain Co. on this side of the Atlantic. Michel, who was in U.S. Army intelligence in France at the time, returned to the task of running the company. Under his leadership, Continental Grain has prospered to the point where it is second in size after Cargill in the agricultural commodities business. It now encompasses more than 100 subsidiary companies and handles about 25 percent of the world's international grain shipments.

Although a naturalized American citizen, Fribourg prefers the life-style of a European aristocrat. He boasts that his Manhattan town house, which he shares with his wife and five children, is "just like a French home." Indeed, it is. The furniture is predominantly

CONTINENTAL GRAIN

The sign in Michel Fribourg's reception room. This is as close as I got to securing a photo of Continental Grain's chieftain. The only existing photos of Fribourg were taken by photographer Ron Appelbe for a March 11, 1972, Business Week *feature. When I asked to buy one of those pictures, Appelbe insisted on querying Fribourg for permission. Permission was not granted.* JACQUELINE THOMPSON

Louis XV and XVI while the walls display the art of such famous European painters as Modigliani, Pissarro, and Chagall. The basement wine cellar would please the most discerning oenophile.

Actually, the cosmopolitan Fribourg, whose European elegance and seeming detachment mask a painful case of shyness, calls a number of places home. The family spends most winter weekends at an upstate New York lodge while a country house in Connecticut claims their attention in spring and fall. In Europe, the Fribourgs have an apartment in Paris, a chalet in the Swiss alps, and a retreat on the Riviera.

Largely self-educated, Fribourg is determined to surround himself with the country's most talented MBAs. To that end, his two foundations finance fellowships at the Harvard and Wharton B-schools and other student scholarships. The *Alliance Française,* an organization fostering international goodwill, and a Franco-American student exchange program are two more of his favorite charities.

Stephen D. Bechtel, Sr., eighty-one, San Francisco: $400+ million

Stephen Bechtel, Sr., may be one of the country's most bland and predictable plutocrats. Now retired, he leaves the day-to-day operations of the privately held Bechtel Group to his son, Stephen, Jr., fifty-five, and haunts the nation's top golf courses when he isn't visiting one of the many blue-blood East and West Coast clubs to which he belongs.

At these exclusive preserves, Bechtel is generally considered part of the inner circle. Stephen Bechtel's charter membership in the "military-industrial complex" is based on his controlling interest in the nation's, and perhaps the world's, largest engineering and construction company, specializing in the building of pipelines and other sophisticated technological projects. If Bechtel were a public company, it would rank in the top twenty-five on the *FORTUNE 500* list.

A drop-out from the University of California—a school which has since awarded him an honorary degree—Bechtel inherited the top spot in his father, Warren's, medium-sized construction company in 1933. Taking over the leadership came naturally to Bechtel as he had virtually grown up in and around his father's building sites. To Bechtel, Sr., falls most of the credit for the firm's enormous growth and prestige. Bechtel, Jr., on the other hand, is considered the epitome of the modern businessman with his engineering and Stanford MBA degrees. He's the ideal manager to consolidate his father's innovative gains.

The Bechtel family still owns nearly half the company through trusts naming the father and son as the voting trustees. The rest is owned by some sixty corporate officers who must sell their holdings back to the company when they leave or retire.

Bechtel, Sr., is an Episcopalian who is still married to the mother of his two grown children. In addition to running the company, Bechtel, Jr., is also an avid golfer and father of five.

(Opposite) Stephen D. Bechtel, Sr. (left), hobnobs with S. Clark Beise, president of the Bank of America, and J. D. Zellerbach, chairman of the board of Crown Zellerbach Corp. These three San Franciscans were among a group of eleven businessmen called to Washington by President John F. Kennedy in 1961 to discuss the U.S. foreign aid program. WIDE WORLD PHOTOS (1961)

Edwin C. Whitehead, a founder of Technicon, is photographed in the medical equipment firm's Tarrytown, New York, offices. MESOPOTAMIA/ BILL KELLY (1978)

Edwin C. Whitehead, sixty-two, Greenwich, Conn.: $300–500 million

Judging by his life-style, Edwin C. Whitehead appears to be just another CEO of a *FORTUNE 500* company. His company, Technicon, hasn't made the *FORTUNE* list, however. Nor will it ever for in 1980, the medical-equipment manufacturing firm was merged into Revlon, Inc., the cosmetics empire.

Until that merger, Whitehead owned approximately 90 percent of Technicon's shares. Those shares had, indeed, made him a paper billionaire for one brief shining moment in 1969 when Technicon went public.

Whitehead's version of Camelot is to seize the holy grail of medical philanthropy from the Rockefeller family and become known as the nation's premier medical research benefactor, if for no other reason than to capture public-relations kudos for his company. In 1974, Whitehead helped his dream materialize by underwriting a $100-million biomedical research institute at Duke University, a facility that he hopes will eventually churn out Nobel-prize laureates at the same rate as Rockefeller University in Manhattan.

Whitehead is the son of Edwin C. Weiskopf, Technicon's other cofounder. He lives in Greenwich with his third wife. (His three children by his first wife are now grown.) A solid citizen, he supports all the usual causes befitting an Eastern liberal executive: the Urban League, College Careers Fund of Westchester, the Cancer Society, and the Association for the Handicapped.

William Herbert Hunt and his older brother Nelson Bunker Hunt (right) are shown here testifying before the House Commerce Committee about

their involvement in the silver futures market crash on March 27, 1980.
RODDEY E. MIMS/TIME (1980)

Nelson Bunker Hunt, fifty-five, Dallas: $300–500 million

The H. L. Hunt family of Dallas has always been an asset-rich, cash-poor clan. Following big brother Bunker's lead, they've traditionally used their assets to secure enormous loans in order to speculate in commodities ranging from sugar to silver. And therein lies the moral to the story of Bunker Hunt's plunge from $2-billion status in early 1980 to anybody's-guess status (including Bunker's) by mid 1980. The moral is this: Even those with legendary financial girth should be asked to flash some cash now and then. Greenbacks on the barrelhead are still the best legal tender when dealing with "billionaires" no matter how dazzling their collateral may appear on paper.

When "Big Bunk"—whose two hundred and forty pounds make him look like Fatty Arbuckle—rang in the New Year in 1980, all signs augured well for his continued prosperity. Bunker's fortune emanated from his father, H. L. Hunt, the famed Texas oil wildcatter once pegged as the wealthiest man in the United States. The old man died in November 1974, leaving his estate to Bunker and Bunker's three brothers and two sisters, as well as Bunker's four half-brothers and -sisters. (The aggregate family holdings in 1980 were estimated at $8–9 billion.)

But besides the money, Bunker inherited something more: the old man's instinct for wheeling and dealing. In league with his brothers Lamar, forty-nine, and William Herbert, fifty-one, Bunker has expanded the family holdings from oil and gas exploration and production into coal, sugar, silver, ranching, thoroughbred horse racing and breeding, and the brokerage business—a veritable cornucopia of assets. Also in keeping with family tradition, Bunker does not flaunt his wealth. He lives in a large, upper-middle-class home in an affluent Dallas suburb and drives around in cars that are always several years old. He usually flies tourist class and he seldom has more than a few bucks in his pocket. Cheap chocolate-brown suits are his trademark and they generally have an unkempt look. One Texas newspaper editor describes him as "the kind of guy who orders chicken-fried steak and Jell-O, spills some on his tie, and then goes out and buys all the silver in the world."

Trying to buy all the silver in the world was Bunker's big mistake. Somewhere along the line, Bunker got it into his head that silver would be a foolproof inflation hedge at a time when the inflation rate was the highest in recent history. So by October 1979, the Hunt interests—Bunker, Lamar, and Herbert—held a net long position in a whopping 12,281+ silver futures contracts with mid-1980 delivery dates. But Bunker claimed he had "no present intention" of taking delivery even though the price of silver was rising steadily.

What happened next P. T. Barnum couldn't have staged with more flair. Bunker and brothers were the principal players in the '79–'80 silver futures spectacular. As the price of silver marched toward its high of $50.35 an ounce on January 18, 1980—almost nine times its level one year earlier—"above-ground silver" in the form of coins, candlesticks and other collectibles began flooding into refineries. In the meantime, the directors of the two major U.S. commodities futures exchanges were getting nervous. In an October 1979 attempt to curb speculation, the Chicago Board of Trade placed "position limits" on the number of silver-futures contracts a trader could own. Three months later, in January 1980, the Commodity Exchange (COMEX) in New York followed suit. Two weeks after that, COMEX delivered the *coup d'état*: It declared an "emergency situation" and limited silver trading solely to the liquidation of existing positions.

The combination of the new rules and overnight glut of melted-down candlesticks on the market created a textbook case of the supply-demand equation in action. On January 22, 1980, the price of silver thudded from $44 to $34 an ounce and continued reeling downward until it hit bottom at $10.20 on March 27, leaving the Hunts strapped for cash to cover margin calls with their brokers and to settle maturing contracts to buy at the old higher prices. To one creditor alone, the Engelhard Minerals & Chemicals Corp., the Hunts owed $665 million in the form of a contract to buy 19 million ounces of silver at $35 an ounce. The Hunts couldn't come up with the cash and called for emergency renegotiation of the debt, offering in settlement 8.5 million ounces of silver bars worth $390 million and a 20 percent interest in some Canadian-based oil and gas reserves. Meanwhile, the brothers were also being called on the Congressional carpet in Washington to defend themselves against accusations they tried to corner the silver market.

By June, with the silver dust almost settled, the Hunts were issuing statements to the press designed to allay any fears about their solvency. The brothers had secured a $1.1 billion loan from a consortium of the nation's largest banks to refinance their debts but in the process had been forced to mortgage practically everything they owned from Bunker's racehorses and Boehm birds to Lamar's Rolex watch and Mercedes-Benz. So what? was the trio's attitude. During the past twenty years we've often used personal assets as collateral to obtain financing.

"For security reasons," their June 3, 1980, press release read, "blanket collateral with extensive property descriptions aren't considered unusual for operating business interests in America today. Doing business on credit properly collateralized is a continuing part of the American business system."

Ray Kroc, seventy-nine, Chicago and La Jolla: $250–500 million

Ray Kroc is one of America's better-known multimillionaires. In the business community his name is synonymous with the best in fast food—McDonald's hamburgers. He's also infamous for his, at times, fiery relationship with his baseball team, the San Diego Padres, which he purchased for $12 million in 1974, "just for the fun of it." (He's been known to berate bumbling players over the stadium's public address system halfway through a game.)

Kroc is a chauvinistic apologist for American capitalism; he strives to communicate his enthusiasm for the system in everything he does. A font of energy, he works around the clock. As proof of his corporate devotion, he's had the McDonald's logo, a pair of golden arches, emblazoned on everything from his gold cufflinks and tie bar to the pockets of his custom-tailored blazers. The doorbell of his luxurious Fort Lauderdale beach home chimes a familiar tune: "You deserve a break today."

While Kroc works and shuttles between his 210-acre ranch in southern California, apartment in Chicago, and homes in La Jolla and Florida, his third wife, Joan, fifty-two, busies herself with charitable good deeds. A former professional organist, she recently gave up what she calls "my dumb boards" to promote her own project, Operation Cork, a $1-million alcohol education program financed by the Kroc Foundation. Neither she nor her husband claim to be anything other than social drinkers, although in January 1980 Kroc's sobriety was called into question when, following a stroke, he entered an alcoholic treatment center in Orange, California. In a statement issued by the family, Kroc was quoted as saying he transferred there from the Scripps Hospital in La Jolla because "I am required to take medication which is incompatible with the use of alcohol."

NOTES

1. In 1971, *FORTUNE* magazine editor Irwin Ross asked self-made multimillionaire Bernard Patrick McDonough to estimate his personal net worth. Ross was surprised to get a forthright reply. "McDonough was happy to tick off the figures," said Ross. It came to $62,500,000.

"At times, his candor is almost embarrassing," Ross wrote. "A caller walked in on him one day when he was examining a run-down of personal expenditures over the last few years. McDonough thereupon read the figures aloud: $24,000 in checks made out to cash in 1970 and $22,000 the year before, other personal outlays of $49,000 in 1970 and $50,000 in 1969. He can afford such sums, for his annual income is over $1 million. 'Not bad for a former cab-driver, is it?' McDonough chuckles." (See *FORTUNE* magazine, July 1971, "A Do-It-Yourself Man from Parkersburg, West Virginia," by Irwin Ross.)

Ray Kroc, the McDonald's hamburger king who owns the San Diego Padres baseball team, inspects his latest addition to San Diego Stadium —an ivy curtain covering the center-field fence. Kroc's other improve-

ments are a nonsmoking section and a special row set aside for the hand-icapped confined to wheelchairs. WIDE WORLD PHOTOS (1979)

HEIRS AND HEIRESSES

2

WORTH MORE THAN $1 BILLION

du Pont family, Wilmington, Del. — Du Pont Company (chemicals); General Motors

Lykes family, Tampa, Fla., and New Orleans, La. — Lykes Bros., Inc. (privately held diversified holding company)

$600 MILLION–$1 BILLION

Ford family, Detroit, Mich. — Ford Motor Co. and Ford Foundation

Pew family, Philadelphia, Pa. — Sun Co. (oil) and Glenmede Trust Co.; Pew Memorial Trust

Phipps family, Old Westbury, Long Island, N.Y. — Bessemer Securities Corp. (family holding company with large investments in steel, real estate, banks, and manufacturing)

$500 MILLION–$1 BILLION

Johnson family, Racine, Wisc. — S. C. Johnson & Son, Inc. (waxes and personal-care products; privately held)

Charles G. Koch, forty-five, Wichita, Kan. — executive, Koch Industries (family-owned chemicals, oil exploration, agricultural products, fiber-glass products)

Forrest E. Mars, seventy-seven, Las Vegas, Nev., and The Plains, Va. — executive, Mars, Inc. (privately held candy company)

Paul Mellon, seventy-four, Upperville, Va. — inheritance (oil, banking, aluminum refining and fabricating, and industrial equipment manufacturing)

$300 MILLION–$600 MILLION

Stephen D. Bechtel, Sr., eighty-one, San Francisco, Calif. — retired executive, Bechtel Group (privately held engineering and construction firm)

Coors family, Golden, Colo. — Adolph Coors Co. (beer)

Marvin Davis, fifty-five, Denver, Colo. — executive, Davis Oil Corp. (privately held exploration and production company)

John T. Dorrance, Jr., sixty-two, Philadelphia, Pa. — inheritance; executive, Campbell Soup Co.

Michel Fribourg, sixty-eight, New York, N.Y. — inheritance; executive, Continental Grain Co. (privately held commodities firm)

Burton E. Green family, Los Angeles, Calif. — inheritance, Belridge Oil Co. sold to Shell Oil

Haas family, San Francisco, Calif. — Levi Strauss & Co. (blue-jean and apparel manufacturers). Three family members own the Oakland A's baseball team.

Hearst family, San Francisco, Calif., and New York, N.Y. — inheritance; Hearst Corp. (media)

N. Bunker Hunt, fifty-five, Dallas, Tex. — inheritance; independent oil operator and venture capitalist (silver, coal, sugar, and ranching)

Ray Hunt, thirty-seven, Dallas, Tex. — inheritance; oil, real estate, and agricultural interests

J. Seward Johnson, eighty-five, Princeton, N.J. — inheritance; retired executive, Johnson & Johnson

Howard B. Keck, sixty-eight, Houston, Tex., and Los Angeles, Calif. — executive, Superior Oil Co.

Kennedy family, Boston, Mass., and New York, N.Y. — real estate, diversified stock and bond holdings

Kleberg family, King Ranch, Tex. — ranching, real estate, oil

MacMillan family, Minneapolis, Minn. — Cargill, Inc. (closely held commodities firm)

Moody family, Galveston, Tex. — inheritance; controlling interest in American National Financial Corp. (insurance) through the Moody Foundation and the Moody National Bank

Murchison family, Dallas, Tex. — Murchison Brothers (diversified investments); Dallas Cowboys football team

Scully family, Lincoln, Ill. — farming and real estate in Illinois, Nebraska, and Kansas

Robert W. Woodruff, ninety-two, Atlanta, Ga. — inheritance; retired executive, Coca-Cola Co.

$200 MILLION–$300 MILLION

Josephine Abercrombie, fifty-five, Houston, Tex. — inheritance; Cameron Iron Works

Walter Annenberg, seventy-three, Philadelphia, Pa., and Palm Springs, Calif. — publisher, Triangle Publications; philanthropist

Blaustein family, Baltimore, Md. — American Oil Co., subsidiary of Standard Oil of Indiana

Chandler family, Los Angeles, Calif. — Times Mirror Co. (media)

Edna McConnell Clark (Mrs. W. Van Alan Clark), ninety-three, New York, and Hobe Sound, Fla. — inheritance; Avon Products

Doubleday family, New York, N.Y. — Doubleday & Co. (family-owned publishing conglomerate); New York Mets baseball team

Cordelia Scaife May Duggan (Mrs. Robert Duggan), fifty-three, Pittsburgh, Pa. — inheritance; Mellon family; venture capital for Roldiva, Inc. (holding company for energy-related land holdings and energy development firms)

Jane Engelhard (Mrs. Charles Engelhard), fifty+, Far Hills, N.J. — inheritance; Engelhard Hanovia, Inc. (conglomerate with international holdings)

Charles Gates, sixty, and siblings, Denver, Colo. — executive, family-controlled Gates Rubber Co. (rubber hoses and V-belts; two-thirds ownership of Learjet; A Bar A Dude Ranch; real estate)

F. Otto Haas, fifty-five+, Philadelphia, Pa. — inheritance; executive, Rohm & Haas (chemicals)

John C. Haas, fifty-five+, Philadelphia, Pa. — inheritance; executive, Rohm & Haas (chemicals)

Amory Houghton, eighty-two, Corning, N.Y. — inheritance; retired executive, Corning Glass

Robert S. Howard, fifty-six, Oceanside, Calif. — executive, Howard Publications (privately held newspapers, TV and radio stations)

Kirby family, Morris County, N.J. — large holdings in Alleghany Corp., Woolworth, IDS, and Pittston

Roger Milliken, sixty-five, Spartanburg, S.C. — executive, Milliken & Co. (privately held textiles)

O'Connor family, Victoria, Tex. — ranching, oil, banking; Victoria Bank & Trust Co.

Pitcairn family, Philadelphia, Pa. — Pittsburgh Plate Glass Co.

David Rockefeller, sixty-six, New York, N.Y. — inheritance (oil, banking, real estate); retired executive, Chase Manhattan Bank

Laurance Rockefeller, seventy-one, New York, N.Y. — inheritance (oil, banking, real estate); venture capitalist (Eastern Air Lines, Reaction Motors, International Nickel, Rock Resorts, etc.)

Richard Mellon Scaife, forty-nine, Pittsburgh, Pa. — inheritance; Mellon family; newspaper publisher.

Vivian L. Smith (Mrs. R. E. Bob Smith), seventy-three, Houston, Tex. — oil, ranching, real estate

C. V. Whitney, eighty-two, New York, N.Y. — inheritance; Vanderbilt and Whitney families

John Hay Whitney, seventy-seven, New York, N.Y. — inheritance; venture capitalist, publisher, diplomat

$100 MILLION–$200 MILLION

Brady family, Far Hills, N.J. — Dillon, Read (investment banking) and Brady Securities & Realty Co. (family holding company)

August A. Busch, Jr., eighty-two, St. Louis, Mo. — inheritance; executive, Anheuser-Busch (beer), owner of the St. Louis Cardinals baseball team

Amon G. Carter family, Fort Worth, Tex. — oil, newspaper/ broadcasting empire

Lammot du Pont Copeland, seventy-five, Wilmington, Del. — inheritance; retired executive, E. I. du Pont de Nemours

Helen K. Copley (Mrs. James S. Copley), fifty-eight, La Jolla, Calif. — inheritance; executive, Copley Press, Inc. (privately held newspaper chain)

Joseph F. Cullman, 3d, sixty-nine, and family, New York, N.Y. — retired executive, Philip Morris Inc. (diversified tobacco, beer and soft-drink company)

Davis family, Forth Worth, Tex. — executives, KenDavis Industries (privately held oil supply and drilling)

Fitz Eugene Dixon, Jr., fifty-nine, Philadelphia, Pa. — inheritance; Widener family (transit systems)

Doris Duke, sixty-nine, Somerville, N.J., Newport, R.I., and Honolulu, Ha. — inheritance (Duke Power and American Tobacco Co.)

Jack M. Eckerd, sixty-eight, Clearwater, Fla. — executive, Jack Eckerd Corp. (drugstores)

Marshall Field V, forty, and siblings, Chicago, Ill. — executive, Field Enterprises Inc. (privately held publishing company)

Malcolm Forbes, sixty-three, Far Hills, N.J. — publisher, Forbes, Inc. (privately held)

Helen Clay Frick, ninety-two, New York, N.Y., and Pittsburgh, Pa. — inheritance (coke and steel)

Katherine Graham, sixty-four, Washington, D.C. — inheritance; executive, The Washington Post Co. (media)

Franklin Groves, fifty, Minneapolis, Minn. — executive, S. J.

Groves & Sons Construction (privately held heavy contracting firm)

Guggenheim family, New York, N.Y. — mining and metallurgy

Jake L. Hamon, Jr., seventy-nine, Dallas, Tex. — inheritance; independent oilman

W. Averell Harriman, ninety, New York, N.Y., and Washington, D.C. — inheritance (railroads); venture capitalist, politician, diplomat

Arthur A. Houghton, Jr., seventy-five, New York, N.Y., and Queenstown, Md. — inheritance; executive, Steuben Division of Corning Glass

Carl C. Landegger, fifty, Bronxville, N.Y. — executive, Parsons & Whittemore (world's largest builder of pulp and paper mills; family owned)

Henry S. McNeil, sixty-four, Philadelphia, Pa. — executive, McNeil Laboratories, division of Johnson & Johnson (drugs)

Elizabeth Meadows (Mrs. Algur Meadows), sixty+, Dallas, Tex., and Palm Beach, Fla. — inheritance; General American Oil Co.

Dellora Angell Norris (Mrs. Lester J. Norris), seventy-eight, St. Charles, Ill. — inheritance from aunt, Mrs. John W. (Bet-a-Million) Gates; major shareholder, Texaco

E. Claiborne Robins, seventy-one, Richmond, Va. — inheritance; executive, A. H. Robins (pharmaceuticals)

William Rosenwald, seventy-eight, New York, N.Y. — inheritance (Sears Roebuck); venture capitalist

Edith Rosenwald Stern (Mrs. Edgar Bloom Stern), eighty-six, New Orleans, La. — inheritance (Sears Roebuck); local philanthropist

Iphigene Ochs Sulzberger (Mrs. Arthur Hays Sulzberger), eighty-eight, Greenwich, Conn. — inheritance (New York Times Co.); philanthropist

Thomas J. Watson, Jr., sixty-seven, Greenwich, Conn. — inheritance; retired executive, IBM Corp.

Keating Zeppa, 50+, Tyler, Tex. — inheritance, Delta Drilling (on and offshore oil drilling)

$50 MILLION–$100 MILLION

Kenneth Stanley (Bud) Adams, fifty-eight, Houston, Tex. — inheritance, Phillips Petroleum; founder, Ada Resources; owner, Houston Oilers football team

Perry R. Bass, sixty-six, Fort Worth, Tex. — inheritance from uncle, Sid Richardson; executive, Perry R. Bass, Inc. (oil) and Sid Richardson Foundation

William S. Beinecke, sixty-seven, Summit, N.J. — inheritance, Sperry & Hutchinson; lawyer

Belk family, Charlotte, N.C. — Belk Store Services, Inc. (privately held department stores)

Bentsen family, Houston and McAllen, Tex. — real estate, citrus groves, cattle, oil; Lincoln Liberty Life Insurance; Bank of McAllen

Elcctra Waggoner Biggs (Mrs. John Biggs), fifties, Vernon, Tex. — inheritance; oil and ranching

Block family, Toledo, Ohio — Block Newspapers (family owned)

Borg family, Tenafly, N.J. — newspapers and TV stations

Carpenter family, Dallas, Tex. — Southland Financial Corp.

William W. Caruth, Jr., sixty-nine, Dallas, Tex. — real estate, hotels, ranching, timber

Leo Corrigan, Jr., fifty+, Dallas, Texas — Corrigan Properties (real estate, hotels, and shopping centers)

Wirt Davis family, Dallas, Tex. — real estate; Republic National Bank of Dallas

Dealey family, Dallas, Tex. — inheritance: *Dallas Morning News*; other newspaper and media properties

Fairleigh Dickinson, Jr., sixty-one, Ridgewood, N.J. — inheritance; former executive, Becton, Dickinson (surgical supplies); executive, National Community Bank of Rutherford

Entenmann family, Bay Shore, Long Island, N.Y. — Entenmann's Inc. (baked goods) division of Warner-Lambert

Farish family, Houston, Tex. — inheritance; Humble Oil Co., subsidiary of Exxon

Ingram family, Nashville, Tenn. — Ingram Corp. (shipping, forest products, pipeline construction, and petroleum trading; privately held)

Belton Kleberg Johnson, fifty-one, San Antonio and La Pryor, Tex. — inheritance, King Ranch; owner, La Chaparrosa Ranch

Edgar Kaiser, seventy-three, Oakland, Calif. — inheritance; retired executive, Kaiser Industries

Kempner family, Galveston, Tex. — U.S. National Bank of Galveston (privately held); Imperial Sugar; real estate; cotton brokerage

Levy family, Dallas, Tex. — executives, NCH Corp. (cleaning chemicals)

S. M. McAshan, Jr., seventy-six, Houston, Tex. — retired executive, Anderson, Clayton & Co. (food processing, insurance, machinery manufacturing)

Margaret McDermott (Mrs. Eugene McDermott), sixty-nine, Dallas, Tex. — widow of founder, Geophysical Services, Inc., predecessor of Texas Instruments

Harvey M. Meyerhoff, fifty-four, Baltimore, Md. — executive, Monumental Properties (insurance, real estate)

John M. Olin, eighty-nine, Alton, Ill. — inheritance; retired executive, Olin Corp. (chemicals)

Spencer T. Olin, eighty+, Alton, Ill. — inheritance; retired executive, Olin Corp. (chemicals)

Edward B. Osborn, seventy-four, Bronxville, N.Y., and St. Paul, Minn. — inheritance; executive, Economics Laboratory (industrial cleaning products)

Helen Regenstein (Mrs. Joseph Regenstein), sixty+, Chicago, Ill. — inheritance; Arvey Corp. and Velsicol Chemical Corp., subsidiary of Northwest Industries

Thomas H. Roberts, Jr., fifty-seven, DeKalb, Ill. — executive, DeKalb AgResearch (hybrid seed and oil exploration)

Schlumberger family, Houston, Tex. — Schlumberger Ltd. (oil drilling services); Schlumberger et Cie (textiles); banking

Shapiro family, Baltimore, Md. — Maryland Cup Corp. (paper cups, straws, plates)

Robert Shelton, forty-five, Kingsville, Tex. — inheritance; King Ranch (ranching, oil, and real estate)

James Sottile, Jr., fifty-five+, Miami, Fla. — inheritance (real estate, citrus groves, banking, and ranching)

John M. Stemmons, seventy-one, Dallas, Tex. — executive, Industrial Properties Corp. (land development)

Arthur Temple, Jr., sixty-one, Diboll, Tex. — inheritance; Temple Industries (forest products), subsidiary of Time, Inc.; Republic Texas Corp. (bank holding company)

Thompson family, Dallas, Tex. — executives, Southland Corp. (convenience stores)

Roy V. Titus, seventy-two, New York, N.Y. — inheritance; son of Helena Rubinstein, cosmetics entrepreneur

Camilla Davis Blaffer Trammell (Mrs. Tex Trammell), sixty+, Houston, Tex. — inheritance from father, Wirt Davis (banking, real estate), and a late husband, John H. Blaffer (Humble Oil Co. heir)

Donald Trump, thirty-five, New York, N.Y. — executive, Trump Organization (privately held real estate)

Mary Hudson Vandegrift, sixty-eight, Kansas City, Kan. — inheritance; Hudson Oil Co. (privately held service stations)

Ella Widener Wetherill (Mrs. Cortright Wetherill), fifty-two, Philadelphia, Pa. — inheritance; Widener family (transit systems)

Leland K. Whittier, seventy-eight, Los Angeles, Calif. — former executive, Belridge Oil Co., sold to Shell Oil; additional inheritance from other oil properties

NOTES

1. The majority of the names on this list was culled from *FORTUNE* magazine, which has published four lists of the richest Americans (see November 1957, May 1968, September 1973, and the February 12, 1979, issues). The remaining names, with the estimates of their personal worth, were taken from various issues of *Business Week*, *Forbes* (November 1, 1976), *Nation's Business*, *Philadelphia Magazine* (March 1974), *Boston Magazine* (November 1972), *Texas Monthly* (October 1978), *New Jersey Monthly* (July 1977), *New York Magazine* (November 6, 1978), *Financial*

World (September 15, 1978), *Time* (July 25, 1960), *Newsweek* (August 2, 1976), *U.S. News & World Report* (August 14, 1978), *Town & Country* (September 1979), *Jewish Living* (September/October 1979), *The Wall Street Journal, The New York Times,* the *Pittsburgh Press,* Associated Press stories, and the books, *The Rich and the Super-Rich* by Ferdinand Lundberg, and *The Very Rich* by Joseph J. Thorndike, Jr. These estimates of net worth include not only the aggregate of an individual's or family's personal holdings, but also those of minor children; and of trusts benefitting the immediate family and foundations.

TWO FALLACIES ABOUT
INHERITED FORTUNES

Fallacy #1: *Instruction in money-management is an integral part of the average inheritor's education.*

3

One might assume that any well-heeled parents about to drop millions into the laps of their progeny when the latter turned twenty-one would have carefully instructed them in the art of personal cash management. One might assume that any self-respecting tycoon would not draw up a will leaving a mint to a favored relative without discussing the legacy's ramifications with the lucky Midas-to-be.

One would assume incorrectly—but that is not to say that young heirs-apparent don't sense their "entitlement," a word used by child psychiatrist Robert Coles to describe rich children's subliminal grasp of their privileged status. They can't avoid feeling it, for once they reach the age when they can be confidently admitted to the family dinner table, they have to endure endless adult banter about the vagaries of the stock market, the latest "hot" collectible, and vacillating real-estate values—in short, conversations about money in the abstract, more specifically, how to make it. But what they won't hear anything about is the flip side of the question—how to conserve money, that rather dull plebeian chore best left to the hired fiduciaries down in the bank trust department.

Stewart Mott, the forty-four-year-old heir to a tidy fortune in General Motors stock, says he wasn't aware of the family money until he was in his teens and then only in a vague way. He explains that he grew up in the middle-American atmosphere of Flint, Michigan, where civic responsibility was considered a duty and the Puritan ethic reigned supreme. He recalls feeling that he had to do something worthwhile with his life, but his father, Charles S. Mott, the well-known industrialist, wasn't willing to point the way.

"Like a lot of people who make their millions in a pioneering way, my father never took the time to teach me about money management or philanthropy," Mott says. "He was loath to even acknowledge the extent of the trust he had set up for me. At age twenty-one, when I became entitled to it, he just asked me to sign a piece of paper that allowed him to act as trustee and I did it without inquiring further. And so my tax returns were filled out and my investments were handled without my involvement.

"It wasn't until age twenty-six that I began inquiring about the nature of the assets and income management and asked about the extent to which I could direct philanthropic gifts. I'll never forget the first time I asked my father about philanthropy and politics in general. He said, 'Well, if you have some particular thing you'd like to give to, then just let me know and we'll consider it.' At this time, I was still living on a monthly allowance. I said, 'I'd like to donate to the Adlai Stevenson campaign.' He blew up. I've forgotten whether he came through or not."

Charles S. Mott is now deceased but that hasn't changed Stewart's situation vis-à-vis his trust fund. Throughout the years, his worth in General Motors stock has fluctuated from $9–$30 million. "If I had control of the assets, which actually belong to my heirs [he's a bachelor], I'd get out of GM," he says emphatically.

In any discussion of heirs and their financial savvy, it's important to distinguish between the ability to manage other people's money and the ability to manage one's own. In a notorious embezzlement/personal bankruptcy case of the late 1930s, Richard Whitney proved that an heir can have a knack for the former without a talent for the latter.

Whitney was a descendant of the Pilgrim Fathers, the son of a respected Boston banker and, as one commentator put it, "seemed to be one of those privileged patricians upon whom Providence could only smile." Providence downright beamed for the first fifty years of Whitney's life. At Groton, he was captain of the baseball team and school prefect and at Harvard he was tapped for membership in the exclusive Porcellian Club. At age twenty-three, he bought a seat on the New York Stock Exchange and eventually became the premier broker for the powerful J. P. Morgan & Co. His role in halting one of the stock market panics of 1929 made him a public hero and catapulted him into the presidency of the Big Board for five years, during which time he became known as "the voice of Wall Street."

But all the while he was garnering laurel wreaths for his work as moral guardian over Wall Street's intricate transactions, he was secretly trying to cover his personal debts by "borrowing" from the accounts of the stock exchange, the New York Yacht Club (he was treasurer), and his father-in-law's estate. His criminal misdeeds, which he did not deny, were exposed in 1938 and he was sentenced to five to ten years' imprisonment in Sing Sing for grand larceny. He emerged three years and four months later, a parolee. At least, his dignity was intact. The whole time he was inside, the guards and his fellow cons referred to him deferentially as "Mr. Whitney."

Fallacy #2: *Heirs exercise firm control over their fortunes.*

A few wealthy families carefully nurture the myth that their offspring all receive austere schooling about money and its value. The Rockefellers come to mind; the third generation—Nelson and David's generation—have fed this story to the press. They claim that when they were children, hand-me-down clothes were the rule, and their father, John D. Rockefeller, Jr., never doled out more than 25 cents a week allowance. However, they could earn extra spending money by killing flies (the going rate was a penny a scalp), shining shoes, and hoeing in the garden. As a young man, Nelson claimed he pedaled his way around Dartmouth College campus on a bicycle while many of his classmates drove cars. He lived on a yearly stipend of $1,500 and was required to send his parents monthly reports on how it was spent. In fact, one would think the Rockefellers were trying to rear accountants. Other Rockefeller heirs have described the meticulously detailed ledgers they were required to keep.

Nelson's second wife, Happy, told *McCalls* magazine in 1975: "Nelson stresses that even if you're a Rockefeller, you have to work to earn money and you have to work to get anyplace. Every Monday he gives each child [Nelson Aldrich, Jr., eleven, and

Mark Fitler, eight] a dollar for toys or candy or other small items. He teaches them to keep records of deposits and withdrawals, so they'll understand the value of money and how to use it." Apparently, Nelson was determined to visit the tactics of his own upbringing on his children.

But lessons in penny-pinching are one thing, while trusting scions with real control over their financial destiny in adulthood is something else. The fourth generation of Rockefellers—Nelson's children's generation—paints a different portrait of life with money. David Rockefeller's daughter, Abby, remembers the time her brother, David, Jr., asked their father straight out exactly how much he was worth. Their father's response was cold and angry. "He said that such talk was *not nice*. The way he said it made me glad I had not been the one to ask."

Abby calls Room 5600 of the RCA Building in Rockefeller Center, the seat of dynastic decision-making for the family, "an institutional replica of my father's manner; it prevents one from asking questions that might explain the inner logic."

Indeed, when the fourth generation of Rockefellers meets each year at the Pocantico Hills compound in Tarrytown, New York— a kind of familial stockholders' meeting—one of the major issues is always how to wrest more information and ultimately control over the communal billions from the trustees in Room 5600. On more than one occasion, a Rockefeller scion has come away from a Room 5600 encounter insulted by the patronizing *in loco parentis* attitude of many of the more than 200 bureaucrats, accountants, analysts, and attorneys who labor there. One mature Rockefeller heiress once put in an application to invade the principal of her trust fund and got a severe lecture from a family accountant. "I was told explicitly that the money was not mine, that the trustees were responsible for what they did and that if they approved something irresponsible they would be held accountable."

The chief villain in this regard is J. Richardson Dilworth, of patrician extraction himself (his great-grandfather was the man who gave the young Scots immigrant Andrew Carnegie his first job in the United States). As the principal Rockefeller family fiduciary, Dilworth says he thinks of himself "more as a family solicitor in the English sense than as a corporate head. Sometimes the problems I deal with are financial; sometimes they're human."

The human problem, of course, is the discontent of the fourth generation. That problem abated slightly in 1968 when a bone was tossed their way in the form of the Rockefeller Family Fund. The third generation had its multimillion-dollar philanthropic plaything called the Rockefeller Brothers Fund; now the fourth had its. But in the long run, creating more financial institutions to link family members together only increases the sense of unreality and isolation from their greenbacks heirs already feel, adding to the enormous guilt many of them experience as the recipients of an unasked-for fortune.

Private family-holding companies and foundations,[1] such as those of the Rockefeller tribe, are the favorite devices of domineering patriarchs intent on guiding their descendants' destiny from the grave. Both these financial instruments have the advantage of keeping the founder's behemoth holdings under central control while simultaneously forging a dynasty. A family holding company is an excellent way to keep progeny in line, for any heir who tries to challenge the administrators' decisions will also have his relatives' wrath to contend with.

The average scion remains content as long as the organizational goose continues to lay periodic golden eggs, enough at least to provide for several homes, perhaps a stable full of thoroughbreds, and sufficient monthly pin money. In the case of the Phipps family, "the Office" even spares steel magnate Henry Phipps' seventy-odd beneficiaries the discomfort of having to write their own checks. Everything from yachts to restaurant tabs are paid for out of the central treasury at 245 Park Avenue, the Manhattan address of the Bessemer Securities Corp.

But sixty-six-year-old Esmond Bradley Martin, one of the seventeen Phipps grandchildren, is one scion who took violent exception to a world where he was constantly shielded from the mundane realities of everyday life. He wanted more than periodic discretionary pay-outs from a family holding company that he felt was grossly mismanaged. (It doled out dividends of only 1.9 percent of capital from 1932 to 1958.) At the very least, he wanted a full accounting of the company's transactions. At best, he wanted to take an active part in the decision-making process.

The in-members of the Phipps family did little to appease Martin. In fact, if they were trying to ignite his ire, they couldn't have done a more thorough job. Defending the *status quo,* a

Phipps' family lawyer, the late Theodore Miller of Dunnington, Bartholow & Miller, said haughtily that family members, Esmond excepted, "want to feel if they die suddenly they are going to have trustees who will . . . fight to protect the beneficiaries against themselves."

Esmond had had enough such protection for one lifetime and launched a one-man rebellion against the entire Phipps clan and its principal surrogates. In a series of lawsuits begun in 1960, he accused company administrators, some of whom were kinfolk, of advancing the interests of key family members and a few of the more influential hired hands while neglecting the long-range financial welfare of other out-of-favor relatives such as he.

To this day $3 million in lawsuits later, the case drags on, keeping a phalanx of attorneys happily employed if nothing else. But Esmond says the litigation has also had a certain therapeutic value for him. "Ten or fifteen years ago, you couldn't have gotten me to open my mouth about the family trust. But now, even if the verdict goes against me, I've gained confidence. My attorneys tell me I should have sued twenty years earlier. The suit has even affected my tennis and my chess—chess has improved ten thousand percent."

NOTES

1. Other dynastic investment vehicles of wealthy American families are the Phipps' Bessemer Securities Corp., Bessemer Trust Co. of Newark, New Jersey, and the Palm Beach Trust Co.; the du Ponts' Christiana Securities Co. recently merged with the Du Pont Co. and the Wilmington Trust Co.; the Fords' Ford Foundation; and Pews' Pew Memorial Trust and Glenmede Trust Co.; and the Kennedys' Park Agency Inc., Kenoil Corp., and Joseph P. Kennedy, Jr., Foundation.

POOR LITTLE RICH KIDS:

A SHRINK'S-EYE VIEW

The Psychological Problems of Heirs and Heiresses

Throughout the world people love fairy tales, especially those related to the lives of the rich. You must learn to understand this and accept it.

—Aristotle Onassis' advice
to his wife Jacqueline

It's a wise piece of advice, but many sons and daughters of the rich have a hard time following it. To many of them, fear, isolation, and guilt surround their fortunes the way an octopus envelops its prey. Once entwined, there seems no escape.

Who is to blame for heirs' emotional misfortunes? Neglectful, social-climbing parents in a majority of cases. According to Dr. Burton N. Wixen, author of *Children of the Rich,* and others who have studied the problem, upper-class Americans tend to raise their children in one of three disastrous ways: They attempt to shield their offspring from anything unpleasant by enveloping them in a fantasy cocoon of material goods. Or they use money to manipulate their children—the dangling carrot syndrome. Or they abandon their progeny completely, remanding them to the professional care of uninterested servants who see child-rearing as just another annoying way to make a living.

In the first two instances, most wealthy kids quickly figure out the rules of the game, smile obediently, and grab all they can get. The end result is foretold in any basic child-psychology text. Unbridled access to anything one's infantile heart desires produces an adult who is monstrously egocentric, lacks any shred of self-discipline, and habitually postpones distasteful responsibilities. Never having had to adapt to anything as a child, such a person also lacks the motivation to change and will most certainly sail off into the money-laden sunset the minute the emotional undercurrent—from a shrink or spouse—gets choppy.

But the most emotionally devastating mode of parenting by far is neglect. It often results in a pathology known as "maternal deprivation." Ironically, its victims commonly come from one of two disparate classes—the very rich and the very poor. In psychological jargon, the symptoms are "a chronic low-grade depression; an acute sense of abandonment; feelings of emptiness; a weak sense of personal or sexual identity; deep dependency needs; the inability to maintain intimate human relations; psychotic-like attacks; and a tendency toward projective defenses, giving a paranoid cast to a person's character." Sufferers have been known to describe themselves as hollow seashells washed up on barren shores. They say they feel like glittering trinkets whose sole purpose is to amuse an occasional beachcomber, who may admire them briefly but will always cast them off eventually, sometimes grinding them brutally into the sand before passing on.

Dr. Michael Stone, associate director of the New York State Psychiatric Institute, has treated a number of heirs and heiresses and cites one of his former patients—the scion of a well-known, aristocratic New England family—as a typical example of the emotional devastation wrought by impersonal parenting.

"Sybil" came to him as a woman in her late thirties who was chronically addicted to the role of "poor little rich girl." As a child, she was kept isolated from other children; she was twelve years old before she was even allowed to venture beyond her parents' 1,000-acre estate or the estate of her cousins next door. Sybil saw her parents so rarely, in fact, that when her mother was once hospitalized for six months for severe depression, Sybil never even thought to question her absence.

Sybil spent her early adult years working at various odd jobs, bumming around Europe, studying briefly any subject that struck her fancy, and getting caught up in two short and unrewarding affairs. She supported herself with the proceeds from her trust fund, which was more a source of anxiety than comfort to her. She was surprisingly naive about money management, was never able to balance her own personal budget, and was so guilt-ridden about her wealth that she lived simply, dressed unobtrusively in cheap clothes, and took no interest whatsoever in the size of her holdings. She felt the only way she could possibly justify her unearned income—and in turn her existence—was by achieving great artistic success of some sort. However, she never put herself to the test because she lacked any confidence in her abilities and feared failure. Her life was in permanent abeyance.

"Sybil's experience comes about as close as any to absolute maternal deprivation with all its horrible consequences," Dr. Stone explained. "She had extremely low self-esteem and great vulnerability to depression. She felt valueless, convinced that if she didn't perform at some magnificent level and finish Schubert's 'Unfinished Symphony' or the like, she would never be able to win the recognition of a man and marry and have a family of her own. As a consequence, she kept a low profile and found it hard to enjoy even the simplest things."

Dr. Stone's analysis: Parental expectations form the backbone of any child's ambition and sense of direction. Sybil, in contrast, had no aspirations because her parents had none for her, beyond seeing her progress from the clutches of a stern governess into the elite ranks of a proper finishing school, and finally into the arms of a suitably prosperous and socially prominent mate. Barring that, her parents expected the family's financial trustees to look after her needs, which they saw in purely monetary terms. As have many multimillionaire parents, Sybil's had arranged for their love to be transmitted to their daughter, like the family money, via fiduciaries.

Dr. Stone claims that Sybil was haunted constantly by a nameless feeling of longing. "The longing, although she didn't know it, was for her mother, any mother, to do the things for her she knew mothers did. But Sybil had no backlog of happy maternal memories which would allow her to fantasize: 'If it could only be like when I was four and my mother used to read to me when I was sick.' Even if one of her parents had, at some time, done a few nice things for her, no matter how meager, there might have been a few memories to reactivate. But Sybil had none. That's an incredibly overpowering vacuum."

How does a doctor try to fill this void? Dr. Stone acknowledges it isn't easy. "If my patients are children or teen-agers, I become a surrogate parent as much as possible. I have to demonstrate the appreciation and enthusiasm of a parent for their drawings and clay models and new efforts and other little spurts of growth. Of course, I try to enlist the aid of the real parents. But often they are the products of similar deprivation themselves and don't understand what loving attentiveness can accomplish. When the parents' cooperation isn't forthcoming and the child is mature enough to comprehend the complexities of his or her situation, I have to make a compact with them. I tell them straightforwardly: "Your home life is terrible. It's not going to get any better. So you might as well make the best of it until you're old enough to leave.' "

In Sybil's case, her mother eventually became a senile eccentric who fired most of the household help because she was convinced she was fast approaching poverty. During Sybil's visits, her mother "parentified" her, making Sybil minister to her like a mother. Some superannuated fathers, who have ignored their daughters most of their lives, mentally transform them into fantasy mistresses to ease the ego-shattering pain of growing old.

"If parents are loving toward their children in the end, for whatever selfish reasons," Dr. Stone claims, "it can mitigate somewhat the rejection of the past. But it's a hard road to travel with or without a loving coda tacked on at the end."

Suicidal Scions

If the suicide rate of an economic class is a valid indicator of happiness, then it would be fair to say that the American upper class harbors some extremely morose people. Although there are no definitive statistical studies of the suicide rate by class,[1] several authorities have expressed opinions on the subject.

Sociologist Emile Durkheim, who wrote the classic text *Suicide*, asserted that "suicide has most victims among the most cultivated and wealthy classes." Professor George Simpson, who edited one edition of Durkheim's treatise, claims: "Suicide rates are relatively high among the highest income groups. Wealth, the touchstone of success in our type of society, is no assurance of immunity."

What makes the elite self-destructive? Dr. Howard Shevrin, a University of Michigan psychoanalyst, feels that many wealthy scions suffer from enormous guilt ". . . because their lives have not been sufficiently marked by [material] deprivation. There is a real and nagging doubt about the source of the comforts they enjoy in life that makes them particularly prone to feelings of extreme unworthiness and depression." The logical extension of such feelings is drug addiction, alcoholism, or total oblivion—death.

Obviously, the specific reasons—and the stories put forth to cover up the reasons—are as varied as the number of suicides.

Herewith is a representative sampling of scion suicides. When family members have used excuses and euphemisms to try to explain away suspicious deaths, I've quoted them verbatim from newspaper accounts:

Roger Annenberg, twenty-two, son of the Philadelphia publishing executive Walter Annenberg, died August 7, 1962, "after a long illness which had caused him to interrupt his studies" at Harvard University and the University of Pennsylvania. He was a cum laude graduate of the Episcopal Academy.

J. Frederick Byers 3d, thirty-eight-year-old realty executive, trustee of the Museum of Modern Art, and son-in-law of CBS founder William Paley, "plunged to his death from his 14th-floor Manhattan apartment" on New Year's Eve 1977. Police said he left a note that talked about "business problems."

Harvey S. Firestone III, thirty-two, grandson of the Firestone Tire & Rubber Co. founder, "was killed instantly when he jumped or fell from the 20th floor of the Havana Hilton Hotel" in May 1960. Firestone, a cripple since birth, was married and had an eighteen-month-old daughter. He had finished third in his law school class at Stetson University and was planning to open a law practice in St. Petersburg as soon as he passed the bar.

Although a cousin, David Firestone, admitted that Harvey III had tried to jump from a speeding car only two months previously in Florida, his two uncles, Leonard K. Firestone and Raymond C. Firestone, vehemently denied their nephew had taken his own life. They released a joint statement to the press that read:

"Harvey Firestone III went to Havana for a vacation trip. It is our feeling that inasmuch as he was capable of standing and walking, he might possibly have wheeled himself to the terrace and stood up to see the view, toppling over the low balcony."

Jerry D. Gamble, a thirty-three-year-old Gamble-Skogmo, Inc., vice president and only son of one of the company's founders, "was found dead about 12:30 P.M. Monday, February 25, 1963, in a car parked in a garage at his parents' home" where he was living in Minneapolis.

Although officials reported that the door to the garage, which could be operated by controls in the car, was closed, the car's gas tank was empty, and the car's ignition was on, the county sheriff's office said its investigation indicated the death was "accidental." It appeared "Mr. Gamble had lain down to rest and fallen asleep." The county coroner's office said tersely, "Mr. Gamble died from carbon monoxide poisoning."

Leo Goodwin 3d, grandson of the Government Employees Insurance Co. (GEICO) founder, died on June 1, 1977, of a "drug overdose."

He had reason to bow out. His father, Leo Goodwin, Jr., who had just filed for bankruptcy listing assets of $26.5 million and debts of $29.9 million, was left to deal with a paternity claim filed by a twenty-six-year-old secretary against the "multimillion-dollar estate" of Leo 3d. Before the suit was settled, Leo, Jr., also died— of cancer. The way he went was ironic since during his lifetime he had funneled all his philanthropic dollars into cancer research at the Leo Goodwin Institute for Cancer Research in Miami.

Clifford S. Heinz III, twenty-six, fourth-generation heir to a Pittsburgh-based pickle fortune, "shot himself in the abdomen and head apparently because he was despondent," according to police. He was a former student at the University of Chicago and under psychiatric care at the time. He left a note addressed to his father, who had battled Clifford's mother and won full custody of him in 1945 when he was four years old.

Keith Wold Johnson, twenty-five-year-old heir to the Johnson & Johnson fortune, "was found dead in his Fort Lauderdale apartment from an apparent drug overdose" on March 30, 1975. "Mr. Johnson was found lying nude in his living room, a belt wound loosely around his arm." In a nearby closet, police found "a suitcase containing a small bag of white powder, a syringe, a spoon and some bloodstained cotton." Police said "a test of the substance was 99% conclusive that it was cocaine but a toxicologist's report was ordered." They also reported that the quantity of the substance was "small enough to be considered the average amount bought for personal use and not for resale."

William L. Mellon III, the grandson of a chairman of Gulf Oil and great-grandnephew of financier Andrew Mellon, "was found dead in his auto parked on a wooded side road two miles from his home in Yarmouthport, Mass." Tests indicated that Mellon, who had "recently been suffering from nervousness and fatigue," had died of barbiturate poisoning.

Mellon was thirty, married, and a pre-med student at Boston University. When he finished his studies, he was expected to work at the Albert Schweitzer Hospital in Haiti. His father, also a doctor, had founded the institution, with much press acclaim, in the mid-1950s.

Henry Ogden Phipps, great-grandson of the Pittsburgh coal baron, "was found dead of an overdose of narcotics in a hotel on New York's upper West Side." He was thirty-one years old. His wife was the daughter of a European nobleman, Count Leopold Sternberg of Czechoslovakia.

Although Phipps had rejected his family's involvement in the thoroughbred racing scene, his thoroughly horsey relatives considered it a fitting memorial to him to cancel a race at Aqueduct on the day of his death.

Harold F. Pitcairn, "noted aviation pioneer, took his life with a single pistol shot. Only a few hours before he had been notably gay at a party celebrating the 75th birthday of his brother. The 62-year-old Mr. Pitcairn killed himself in the study of his medieval-style stone home, Cairncrest, in suburban Bryn Athyn" outside Philadelphia on April 23, 1960.

Pitcairn, second-generation heir to the Pittsburgh Plate Glass Co. fortune, was the father of eight children and founder of the Autogiro Co. of America, which introduced the "flying windmill" into the United States.

Ethel du Pont Warren, forty-nine, a du Pont heiress and former wife of Franklin D. Roosevelt, Jr., "was found dead, hanging by the neck from a braided bathrobe belt looped over a shower curtain rod in a second-floor bathroom of her Grosse Pointe Farms home. A maid told police that Mrs. Warren complained of feeling ill and appeared gloomy when she was served breakfast in bed about 9 A.M."

A family spokesman said Mrs. Warren "had been in good spirits lately, had just returned from a Florida vacation, and was looking forward to the forthcoming marriage of her son, Christopher du Pont Roosevelt, to Rosalind Havemeyer in June [1965]."

Mrs. Warren, who was estranged from her second husband, attorney Benjamin S. Warren, Jr., was hailed as "the most beautiful and eligible wealthy bachelor girl in America" by artist Don Flowers during the 1934 debutante season. She had three children from her two marriages.

NOTES

1. There is no simple, comprehensive way to calculate the actual number of suicides that take place in this country every year because of the pervasive taboo against the taking of one's own life. Relatives, especially if they are rich, influential, and have the family's good name to protect, will go to great lengths to disguise self-destruction, calling it "an accidental shooting while cleaning his gun," or "an unintended fall from a thirty-story window," or "a fatal car crash"—anything to prevent the grisly word "suicide" from appearing on the death certificate.

In his article "Suicide Among Civilized and Primitive Races" (*American Journal of Psychiatry,* Vol. 92, 1935–1936), Dr. Gregory Zilboorg, who combines experience in treating wealthy patients and extensive theoretical knowledge of suicide, writes: "Statistical data on suicide as they are compiled today deserve little if any credence; it has been repeatedly pointed out by scientific students of the problem that suicide cannot be subject to statistical evaluation, since all too many suicides are not reported as such."

Nevertheless, census figures show that of the 50,000–70,000 suicides that are reported every year in the United States, nearly 80 percent of the victims have incomes in the higher brackets.

THE MILLION-
DOLLAR BABY GROWS UP:
NINE WAYS HEIRS FILL THEIR DAYS

5

What should I be when I grow up?

The sons and daughters of the rich have three broad options: They can take up where their ancestor, the empire builder, left off and try to increase the family fortune. If the hustle of commerce strikes them as too crass and demeaning, they can go into more public-spirited work as "concerned" philanthropists or politicians. Or they can reject worldly matters entirely and focus on aesthetic, athletic, or academic occupations.

These are the acceptable choices. But the upper crust, as has the lower, has its fair share of bums, misfits, murderers, and petty criminals who favor immediate gratification to long-term career planning.

What follows might be termed a guide to the plutocratic professions. It sketches the respectable as well as nefarious pursuits of America's hereditary elite.

The Business Heads

How do the sons and daughters of famous tycoons feel about succeeding their dynamic dads in the family business?

The second generation often feels totally inadequate.[1] Studies have shown that many scions purposely avoid placing themselves in competition with dear old dad for fear of falling short of his revered memory. The list of intimidated sons is long: Henry Ford's son, Edsel; Henry Clay Frick's son, Childs; Horace Dodge's son, Horace, Jr.; Henry Phipps' three sons; Andrew Mellon's son,

Paul; and John D. Rockefeller's son, John, Jr.

By no means were these men all wastrels and playboys. Some, in fact, devoted their lives to philanthropy. The point is they recognized that they couldn't top their fathers' reputations in the world of commerce so, to avoid unpleasant comparisons, they didn't try.

If it's any consolation to them, some psychologists have pointed out that the sons of fortune builders could have it worse. Dr. Michael Stone, who specializes in treating the progeny of the very rich, as mentioned earlier, claims that children whose parents are intellectual or artistic giants of the sort that appears only once in a generation—a Winston Churchill or Albert Einstein, for example—are in a much worse position. "They might as well give up," he says. "There is no way for them, or anyone else, to emulate that kind of talent. However, if the father or grandfather was a captain of industry, the sons and daughters still stand a chance of making their own mark. They can at least try their hand at the family business and see how they like it."

These days, when it's considered fashionable to work, more and more scions are again taking up posts in the family corporation. But today, the "family business" is probably publicly owned and run by professional managers and highly trained technocrats, so any aspiring pretender to the corporate throne had better have talent.

In fact, according to David Rockefeller, grandson of John D. and Chase Manhattan Bank chairman, a ladder-climbing heir must be better than the best. He admits the Rockefeller name has sometimes been an advantage, but he claims it also makes people more suspicious and cynical. "It means they assume anything you achieve is the result of the name rather than doing something yourself. So it makes it doubly important that you do twice as well as the other person to justify things. It also meant being doubly sure that what I did I did well."

Knowing that their succession to the presidency is no longer automatic, the current generation of inheritors tends to come to their jobs armed with the best business or legal education money can buy. Many enjoy a credible degree of success (see the following list). And those who do make it to the top often turn out to be daring and outspoken corporate titans—and far more concerned about social-responsibility issues than the average money-grubbing hired manager with no family reputation to uphold.

The Rescue Artists

If the family name can be an inhibitor to some timid scions, it can also be a great motivator to others should the source of familial pride and glory—"the company"—start to founder. While the list of crown princes who copped out is sizable, there is also a number of heirs to modest corporate fortunes who proved they had more of a knack for empire building than their antecedents.

Charles Koch, now one of the country's wealthiest citizens, took over his father's medium-sized oil exploration and refining venture when his father died in 1967 and has since transformed it into a diversified holding company with more than $6 billion in sales each year. The Bechtel Corp. was still a one-horse operation when Warren Bechtel's son Stephen took up the reins in 1933. Now it's the nation's premier high-technology engineering construction firm. The late Charles W. Engelhard, the industrialist after whom Ian Fleming patterned his character Goldfinger, built a $20-million precious metals business founded by his German-immigrant father into an empire that straddles the globe. He was only fifty-four when he died of a heart attack in 1971, and was worth an estimated $300 million.

When J. Irwin Miller became general manager of the fledgling Cummins Engine Co. in 1934, his purpose was to rescue his father's sizable investment in this tiny diesel-engine manufacturing concern, the brainchild of his father's chauffeur, Clessie L. Cummins. When Miller retired in 1977, it was a billion-dollar enterprise with 46 percent of the U.S. market in diesel engines for trucks and $380 million in overseas sales.

The Ingram brothers of Nashville, fourth-generation heirs to the Weyerhaeuser timber fortune, performed a similar feat. Frederic (Fritz) and Bronson Ingram built a $2-million, money-losing inland barge company that was part of their inheritance into the Ingram Corp. with revenues of almost $1 billion, and a profitable acquisition program underway. The middle-aged brothers' greatest hope is that one of their five sons will be equally adept. "Dad made it very clear to us that Bronson and I could spend our whole lives on the beach if we wanted," Fritz told a *Forbes* magazine reporter in 1976. "By his example, however, he convinced us that we'd get bored pretty quickly if we chose that route. Watching him run his oil company, the thought of *not* working just never crossed our minds. But if Dad had sold out when we were eighteen or twenty, God knows what would have happened."

And finally there's Henry Ford II who was only twenty-seven when he led the family coup that forced his aging grandfather and namesake out of the driver's seat of the Ford Motor Co., which was then losing $10 million a month because of bad management. The young Henry completely revamped the ailing company, a company which in its halcyon days had prospered by introducing the innovative concept of assembly-line production. Henry II pushed the company further into the twentieth century. He instituted modern cost-accounting procedures, established a working relationship with the union, and hired a battery of brilliant business-school-trained managers (Robert McNamara, Arjay Miller, Bunkie Knudsen). Although the Ford Motor Co.'s profits have had their ups and downs during his tenure, no one will ever accuse Henry Ford II of timidity.

Entrepreneurs in Their Own Right

Not all heirs who work for the family enterprise find the experience as gratifying. Ward Lay, son of the Frito-Lay potato-chip mogul, is an example. Ward spent the first few years of his working career with his father's company. "I never noticed any resentment," the younger Lay confesses, "but working for my father kept me wondering if I could make it on my own."

As have an increasing number of resourceful heirs, Lay decided to test his money-making mettle on the outside. Lay, whose background was in marketing and finance, teamed up with a twenty-five-year veteran builder and together they formed a small construction firm. Within three years, the Rucker Construction Co. of Dallas had completed building projects worth more than $10 million and Lay, at twenty-eight, was one of the younger board chairmen in the industry.

Benson Ford, Jr., great-grandson of the auto tycoon, is another young member of the elite who struck out on his own, a decision heavily influenced by the fact that neither his late father Benson nor Uncle Henry ever invited him to launch his career at Ford Motors. For sound reasons. "Ben," as he's called, was an indifferent drama major at Whittier College. As he puts it, "I didn't want to rack my brains too much." Next, he did a stint as a laborer in a plastics plant while searching for something "worthwhile" to do. It all came together in the person of Bill Stroppe, a friend and contemporary of his father and well-known figure in off-road racing. At the time, racing was Benson, Jr.'s only abiding passion. He and Stroppe turned it into a lucrative business. Then in 1975, Benson and another friend, Louis Fuentes, formed Luben Industries, Inc., which manufactures parts for recreational vehicles and has grown from a venture with gross sales of $50,000 in 1976 to one pulling in approximately $10 million at the end of 1978. Benson eventually returned to Whittier and earned a B.S. in business administration. Now he's using that sheepskin, his successful business record, and the argument that "my father would have wanted it" to try to force his way into a management position or board seat at Ford Motors.

Sounds impressive, doesn't it? But in all fairness, Lay and other heirs who venture forth in the business world to "prove" themselves have two things going for them that the average entrepreneur doesn't: seed money and influential friends.

In certain businesses such as fashion, cosmetics, interior decorating, and venture capital these two commodities are absolutely essential. Thus, it is with serious reservations that we hail the apparent success of that pedigreed group of designing women: in the apparel trade, Gloria Vanderbilt Cooper (Gloria Vanderbilt, Ltd. failed in 1977 because of poor management); Diane von Furstenberg; Lilly Pulitzer; Henry Ford II's daughter, Charlotte; and Mary McFadden; in the chi-chi world of interior decor, Justine Cushing, Mica Ertegun, and Lee Radziwill; and in fragrances, Raymond K. Mason's daughter, Marcy. After all, how can a Charlotte Ford bomb when her line of clothes is featured in a five-page, four-color advertising spread in *Town & Country* with her father's luxurious LTDs as the backdrop?

One heir—if you can rightfully call him that—who deserves full credit for his millionaire status is J. Roderick MacArthur, the sixty-year-old son of the recently departed billionaire, John D. MacArthur, who remained stingy to the very end. Roderick was no pampered playboy. After scraping out a meager living as a reporter, self-taught photographer, and public relations man, he finally took a job in one of his father's companies where he labored long and hard, came up with several winning mail-order ideas and by age fifty was still earning only $25,000 a year. When he asked the old man for a raise, MacArthur remained true to his Scots ancestry. "You don't need a raise," Rod recalls his father saying. "You'd just have to pay more taxes."

Rod vowed to keep the majority of the proceeds of his next good idea for himself. The idea was the direct mail marketing of limited-edition plates. Once again, Rod approached his father for start-up capital. The old man agreed to assume the advertising expenses in return for one half of the profits for a single series of plates commemorating Lafayette's contribution to the American Revolution. His father also sold him the rights to a dormant corporation for $700. Rod renamed it the Bradford Exchange.

When the company took off, the elder MacArthur got more interested, claiming that their contract entitled him to 51 percent of everything the company did, not just half the profits from one lousy line of Lafayettes. The brouhaha that ensued left Roderick in full control although Rod did end up paying his father $175,000 for his interest in the business. In just six years, the company, based in Niles, Illinois, has cornered about 25 percent of the market, doing ten times the volume of its nearest competitor. In 1978, the firm's sales exceeded $40 million and in 1980, it bought the renowned New York store Hammacher Schlemmer for an undisclosed amount.

How did he do it? By relying on sophisticated computerized marketing techniques, slick promotions, and a brilliant gimmick to stimulate the resale market, *The Market Bradex Current Quotations*. This bimonthly publication imitates the stock market, listing the high, low, and current quoted values for hundred of plates. It's the bible of an industry that has made MacArthur the Younger a mini-mogul.

Business Executives by Birthright

Usually the fourth generation of a successful family spends its time on sports cars and jet planes. We haven't, and it looks like we have a fifth generation coming along that has the same attitude we've had.

—Walter A. Haas, Jr., chairman, Levi Strauss & Co.

Rating America's Corporate Royalty

Second-, third-, and fourth-generation scions are not all incompetent corporate managers as those who are fond of clichés would have us believe. In fact, many a family-controlled company might have languished indefinitely or ended up in bankruptcy were it not for the founder's son or grandson, who put his Harvard MBA to good use and saved the day.

There are exceptions, of course, heirs who took over a fiefdom and would have dismantled it completely if saner heads hadn't taken over the daily management in the nick of time.

In an attempt to set the record straight concerning inheritors and their business acumen, we have rated the performance of those descendants of American corporate dynasties who either currently hold, or have held, responsible positions in the enterprise that made the family name famous.[2] The companies they command are generally industry leaders—established firms in mature industries —where "teamwork" and consensus decision-making are the rule. Promotion is usually from within by way of comprehensive management-training programs.

In keeping with corporate tradition, most of the following heirs-apparent started in menial posts and worked their way up, trying their best to overlook the snickers of other employees who automatically assumed every promotion they got was preordained and had little to do with merit. (The backbiting was occasionally justified.)

Strong Leaders

August A. Busch, Jr., 82 — third generation, Anheuser-Busch
Otis Chandler, 54 — fourth generation, Times Mirror Co.
Joseph F. Cullman, 3d, 69 — third generation, Philip Morris, Inc.
George S. Eccles, 81 — second generation, First Security Corp.
Henry Ford II, 64 — third generation, Ford Motor Co.
Michel Fribourg, 68 — fourth generation, Continental Grain Co.
Robert W. Galvin, 58 — second generation, Motorola Corp.
J. Peter Grace, 68 — third generation, W. R. Grace & Co.
Walter A. Haas, Jr., 65 — fourth generation, Levi Strauss & Co.
H. J. Heinz II, 73 — third generation, H. J. Heinz Co.
Edgar F. Kaiser, Jr., 39 — third generation, Kaiser Industries
Howard B. Keck, 68 — second generation, Superior Oil Co.

E. Claiborne Robins, 71 — third generation, A. H. Robins
David Rockefeller, 66 — third generation, Chase Manhattan
Winthrop Paul Rockefeller, 32 — fourth generation, Winrock Farms
Willard F. Rockwell, Jr., 67 — second generation, Rockwell International
Joan Irvine Smith, 48 — fourth generation, The Irvine Co.
Paul H. Smucker, 63 — third generation, J. M. Smucker Co.
Arthur Ochs Sulzberger, 55 — third generation, N.Y. Times Co.
Thomas J. Watson, Jr., 67 — second generation, IBM Corp.

Competent Executives

Stephen D. Bechtel, Jr., 56 — third generation, Bechtel Group
August Busch III, 44 — fourth generation, Anheuser-Busch
Marshall Field V, 40 — third generation, Field Enterprises, Inc.
Edsel B. Ford 2d, 32 — fourth generation, Ford Motor Co.
Randolph A. Hearst, 65 — third generation, Hearst Corp.
Christie Hefner, 29 — second generation, Playboy Enterprises
Amory Houghton, Jr., 54 — fifth generation, Corning Glass
Howard B. Johnson, 49 — second generation, Howard Johnson
Peter O. Lawson-Johnston, 54 — fifth generation, Guggenheim Brothers, Guggenheim Museum, Anglo Co., Pacific Tin Consolidated
Samuel C. Johnson, 53 — fourth generation, S. C. Johnson & Son
Edgar F. Kaiser, Sr., 73 — second generation, Kaiser Industries
Fred M. Kirby, 61 — second generation, Alleghany Corp.
J. W. Marriott, Jr., 49 — second generation, Marriott Corp.
John B. Reece, 63 — third generation, Reece Corp.
David Rockefeller, Jr., 40 — fourth generation, Rockefeller Family Fund
Rodman Rockefeller, 46+ — fourth generation, international Basic Economy Corp. (IBEC)
Randall Rollins, 50 — second generation, Rollins, Inc.
Peter Storer, 52 — second generation, Storer Broadcasting Co.
William Wrigley, 48 — second generation, William Wrigley Jr. Co.

Undistinguished Managers

William Coors, 64; Joseph Coors, 63 — third generation, Adolph Coors Co.

Edgar M. Cullman, 63 — third generation, Culbro Corp.

Kimball C. Firestone, 47 — third generation, Firestone Tire & Rubber Co.

William C. Ford, 56 — third generation, Ford Motor Co.

Donald E. Graham, 35 — third generation, Washington Post Co.

Richard Manoogian, 45 — second generation, Masco Corp.

Sanford N. McDonnell, 59 — second generation, McDonnell Douglas Corp.

E. Claiborne Robins, Jr., 38 — fourth generation, A. H. Robins

Gary Rollins, 37 — second generation, Orkin division of Rollins, Inc.

Robert W. Sarnoff, 63 — second generation, RCA Corp.

Daniel C. Searle, 55; William L. Searle, 53 — fourth generation, G. D. Searle

Titular Posts With Little Power

John T. Dorrance, Jr., 62 — second generation, Campbell Soup Co.

Michael J. Paulucci, 32 — second generation, Jeno's, Inc.

W. Clement Stone, Jr., 40s — second generation, Combined Intl. Corp.

The Laughable Financial Losers

It takes a unique cluster of personality traits to make a business leader of the stature of Henry Ford II or David Rockefeller, two heirs who managed to fulfill the family destiny. Unfortunately, many scions aren't born with a knack for juggling big bucks and become public laughingstocks instead, often seriously depleting the familial resources. That old chestnut, "Shirt sleeves to shirt sleeves in three generations," should not be discounted.

The biggest blue-blood bankruptcy in recent years—indeed, one of the largest personal bankruptcies in history—was that of Lammot du Pont Copeland, Jr., great-great-great-grandson of the founder of the world's largest chemical company. This forty-eight-year-old Harvard-educated businessman listed assets of $25.6 million and liabilities of $59 million when he went before the bankruptcy judge in 1970. More than half of Copeland's debts were in the form of accommodation paper in which "Motsey," as his friends call him, undertook an obligation on someone else's behalf. His bereft investments spanned newspaper publishing, toy manufacturing, film distribution, real-estate development, shopping centers, a car wash, a major van line, insurance, proprietary colleges, and school dormitories. He had more than 100 creditors including his father, Lammot du Pont Copeland, Sr., who had advanced his son about $8 million between July 1969 and June 1970 in a last-ditch attempt to stave off the inevitable. Copeland, Sr., was so embarrassed by his son's malfeasance that he resigned as chairman of the Du Pont Co. in 1971 to devote the major portion of his time to cleaning up the mess.

The financial wreckage took four years to sort out with creditors finally settling for 10 to 20 cents on the dollar to be paid over a ten-year period. During the bankruptcy proceedings, Motsey depicted himself as the victim of "a shrewdly conceived confidence game." In the only statement Motsey made to the press, he said, "In recent months I have become aware of the character of some of my business associates. And I have become increasingly concerned over the consequences of my relationship with these unscrupulous individuals who have exploited me and the people who have placed their business trust in me."

The characters in this financial drama were certainly as colorful as they were unscrupulous. They included an ex-convict who collected pornographic dolls and a high-living "money broker" who jumped bond and disappeared abroad. But shed no tears for their victim. Motsey is still living comfortably because of three unassailable facts: 1) the lien on Motsey's real property held by his father; 2) Motsey's share in eighty-three "spendthrift" trusts that are off limits to creditors while providing him with an income of at least $400,000 a year; and 3) a unique Delaware law making bank accounts unattachable. If you are going to go bankrupt, it would seem that the du Pont fiefdom of Delaware is the place to declare it. Meanwhile, Motsey keeps himself busy and amused as president of the Comedy Center, Inc., a joke-writing service that once offered to sell its inventory of one-liners for $2.00 a pound. Motsey considered it a coup: "We got rid of a lot of inventory that way."

Not to be upstaged, Motsey's cousin, Henry E. I. du Pont, declared his insolvency a few years later—which was no mean feat since he had inherited $48.5 million from his father William, Jr.

(Henry's name also appears as "William" on his birth certificate. But, in a fit of pique over his grandfather, William, Sr.'s will, he had it legally changed to the moniker of an early du Pont.)

Where did Henry's money go? It paid for two lavish homes; a 1,700-acre farm in Maryland; three wives, two of whom departed decidedly richer than they arrived; and his current mate's irrepressible whims. His wife Muffin's most extravagant project was the conversion of a Delaware château-country estate into a home for wayward children. Henry's penchant for backing business ideas whose time has not yet arrived also contributed to his downfall. But he's not particularly worried about the disheveled state of his financial affairs since he expects to replenish his dry well on the $35 million due him from his octogenarian aunt, Marion du Pont Somerville Scott. Besides, if the drought continues, he can always return to his old working-class job as a middle manager in the computer field.

Perhaps the opposite of the Midas Touch should be dubbed the Huntington Hartford Hunch, a tribute to the litany of foolish monetary moves made by this aging New York City playboy, the seventy-year-old A&P heir George Huntington Hartford II. During the past two decades his name has become virtually synonymous with failure. It's reached the point where the surest way to scare potential investors is to intimate that "Hunt" is involved in the enterprise. His ill-starred ventures include an autobiographical novel that was never published; a $100,000 investment to shore up the liberal New York daily, *P.M.*, now long defunct; a model agency that folded; various film and legitimate theater productions of "classics" that all bombed at the box office; pamphlets and a Doubleday-published book in which he characterized abstract art as a Communist plot to bring down Western civilization; $12 million spent to build and maintain an impressive modern art museum in Manhattan, a white elephant that was finally purchased by Gulf + Western in 1976 as a gift to the city; at least $6 million lost in backing *Show* magazine; and many thousands dumped to promote handwriting analysis as the true key to understanding the human personality.

By pure accident, Hunt almost lucked into a gold mine, but true to form he lost it and Resorts International became the beneficiary. That spine-tingling tale of another investment gone sour started in 1959 when Hunt bought Hog Island in the Bahamas. For $25 million, he transformed it into Paradise Island, a tropical hideaway that never made it with the tourist trade—that is, until Hunt sold about 75 percent of his interest to Resorts International for $11 million, much of it in Resorts stock. Resorts officials knew how to get what they wanted in the bribe-filled Bahamian underworld and soon had procured the gambling license that put Paradise Island on the map. All Hunt had to do to make his killing on this deal was to hold on to his Resorts International stock, which skyrocketed after 1977 when Resorts opened the first gambling casino in Atlantic City, New Jersey. But in 1974, Hunt had settled a dispute with Resorts in which he got cash for his remaining stock.

Also working against Hunt were his three ex-wives and their greedy divorce lawyers and the Great Atlantic & Pacific Tea Co. whose stock has consistently plunged. Likewise, Hunt's personal financial statement has dropped from $100 million to less than $30 million. The quixotic Mr. Hartford does not despair. He says there are two ways of looking at his life's work. "One way is the American way, to look at how much money it makes. The other way is, what is it that I'm doing? What have I accomplished?" His final word on the subject: "You can't judge everything by its dollar value."

The Culture Vultures

How do those at the top dictate *haute* culture (as opposed to low or popular culture) to those at the bottom? Through their financial and administrative control over the country's major cultural institutions: influential museums, art galleries, landmark preservation sites, opera and ballet companies, and symphony orchestras.

Next time you attend a function at one of these august institutions, scan the list of patrons which you'll find in the program or on gold plaques scattered throughout the building. The list will read like a page out of the Social Register. And let me disabuse you of the naive notion that those names are plastered all over the walls solely because the person in question has a passion for opera or Rembrandt. While that may or may not be true, the person's name is probably there for one reason only—it was preordained since childhood. Many diamond-in-the-rough fortune builders actively encourage and educate their offspring to take a serious interest in "the finer things in life," knowing full well their children's refined sensibilities will help smooth the sharp edges off the family's philistine reputation.

Walt Whitman Rostow, one of John Kennedy's New Frontiersmen, calls the phenomenon the "Buddenbrooks Dynamic." The first generation seeks money; the second, social and civic position; and the third, music and arts patronage in general.

But while the moneygrubbing family patriarch may see the arts as merely a means to a social end, their children and children's children often see music, art collecting, and historic restoration as a way to gain a very real sense of personal fulfillment. That certainly can be said of Paul Mellon, Andrew Mellon's son, who is perfectly adapted to the role of connoisseur. Indeed, it has been said of him that he lives his life like a work of art. He has used his money to conjure up a world of English gentility and urbanity that he remembered from his childhood when he and his now-departed sister, Ailsa Mellon Bruce, would romp through the British countryside on their annual summer visits with their mother. (Their mother lost custody of them during an acrimonious divorce suit, settled in 1912, and returned to her native England.)

Mellon has explained his love of eighteenth-century English art. To him, it conjures up remembered images of "huge dark trees in rolling parks, herds of small friendly deer, flotillas of white swans on the Thames, dappled tan cows in soft green fields, soldiers in scarlet and bright metal, drums and bugles, troops of gray horses, laughing ladies in white with gay parasols, men in impeccable white flannels and striped blazers, and always behind them and behind everything the grass was green, green, green . . . There seemed to be a tranquillity in those days that has never again been found."

"Tranquil" is an ideal word to describe Paul Mellon's days spent on his rolling hunt-country estate ("Oak Spring") and thoroughbred horse farm ("Rokeby") in Upperville, Virginia, his primary residence (he has four others). There he has created a life-style confirming his belief that "at least part of the purpose of life is enjoyment"—and privacy. "There is an inherent duty [in life]," he once told a prep-school graduating class, "to be aware, to do something, to care. The only thing that I want to add . . . is something I think many people tend to subtract. This is the element of, the principle of, pleasure. . . . To see, to hear, to smell, to taste, to feel—these are privileges all too often neglected, or even forgotten in our preoccupation with being students or writers or business people or lawyers or critics or even mothers and fathers. . . . What we often really need is an hour alone, to dream, to contemplate, or simply to feel the sun."

Mellon admits to being a "galloping Anglophile" who consciously envelops himself in sensual stimuli. He might begin a typical day by walking over to the solid-brick manor house—his home during his first marriage—that currently houses much of his rare-book and -manuscript collection of more than 20,000 volumes. He'll run his fingers over the gold-leaf lettering on the spine of a book before he opens it to meditate briefly on a particularly well-turned phrase.

Later, he'll return to the graystone farmhouse with the white trim and ivy growing up the sides where he lives with his second wife. In his book-lined study, he may attend to administrative matters concerning his father's philanthropic tribute to the nation, the National Gallery of Art in Washington. Or he'll answer correspondence about the multimillion-dollar art center he donated to his alma mater Yale University; it contains, according to *Time* magazine, "the most systematic collection of British art, mainly eighteenth and early nineteenth century, in existence outside London's Tate Gallery." Or Mellon might consider some worthy candidate for a grant from the Andrew W. Mellon or Bollingen foundations. (Bollingen honors excellence in the field of arts and letters and awarded its first poetry prize to Ezra Pound in the late 1940s. Mellon and his first wife were also instrumental in having Carl Jung's work translated into English.)

When he's ready for a break, Mellon might peruse for the thousandth time one of the British hunting and sporting prints and paintings that decorate the walls of his home. Or he might take a jaunt around the fields himself on his favorite mount. At seventy-four, he still rides almost daily to keep in shape for the various hunts and steeplechases he continues to enter—and often wins. And twilight usually finds him lost in his own thoughts on a stroll through his pastures and woods accompanied by his Norwich terriers.

Bunny Mellon describes her husband as simultaneously "very sensitive" and "very remote." Perhaps some verse Mellon wrote during his undergraduate days at Yale provides the best clue to his inner landscape:

I built a temple in my inmost mind
Of pure white marble, its stern
   symmetry
Became the symbol of tranquility
How calm it was, and peace, and
   no wind
Ever disturbed its stillness . . .

Don't think the prestige nonprofit institutions in this country are ever that hard up for cash that they'll take it from just anyone. A large benefaction from a singer whose name has been associated with the underworld was rejected outright. Gifts—more properly termed "bribes"—stipulating that the name of a commercial enterprise, such as McDonald's hamburgers, must adorn the front door are another no-no. The name of McDonald's founder, Ray Kroc, might be acceptable, but only in a financial pinch. He made his money himself. Blue-blood names are always preferred.

The ancient aristocrat Alice Tully, whose name is now synonymous with a concert hall in New York City, was asked by her cousin, Arthur Houghton, Jr., if she would underwrite a home for chamber music at Lincoln Center. "Nothing would please me more," she reportedly replied. She was to be an anonymous donor —although the people who count would know—until John D. Rockefeller 3d suggested that she really ought to get the credit for such a sizable gift. "I just couldn't refuse," she recalls.

Sometimes a *doyenne* herself comes up with the idea for a new cultural project and because of her money and connections, loosens others' purse strings. John D. Rockefeller, Jr.'s first wife, Abby, dreamed of starting a gallery of modern art. The result was New York's Museum of Modern Art. The eighty-five-year-old Catherine Filene Shouse, backed by a Boston department-store legacy, was the guiding spirit behind Wolf Trap Farm Park for the Performing Arts outside Washington, D.C., now the city's premier summer cultural center. Mrs. Dorothy Buffum Chandler of the newspaper family was the force that brought the $24-million Los Angeles Music Center to fruition, its ulterior purpose being to help erase the city's frivolous image as a "clown town" and lowbrow "movie mecca." Mrs. Chandler had so much clout among prospective donors that she claims proudly, "I was only turned down flatly once, although some prospects did take a long time to make up their minds."

The Easy-Street Eccentrics

Money gives you the freedom to be yourself. If your real self is a shade off-beat, so be it.

That's fine in England where the aristocracy can do little wrong, having roots reaching back through the centuries. There, aristocratic foibles are a source of general amusement. But, as Donal Henahan of *The New York Times* has noted, "The full-blown eccentric is not regarded as a national treasure by most Americans. True spawn of the Puritans, we tend to look askance at unconventional people."

The American rich, who are less secure about their social position than their English counterparts, are aware of this New World stigma against the oddball and generally go to great lengths to keep any nutty family skeletons locked up in the closet.

But skeletons have a way of ambling into the spotlight just when "respectable" relatives least expect it. Imagine how retired U.S. Secretary of the Treasury Andrew Mellon felt in 1934 when a newspaper revealed that his cousin, William Andrew Mellon, was living in ramshackle rooms over a coffee store in downtown Pittsburgh. He had been on the local relief rolls for a while when he wasn't living off a small Mellon-family allowance. He told the reporter about the dream that had kept him going for the last twenty-five years—to develop a gold mine he knew about in Colorado. Control of the mine would be his for $15,000, and his cousin "Andy" had promised to help him "after I complete some work for him. I am working on that now—a new genealogy of the Mellon family."

To the Mellon family's credit, they had tried to get Mr. William Andrew Mellon into more suitable digs, but he would have none of it. "I like it here," he told another cousin, Fred Mellon, and the family attorney when they visited him.

Whether the Biddle family of Philadelphia ever tried to do the same for Winthrop L. Biddle remains a guarded family secret. The only comment on the subject was made by Nicholas Biddle, Winthrop's older brother, when the seventy-four-year-old drifter was found dead on a rural road near Camden, New Jersey, in 1971: "Money meant nothing to him," Nicholas said. "He had no more idea than the man in the moon of what to do with it except get rid of it."

Winthrop was the victim of a hit-and-run driver. The police said he was wearing four pairs of pants and a sport coat, and was pushing a shopping cart containing a suitcase when he was struck. Although he had a number of addresses, including one at the Camden YMCA, his sleeping quarters were usually abandoned buildings, park benches, and occasionally even jail cells. Through the years he'd been accused of petty crimes ranging from passing worthless checks to stealing from a Biddle family servant.

These are the sad cases of aberrant behavior bordering on the psychotic. Most scions' looniness is far more whimsical.

Irénée du Pont, who was president of the E. I. Du Pont de Nemours Company from 1919 to 1926 and stayed active in the family firm until 1959, had a fascination with iguanas, nurtured during his long stays in the tropics. In the garden of his Cuban home Xanadu, he devoted many hours to the training of his reptilian pets, who eventually learned to respond when called and to stand at attention on signal.

The late Marjorie Merriweather Post had a craving for sweets. She employed huge staffs of servants to keep her lavish Palm Beach and Washington, D.C., residences in top form. But, perhaps the servant she found the most indispensable was her very own candymaker, who kept her supplied with fresh-made delicacies on a twenty-four-hour basis.

Jefferson Seligman, grandson of the eminent New York banker David Seligman and uncle to the art-collecting Peggy Guggenheim, had a whole catalogue of idiosyncrasies. After a bad first marriage, "Jeff" closeted himself in two small hotel rooms on Manhattan's East Side which he stocked with expensive fur coats and, later, dresses from Klein's. Lady visitors were allowed to choose whatever garment struck their fancy. With a perfectly straight face, he once told a reporter that kissing should be substituted for handshaking because the latter custom spread germs, and that the New York sanitation department should program its street-sweeping machines to leave dry gaps every block so little old ladies could cross without getting their shoes wet. Seligman ended his years as a nonworking member of the J. & W. Seligman & Co. partnership. Instead of tending to high-echelon financial matters, he spent his days distributing fresh fruit and ginger to his colleagues. This dietary supplement was supposed to keep body and mind in tip-top shape.

Although Henry Ford, the auto maker, was not an heir, he was plenty odd. He kept his dear friend Thomas Edison's dying breath in a bottle and habitually used new dollar bills as bookmarks. He never took a walk around his Dearborn estate "Fair Lane" without an ax, which he referred to as his "key." Once he explained that "some of these people around here have been locking the doors of the outbuildings. When I find a door I can't open, I use my key."

The Rich Recluses

> *Money* doesn't *make you different. It makes your circumstances different. Money enables you either to do more with your life or to insulate yourself more from life.*

> —Malcolm Forbes
> chairman, Forbes, Inc.

Reclusiveness seems to be part of the birthright of the well-to-do.

One theory, advanced by Thomas Wiseman in his book *The Money Motive*, is that reclusiveness "may be an attempt to recreate that imaginary condition of total isolation and total safety and comfort of the womb." He claims opulent surroundings and around-the-clock maid service are all part of an intense psychological need for instant gratification and complete control over the environment. "In this luxury cocoon, they have created an artificial inexhaustible breast, and feel safe."

Howard Hughes was an extreme example of this phenomenon but certainly not the only one. A prime case of the living dead is Sandra Ferry Rockefeller, the late John D. 3d's oldest daughter. Sandra has become a desperate woman in her determination to escape her heritage. In 1959, this Vassar-educated artist stopped using her surname, introducing herself simply as Sandra Ferry; and tried, unsuccessfully, to disown her multimillion-dollar trust fund. Today, she accepts the money because it helps her hide out. She lives alone in Cambridge, Massachusetts, behind multiple locks like a woman twice her forty-five years. Family lore has it that she once spent two years recovering from a broken toe and admits only two regular visitors, a psychiatrist and a music therapist.

When Mellon heiress Cordelia Scaife Duggan named her Ligonier, Pennsylvania, estate "Cold Comfort," she might just as aptly have been describing the barren emotional terrain of her life. Tyrannized by a $300-million inheritance from her mother, she chose to recede into the shadows after a short-lived society marriage to Herbert May, Jr., a highborn gentleman whose father was one married to Post cereal heiress, Marjorie Merriweather Post. Cordelia's second marriage—reputedly one of convenience rather than love—ended in tragedy when her childhood companion-turned-husband shot himself after learning he'd just been indicted for tax fraud. At the time, he was Pittsburgh's controversial district attorney. "Corgy," now fifty-three, continues to spend most of her time traveling abroad and donating to her favorite cause: birth control.

Mrs. Lester J. Norris' (née Dellora Angell) cocoon is St. Charles, Illinois (population 15,144), the country town where she was born, reared, and which she never leaves. Dellora Angell was only sweet sixteen when she inherited about $25 million from her aunt, the wife of John W. (Bet-a-Million) Gates, a barbed-wire salesman who wheeled and dealed and gambled—thus the nickname—his way to fame and a fortune in Texaco and U.S. Steel stock. The press had a field day, dubbing her "America's No. 1 heiress" and "the richest little girl in the world." In their exaggerated reports, they had her engaged to all manner of glamorous figures from European noblemen to Texas oil wildcatters. Dellora was repulsed by this "tiresome show of bad taste" and foiled them all by marrying her childhood sweetheart, the local undertaker's son, who was then working as a cartoonist for the *Chicago Tribune*. Once they were wed, he settled down to babysit her bankroll (her majority holdings in Texaco afforded him a seat on the board), and she settled down to mother three sons and two daughters.

With one son now dead, the seventy-eight-year-old Mrs. Norris is even less in evidence on the streets of St. Charles. When I wrote asking for an interview, her administrative assistant politely demurred, explaining that Mrs. Norris hasn't had much luck with interviews throughout the years.

"Even if the stories are well done and favorable, they still wind up giving her a lot of headaches—floods of phone calls and letters

and people wanting money and knocking on the door. Besides,"
he said apologetically, "she's kind of shy—well, I suppose 'shy'
isn't the word and I hate to use the word 'recluse' because she does
get out some but very little. When she got your letter, she said,
'I'm going to go off somewhere when this person is in town. I don't
want to be around.' "

The same hermetic policy characterizes the life of Helen Clay
Frick, the spinster daughter of Andrew Carnegie's crony, Henry
Clay Frick. Miss Frick, who inherited the bulk of her father's $100-
million estate, has made a fetish of eluding reporters. (The only
existing photos of her show pocketbooks covering her face.)
About her, it can truly be said that her flinty old heart belongs
to daddy. At ninety-two, she still devotes all her remaining energy,
which is considerable, to one unattainable goal: clearing her father's besmirched reputation.

Miss Frick is every bit as stubborn and pugnacious as the old
man ever was. Although she was rarely seen in public after her
father's death in 1919, out of sight was not out of trouble. A chro-
nology of her showdowns reads as follows:

> *1935:* She successfully defends herself in a libel/slander suit
> pressed by a former secretary to her father who claimed
> he had been curator of the Frick Museum in Manhattan.
> Miss Frick claimed he was merely "somebody hired to
> show people through the galleries."

> *1936:* She spearheads a hush-hush drawing-room drive to get
> wealthy women such as herself to "work, pledge money,
> and vote" against President Roosevelt and his New Deal
> cohorts. In typical H.C.F. style, the letter soliciting sup-
> port read, "We wish to keep this movement very quiet.
> . . . We are taking precautions about telephone conver-
> sations and avoiding all publicity in newspapers. This is
> important."
>
> (In 1973, she was rounding up Republican support
> once again, this time to keep a beleaguered President
> Nixon in office.)

> *1940:* She refuses to answer what she considers overly per-
> sonal questions on the 1940 census, questions about her
> age, the value of her home, and her education. Her final

comment: "Let them refer the matter to Washington if they wish."

1948: She is sued by the other Frick Museum trustees who wish to allow John D. Rockefeller, Jr., to contribute some of his artworks to the Frick Museum. She loses the battle to keep out the "inferior" art and, thirteen years later, quits the board over the same issue.

1963: She writes a heated letter to the editor of the *Pittsburgh Press* protesting the Supreme Court ruling striking down prayer in the schools: "Now we can be certain that out of the 'Nine Old Men,' the eight who have cast their vote to outlaw the Lord's Prayer in the schools, and who so often protect Communists in their suits, will ruin the country that was founded by Christian men and women. The American people must fight to preserve their beliefs!"

1967: She settles a suit brought to suppress a Pennsylvania historian's unflattering appraisal of her father. After an expensive three-year legal wrangle, she only manages to get the author to make a few minor "corrections"— rather than have the book taken off the market completely as she'd asked.

The Cumberland County (Pennsylvania) judge who heard the case scolded Miss Frick at one point, saying "by analogy Miss Frick might as well try to enjoin publication and distribution of the Holy Bible because, being a descendant of Eve, she does not believe that Eve gave Adam the forbidden fruit in the Garden of Eden, and that her senses are offended by such a statement about an ancestor of hers."

1967: She withdraws her financial support from the University of Pittsburgh's Henry Clay Frick Fine Arts Building because school officials refused to abide by all the stipulations that go along with it. The university's vice chancellor indignantly declares that "no university can maintain this domination from the outside and remain a university."

1975: She refuses to let a woman clad in pants do research at the Frick Art Reference Library adjoining the museum. Miss Frick's dress code, printed on a sign in the lobby, reads: "Ladies wearing very short skirts, shorts, slacks or spike heels will not be admitted. Gentlemen must wear jackets or coats in reading room."

As you ponder all this, Miss Frick is probably holed up in her secluded estate in Roslyn, Long Island. But guards at her father's Manhattan memorial, The Frick Collection on Seventieth Street and Fifth Avenue, report that she still makes occasional pilgrimages there, and, according to some rumors, may even have moved to Manhattan full time to live in an apartment over the collection.

The Diligent Dilettantes

Very few people possess true artistic ability. It is therefore both unseemly and unproductive to irritate the situation by making an effort. If you have a burning, restless urge to write or paint, simply eat something sweet and the feeling will pass. Your life story would not make a good book. Do not even try.

—Fran Lebowitz
Metropolitan Life

That advice from a pop journalist has been universally ignored by the pseudo-artistic types in the moneyed set. Unlike the rest of us, they have the wherewithal to showcase their lack of talent, becoming in many instances the most diligent—and ridiculous—of all dilettantes.

Most of the inheritors I will mention in this section are people you've probably never heard of—for good reason. They've done nothing to merit artistic acclaim although some have certainly tried hard enough.

Are you familiar with the names Cornelia Sharpe or Andrea De Portago? Of course not. They're two socialites trying to make it as actresses. Dina Merrill (Marjorie Merriweather Post's daughter), Grace Kelly, and Katharine Hepburn are three socialites, of all the hundreds who have tried, who managed to make it big in that cutthroat profession.

Cindy Firestone, thirty-two, is a well-heeled young woman with reformist tendencies who is trying to make it behind the camera—with some initial success. In 1974, *People* magazine described her as "a new filmmaker with unlikely credits: she is a scion of the tire-and-rubber fortune, an alumna of Jacqueline Kennedy's finishing school (Miss Porter's), of Sarah Lawrence College, and of the Detroit city jail." (Cindy was arrested on charges of trying to enter a Chrysler Corporation factory illegally to film a United Auto Workers' strike. This was but three years after she bowed to Philadelphia society decked out as a debutante.)

Cindy's *oeuvre* may not rival Steven Spielberg's at the box office or Ingmar Bergman's for consistent critical acclaim, but it gets plenty of currency in private screening rooms and raves from armchair Socialists. Her first solo endeavor was a polemic about the Attica prison uprising, called succinctly *Attica*. The event took place just after she'd apprenticed herself to an established moviemaker to develop her skills. But with the arrogant self-confidence of a third-generation heiress, she plunged ahead even without the requisite experience and know-how. She admitted later, "I was really learning how to make a movie as I made a movie."

As luck or talent would have it, the result was commendable. Vincent Canby of *The New York Times* wrote that it was "an exceptionally moving, outraged recollection of that terrible event." It was also hailed at two international film festivals as a hot new property that promised to attract campus *cognoscenti* in droves.

Class-consciousness seems to dominate Firestone films as well as Ms. Firestone's thoughts. She says, "I refuse to feel guilty about my class background" and capped off that remark by describing her mother, who financed the *Attica* footage to the tune of $40,000, as "slightly to the right of Louis XV."

Plenty of upper-class *artistes* have apologized in one way or another for their origins. Amy Lowell, the American Imagist poet, complained that her greatest handicap was being born into a class which is commonly assumed incapable of artistic creativity. Cornelius Vanderbilt, Jr., five generations removed from the Commodore, struggled all his life to gain acceptance as a journalist and novelist. "The most difficult thing I have found in my individual case," he said, "is that of trying forever to convince everybody that I am in earnest." His seven marriages did not help his image as a serious writer. One of his books, however, got plenty of attention. Published in 1935, it was a memoir entitled *A Fare-well to Fifth Avenue*. The title couldn't have been more apt. For "exposing" the great and near-great in much the same manner as Truman Capote did in some *Esquire* magazine pieces in the mid-1970s, "Neely"—as he was called—got booted out of the Social Register.

The question of whether the upper class can produce fiction of any merit has been considered by several writers who take a personal interest in the subject. Louis Auchincloss, lawyer-scion-novelist-social chronicler, commented in his introduction to *The Edith Wharton Reader*: "It is true, of course, that an upper class training may hamper an incipient artist by inhibiting his emotions, and in fields of direct personal exhibition, as the stage and the dance, it may well be fatal. But the novelist need expose no more of himself than he wishes." That could be a biased observation since Auchincloss has more than twenty novels to his credit and isn't exactly poverty stricken.

Geoffrey T. Hellman, who isn't starving either, tackled the subject in a long *New Yorker* piece in 1963 called "Can the Rich Write?" He surveyed more than fifty wealthy American novelists (nineteenth and twentieth century) and came to the conclusion that "rich writers tend to be related to other rich writers, to get going relatively late, and to start their books with the weather." Furthermore, "about a tenth of our rich writers have resorted to anonymity or pseudonymity . . . quite a few have been in the diplomatic service and . . . more have been associated with the law than with any other profession." He singled out Edith Wharton as one of the few "rich writers who could really write" and generally dismissed the rest as "crypto-novelists." Henry James and James Fenimore Cooper were left out of the discussion entirely because of their lack of sufficient resources, Hellman's definition of "rich" being "that fiscal condition in which the writer, from his (or her) avocado-salad days on, is sufficiently in clover—a mixed metaphor but herbivorous throughout—not to give a damn financially whether his (or her) books sell."

Charlotte Bergen is a genteel geriatric conductor who doesn't seem to care whether her concerts sell. In fact, each time she enacts her Walter Mittyesque fantasy with the American Symphony at Carnegie Hall, it costs her about $40,000. But she knows plenty of enthusiastic people will show up to listen since the events are free—and of late well publicized.

The spectacle of a frail eighty-two-year-old Gardiner heiress with a heavy back brace conducting a major orchestra just because she loves music and decided, rather late in life, that she wanted the experience before she died was enough to intrigue even jaded *Time* magazine and *New York Times* critics. The *Time* reviewer was characteristically flip: "Bergen proved to be no Solti on the podium —she gave few entrance or dynamic cues—but she kept the symphony marching along smartly to her emphatic beat through the Brahms and Schumann program." Reviewing a follow-up concert six months later, *The New York Times'* Peter G. Davis was somewhat kinder: "Miss Bergen took on nothing less than Beethoven's Missa Solemnis and gave a performance that was an entirely worthy statement of this towering masterpiece. . . . Bergen coordinated all the elements authoritatively, faltering only slightly during the more hectic moments of the Gloria and Credo movements, which did threaten to come a bit unglued."

Ms. Bergen, whose father was a wealthy corporation lawyer who helped forge the vast Public Service Electric & Gas Co., New Jersey's largest utility, wants it clearly understood that she's not trying to accomplish anything more than to make beautiful music. "I've been making music since I was five [on the piano and the cello]. I do this only because I love music. I'm not seeking to make a career, I don't want to exploit anyone."

Only Doris Duke knows what her motives were when she got her hair bobbed Afro-style and started singing each Sunday in a black Baptist church choir in Nutley, New Jersey, about twenty-five miles from her 2,500-acre estate in Hillsborough. Ms. Duke, an avid jazz enthusiast who once started her own record company to turn out popular music discs under the direction of her pianist-beau at the time, Joe Castro, somehow managed to keep her Sabbath activities a secret for several years. When a local reporter did come nosing around, the congregation, which included some of the most prominent blacks in the state, closed ranks and refused to talk or let him near her to take a picture. Their unwavering loyalty to a Southern tobacco heiress is an amusing irony.

But the press had no trouble getting an audience with Rebekah Harkness when this professional heiress (Standard Oil) and amateur everything-else came on the scene like an explosion in 1974. Over the sixty-six-year span of her life, Rebekah Harkness has dabbled in almost every form of artistic endeavor there is, including piano playing, composition, and orchestration. Never being one to hide her talents, such as they are, under a bushel, Rebekah told a *Harper's Bazaar* reporter: "Gian Carlo Menotti told me I was a fool not to study music seriously. He said, 'You'll probably be dead before anyone cares about it, but do it anyway for your own satisfaction.'" Posterity has not had a chance to assay Ms. Harkness' musical gifts as yet but when the time comes, there'll be enough artifacts of her compositions available for inspection since the willful heiress has paid a number of orchestras to make recordings of them. The albums carry Mercury, Vanguard, and Westminster labels.

Rebekah's late mother, a St. Louis dowager of the country-club set, always felt her daughter's major talent lay in sculpting. But at the mature age of forty-two, Rebekah decided it was dance. Her daily ballet class probably accounts for her unduly erect posture and slender figure to this day. She made her stage debut as a dancer at age fifty-eight and none other than dance critic Walter Terry called her "a fairly accomplished and very hard-working dancer."

He also likened her to the domineering Catherine de Médici, the sixteenth-century French queen who was a major force in the world of dance, dipping into the royal till to finance the world's first ballet extravaganza.

Ms. Harkness' twentieth-century contribution to the world of dance was nothing less. Picture, if you will, this imperial patroness parading majestically into the New York City theater, which she had just remodeled with $5 million of her own money, on the night of April 9, 1974. A string of real diamonds encircled her blond hair, more diamonds fell from her ears, and she clutched a diamond-studded evening bag worth a quarter million dollars as she regally acknowledged the applause of the exuberant opening-night audience assembled to witness the debut of her very own Harkness Ballet troupe. But the ostentation of her costume was nothing compared to the interior decor of her theater. One observer termed it "Rebekah's boudoir" and said it reminded him of a bedroom scene from a Norma Shearer movie. The basic color scheme was baby blue, antique gold, and a striking white; and the predominant fabric was velvet in draped, upholstered, and carpeted form. The floor was covered wall to wall in plush baby blue and the front curtain was a gauzy apricot. Enormous crystal chandeliers hung from the elaborately filigreed ceiling, and on either side of the stage rose two huge surrealistic murals depicting nudes and semi-nudes of both sexes in languid poses. Rising up phoenixlike from the center of this orgy was an imposing blond goddess figure, fully clothed, representing the benefactress herself.

As to the energetic exhibition that took place *on* the stage, the critics were not suitably impressed nor, apparently, the ticket-buying public, for the whole shebang closed within a matter of months. The stated reason was lack of financing. Ms. Harkness once said that her second husband, William Hale Harkness, had tried to teach her about business. "He used to say, 'If you're going to have money, you'd better know how to handle it.' I've learned a little about it, which is very helpful." Damned little and not helpful enough, unfortunately. Whether she truly overextended her resources or got caught in a liquidity bind due to the '74–'75 recession was never clear. She consoled herself with a fourth marriage, this time to Dr. Neils H. Lauersen, but that didn't survive the recession either. Except to put some of her residential real estate on the block, the once-resplendent Lady Bountiful hasn't been heard from since.

Before she vanished, Rebekah voiced a lament reminiscent of all her wealthy predecessors: "If I were starving to death for my art in a one-room apartment, the heart of the world would go out to me and everybody would say, 'I hope she makes it.' But because I'm loaded, they all look at me and say, 'Show me.' It's a very hard thing to face the fact that people almost wish you ill."

How did she muster up the courage to ignore the snickers and forge ahead? Before her house came crashing down around her, she told Walter Terry, "People of means have a responsibility to leave something behind. I'd like to leave something behind other than a hangover when I depart, if that's possible. But I can't do it all myself. I'm given credit for having a helluva lot more money than I've got." On that subject, the lady apparently spoke the truth.

The Millionaire Misfits

They say money buys everything but happiness. Unfortunately, there's one other thing it doesn't guarantee—the good behavior of the beneficiary. Indeed, legacies and petty criminal acts are hardly mutually exclusive as the following cases will illustrate.

With a grandfather worth more than a billion, John Paul Getty 3d was booked in 1975 for the theft of a pick-up truck. He was released on $2,000 bail. The Los Angeles sheriff claimed Getty smashed his small foreign sports car against a guardrail, abandoned the car, stole a truck parked nearby, and then got stopped for speeding.

This incident pales next to the mess young Getty had already made of his personal life by the tender age of twenty-four. This U.C.L.A. dropout is married, the father of a small son; and, according to the courts, he is legally incapable of managing his own money. Shortly after he turned twenty-one, he had to listen to his maternal grandfather, Judge George Harris of the U.S. District Court in San Francisco, tell the court his grandson was easily victimized, financially improvident, and in danger of going broke. The young Getty's comeback was weak: "I managed the best way I could. After all, I *was* a business administration major." In case you didn't recognize the name, this is the same young man who gained worldwide sympathy in 1972 when he was kidnapped in Italy. The abductors cut off his right ear and mailed it to his family before the Gettys finally coughed up his ticket to freedom —a $2.2 million ransom.

Industrialist Armand Hammer may be proud of his priceless art collection and his well-publicized efforts to bring detente between the U.S. and Russia, but he's certainly not proud of his only son. In 1976, Julian A. Hammer, then forty-seven years old, was charged with receiving stolen property after Los Angeles police searched his home and found an antique dagger and ring that matched the descriptions of items filched during a series of Malibu burglaries. And this wasn't Julian's first brush with the law. In 1955, he was charged with the fatal shooting of a friend. The charges were later dismissed after Hammer successfully argued that he'd acted in self-defense.

A number of young heirs who came of age in the psychedelic '60s have been arrested for possession of drugs. Among them are Robert F. Kennedy, Jr., and his cousin, R. Sargent Shriver III; Leo Goodwin 3d, who died of an overdose; Benson Ford, Jr.; and one of drugstore tycoon Jack Eckerd's sons.

But their petty offenses were nothing compared to the enterprising multimillion-dollar acid manufacturing operation of William Mellon Hitchcock, the forty-one-year-old grandnephew of Pittsburgh financiers Andrew and Richard B. Mellon. The front "Billy" Mellon Hitchcock presented to the world was 100 percent patrician: fifth-generation descendant from Judge Thomas Mellon, the Mellon-family patriarch; beneficiary of a $160-million trust fund that yielded anywhere from $5 million to $7 million a year; a special arrangement with the blue-blood securities firm of Delafield and Delafield that allowed him to act as the broker for his own account and that of a few relatives and friends; a fashionable wife and children; and a 2,650-acre estate in Millbrook, New York. That estate became infamous as the communal outpost of ex-Harvard professor Dr. Timothy Leary. A *Village Voice* reporter who spent a weekend there in mid-1968 described it as the "Eastern version of the electric koolaid acid test."

Hitchcock's motives for helping to mastermind and bankroll the largest acid production and distribution ring in history have never been clear. While his partners in crime—Leary; Case Western Reserve chemistry professor Lester Friedman; boy scientific genius Tim Scully; Brooklyn manipulator Nick Sand; and the "king of LSD" himself, Augustus Owsley Stanley III, the grandson of a former governor of Kentucky and U.S. Senator—saw Hitchcock as an ideological ally who, like themselves, wanted to kick the establishment in the teeth, there is some evidence that Hitchcock had the profit motive uppermost in his thoughts the whole time. There were rumors that he had lost a bundle in the stock market and wanted to replenish his capital.

LSD, sold under the name of "Orange Sunshine," was Hitchcock's passkey into paradise. The scheme had the added benefit of saving him thousands in taxes. While Leary functioned as the group's public relations and advertising head and the Hell's Angels handled distribution, Hitchcock was responsible for the financial and legal end of the business. He underwrote the conspirators' research and development efforts in the production of LSD, STP, DMT and mescaline; found "safe banks" for stashing profits; and provided lawyers whenever their best-laid plans went awry, as they did with increasing frequency after 1969.

The feds finally nailed Hitchcock in 1972 thanks to carelessness on the part of an international errand boy and an estranged wife who was feeling vindictive. The charge was tax evasion. Under indictment, Hitchcock freaked and began describing himself as an ignorant investor who was misled. To save his family's good name and trust fund, he turned state's evidence and ended up with a five-year suspended sentence and $20,000 in fines. His friends got sentences ranging from stiff fines to twenty years behind bars. Needless to say, he is no longer on speaking terms with his double-crossed associates.

Drugs also figured heavily in the story of Michael James Brody, Jr., grandson of John F. Jelke, the Good Luck margarine magnate. Brody is tied with or competes with Hitchcock for the million-aire-misfit-of-the-decade award. It could be said of Hitchcock that he helped transform a cottage industry into a grand international enterprise. Brody, on the other hand, made an ass of himself on a much smaller scale.

On his twenty-first birthday in October 1969, Brody watched his personal worth soar to between $3 million and $4 million. With more than 400 LSD trips to his credit (so he claimed), Brody's wits gave out under the strain of his newfound wealth. He proclaimed himself the Messiah of Money—what *Time* magazine called "a combination of Terry Southern's Guy Grand in *The Magic Christian* and Kurt Vonnegut's saintly, alcoholic millionaire in *God Bless You, Mr. Rosewater*"—and passed out more than $100,000 to complete strangers before frantic trust officers shut off his supply.

A pop-religious sermon accompanied each handout. After giving a heroin addict $500, he intoned: "You want love? You'll get love. Money. Cars. If you want my death, you can have that too." His Scarsdale, New York, home became the Mecca for thousands of suppliants who were alternately blessed ("Anyone who believes in me can never die. . . . I need seven days, and I'll save the world") and reviled ("I'm sick of hard-luck stories. If you don't leave me alone, I'll kill myself—and you'll all die!"). At one point, he claimed he had forty-eight missiles that he intended to use to obliterate mankind ("I can destroy as well as create") and made an unsuccessful pilgrimage to the White House to confer with President Nixon about his plan to end the Vietnam war. (Brody's plan was to have Nixon make him a general in the United States Army.)

Brody's credibility cracked when his checks began to bounce, and it became clear that an RCA record contract as a rock singer was his real goal. (He signed one for more than $10,000 but it was later canceled by mutual agreement.) But maybe it wasn't his objective, after all. In one of his last hallucinatory statements, he proclaimed: "I'll never be happy as long as there are wars and starving children. I'm just a big put-on. The world is one big put-on."

The Haughty Horticulturists

Horticulture, the fancy term for gardening, is probably the number one avocation of the female *crème de la crème* in this country. Peruse the membership list of the New York Horticultural Society sometime and you'll think you're reading a print-out of the account-holders at Morgan Guaranty Trust Co., where you don't bank unless you plan on leaving a minimum balance of $10,000 in your checking account.

These dedicated tillers of the soil are in the tradition of Marie Antoinette who used to seek temporary sanctuary at Le Petit Trianon, a make-believe farm on the grounds of Versailles. There she would cleanse her soul by simulating the idyllic life of a simple peasant lass. Indeed, it could have been Marie Antoinette herself talking when social butterfly C. Z. Guest (Mrs. Winston Frederick Churchill Guest) told an interviewer recently: "The best thing in the world is simplicity. . . . Some people are afraid to put their hands into the earth. They don't realize how lucky we are to live here. Plants do so much for us; they give us medicine and vitamins." In short, pruning, potting, transplanting, and weeding are next to godliness and the dirtier you get, the better.

Mrs. Guest failed to mention, of course, that plants have also launched her on a whole new career—that of socialite gardener *par excellence*. Her 1976 how-to book *First Garden*—with its charming children's-book format, flowery introduction by her pal Truman Capote, and handsome illustrations by Cecil Beaton— has put her in great demand as a syndicated garden columnist and lecturer on the women's club circuit. It has also helped her publicize her other venture, a chic line of Italian garden furniture known as C. Z. Guest-Cittone Ltd., sold only through decorators for very high prices.

Mrs. Guest is the latest of a long line of aristocratic American matrons who have made a name for themselves on their hands and knees. The late Mrs. Roy Arthur Hunt, the wife of an Alcoa founder, got honorary degrees from the University of Pittsburgh and Carnegie Tech for her contribution to the fields of horticulture and botany. She reciprocated by presenting Carnegie Tech with the Rachel McMasters Miller Hunt Botanical Library, said to be the largest private collection of gardening literature in the world. Mrs. E. Claiborne Robins, the wife of the head of A. H. Robins, drug manufacturer, is so skilled with a trowel that she was given *carte blanche* when it came time to landscape the firm's Richmond plant. For her handiwork, the Central Richmond Association honored the company with its turnpike-beautification award.

But the gentlewoman with the biggest green thumb of all is still Paul Mellon's second wife, "Bunny" (Rachel Lambert Lloyd Mellon), the Listerine mouthwash heiress. Bunny became the nation's premier arbiter of horticultural good taste when First Lady Jackie Kennedy put her in charge of caring for the White House Rose Garden which President Eisenhower had used as a putting green. (Jackie and Bunny were very old and dear friends.) In addition, Bunny was one of twelve patricians Jackie named to her blue-ribbon White House committee to locate antique furniture for the restoration of the executive mansion. At Jack Kennedy's funeral, Bunny was also there arranging all the floral tributes that arrived from all over the nation and the world. When Kennedy's gravesite needed landscaping, Bunny again stepped in.

During Lyndon Johnson's administration, Mrs. Mellon completed her tenure as the unofficial White House groundskeeper with her design of the Jacqueline Kennedy garden. The garden features a pool that shoots water ten feet in the air, a croquet area, a teak table where guests can sit awestruck by the floral splendor surrounding them, an herb garden, grape arbor, and plenty of flowers suitable for cutting. Bunny's reward for all this work was the 1966 U.S. Interior Department Conservation Service Award for "outstanding efforts in furthering the conservation of natural resources."

Mrs. Mellon is not 100 percent workhorse. She's at least 50 percent clotheshorse, spending more than $100,000 on her wardrobe each year. Givenchy, her favorite exponent of *haute couture*, designs underwear especially suited to her body's topography.

NOTES

1. If you've any doubt that self-made moguls cast a forbidding shadow over their progeny, consider the existence of an organization called Sons of Bosses International. It's dedicated to solving the psychological conflicts and bruised egos of sons, daughters, and even sons-in-law who labor under the stern eye of the family patriarch. It is the stated belief of the founders of this organization that fathers who build up and run their own businesses are invariably intense, competitive people who are emotionally bound up in their enterprise to the point of neurosis.

Harry Levinson, a psychologist who has studied father-son relationships in closely held companies, says: "For the entrepreneur-father, the business comes to define his position in life. When a son is brought into the business, the father has all the problems of a man who introduces his rival to his mistress." In short, the son becomes a threat, or potential embarrassment, or worse still, someone to be tolerated to keep peace in the family. Levinson claims it's rare that a son is welcomed open-heartedly and given a free rein.

New York City psychiatrist Dr. Milton R. Sapirstein has a different view. "When a father's wealth reaches well beyond a certain point, the man has a rough time raising his children. The thing that most people would like to believe is that the father crushes the son and the son, therefore, ends up a spineless idiot. That is not the case at all. It happens, of course, that a powerfully motivated father by his very nature becomes an example of achievement that the son cannot hope to emulate. How many successes can there be in one or two generations? Sometimes, it is a pathetic situation for the second generation. They have no place to go. But it is not because the father wants to hold his son down. He wants to be proud of him but he is usually disappointed." (Isadore Barmash, *The Self-Made Man*. New York: Macmillan, 1969, pages 249-250.)

2. The ratings are based on management articles that appeared in prominent business publications: *FORTUNE*, *Business Week*, *Forbes*, the *Wall Street Journal*, as well as *The New York Times*, *Time* magazine, *Newsweek*, *Philadelphia* magazine, *The New Yorker*, and *New York* magazine.

6

A rich man without heirs is like an unmilked cow.

—Aunt Dagmar
Portrait in Brownstone,
by Louis Auchincloss

The following list of childless multimillionaires is dedicated to the country's elite fraternity of professional fund-raisers. They'll know what to do with it.

Edward Ball, 93, Jacksonville, Fla.
Cordelia Scaife Duggan, 53, Pittsburgh, Pa.
Doris Duke, 69, Somerville, N.J., and Hawaii
Helen Clay Frick, 92, Pittsburgh, Pa., and Long Island, N.Y.
Harry B. Helmsley, 72, New York, N.Y.
Mary D. Lasker, 70s, New York, N.Y.
William Rosenwald, 78, New York, N.Y.
Anthony T. Rossi, 81, Bradenton, Fla.
DeWitt and Lila Acheson Wallace, both 92, Chappaqua, N.Y.
Robert W. Woodruff, 92, Atlanta, Ga.

SELF-MADE MEN

MODERN MOGULS WHO'VE
MADE MORE THAN $50 MILLION[1]

WORTH $2 BILLION–$3 BILLION

Daniel K. Ludwig, eighty-four, New York, N.Y., and Bahamas — founder, National Bulk Carriers (shipping); diversified holdings (real estate, natural resources, and savings and loans)

$500 MILLION–$1 BILLION

Pritzker family, Chicago, Ill. — venture capitalists; controlling interest in Hyatt Corp. (hotels)

Leonard Stern, forty-three, New York, N.Y. — executive, Hartz Mountain Industries (pet supplies and New Jersey real estate; privately held)

$300 MILLION–$500 MILLION

Kenneth W. Ford, seventy-three, Roseburg, Ore. — founder, Roseburg Lumber Co. (forest products; privately held); Ford Industries (auxiliary telephone equipment)

Ray Kroc, seventy-nine, Chicago, Ill., and La Jolla, Calif. — executive, McDonald's System (fast-food chain); owner, San Diego Padres baseball team

Malcolm P. McLean, sixty-seven, Mobile, Ala. — founder, Mc-

Lean Industries; majority owner, Diamondhead Corp. (real estate development); U.S. Lines (shipping); First Colony Farms (corporate farming); Loyal American Life Insurance Co.

Milton J. Petrie, seventy-nine, New York, N.Y. — founder, Petrie Stores (women's clothing shops)

Laurence A. Tisch, fifty-eight; Preston Tisch, fifty-five (brothers), New York, N.Y. — executives, Loews Corp. (conglomerate in hotels, theaters, tobacco, and insurance)

Edwin C. Whitehead, sixty-two, Greenwich, Conn. — cofounder, Technicon (medical equipment manufacturer), subsidiary of Revlon

$200 MILLION–$300 MILLION

Charles Allen, Jr., seventy-eight, New York, N.Y. — founder, Allen & Co. (investment banking)

Olive Ann Beech (Mrs. Walter H. Beech), seventy-eight, Wichita, Kan. — cofounder, Beech Aircraft, subsidiary of Raytheon Corp.

Loren M. Berry, ninety-two, Dayton, Ohio — founder, L. M. Berry & Co. (privately held advertising agency)

Harvey R. Bright, sixty, Dallas, Tex. — executive, East Texas Motor Freight Lines (privately held common carrier)

Roy J. Carver, seventy-one, Muscatine, Iowa — founder, Bandag, Inc. (tire retreads and equipment)

Henry Crown, eighty-five, Chicago, Ill. — financier/industrialist; philanthropist

Joyce C. Hall, ninety, Kansas City, Mo., and Malibu Beach, Calif. — founder, Hallmark Cards (privately held)

Harry Helmsley, seventy-two, New York, N.Y. — founder, Helmsley-Spear (real estate)

Leon Hess, sixty-seven, New York, N.Y. — executive, Amerada Hess (oil)

William R. Hewlett, sixty-seven, Palo Alto, Calif. — cofounder, Hewlett-Packard (electronic equipment)

Kirk Kerkorian, sixty-four, Los Angeles, Calif. — financier (entertainment industry); real estate

Sam Lefrak, sixty-two, New York, N.Y. — real estate

Mitchell family, Houston, Tex. — founders, Mitchell Energy & Development (oil and gas exploration, real estate)

David H. Murdock, fifty-seven, Los Angeles, Calif. — executive, Pacific Holding Corp. and David H. Murdock Development Co. (privately held real estate, meat processing, and diversified manufacturing company); finance chairman for John Connally's 1980 presidential campaign

David Packard, sixty-nine, Palo Alto, Calif. — cofounder, Hewlett-Packard (electronic equipment)

Jackson T. Stephens, fifty-seven; Wilton R. Stephens, seventy-three (brothers), Little Rock, Ark. — cofounders, Stephens, Inc. (investment banking); public utilities, insurance

DeWitt Wallace, ninety-two; Lila Acheson Wallace, ninety-two (married), Chappaqua, N.Y. — cofounders, *Reader's Digest*

Dr. An Wang, sixty-one, Lowell, Mass. — founder, Wang Laboratories (small-business computers, word processors)

Harry Weinberg, seventy-two, Honolulu, Hi. — real estate in Hawaii; former owner, Fifth Avenue Coach Line; investor

$100 MILLION–$200 MILLION

Albert B. Alkek, sixty-nine, Victoria, Tex. — founder, Alkek Oil Corp. (privately held production and transportation company); executive, American Bank of Commerce

Joseph L. Allbritton, fifty-six, Houston, Tex. — executive, Perpetual Corp. (privately held communications and banking)

Gene Autrey, seventy-three, Hollywood, Calif.—actor/singer dubbed the "Singing Cowboy"; owner, Golden West Broadcasting Co. (radio-TV holding company), California Angels baseball team, cattle ranch in Arizona, and the Gene Autrey Hotel in Palm Springs

Donald Bren, forty-seven, Orange County, Calif. — executive, Bren Co. (privately held real estate)

Curtis L. Carlson, sixty-seven, Minneapolis, Minn. — founder, Carlson Cos. (privately held holding company for trading stamps, hotels, restaurants, candy and tobacco wholesaling; optical and tennis gear importing enterprises, etc.)

Edwin L. Cox, fifty-nine, Dallas, Tex. — founder, Cox Oil Co. (privately held exploration and production company)

Nathan Cummings, eighty-four, Chicago, Ill., and New York, N.Y. — retired founder, Consolidated Foods

Edward J. Daly, fifty-nine, Oakland, Calif. — founder, World Airways

Barrie Damson, forty-five, New York, N.Y. — founder, Damson Oil Corp.

Leonard Davis, fifty-seven, Philadelphia, Pa. — founder, Colonial Penn Group (low-cost insurance for the elderly)

Richard DeVos, fifty-five, Ada, Mich. — cofounder, Amway Corp. (privately held household products and cosmetics sold door-to-door)

Thomas Mellon Evans, seventy, New York, N.Y., and Pittsburgh, Pa. — executive, H. K. Porter Co. (diversified holding company); Crane Co. (plumbing fixtures and valves); and Evans & Co. (brokerage)

Sol Goldman, sixty-three, New York, N.Y. — real estate

Gerald D. Hines, fifty-five, Houston, Tex. — founder, Gerald D. Hines Interests (real-estate development and ownership)

Joseph Hirshhorn, eighty-two, Washington, D.C. — retired stockbroker; minerals entrepreneur; philanthropist

Oveta Culp Hobby (Mrs. William Pettus Hobby), seventy-six, Houston, Tex. — executive, *Houston Post*, and head of family-owned communications empire; real estate; U.S. Secretary of HEW in Eisenhower's administration

Bob Hope, seventy-eight, Hollywood, Calif. — entertainer; investor

Lauder family, New York, N.Y., and Palm Beach, Fla. — founder, Estée Lauder (cosmetics)

Carl H. Lindner, sixty-one; Robert Lindner (brothers), Cincinnati, Ohio — executives, American Financial Corp. (diversified holding company); United Dairy Farmers (convenience stores)

Long family, Walnut Creek, Calif. — founders, Longs Drug Stores (self-service)

Alex Manoogian, eighty, Detroit, Mich. — founder, Masco Corp. (faucets and metal products)

Raymond K. Mason, fifty-four, Jacksonville, Fla. — executive, Charter Co. (oil and energy; publishing)

W. A. (Monty) Moncrief, eighty-six, Fort Worth, Tex. — independent oil operator

Robert A. Mosbacher, fifty-three, Houston, Tex. — executive, Mosbacher Production Co. (privately held oil exploration and production company)

Kenneth H. Olsen, forty-five+, Boston, Mass. — founder, Digital Equipment Corp. (computer manufacturer)

William G. Reed, seventy-three, Seattle, Wash. — executive, Simpson Timber (privately held wood products, chemicals, plastics)

Roy Richards, sixty-eight, Carrollton, Ga. — executive, Southwire Co. (privately held wire and cable manufacturer)

O. Wayne Rollins, sixty-nine, Atlanta, Ga. — founder, Rollins, Inc. (broadcasting, advertising, cosmetics, exterminating, etc.); Florida real estate

John S. Samuels 3d, forty-eight, New York, N.Y. — founder, Carbomin International Corp. (privately held holding company with diversified interests)

Norton Simon, seventy-four, Los Angeles, Calif. — retired founder, Norton Simon, Inc. (conglomerate)

Jules Stein, eighty-five, Los Angeles, Calif. — founder, MCA, Inc. (records and films)

W. Clement Stone, seventy-nine, Chicago, Ill. — executive, Combined International Corp.

S. Mark Taper, eighty, Los Angeles, Calif. — founder, First Charter Financial Corp.

Juan Terry Trippe, eighty-two, New York, N.Y. — founder, Pan American World Airways

---

Jay VanAndel, fifty-six, Ada, Mich. — cofounder, Amway Corp. (privately held household products and cosmetics sold door-to-door)

$50 MILLION–$100 MILLION

J. A. Albertson, seventy-six, Boise, Idaho — executive, Albertson's (supermarket chain)

Robert O. Anderson, sixty-four, Roswell, N.M. — executive, Atlantic Richfield Co.; investor (real estate, ranching, farming; Bank Securities Inc.; Hyer Boot Company)

Lucille Ball, seventy, Hollywood, Calif. — entertainer; executive, Lucille Ball Productions, Inc.; investor

Erol Beker, sixty-three, Greenwich, Conn. — founder, Beker Industries (fertilizers)

Curtis L. Blake, sixty-four, West Hartford, Conn. — retired cofounder, Friendly Ice Cream Co., subsidiary of Hershey Foods Corp.

S. Prestley Blake, sixty-seven, Wilbraham, Mass. — cofounder, Friendly Ice Cream Co., subsidiary of Hershey Foods Corp.

Block family, New York, N.Y. — founders, Block Drug Co.

Ivan F. Boesky, forty-four, New York, N.Y. — founder, Ivan F. Boesky & Co. (investment management)

Dolph Briscoe, fifty-eight, Uvalde, Tex. — real estate in southwest Texas; ranching; former Texas governor

Eli Broad, forty-eight, Los Angeles, Calif. — executive, Kaufman & Broad (homebuilders)

George R. Brown, eighty-three, Houston, Tex. — cofounder, Brown & Root (construction)

Edward M. Carey, sixty-four, New York, N.Y. — founder, Carey Energy Corp. (holding company) sold to Charter Co.

Johnny Carson, fifty-six, Hollywood, Calif. — entertainer, host of NBC's "Tonight Show"; executive, Carson Productions, Inc.; diversified investments

Thomas L. Carter, fifty-three, Houston and east Texas — executive, W. T. Carter & Brothers (investments); Texas Commerce Bancshares

W. P. Clements, Jr., sixty-four, Dallas and Austin, Tex. — Sedco (independent oil drilling); politician

John F. Connelly, seventy-six, Philadelphia, Pa. — executive, Crown Cork & Seal and Connelly Containers

Trammell Crow, sixty-six, Dallas, Tex. — founder, Trammell Crow Co. (real estate)

William M. Davidson, fifty-eight, Novi, Mich. — executive, Guardian Industries (auto and architectural glass manufacturers)

Edward M. Davis, forty-eight, Houston, Tex. — executive, Tiger Oil International (exploration and production), division of Cleveland-Cliffs Iron

Heinz Eppler, fifty-two, Secaucus, N.J. — executive, Miller-Wohl Co. (retail apparel chain)

Epstein family, Chicago, Ill. — A. Epstein & Sons International (privately held construction and engineering firm)

Harold Farb, fifty+, Houston, Tex. — furniture, real estate, and apartment development

Manny Fingerhut, sixty-six, Minneapolis, Minn. — cofounder, Fingerhut Corp. (mail-order sales of consumer products)

Max Fisher, seventy-three, Detroit, Mich. — executive, Aurora Gasoline Co.

Thomas J. Flatley, forty-nine, Boston, Mass. — executive, Flatley Enterprises (privately held real estate development)

Edward J. Frey, seventy-one, Grand Rapids, Mich. — cofounder, Centennial Corp. (insurance for mobile homes)

J. B. Fuqua, sixty-three, Atlanta, Ga. — founder, Fuqua Industries (conglomerate with recreation/leisure orientation)

Bertin C. Gamble, eighty-three, Minneapolis, Minn. — cofounder, Gamble-Skogmo, Inc. (wholesale and retail merchandising), division of Wicks Cos.

Gordon family, Houston, Tex. — founders, Gordon Jewelry (retail stores)

Cecil H. Green, eighty-one, Dallas, Tex. — cofounder, Geophysical Services, now Texas Instruments

Maurice R. Greenberg, fifty-six, New York, N.Y. — executive, American International Group (insurance holding company)

Frank K. Greenwall, eighty-five, New York, N.Y. — retired executive, National Starch & Chemical Co.

Ben Hill Griffin, Jr., seventy, Frostproof, Fla. — executive, Griffin Co. (privately held citrus products company)

Bud Grossman, fifty-nine, Eden Prairie, Minn. — executive, Gelco Corp. (privately held soft-drink bottling, vehicle-leasing, petroleum-marketing firm)

Bob Guccione, fifty, New York, N.Y. — founder, Penthouse International Ltd. (privately held magazine publishing company); venture capitalist in leisure-entertainment industry

Patrick E. Haggerty, sixty-seven, Dallas, Tex. — retired executive, Geophysical Services, now Texas Instruments

Michel T. Halbouty, seventy-two, Houston, Tex. — executive, Halbouty Alaska Oil Co.; independent oil and gas operator

Dr. Armand Hammer, eighty-three, Los Angeles, Calif. — executive, Occidental Petroleum

Irving Harris, seventy-one, Chicago, Ill. — cofounder, Toni home permanents; executive, Pittway Corp.; Standard Shares

Ralph Ingersoll, eighty, Sharon, Conn. — executive, Ingersoll Publications (privately held newspapers)

Irwin Jacobs, thirty-nine, Minneapolis, Minn. — executive, Jacobs Industries, Inc. (privately held diversified investments)

J. Erik Jonsson, eighty, Dallas, Tex. — cofounder, Texas Instruments; politician

Ewing Kauffman, sixty-one, Kansas City, Mo. — founder, Marion Laboratories (drugs); owner, Kansas City Royals baseball team

Robert Krieble, sixty-five, West Hartford, Conn. — executive, Loctite Corp. (sealants and adhesives)

Dr. Edwin H. Land, seventy-two, Cambridge, Mass. — founder, Polaroid Corp.

Herman Lay, seventy-two, Dallas, Tex. — founder, Frito-Lay (snack foods); executive, PepsiCo.

Thomas E. Leavey, eighty-four, Los Angeles, Calif. — cofounder, Farmers Group (insurance)

William J. Levitt, seventy-four, New York, N.Y. — cofounder, Levitt & Sons (home builders)

C. K. McClatchy, fifty-three, Sacramento, Calif. — executive, McClatchy Newspapers, Inc. (privately held newspapers, radio and TV stations)

Billy J. "Red" McCombs, fifty-three, San Antonio, Tex. — venture capitalist (Mr. M. convenience stores; seven radio stations; oil exploration and drilling; real estate; ranching; Rolls-Royce dealership; insurance; Subaru distributorship; Houston bank; pay television company; commuter airline; and minor league football team); partial owner, Stanford Court Hotel, San Francisco, and San Antonio Spurs basketball team

John H. McConnell, fifty-seven, Worthington, Ohio — executive, Worthington Industries (steel processing)

Bernard Patrick McDonough, seventy-eight, Parkersburg, W. Va. — executive, McDonough Co. (mini-conglomerate)

Patrick McGovern, forty+, Waltham, Mass. — executive, International Data Corp. (privately held computer software and market research firm)

John W. Mecom, Sr., seventy, Houston, Tex. — independent oil operator

Fred Meyer, ninety-five, Portland, Ore. — founder, Fred Meyer, Inc. (shopping centers, food stores)

Gordon Moore, fifty-one, Santa Clara, Calif. — executive, Intel Corp. (semiconductor memory circuits and microcomputers)

C. H. Murphy, Jr., sixty, El Dorado, Ark. — executive, Murphy Oil Corp. (integrated oil company)

Roy R. Neuberger, seventy-eight, New York, N.Y. — cofounder, Neuberger & Berman (brokerage); Westchester County, N.Y., real estate

Wayne Newton, thirty-eight, Las Vegas, Nev. — entertainer/singer; diversified investments (real estate, Arabian horses, hotels, casinos)

Obering family, Denver, Colo. — Warrior Oil Co. (privately held exploration and production company)

William O'Donnell, fifty-eight, Chicago, Ill. — founder, Bally

Manufacturing (pinball and slot machines); casino real estate

Max Palevsky, fifty-six, Los Angeles and Palm Springs, Calif. — founder, Scientific Data Systems; venture capitalist

William S. Paley, eighty, New York, N.Y. — founder, Columbia Broadcasting System

Roy Park, seventy, Ithaca, N.Y. — sole owner, Park Broadcasting, Inc.

Jeno Paulucci, sixty-three, Duluth, Minn., and New York, N.Y. — founder, Chun King and Jeno's, Inc. (fast foods); executive, R. J. Reynolds and Paulucci Enterprises

Frank Perdue, sixty, Salisbury, Md. — founder, Perdue, Inc. (privately held chicken processor)

H. Ross Perot, fifty-one, Dallas, Tex. — founder, Electronic Data Systems (computer software)

B. J. Pevehouse, fifty-five, Midland, Tex. — executive, Adobe Oil Co. (exploration and production; mining)

Victor Posner, sixty-two, Miami, Fla. — venture capitalist, Sharon Steel, NVF Industries, and several other companies; diversified industrial enterprises

Samuel N. Regenstrief, sixty-nine, Connersville, Ind. — executive, Design & Manufacturing Co. (privately held dishwasher manufacturer)

Donald W. Reynolds, seventy-two, Fort Smith, Ark. — executive, Donrey Media Group (privately held newspapers, TV and radio stations, cable TV, billboards)

Richard E. Riebel, fifty-eight, Grand Rapids, Mich. — cofounder, Centennial Corp. (insurance for mobile homes)

Corbin J. Robertson, sixty, Houston, Tex. — executive, Quintana Petroleum (privately held exploration and production company)

Chapman S. Root, fifty-six, Daytona Beach, Fla. — executive, Associated Coca-Cola Bottling (bottling and distribution)

Anthony T. Rossi, eighty-one, Bradenton, Fla. — founder, Tropicana Products (fruit juices), subsidiary of Beatrice Foods

Louis J. Roussel, Jr., seventy-five, New Orleans, La. — independent oil operator; banks and insurance companies

Eddy C. Scurlock, seventy-six, Houston, Tex. — founder, Scurlock Oil Co. (privately held transportation, refining, and production company)

R. Y. Sharpe, seventy-five, Charlotte, N.C. — executive, Pilot Freight Carriers, Inc. (privately held common carrier)

Charles E. Smith, Washington, D.C. — founder, Charles E. Smith Companies (real estate)

Smith family, Houston, Tex. — executives, Big Three Industries (industrial gases and welding equipment)

Oscar Stauffer, ninety-four, Des Moines, Iowa — founder, Stauffer Communications (privately held newspapers, radio and TV stations)

Robert W. Stoddard, seventy-four, Worcester, Mass.—executive, Wyman-Gordon Co. (metal forgings)

Jimmy Storm, sixty-seven, Corpus Christi, Tex. — executive, Marine Drilling Corp. (privately held exploration and production company)

Daniel J. Terra, seventy, Northbrook, Ill. — founder, Lawter Chemicals (inks and resins for printing); finance chairman for Ronald Reagan's 1980 presidential campaign

R. David Thomas, forty-eight, Dublin, Ohio — founder, Wendy's International (hamburger chain)

Tom E. Turner, sixty-eight, San Antonio, Tex. — founder, Sigmor Corp. (gasoline retailers)

Albert Ueltschi, sixty-three, New York, N.Y. — executive, Flightsafety International (pilot-training centers)

Alan Voorhees, fifty-seven, Maynard, Mass. — executive, Data Terminal Systems (terminals and control systems)

Sam M. Walton, sixty-two, Bentonville, Ark. — founder, Wal-Mart Stores (discount and variety stores)

Lew Wasserman, sixty-eight, Los Angeles, Calif. — executive, MCA, Inc. (films and records; other media)

D. J. Witherspoon, sixty-nine, Omaha, Neb. — founder, Pamida, Inc. (regional discount store chain)

Ervin Wolf, fifty-five, New York, N.Y. — executive, Inexco Oil (offshore oil production)

John Wolfe, forty+, Columbus, Ohio — executive, *Columbus Dispatch* (privately held newspaper)

Henry Bartell Zachry, eighty, San Antonio, Tex. — founder, H. B. Zachry Co. (construction, privately held); oil

Zale family, Dallas, Tex. — founders, Zale Corp. (retail jewelry stores)

NOTES

1. The majority of the names on this list were culled from *FORTUNE* magazine, which has published four lists of the richest Americans (see November 1957, May 1968, September 1973, and the February 12, 1979, issues). The remaining names, with the estimates of their personal worth, were taken from various issues of *Business Week, Forbes* (November 1, 1976), *Nation's Business, Philadelphia* magazine (March 1974), *Boston* magazine (November 1972), *Texas Monthly* (October 1978), *New Jersey Monthly* (July 1977), *New York* magazine (November 6, 1978), *Financial World* (September 15, 1978), *Time* (July 25, 1960), *Newsweek* (August 2, 1976), *U.S. News & World Report* (August 14, 1978), *Town & Country* (September 1979), *Jewish Living* (September/October 1979), *The Wall Street Journal, The New York Times,* the *Pittsburgh Press,* Associated Press stories, and the books *The Rich and the Super-Rich* by Ferdinand Lundberg, and *The Very Rich* by Joseph J. Thorndike, Jr.

These estimates of net worth include not only the aggregate of an individual or family's personal holdings, but also those of minor children; and of trusts benefitting the immediate family and foundations.

HOW TO MAKE A MILLION:
ELEVEN RULES FOR THE WOULD-BE RICH

8 Most people who aren't rich daydream about *being* rich. But only a certain kind of person fantasizes about *becoming* rich. Of this group, only a small number *seriously try to get* rich and a tiny minority, indeed, eventually says, *"I am rich."*

If wealth is your goal, you'd best take stock of the human equipment at your disposal—you, that is. Most "self-made" men and women are born with a set of personality traits that predisposes them for business success. While it's true that they might have made it to the top without these hereditary green lights, their climb would have been exceedingly more difficult and precarious.

For the aspiring Croesus, here is a checklist of the primary character traits that usually accompany financial derring-do:

• *Excessive Energy.* Most tycoons can't sit still. They flail around like a hurricane, stirring up motion in every living thing within earshot. Typically, they abhor vacations because they don't want to relax. They find it almost physically painful.

Jeno Paulucci, the fast-food dynamo from Duluth, complained to a reporter, "I never learned to relax. I can't relax. Never could." His fishing buddies say he has no patience with fish that won't cooperate. When the fish are balking, one friend says, Paulucci can "cover more territory than a teen-ager with his first car." As a golfer he's no better. He's quit the game completely several times and usually walks off the course in disgust after three or four holes if he's playing poorly.

In 1966 at the age of forty-eight, Paulucci sold his Chun King

Corp. to R. J. Reynolds Tobacco Co. for $63 million and could have retired to enjoy his windfall. Not Jeno. "I wish I could slow down but I have to have something of my own," said Jeno at the time, explaining why he decided to revive a dormant pizza producer called Jeno's, Inc. ". . . As soon as I sold Chun King I moved over here, remodeled the office, and told our people to take down those signs that said, 'Walk, don't run,' and put up signs that said, 'Run, don't walk.' "

If a tycoon can sit still—a few can—they usually find it impossible to keep their minds still. Dr. Edwin Land, the inventor of the Polaroid self-developing camera, is a voracious reader and claims he never goes to bed with a hypothesis untested. He also admits that makes for a lot of sleepless nights.

• *Ambition* . . . variously described as "drive," "dedication," "an addiction to winning," and "a need to put one's stamp of identity on something." What is the source of this compulsive craving for success? Psychological theorists say it is the need for love and constant approval. Others admit they aren't sure. Says George Kirstein who interviewed a number of psychiatrists on the subject for his book *The Rich: Are They Different?*:

"Despite the often-repeated theories that hard work, sacrifice, luck, and brains are all required to amass wealth in today's America, the true explanation, while scientifically vague in outline, lies elsewhere. Difficult as they are to describe, elusive as they are to study, the keys to the treasure chest lie hidden in personality traits springing from a compulsive inner drive . . . the tireless expenditure of narrowly focused energy."

Highfalutin theories aside, the motive for success sometimes amounts to little more than petty revenge, an I'll-show-them attitude. Paulucci once became so outraged at the tactics of a former business associate who made pie fillings that he decided to start a competitive pie-filling operation. The outcome was the thriving Jeno's, Inc.

• *Emotional and Cardiovascular Stamina* (or the ability to take risks and withstand the resulting stress). Texas oil wildcatter Sid Richardson is the supreme example of the high-stakes player who never gets ruffled. He claimed he never let money, or its absence, worry him.

"I been broke so often I thought it was habit-formin'," he confided to an interviewer shortly before he died. "But there was only one night when I didn't turn the light off and my mind off at the same time. It was thirty-three years ago. I'd just lost a million dollars, and that day I'd had a dry well; I knew I was flat broke.

"But it wasn't those thoughts was keepin' me awake—it was a kidney infection hurtin' me. I had to drink two glasses of buttermilk 'fore I could go to sleep."

Why are some people able to keep their cool in the midst of personal catastrophes? Albert Z. Carr, a management consultant who served on the White House staff under President Truman, claims that the most successful businessmen approach their work like they'd approach a game of poker. In an article entitled "Is Business Bluffing Ethical?" (*Harvard Business Review,* January-February 1968), he delineates the similarity between the special type of ethical attitude shown by successful *stress-free* business executives and good poker players:

"We can learn a good deal about the nature of business by comparing it with poker. While both have a large element of chance, in the long run the winner is the man who plays with steady skill. . . . This does not mean that he must be ruthless, cruel, harsh, or treacherous. On the contrary, the better his reputation for integrity, honesty, and decency, the better his chances of ultimate victory. But from time to time every businessman, like every poker player, is offered a choice between certain loss or bluffing within the legal rules of the game. If he is not resigned to losing, if he wants to rise in his company and industry, then in such a crisis he will bluff—and bluff hard. . . . Whatever the form of the bluff, it is an integral part of the game, and the executive who does not master its techniques is not likely to accumulate much money or power."

Carr's definition of "bluffing" incorporates outright lying which, according to him, the genius businessman/poker player can lightheartedly dismiss as "an integral part of the game." Carr may be on to something because an inordinate number of modern moguls, including Sid Richardson, has admitted an addiction to gambling.

William Benton, cofounder of the advertising agency Benton & Bowles and publisher of the *Encyclopaedia Britannica,* worked his way through Yale on his winnings from auction bridge. He once told a friend, "It's a demonstrable fact that for ten years I was one of the ten or twenty best card players in the world."

Kansas City Royals' owner Ewing Kauffman emerged from the Navy after World War II with more than $50,000 in poker winnings stuffed in his pocket, then went on to build a multimillion-dollar pharmaceutical empire using, no doubt, much the same game strategy. It's been said that the legendary H. L. Hunt entered the oil business by way of the poker table, oil leases being the stakes. Although Hunt denied this, he did say he never met a poker player who was his match. Later in life with his billion-dollar fortune secured, he would bet $50,000, $100,000, up to $300,000 on a single sports event.

A hardness comes into potato-chip potentate Herman Lay's voice when he talks about his obsession with gambling, especially the ten-year-long poker battle he engaged in as a young businessman in Atlanta:

"It was so-called friendly gambling for heavy stakes," he recalls. "There were fifteen people involved and there would be six or seven playing at one time. It started out once a month, then it went to every week, then twice a week. I won on balance, but I won because I stayed sober and watched the game and was a better player than the average. And I would have won considerably over balance if I had been as hard-nosed as one or two of my friends who took $50,000, $75,000, and $150,000 out of it a year. You've got to have no sympathy to do that. No sympathy. When you've got a guy, you've got to grind him. Grind . . . grind . . . grind. When the chance comes, you gotta get it regardless of whether you know the man's in the tank or shouldn't be gambling or anything else. I played the game too well to lose. But it can hurt people badly and that's why I quit. Plus the hours I was spending on it that I needed to spend on rest and work. Later, I got to betting $1,000 to $5,000 a week on football and boxing. Now I doubt that I average $50 or $100 a week, but I enjoy that $50 or $100 just as much. As you get older, I guess you get a little more moderate."

• *Supreme Self-confidence.* Mark Twain once quipped that "A crank is a man with a new idea—until it succeeds." Then, he automatically becomes a genius, of course. Until that time, the striving entrepreneur needs courage and the inner resources to thumb his nose at the world.

Leon Hess, who rose from a fuel truck driver to czar of the

Amerada Hess oil empire, has this kind of steely resolve. An ex-member of the Hess Oil board of directors once observed that there was no way to dissuade Hess once he decided a project was viable. "He becomes so possessed by a goal that he can't let loose even if wisdom suggests that it's the better course. It's his great shortcoming, and maybe his greatest strength."

• *Disciplined Mind.* The late J. Paul Getty referred to this asset as a "millionaire mentality." He said it was "that vitally aware state of mind which harnesses all of an individual's skills and intelligence to the tasks and goals of his business."

You don't need intellectual brilliance to amass a fortune. You do need basic intelligence, common sense, and the ability to concentrate and devise innovative solutions to problems. This knack for problem-solving usually requires a fair degree of creativity and mental agility.

John F. Cuneo, the multimillionaire Chicago printer now deceased, once explained that the only reason he studied engineering for two years was "as a means of training my mind for business. Along that same line I hire young men who have had law training because they have been taught to think logically."

But getting an expensive education is no guarantee that you'll end up with a mind that functions better. You could graduate with a brain overloaded with trivia and be worse off than when you entered. It's the ability to make the right connections between seemingly disparate elements that's important in empire-building.

• *Outer-directed Personality.* One thing most money-makers are *not* is introverted. It is not a part of their nature to relax and reflect and take the long view. They are action oriented.

A Princeton University psychology student once sent Joseph P. Kennedy a long questionnaire intended to probe his psyche for the secret of his success. Typically, Kennedy wasn't wasting any of his precious brainpower answering a bunch of nonsense questions. Instead, he wrote the young man a curt note that said it all as far as he was concerned: "Dear Mr.———: I am rich because I have a lot of money."

While it is accurate to say that moguls are seldom introverted, they aren't universally possessed of an extroverted, backslapping, salesman personality either. But if they've got it, it helps enormously. Being able to impart a contagious enthusiasm to prospective backers, customers, or clients is an important factor when starting a business. Shyness and false modesty are liabilities for those seeking aggrandizement.

The foregoing components of the success formula are largely a matter of genes and chromosomes. Count yourself as fortunate if you've been blessed—or cursed, depending on how you look at it—with this special complex of traits. But keep in mind that in and of themselves they'll get you nowhere.

To be a big winner in the monetary sweepstakes, you must build on heredity, harnessing your particular strengths and weaknesses to the task at hand: making a mint.

The following guidelines will help you channel your potential in the direction of maximum financial gain. Think of these rules as stepping-stones leading you over the rainbow to that proverbial caldron of gold at the other end:

Rule #1: Work for Yourself. In a recent article entitled "Where Big Money Is Made," Marshall Loeb, the economics editor of *Time* magazine, pointed out that despite contemporary headlines disclosing huge salaries for corporate executives—what Loeb calls "higher-up hired hands"—an old fact remains true: "America still reserves its richest rewards not for those few who climb in corporate hierarchies, but for the many who dare, who risk, and who go into business for themselves."

Author George Kirstein seconds the notion: "Anyone who thinks that the average man of today starting at the bottom of the large corporation, gradually rising through hard work and strict obedience to orders to emerge a highly paid executive, can turn his savings into a fortune is sadly mistaken. With exceptions so rare as to be noteworthy, today's self-enriched eschew the savings route to wealth."

And keep in mind that old Benjamin Franklin was only trying to make a buck himself with his *Poor Richard's Almanack* when he propagated the cornball idiocy that thrift leads to riches, that savings accounts eventually swell into fortunes, that "a penny saved is a penny earned." If it were ever true, which is doubtful, it's certainly not true now. Modern magnates do not build fortunes on accumulated savings. Modern moguls build fortunes on borrowed money or O.P.M., "other people's money."

However, don't think starting your own business will be easy. Most financial experts agree that the climate for the bootstraps entrepreneur is growing cloudier because of increasing government red tape and regulation. On the other hand, the extent to which you'll be burdened with government interference depends in great measure on the industry you choose, whether the product you manufacture may be harmful or hazardous, whether noxious by-products are emitted during the manufacturing process, whether you employ enough minority-group members in important jobs to satisfy the authorities.

There are ways to circumvent government watchdoggery. To avoid heavy SEC scrutiny, for instance, keep your company privately held. If you issue shares at all, make sure it's to relatives and close business associates; in short, keep it "in the family." This route has its disadvantages as well. If you've got cash-flow problems, going public is certainly one method for gaining access to a large chunk of working capital—and you can always go private again when the stock bottoms out. The bugaboo here is nosy stockholders.

I once asked John D. MacArthur, the Chicago insurance billionaire, why he insisted on maintaining Bankers Life & Casualty as a sole proprietorship. He exploded. "Go public! Why should I go public and have some son of a bitch with five shares of stock sue me because of my accounting procedures or because I use my company plane to go on a trip somewhere. Hell no! I'll *never* go public."

Such resolves are fine while the Midas lives. But when he dies, huge inheritance taxes invariably force the heirs to take the company public—the IRS wants to be paid in cool, hard currency, not in unissued stock certificates—and the corporate leadership vacuum is usually filled by committee group-think. In 1976, *FORTUNE* magazine referred to MacArthur and his billionaire peers as "magnificent relics of an earlier age of capitalism," noting that today's typical entrepreneur is more likely to hold an MBA degree and adopt the teamwork style of the organization man. As Osborne Elliott put it in his book *Men at the Top*: "The curtain is coming down on the one-man show, and the law is looking over the corporate shoulder every minute of every working day."

Rule #2: Do Something You Enjoy. Pick a road to riches that you'll enjoy exploring because if you don't, you won't be willing to invest the necessary time and energy to make your journey a success.

MacArthur defined work as "something you have to do. Play is something you want to do. I try to give all the work to someone else to do."

Fortunately for him, bossing his insurance company lackeys around and haggling over Florida real estate (he was the largest landowner in the state when he died in 1978 at age eighty) was his idea of fun. It consumed his whole life. "I enjoy what I do," he told me, defending his single-mindedness. "I am a perfectionist. I want any business that I'm connected with to be well managed so I snoop around every so often to make sure everything's running smoothly, and that takes me from coast to coast. I'm very busy. I haven't got time to do anything else. I'm very happy. I don't want to change my life or I would."

Rule #3: If You Have a Specialized Education, Use It. While the majority of today's "self-made men" are educated men, there are still plenty of school-dropouts around—increasingly status-weary school-dropouts. These seat-of-the-pants boys have grown more and more defensive about their truncated schooling as they've watched that nineteenth-century hero, Horatio Alger, downgraded in the public's estimation to a comic figure.

This is a latter-day development for there was a time not long ago when captains of American industry were proud of their sophistry. They say Commodore Vanderbilt was more amused than offended when he heard that Britain's prime minister had expressed dismay at the railroad magnate's abbreviated education. The Commodore supposedly replied, "You can tell Lord Palmerston for me that if I had learned education I would not have had time to learn anything else."

Ferdinand Lundberg is one of the few contemporary observers of the rich who opines, perhaps facetiously, that a formal education is a drawback when it comes to fortune-building. Why? "The reason for this is that in the process of being educated there is always the danger that the individual will acquire scruples. . . . These scruples, unless they are casuistically beveled around the edges with great care, are a distinct handicap to the full-fledged money-maker, who must in every situation be plastically opportunistic."

The modern money-maker must also deal with a far more complex world than that of his predecessors. Even those old-line tycoons who graduated from the school of hard knocks are recommending book learnin' to their protégés these days. Oil speculator Clint Murchison, who proudly proclaimed that experience was his best teacher, insisted that his two sons go to college. One went to MIT, the other to Yale. Murchison claimed his goal was to get them to think better.

Rule #4: Find a Vacuum and Fill It. As people become more affluent and sophisticated, they crave a wider range of goods and services. If you are the first to offer the public something it wants and can't get anywhere else, you stand a good chance of striking it rich, especially if you've got the field to yourself for a while before the competition jumps in and steals some of your market share.

A new invention with a practical application is a sure-fire bonanza. The history of the United States is crammed with examples of tinkerers-turned-titans: Eleuthère Irénée du Pont (gunpowder); Cyrus Hall McCormick (reaper); Isaac Merrit Singer (sewing machine); King Gillette (disposable razor blades); Henry Ford, John and Horace Dodge (automobiles); George Eastman (Kodak camera); Charles Kettering (self-starting engine); William R. Hewlett (audio-oscillator/electronic equipment); Chester Carlson (xerography); James S. McDonnell (aircraft manufacture); and Roy J. Carver (process for retreading tires).

Another category of money moguls made their pile anticipating demographic trends: Julius Rosenwald of Sears Roebuck (mail-order merchandising); William S. Paley of CBS (television as home entertainment); Juan Terry Trippe of Pan American World Airways (growth of air transportation); William J. Levitt of Levittown (flight to suburbia); Leo Corrigan (development of Dallas real-estate market); Jeno Paulucci and Herman Lay (popularity of snack and convenience foods); Ray Kroc of McDonald's hamburgers (franchising); John K. Hanson of Winnebago Industries (recreational vehicles and mobile homes as a way of life); Leonard

Stern of Hartz Mountain Industries (explosion in family pet ownership and care); and Curtis L. Carlson of Gold Bond (trading
stamp vogue).

Still, a genuine vacuum is hard to come by these days—after
all, what's really new under the sun?—so you may have to settle
for improving on goods or services already available. Variations
on an insurance theme, for instance, have yielded a number of
millionaires: MacArthur pioneered mail-order insurance. Leonard
Davis' Colonial Penn Group specializes in low-cost insurance for
the elderly. Edward J. Frey and Richard Riebel came up with
special insurance for mobile-home owners. And Leo Goodwin, Sr.,
discovered a gold mine selling auto insurance to government employees under the acronym GEICO (Government Employees Insurance Company).

Rule #5: Research Your Idea Carefully. You're probably saying
to yourself, "Where am I going to get this stroke-of-genius idea,
this hunch that's going to make me a million?"

You're going to get it from the same place that all moguls get
it—from inside yourself. Real-estate entrepreneur Leo Corrigan
defined a hunch as "inbred knowledge guaranteed from experience"
and admitted his career was like a giant monopoly game with his
hunches directing all his moves. Einstein defined original ideas—
he claimed he had only two during his whole life—as the products
of intuition combined with reason. He said he spent most of his
time acquiring and organizing the incredible amount of knowledge
he needed in order to make those two great intuitive leaps.

Clearly, the first step is stuffing your brain, your own personal
data processing unit, with all there is to know about a subject.[1]
Henry Mintzberg, a business management professor at McGill
University, has dissected the intuitive process and postulates that
idea production takes place in four interrelated stages: preparation
("creativity favors the prepared mind"); incubation ("letting the
subconscious do the work"); illumination ("waking up in the middle of the night and shouting, 'Eureka, I've got it!' "); and verifica-
tion ("working it all out linearly").

In short, laziness produces lousy hunches. Engineer John
Mihalasky and parapsychologist E. Douglas Dean have also examined human idea-generation and devised a broad formula for
turning on the proverbial light bulb: (1) Concentrate on what is

unique. (2) Be aware of the gaps in your knowledge. (3) Make connections between diverse factors. (4) Avoid becoming overloaded with information.

Never confuse hope with a true gut feeling, however. Max Gunther pointed out in *The Luck Factor* that "the facts on which the hunch is based are stored and processed on some level of awareness just below the conscious level. This is why the hunch comes with that peculiar feeling of almost-but-not-quite knowing."

Hamburger nabob Ray Kroc says his storehouse of experience as a paper cup and milkshake mixer salesman paved the way for his multimillion-dollar business gamble—buying into the short-order food emporium owned by the McDonald brothers of San Bernardino, California. "I went to see the McDonald operation [which had purchased enough Multi Mixers to make forty milkshakes simultaneously] and suddenly, the seventeen years with the Lily Cup Company and the seventeen years of selling Multi Mixers came together. I can't pretend to know what it is—certainly, it's not some divine vision. Perhaps it's a combination of your background and experience, your instincts, your dreams. Whatever it was, I saw it in the McDonald operation, and in that moment, I suppose, I became an entrepreneur. I decided to go for broke."

That was in 1954. Kroc was fifty-one. In 1960, after running the first McDonald's offshoot in a suburb of Chicago for five years, he decided to buy the McDonald name outright for $2.7 million. He needed heavy financing and his lawyer called it a bad deal. Kroc says: "I closed my office door, cussed up and down, threw things out of the window, called my lawyer back, and said 'Take it!' I felt in my funny bone it was a sure thing." By 1978, the total revenues of Kroc's fast-food chain topped $4.5 billion.

Rule #6: Experiment with New Approaches. Innovation has always ruled this nation and that's what you've got to do if you're determined to propel yourself into the financial stratosphere.

Jeno Paulucci is the master of the wild idea that makes a killing. One of the famous Sayings of Jeno, posted around his plants, is: "It pays to be ignorant. If you're smart, you already know it can't be done." Jeno uses himself as an example. "If I had been smart, I would have known it was impossible for a man with a name like Jeno Francisco Paulucci to start a Chinese-food business on borrowed money in Scandinavian Minnesota and in less than twenty years sell it for $63 million to a tobacco company."

If Jeno had been a traditionalist he never would have allowed comedian Stan Freberg to poke fun at Chun King in its commercials. "I was scared to death," Jeno recalls, "particularly when the first one opened with the line, 'Ninety-five percent of the people in the U.S.A. don't eat chow mein.' But I stuck with it and it worked."

Advertising ace William Benton was credited with inventing the singing commercial, certainly a radical departure from precedent. Other Benton & Bowles innovations included the use of live audiences on radio programs and the first cuing of audiences with placards reading "Laugh," "Applaud," "Sigh," "Groan." Benton & Bowles radio commercials also featured actors smacking their lips and clinking their coffee cups to give listeners an acoustical "picture" of what was happening.

Manny Fingerhut, the Minnesota magnate who made a mint in mail-order with his family-controlled Fingerhut Corporation, brainstormed his way to the top. He and his brother William made a modest living manufacturing and selling automobile seat covers until Manny got the idea to do it by mail. It worked. But a few years later Detroit botched up their bonanza by producing cars with seats already covered in durable attractive vinyl and nylon. Manny met that challenge by producing transparent seat covers that wouldn't hide Detroit's artistry. The Fingerhut Corp. has since broadly diversified its merchandise, but it continues to appeal to lower-middle-income customers and it continues to sell clear-plastic seat covers. In 1973, they were still selling at the rate of $7.9 million a year.

Rule #7: Recognize the Lucky Break and Use It to Your Advantage. "I'd rather be lucky than smart 'cause a lot of smart people ain't eatin' regular." So said Sid Richardson and just about every other self-enriched money monger of the crackerbarrel school. MacArthur claimed his success was "more luck than anything else. The smartest guys can be driving trucks because they've never got the breaks."

Although many tycoons have this almost mystical feeling about luck, few have any real understanding of how it operates. To hear them describe it, luck consists of a series of *deus ex machina*-type coincidences, little more. Their faith in its magic remains pure and childlike and they seem to feel that analyzing it further might destroy its power.

Armand Hammer, who studied to be a doctor and became instead an oil and art speculator and Soviet go-between, summed up his career in typical tycoon fashion: "One thing leads to another. You see an opportunity, and everything after that falls into place." Not very illuminating.

Others, with less to lose, have given the phenomenon more sustained thought. In a 1952 book called *How to Attract Good Luck*, Albert Carr made the point that you can't win a game without entering it; i.e., you can't attract opportunities unless you are fully involved in life. He exhorts the M.I.T. (mogul-in-training) to "expose yourself as fully as possible to the fluid circumstances of life." Here's where the extroverted salesman has the edge over the armchair professor, since contact with as many people as possible is bound to increase your chances of stumbling upon a fortuitous set of circumstances, particularly if your acquaintances are a notch above you socially and financially.

Quite simply, luck is being in the right place at the right time. But are the so-called lucky, anointed people upon whom fate smiles brightly or are they merely average slobs who are alert enough to recognize a good thing when it comes along? Perhaps the most common trait among lucky people is that they make the most of *all* opportunities as they present themselves, for good fortune is not something you should wait for but something you must seize.

And finally, psychiatrist Leon Tec, author of *The Fear of Success*, describes lucky people as people willing to make drastic changes in their lives. Lady Luck works like a tornado. She destroys the *status quo*.

Rule #8: Expect to Work Long Hours and Make Personal Sacrifices. Blood, sweat, and tears. This is the bromide describing what it takes to get ahead in the business world. While not all self-made men are neurotic workaholics with broken marriages, enough are to warn you it's a distinct possibility. Those who can be classified as workaholics are invariably *happy* workaholics. For them, work is an addiction, a way to burn off their nervous energy. It soothes them like a daily fix.

Eighty-three-year-old Armand Hammer, for instance, still works seven days a week, fourteen hours a day by his own admission. (He's also had three wives.) "I carry my weight" was his stubborn retort when questioned about rumors that Occidental Petroleum's forty-six-year-old president Joe Baird thought the company's octogenarian chairman had outlived his usefulness around headquarters and ought to retire to make room for younger turks.

Apparently, there's nothing quite like the thrill of mammon-stockpiling to keep an aging mogul fit. Hammer was croaking a different tune back in 1976 when he was charged with making an illegal $54,000 contribution to Nixon's re-election campaign. Hammer—a feeble worn-out old man (so it appeared)—was taken into court in a wheelchair to hear his doctors testify that his "irreversible and progressive heart condition" would surely kill him should he land in jail. Hammer didn't. Instead he got probation, a fine, and, somewhere along the line, a miraculous recovery.

Seventy-two-year-old Herman Lay hasn't really retired either, but he at least tried. "I'm technically retired from my company [PepsiCo., Inc., parent company to Frito-Lay, Inc.], but I still spend about fifteen percent of my time there," he explains. "I also own two businesses here in Dallas. I work in real estate and have joint-venture investments, mostly with young people. I'd say I work as hard now as the average person works at the peak of his career. But I only put in about seventy-five percent of the hours that I worked years ago. I worked far harder and longer than the average person then. Far more. I find I've got to be busy or I'd shrivel up. I'm still playing the game and the name of the game is the bottom line."

Rule #9: Recognize a Failure Early and Go on to the Next Idea. Grierson's Law of Minimal Self-Delusion states that . . . "Every man nourishes within himself a secret plan for getting rich that will work." This truism applies equally to those who eventually cross the Rubicon—and get rich!

MacArthur, for example, had so many false starts that his career threatened to turn into a comedy routine. By 1927, he had saved $30,000 from a series of sales jobs, mostly in insurance, and he was ready to pry open his oyster. His oyster clammed up. His first two investments in a gas station and bakery were miserable failures and his purchase of the Marquette Life Insurance Company in 1928 for $7,500 wasn't much better. Marquette had a premium income of $15,000 a year from its 600 policyholders, most of whom were in their seventies and eighties and dying rapidly.

MacArthur, being Scots and stubborn, did not give up, however, and his persistence—bordering on malfeasance—and bookkeeping legerdemain gradually turned the company around. But it was a big-mouth insurance examiner who was really responsible for changing MacArthur's luck which had been consistently rotten for fifteen years. The examiner tipped him off that the state insurance department had just closed down Bankers Life & Casualty Company of Chicago because of a $2,500 impairment. Its management had been poor but its business was essentially healthy. MacArthur pounced. He borrowed the money to pay off the impairment, thus becoming the company's sole stockholder. That was 1935 and from that time on, the MacArthur insurance machine steamrolled along in high gear.

MacArthur was the first to admit that he had setbacks all along the way. In fact, MacArthur's image of himself was always that of the irrepressible White Knight in the ill-fitting armor who keeps tumbling off his broken-down steed to Alice's amusement in *Through the Looking Glass.* It is indeed true that he clanked cacophonously throughout his lifetime as he battled foes large and small to protect and enrich his glittering pile of gold.

John W. (Bet-a-Million) Gates was another bootstraps millionaire willing to concede his mistakes. He said he always remembered something Marshall Field had told him about trying to be right only 51 percent of the time. "There's a lot in that," he said. "The fellow who makes up his mind to be right all the time will be busted, in the long run, by the man who insists on being right only fifty-one percent of the time."

It is a characteristic of big-money men that they can spot a disaster early and make for the nearest exit. It's been said that Charles Allen, the Wall Street wizard, is as quick to pull out of a bad deal as a cat is to run from rain. Allen never lets sentiment or stubborn pride contaminate his decisions. They are usually swift and instinctive (he admits he plays hunches).

But when the big bucksters do blunder—it happens to the best of them—they don't sulk for long. They chalk it up to a learning experience and bounce back quickly, at least psychologically; it may take somewhat longer to revive their bank balance.

Cleveland wheeler-dealer Cyrus Eaton lost a cool $100 million in the 1929 crash. According to his stockbroker, his only comment when he came into the brokerage concern to settle up was, "Well, tomorrow is another day."

Rule #10: Publicize Your Successes. The person who gets ahead is often the person who knows how to attract favorable attention, either through word-of-mouth or media mentions.

John MacArthur learned this lesson early when he was a callow Navy enlistee during World War I. Chafing under military discipline, he went AWOL twice, finally ending up in New York City where he latched on to a female companion for a few hours before attempting to stow away on a troop transport ship heading he knew not where. He was discovered before the ship weighed anchor. Meanwhile, his short-order girl friend, who was a newspaper reporter, wrote a piece about this brave young American, so determined to serve his country that he ignored his injuries (sustained when he demolished three planes as a harebrained flight instructor in Texas) to board a ship destined for the combat zone. It made a great story even if it was pure fiction, and was picked up by every major newspaper in the United States. Instead of a court martial, MacArthur the hellion was hailed as a hero and hired by the War Department to tour the country making patriotic speeches and selling Liberty Bonds.

It was MacArthur's first brush with the power of the media and the moral was not lost on him. He became a master at self-promotion and spent the rest of his days providing journalists with "good copy." While he was building his fortune, he created the image of the maverick up-from-under millionaire with street-corner smarts. He claimed to be "as ordinary as apple pie"—although he was always ten times as colorful. He made sure he was the most unforgettable character any reporter ever wrote about.

Truism: The successful person is the one who seizes credit as the man of the hour and leaves the right people with a positive, perhaps even zany, impression (eccentric people are easier to remember). The point is not whether you deserve the credit for a triumph, business or otherwise, but whether you can get people to *believe* you deserve the credit.

Rule #11: Don't Think About Making a Million. After all that's come before, this may seem like contradictory advice. Not really.

If you're sitting around wondering what your cash register will sound like when it finally chimes, you won't be concentrating on the things that will make it chime. The main chance will pass you right by.

Plutologists,[2] while they disagree on many issues concerning tycoonery, all agree on one point: Greed is seldom the goad spurring on the self-made. Says Kirstein, "The paradox is that the accumulation of money for its own sake is a by-product, not the main objective, of their exertions. The necessity to be active, to be what many of [the self-enriched] call 'creative,' plays a far larger role than the desire to accumulate money."

Getting back to the poker analogy, it's the "game" of business— the challenge of winning—that fascinates the heavyweight accumulator. Magnates themselves admit as much.

Joseph Hirshhorn, the minerals and stock-market speculator, says ". . . just to test my judgment—that's what gives me the great kick. The money doesn't matter—not after the first million. How could it? You can't wear more than two shirts a day, or eat more than three meals."

The same logic was trotted out by Ed Ball, the administrator of the Alfred I. du Pont estate who's made $20 million in his own right, and Leo Corrigan. "It's the challenge I like," Corrigan told an interviewer. "I get the biggest kick in life out of making deals. After all, how many meals can you eat at once or how many suits can you wear at one time?"

They must teach them that line in tycoon school. Louis J. Roussel, the New Orleans oil-bank-insurance-real estate manipulator, is the latest mogul to parrot the same idea in an interview I conducted with him in 1974. A cantankerous Cajun, the mustachioed Roussel airs his opinions freely at the drop of a seemingly innocent question. He told me that money, as such, doesn't interest him. "It's what you can do with it," he says. "I'll tell you what. . . . I love to build stuff. I don't like anything old. I have a very modern house that I built and I have a quarter million dollars sunk in it. And everybody was tellin' me I should build a house a long time ago. I said I'd never build one until I could pay for it and wouldn't owe a quarter on it. And that's what I did. I built it in 1957. I just have one house. After all, I can only live in one."

And the seventy-five-year-old Louie, the oracle of New Orleans, also claims that he'll never retire. "You see, it's not just makin' money, honey. I spend a lot of my time givin' people free advice."

Note: A word to the wise from Bernard Patrick McDonough, the West Virginia industrialist, hotelier (Dromoland Castle and other inns in Ireland), and owner of the largest shovel factory in the world: "Stay away from lawyers. They only louse things up." (McDonough holds a law degree from Georgetown University Law School. He never sat for the bar exam.)

NOTES

1. "Those Business Hunches Are More Than Blind Faith," Roy Rowan. *FORTUNE* (April 23, 1979).

2. The word "plutologist" is a neologism meaning student or observer of the rich. It sometimes appears as "plutonomist."

THREE MULTIMILLION-
DOLLAR IDEAS:
YOU GOTTA HAVE A GIMMICK

9 There's an old adage in the marketing field that states: If you can't be the first with a new product or service, then you've got to be the best. In other words, either introduce a new gimmick before your competitors, or find a new application for an old idea that's been lying around a while.

The following success stories demonstrate how novelty or the well-executed theft of other people's ingenuity propelled four hard-working entrepreneurs (two men and a husband-wife team) across that big financial finish line.

Carlson, the Copycat Croesus

Curtis L. Carlson is a guy who may never have had an original idea in his life. But that hasn't held him back because he's got something almost as good—an absolute genius for spotting other people's ideas. Every business move Carlson ever made illustrates his imitative artistry and superb sense of timing.

Carlson once quipped, "Almost any large diversified company starts with one little idea that works." His certainly did. The idea was trading stamps.

In 1938, a year after his college graduation, Carlson founded the Gold Bond Stamp Co. Today, it's the cornerstone of his empire, an empire that spans all types of incentive marketing; catalogue showrooms; restaurants; hotels; candy, tobacco, and diamond wholesaling; gold-jewelry manufacturing; natural gas exploration and production; real estate; and optical and sporting-goods importing. That first year, Gold Bond grossed less than $500. In 1979, the privately held Carlson companies grossed more than $1 billion, with the profits going straight into Carlson's pocket. Clearly, this portly, pink-cheeked former $85-a-week soap salesman for Procter & Gamble has come a long way.

Why trading stamps? Carlson says the light bulb went on in his mental attic the day he learned that a Minneapolis department store had increased its sales appreciably by offering a new-fangled kind of incentive: trading stamps. Carlson reasoned—correctly, as it turned out—that the trading stamp lure would appeal mightily to small neighborhood-grocers whose customers were beginning to respond to the siren-song of the large, full-service supermarket.

With his customary diligence, Carlson investigated carefully before he plunged in. To find out more about the workings of a stamp-company operation, Carlson paid a secretary at the Security Red Stamp Co. a $10 "incentive" to let him see the firm's client contract. "I kept it overnight and read it and got the format down pat," he recalls. Carlson, who had been a business major at the University of Minnesota, then drew up his own incorporation papers *sans* attorney, and the Gold Bond Stamp Co. was born.

Hedging his bets, Carlson held on to his full-time job at Procter & Gamble and spent nights and weekends convincing grocers to buy his stamps. The grocers, in turn, would give the stamps away to customers—so many stamps per so many dollars in purchases. At first, the stamps had a cash redemption value, but later they could be turned in for merchandise at a Gold Bond redemption center.

Competition was keen since there were already twelve stamp companies in existence. But Carlson gradually prospered by thinking small and concentrating on local merchants. Within two years, he had enough takers to quit his soap-peddling post and hire an assistant, a man who has now risen to a Carlson companies vice presidency.

In the 1940s, Gold Bond's growth was slow but steady despite America's wartime shortages and sacrifice mentality. In such an economy, it wasn't easy to stimulate sales. But Carlson held on and reaped his reward in the 1950s and '60s. In 1952, Gold Bond nabbed its first national account, the Super Value supermarket chain. Sisyphus had finally gotten the rock over the crest. Other grocery chains followed suit and by 1960, the trading-stamp phenomenon was sweeping the country. Gold Bond emerged as the biggest independent stamp company in Canada, a market it had moved into in 1957; and the second largest in the United States, behind Sperry & Hutchinson. Curtis L. Carlson emerged a centimillionaire.

But the glitter coming from Carlson's hard-won pile of gold did not blind him to the reality of his situation: Stamps are a fad and it's only a matter of time before a fad becomes passé. Sure enough, from the early 1960s when 70 percent of all food stores in the United States were rewarding their customers with stamps, the figure dropped to less than 50 percent by 1971.

Long before the nadir, however, Carlson had latched on to several new trends, decreeing that conglomeration was his long-term goal. Soon he was renovating once-grand downtown hotels bearing famous old names, developing resorts in the Caribbean and other far-off places, acquiring discount catalogue showrooms specializing in the retailing of carry-out, name-brand hard goods (small appliances, jewelry, TV sets, sporting equipment and toys), and creating incentive programs for companies wishing to reward their high achievers.

Carlson's stringent sales goals—the latest is $2 billion in revenues by 1982 or bust!—is one reason why the company's executive corridor is nicknamed "Ulcer Alley." Carlson is volatile and demanding and shows no mercy when managers fall short of their monthly profits target. When they do, they are required to explain why in a "deviation report." A former Carlson companies executive says, "Curt has a computer mind and is probably the smartest businessman I've known, but I couldn't handle the way he treated some of his people," referring to the grilling Carlson inflicts on his managers at company conferences. Carlson justifies his methods with a throwaway line: "You have to keep a little tension in the air, or things get too lackadaisical."

Clearly, what Carlson wants are carbon copies of himself, men who work long hours—Carlson frequently works on into the night and on weekends—and seldom take vacations. "Leisure is very important for people today—not like in the thirties when everyone seemed to be willing to work long hours," Carlson points out. "So the person who is willing to make the sacrifices and put in the time has a better chance of making it."

With his staff, Carlson's rallying cry is "Momentum—a business that isn't growing is a no-good business." He believes the way to gain momentum is to constantly escalate your goals. Carlson has always made a habit of writing his current business goal on a slip of paper which he tucks away in his wallet. When it's achieved, he throws it away and replaces it with another.

"I believe you should never be content with reaching a goal," he says. And to sustain a company's growth, he feels, the head man has to set higher goals for his subordinates than they would set for themselves. Carlson has surrounded himself with professional managers to whom he delegates responsibility for financial planning, acquisitions, and legal affairs—basically staff functions. "But I'll never delegate goal-setting," he vows.

Carlson claims his top executives will retire as millionaires, but disavows any interest in making them part-owners of his enterprises even though a local reporter once quoted him to that effect in 1959: "My dream is that someday the employees will become owners of the business," he supposedly said.

When asked about that quote years later, Carlson had no memory of it and showed distinct signs of discomfort. If it ever was a goal, it's one he'd like to forget. He maintains that the Carlson companies will remain private because "I really don't know if I'd ever be happy without calling my own shots. I make mistakes and I'm very thin-skinned about making mistakes. I'm not good at taking criticism."

A Land-Office Business

Dr. Edwin Land, an aging Cary Grant look-alike with dark circles under his eyes from years of all-night work sessions in his Cambridge, Massachusetts, lab, says: "Every creative act is a sudden cessation of stupidity." (Incidentally, the "Dr." that Land has tacked on to his name is strictly honorific. Land never even bothered to complete his course requirements at Harvard College although he was just a few points short of his undergraduate degree.)

Land has had several hundred of these stupidity-abatement spells during his fifty-one-year-long career as an inventor, resulting in more than 400 patents in his own name. But by far his most marketable, creative act was the invention of the Polaroid Land camera, that ingenious mechanical device that takes photos and develops them in one mess-free process. When Land's self-developing camera was introduced by the Polaroid Corp. in 1948, it was eagerly snapped up by hobby-happy, leisure-fatigued, gadget-prone Americans obsessed with speed and instant gratification in any form.

Typically, Dr. Land's version of why the camera appealed to the American masses was considerably more highbrow. Land, who thinks of himself as a scientist with an artist's awareness, brushed aside the accusation that his simple, one-step camera was little more than a hot commercial property, describing it instead as "a new medium of expression." It was designed to "enlarge the horizons" of people with a visual sensibility who didn't paint, sculpt, or draw but needed a creative outlet.

While the instant camera was the artifact that made Land and his investors rich, it was not the product that launched his company in 1937. Back then, Land was betting on a new system of polarized headlights and windshields which would eliminate the dangerous glare that cost 40 drivers a night their lives. Land was sure the automobile industry would welcome his contribution. It didn't. Detroit's business was booming and no one there could justify the cost of adopting the new optical technology in those pre-Nader days. The Polaroid Corp. prospered anyway by incorporating its polarizer know-how into sunglasses, filters, and other products, but Land had learned an important lesson: Never again would he develop a product that couldn't be marketed directly to consumers.

During World War II, the company forged ahead manufacturing lenses and gunsights for the military. In the meantime, Land was spending most of his time in his lab trying to invent an "instant" camera to please his little daughter who had complained about the lag time between a shutter's click and the production of the photograph. Her plaintive lament was voiced on a family vacation to the Southwest in 1943 and by 1947 Daddy had come up with the solution. The "Land" camera was in stores by the following Christmas.

Perhaps the most remarkable aspect of Land's breakthrough was the fact that he had seized upon the idea for a self-developing camera in the first place. Wouldn't any sane person have dismissed his daughter's wish as a silly figment of a child's unbridled imagination? Land is proud to point out that he brought an idea to fruition before that idea was even mentioned in photographic literature.

Land believes that the only significant inventions, such as his camera, are ones that are "startling, unexpected, and come into a world that is *not* prepared for them."

Members of the Harriman and Warburg families came up with the initial scratch, ignoring the predictions of conservative stock analysts who branded Land a "nut" who would eventually get the company into trouble.

During the go-go years of the 1960s, Polaroid stock was selling for as high as $256.50 a share and the Harriman, Warburg, and Land families were laughing all the way to their brokers' offices. But during the next decade, the picture grew murky. Polaroid spent more than a half-billion dollars developing the SX-70 camera (a 24-ounce wonder that allows users to watch as their color photos develop themselves in a matter of seconds) only to get bogged down with severe production problems. The 1974 recession didn't help matters either. Land and his wife, Helen, the owners of 2.5 million shares worth an incredible $719 million at their peak, saw their fortune plunge from $336 million in 1973 to less than $90 million in 1974. By 1980, Polaroid stock was selling at about 20, leaving the Lands with a paper fortune of $50 million.

Lofty aspirations are characteristic of Land. Throughout the years, he has vetoed many of the ventures urged on him by his executives because they are "ordinary, not the extraordinary. Our motto is that we won't do anything anyone else can do, for this company works only on things that are manifestly important and nearly impossible." This is in keeping with Land's belief that science should be used to create new industries, not just to improve on existing technologies.

Like Thomas Edison and George Westinghouse, Land is an inventor/industrialist, one of those rare individuals who is part prophet, part promoter, and part executive. A former associate at Polaroid observes that Land has the peculiar ability to transform himself from an egghead idealist into a skeptical businessman momentarily. "He would sit back, shut his eyes, think of the absolute ideal way to make something, the ideal function or purpose. Then, he would suddenly change hats and become absolutely practical and realistic. There was always this sudden shift, and people would either be amused, pleased, or annoyed."

FORTUNE has called Land "the advocate of the un-*status quo*." His staff at Polaroid would certainly second the description. Land says, "My whole life has been spent trying to teach people that intense concentration for hour after hour can bring out resources in people that they didn't know they had."

While "Din" (Land's nickname) secretly delights in his public image as a reclusive laboratory habitué with a near-genius mentality, his subordinates daily bear the brunt of his impossibly high standards. Land, the manager of men, says he is dedicated to creating an environment "in which people with my kind of pace and competence will sprout." Sprout? He may not be kidding. He once told a *FORTUNE* reporter that his successor would have to be such a paragon of wisdom, intelligence, and judgment—"that we're having him made down in the laboratory."

Bite-Sized Sermons in a Pocket-Sized Format

In 1922, thirty-three-year-old DeWitt Wallace, son of a Presbyterian minister and college president, introduced one of the most unforgettable publishing ideas the world has ever known. With Lila Acheson, his wife of one year, urging him on—she also was the offspring of a Presbyterian clergyman—Wallace self-published 5,000 copies of a slim, pocket-sized magazine that regurgitated articles, in condensed form, from such prestigious publications as *Scribner's, The Atlantic Monthly, American*, and the *Saturday Evening Post*.

The 1920s was an era during which the short story and magazine fiction reigned supreme; thus, nobody in publishing circles thought Wallace's harebrained idea of repackaging nonfiction in a shorter, easy-to-skim format stood one chance in a hundred of succeeding.

Not only did it succeed—and rather rapidly—but today the Wallaces' *Reader's Digest* is the most widely disseminated periodical in the world with a circulation of 18.3 million in the United States, 11.7 million abroad, and an estimated pass-along readership of 100 million. It has thirty-nine editions in fifteen languages and is edging up on the Bible in worldwide sales. What was probably the most telling proof of the *Reader's Digest*'s widespread appeal and durability came in the 1950s when television systematically insinuated itself into the minds and hearts of the Wallaces' countrymen and the advertising budgets of the nation's major consumer-products companies. After the dust had cleared on Madison

Avenue, the *Reader's Digest* was the only mass-circulation, general-interest magazine to survive.

What was, and still is, the secret of the Wallaces' success? Quite simply, they seem to understand what tantalizes the minds and tugs at the hearts of their fellow citizens better than anyone else. A friend of DeWitt once told a reporter, the man has a "perfect understanding of the herd mind. He's a genius, all right, and a greater genius than Hearst. Wallace looks at the universe constantly through the wrong end of the telescope, and so does the herd. He sees everything neat and tidy, and so do they. He knows what they want, and he lets them have it."

Wallace conceived the idea for a digest-format publication when he was a young man working as a sales promotion writer for the Webb Publishing Company in St. Paul, his hometown. Webb published a number of farm magazines and agricultural texts and Wallace began to notice that the U.S. Department of Agriculture and various state agricultural divisions were among the company's biggest competitors, publishing as they did literally hundreds of pamphlets on a wide variety of subjects.

Wallace's first digest was a 124-page booklet called "Getting the Most Out of Farming," which listed the titles and brief summaries of the government's free pamphlets. To his own surprise, he managed to sell 100,000 copies of the booklet, mostly to banks for distribution to their rural customers.

Wallace tackled marketing trade journals next, hoping to sell that booklet to department stores, but World War I intervened before he ever completed the project. He was seriously wounded in the war but the injury never killed his almost obsessional preoccupation with the idea of condensations. Wounded in the Meuse-Argonne offensive in 1918, Wallace spent his four-month convalescence applying his rather mundane talent for abstracting to a new sphere—the compression of general-interest magazine articles into punchy, once-over-lightly prose.

Back home, Wallace put together a dummy issue of a magazine containing his best condensations, called it the *Reader's Digest*, and took it around to publishers, offering his services as an editor to any who would support his idea and hire him to implement it. They all laughed, as the song goes. After all, how could a publication without fiction, carrying no advertising or artwork, and devoted only to serious articles possibly attract more than a few readers?

Lila Bell Acheson, the sister of one of Wallace's Macalester College classmates, didn't laugh. When they met, Lila was a social worker for the YWCA. They were married on October 15, 1921, in Pleasantville, New York, and soon after returning from their honeymoon, they launched their baby in the basement of a Greenwich Village speakeasy. Total capitalization for the venture was a borrowed $1,800.

From that day to this, little has changed about the *Reader's Digest*. The magazine's original statement of editorial policy still holds. An article must: (1) apply specifically to the reader so he or she feels the subject concerns him or her personally; (2) be of lasting interest (worth reading a year hence); and (3) be constructive—defeatism is taboo. One big change, however, is advertising, which the magazine began accepting in 1955 to forestall an increase in the cover price. Ads for tobacco, liquor, and medical remedies were verboten, however, even though Mr. Wallace puffed away on two packs a day. Today, the *Digest*'s average reader is older, of course—45.6 years with a median income of $16,697—but the magazine's content is still consistently middle-brow. Critics have called it everything from "anachronistic" and "jingoistic" to "bland" and "middle-American." It may be all that but no one can deny that the Wallaces' small-scale, up-beat view of American life has been the *Reader's Digest*'s greatest editorial asset. Throughout the years, the Wallaces' pleasant myopia has helped them create a magazine dispensing more medical opinions than the AMA *Journal*, more sex than Masters and Johnson, more jokes than Bob Hope, more adventure stories than Walt Disney, and more faith than Billy Graham. It's also a magazine chock full of more unforgettable characters than Charles Dickens would have ever dreamed possible.

Perhaps the two most unforgettable are the Wallaces themselves. Even though the duo formally retired from active editorships in 1973, a week never goes by that the folks down at the headquarters in Chappaqua, a Westchester County suburb of New York City, don't get some missive from one of the nonagenarians inhabiting "High Winds," the Wallaces' hilltop estate in Mt. Kisco. Typical of the Wallaces' sense of humor was a memorandum sent to the

Digest's editorial staff in February 1976. The subject: a recent *New York Times* reference to "the late DeWitt Wallace." It read:

"Here we are in the glorious 'Out Yonder,' looking over your shoulders and applauding the work you are doing, just as we did in our previous incarnation. We are happy to be able to confirm the findings of psychic research, proving the reality of communication with those who have passed on to another world. Happy days to you."

MR. MONEYBAGS ARRIVES: FOUR
TYPICAL LIFE-STYLES OF A
STRIKE-IT-RICH
CAPITALIST

The Recluse

10 What's there to say about a self-made tycoon who steadfastly refuses to be interviewed and makes a practice of eluding everyone except his family and a few trusted business associates?

Howard Hughes fell into this category—indeed, he was an extreme example. But there are others.

Daniel K. Ludwig, the shipping lord-turned-land baron who is now reputed to be the richest living American, claims he's not a recluse. He's always accessible to legitimate business colleagues and even answers his own telephone—if you're one of the select few who have his number. It's mass visibility he wants to avoid. According to an aide: "Ludwig is interested neither in publicity nor in mystery."

Punishing employees who talk too much is one way Ludwig has adroitly managed to maintain his moatlike existence throughout the years. Frederic V. Malek, a White House headhunter for President Nixon who was later hired by Ludwig, learned about this stonewalling policy too late, unfortunately. Malek make the mistake of holding a press conference, announcing to the world at large the name of his new employer. He immediately became an ex-employee (although Ludwig did pay him for some consulting work). Paying money to former aides long after they've left his employ is another way Ludwig seals flapping mouths.

But since Ludwig's estimated net worth ($2–3 billion) became public knowledge following the deaths of celebrity-moguls H. L. Hunt and John D. MacArthur, the eighty-four-year-old magnate has failed in his efforts to keep his penumbral presence out of the spotlight. A few details about his life-style have now become known, much to his chagrin. Unfortunately, there's not much about the way Ludwig lives that's worth exposing as it turns out.

Divorced, Ludwig lives alone in a Fifth Avenue penthouse in Manhattan and reportedly has no lady friends. He has no chauffeured limousine to whisk him around the city and takes public transportation or taxis when necessary. He walks to his Burlington House office at Fifty-fourth Street on the Avenue of the Americas each morning and often indulges in a swim before he begins his business day. (As partial owner of the building, he had a swimming pool built in the basement that only he can use and few building employees even know about.)

Ludwig travels frequently and always takes commercial flights, usually tourist class, carrying his own luggage. He had a yacht once, but sold it to Charles Revson (who renamed it *Ultima*). Politically, he's been described as somewhere to the right of Ronald Reagan—although you might never know it from his lackluster history of making financial contributions to politicians. If he's got to part with his money, he prefers funneling it into cancer research.

Except for the fact that he's surrounded by a large and energetic family, investment banker Charles Allen has a life-style similar to Ludwig's. Twice married with three children by his first wife, Allen lives in a suite at the Hotel Carlyle in New York City and takes taxis to his office on lower Broadway. He neither smokes nor drinks, but does not oppose the routine champagne birthday parties for Allen & Co. employees—they tend to boost morale. Allen is no cheapskate. When the firm has had a good year, employees are often rewarded with surprise bonuses, and Allen, himself, is said to tip well in the restaurants that he frequents. Aside from golf which a doctor once prescribed for health reasons, Allen's only interest is prowling around the corporate landscape looking for bargains. He gets help from his brother, Herbert; his nephew, Herbert, Jr.; his son, C. Robert; and his son-in-law who all work for the company.

Allen rarely gives interviews, but stories keep cropping up about him anyway. The one that almost drove him into court was a 1978 *New York Times Magazine* piece called "Hollywood's Wall Street Connection." The message was that Allen controls Columbia Pictures, which is up for sale and, to keep Columbia salable, Allen did his level best to keep the David Begelman scandal under wraps. The subtheme was that Allen's actions in the Begelman affair were consistent with his history of dealing with disreputable people, including criminals. In a caption under one of the few existing pictures of Allen, the reporter dubbed him "the reclusive Godfather of the New Hollywood." Allen's attorneys characterized the piece as "false and defamatory" but managed to reach an accord with the *Times* before charges were filed.

The volatile Leon Hess, chief honcho of a vast oil empire, shuns publicity because he's not a smooth spokesman and tends to express himself in off-color language that doesn't look good in print.

Hess is so secretive that his company, Amerada Hess—the forty-first largest industrial corporation in the United States in *FORTUNE*'s 1979 ranking—does not even have a public relations department. Hess does make speeches occasionally before elite business audiences, and when the words are written down in front of him, it's said he's both eloquent and well supplied with facts. The only time photographers ever get near him is in his box at New York Jet football games. (He owns 50 percent of the Jets and 13 percent of Monmouth Park racetrack in New Jersey. He's also on the boards of the Metropolitan Opera and New Jersey Symphony.)

Hess' ties to New Jersey are strong: He was born and reared there; one of the Amerada Hess refineries is there; and Mrs. Hess, the former Norma Wilentz, is the daughter of one of the state's most powerful Democrats. Still, the couple prefers living in a co-op occupying the entire floor of a Park Avenue apartment building in New York City although they do maintain a beachfront home in Deal, New Jersey. The couple has three grown children. Hess plays a mediocre game of golf and moves around Manhattan in a chauffeur-driven Cadillac that never lacks for gas during shortages. Little more is known about his personal life.

Forrest E. Mars, the shadow who heads the largest candy concern in the country, is feisty, hot-tempered, autocratic, and has granted only one interview in his life. The winner was the *Candy Industry and Confectioners Journal*. The story appeared in 1966 and the editor claims it took him five years of badgering before the meeting was arranged.

Why is Mars so adamantly opposed to press coverage, both for himself and Mars, Inc.? One of Mars' friends suspects it's because of a bad scare he got in 1944 as the result of a *Reader's Digest* article. The story described Mars' marvelous new process for "converting" rice (Uncle Ben's). The U.S. government liked the idea so much that certain federal officials suggested the company should share its patented secrets with competitors to help feed American troops in tropical areas. The war was over before anything came of the "suggestion," which Mars saw as a dire threat.

Mars runs Mars, Inc., like an absentee business-school professor. Until his recent move to Las Vegas (to oversee the construction of a candy factory), Mars issued orders by telephone each day to the company's McLean, Virginia, headquarters from his home forty miles away in The Plains. That home is a 740-acre estate called "Marland" situated in northern Virginia's bucolic hunt country. Mars raises horses and cattle there.

Mars' management decisions are always carefully thought out and diagrammed in chart or graph form. Mars reads constantly and has been known to supply his subordinates with lists of books bearing such names as *The Principles of Organization* and *General and Industrial Management*, all works supporting Mars' belief that good management is quantifiable and more science than art. In addition to their emulating his intellectual approach to business, Mars also expects his "associates" to emulate his enthusiasm for egalitarianism. Everybody from Mars' two sons, who share the president's title, on down must punch a time clock. Most executives don't even have private offices.

Despite the clamp on public utterances, a few amazing anecdotes occasionally leak out, such as the story about the time Mars interrupted an impromptu executive meeting to declare, "I'm a religious man." Next thing everyone knew, Mars had dropped to his knees at the head of the long conference table and was intoning the litany, "I pray for Milky Way. I pray for Snickers. . . ."

The Social Climber

The entrepreneur-turned-social climber uses money as a means to an aristocratic end. His fortune is a way to acquire class and entrée into the higher circles, if not for himself then for his progeny. With no pedigree after his name, the aspiring *parvenu* can't afford to deviate one iota from upper-class norms—once he figures out what they are. His life-style is about as freewheeling as a minuet.

Nobody but nobody is as self-conscious as a new-money millionaire seeking to acquire an old-money veneer. He's discomfited about his background, which often includes his ethnic origin; his education, or lack thereof; his children's education; his home (its facade, interior decor, and location); his recreational activities; his wife's interests; their "personal investments" (art and other fine collectibles); their club memberships; and his cultural, civic, and governmental appointments. The *arriviste* is especially sensitive about the line of work that made him rich, for he is deathly afraid one of those highborn ladies and gentlemen he is trying desperately to cultivate will notice that his cash still carries the rancid odor of his own sweat.

One way to spot a social climber is to notice whom they wed. The two marriages of William S. Paley, the man who brought the Columbia Broadcasting System to its present eminence, certainly qualify as socially astute moves.

Paley married for the first time in 1932 after enjoying a decade's worth of publicity as a *bon-vivant* young-man-about-town. Those carefree bachelor days had taught him one valuable lesson: New money will gain a Russian Jew entry into Café Society but only ancient money and German-Jewish ancestry will gain him membership into "our crowd" and the exclusive Harmonie Club. Stung by rejection from that corner of ethnic society, Paley did an about-face and chose a bride with built-in WASP respectability —Dorothy Hart Hearst, the former daughter-in-law of William Randolph Hearst, the newspaper mogul.

Beautiful, bright, witty, and liberal, Dorothy created not so much a home for Paley but a salon. Passing through it were people such as David O. Selznick, Herbert Bayard Swope, and a number of FDR brain trusters. But Dorothy may have been too intelligent for her own good: she developed the unfortunate habit of correcting her ambitious young husband in front of people. Exit Dorothy in July 1947 clutching a divorce-settlement check for $1.5 million.

Paley did even better in the marital marketplace the second time around. Five days after his divorce became final, he married Barbara ("Babe") Cushing Mortimer. Babe was one of the three socialite daughters of the famous Boston surgeon, Dr. Harvey Cushing. With her came not only impeccable taste and style but also acceptance into the innermost circles of the American Protestant aristocracy, such as it is. That trip to the altar brought

Vincent Astor and John Hay Whitney as brothers-in-law and a very elegant and very rich set of conservative friends, the kind of people who played golf a lot and voted Republican and belonged to the country's most elite clubs, some of which still rejected Paley's membership application.

In *The Powers That Be*, David Halberstam writes about Paley's ambivalence about his Jewish origins. "He was proud of his background," Halberstam claims, "but as he grew older and more successful he did not necessarily want to be reminded of it. As he tried to put it aside, hang around not just with Wasps but with super-Wasps, it somehow always lurked in the background." It also clouded his business judgment on occasion. He didn't exercise his option on the Broadway musical *Fiddler on the Roof* because he felt it was "too Jewish."

An appointment as American ambassador to the Court of St. James's would have placed Paley squarely at the apex of patrician High Society, but, alas, he never captured that plum. Instead, he had to settle for a seat on the board of the Museum of Modern Art, nothing to sniff at since it brought him into proximity with the Rockefellers, among others; and a private life that he once described as "attractive." That life was filled with the appurtenances of wealth. The Paleys maintained an apartment in Manhattan; an eighty-five-acre Manhasset, Long Island, estate called "Kiluna Farm" that is contiguous with the property of Jock Whitney and his late sister, Joan Payson; a Caribbean hideaway in Lyford Cay; and a summer place at Squam Lake in New Hampshire. All of their homes were decorated with quiet good taste and valuable antiques and had walls sporting an impressive collection of mostly post-Impressionist paintings.

Since Babe Paley's death in 1978, Paley has once again returned to his former status of eligible bachelor around town. Rumors abound concerning the next Mrs. Paley. Whoever she is, she will be hard pressed to top the social dowry of her predecessors—which is probably why Jacqueline Kennedy Onassis is frequently mentioned as a contender.

Besides marriage, another powerful social elevator is important governmental appointments, a guaranteed way to transform a mere person into a personage. Clarence Dillon, the recently departed wizard of Wall Street who headed the investment banking firm of Dillon, Read & Company, Inc., in the 1920s and '30s, was the recognized master of this technique.

Like Paley, Clarence Dillon was no pauper-turned-overnight-plutocrat. His childhood was comfortable, bordering on affluent. His father, Sam Dillon, was a prosperous clothing merchant who moved his family from San Antonio to Abilene, Texas, and finally settled in Milwaukee. But there was always a skeleton in the family closet. Sam Dillon's real name was Sam Lapowski. He was the son of a Polish-Jewish father and a French-Catholic mother whose maiden name was "Dillon." (Sam adopted her maiden name early in life.)

As that name-change proved, Sam Dillon had excellent instincts for assimilation. He sent his son, Clarence, to posh Eastern schools (Worcester Academy and Harvard) where he would develop the proper interests (art, classical music, literature, European travel) and mingle with the right people.

Sam's plan worked. After being rejected by all the family-tree-conscious clubs at Harvard, Clarence did manage to make it into the Hasty Pudding Club by his senior year. Soon after graduating, he married Anne McEldin Douglas of prominent Midwestern stock, and the couple retired to Europe on a two-year-long honeymoon during which Clarence toyed with the notion of studying art and somehow making a career of it. When that proved impractical, he returned to the States and went into partnership with his brother-in-law, founding the Milwaukee Machine Tool Company. The two eventually sold the business for a sizable profit and Dillon headed for New York City to invest his share.

On a Manhattan street corner, Dillon ran into his Harvard roommate, William A. Phillips, who was working for the firm of William A. Read & Co. Phillips encouraged his old school chum to enter banking and introduced him to Mr. Read.

The rest is the tale of any fast-track organization man with a strong personality. Dillon accepted Mr. Read's job offer and immediately streamlined the firm's securities distribution system and brought in a large chunk of new business. In short order, Dillon attracted the endorsement of such *éminences grises* as Bernard Baruch and Jacob H. Schiff and within four years at age thirty-four, he was made a partner in the firm. As fate would have it, Mr. Read dropped dead six days later and Dillon was unexpectedly elected managing partner. The firm's name was changed to Dillon, Read & Co. in 1920 to reflect his ascendancy.

While he was boosting the family bank balance, Dillon also boosted the family's snob appeal by purchasing the world-famous Bordeaux vineyard of Château Haut-Brion and a 300-acre estate called "Dunwalke Farm" in the fashionable hunt country around Far Hills, New Jersey. Dillion was too busy to devote much time to nonfinancial interests, although he did sit on the boards of the Metropolitan Opera, the chic Foxcroft School for girls, and the Post Graduate and Neurological Hospitals.

But if Dillon failed to devote the requisite amount of time to high-minded endeavors, he saw that his only son, C. Douglas Dillon, made up for it.

After graduating from Groton, C. Douglas Dillon followed his father's precedent and went to Harvard, where he was manager of the football team and a member of the Spee Club, which admitted John F. Kennedy more than a decade later. Dillon graduated magna cum laude and promptly married a Boston Brahmin young lady named Phyllis C. Ellsworth.

Clarence bought his son a $185,000 seat on the New York Stock Exchange and took him into his investment firm. A dutiful son, C. Douglas stuck with it, interrupting his business career only once to distinguish himself in the Navy during World War II. After the war, he became chairman of Dillon, Read and gradually turned his attention to matters more cultural and governmental.

A Republican, C. Douglas worked for Dewey in 1948 and led New Jersey's draft-Eisenhower drive in 1952. For his devotion, he was amply rewarded with the much-sought-after post of ambassador to France; and, as Harold Callender pointed out in a *New York Times Magazine* piece, Dillon's background and skills nicely matched the job's requirements:

> An ambassador should be a diplomat, a historian, a linguist, a political reporter, an executive, a public speaker, a traveler, a gracious host, a good mixer capable of enduring endless ceremonies and hand-shaking, not without being bored (which would hardly be possible) but without *appearing* bored; and in France he should be a gourmet. . . . The United States does not invariably get all these assets for the $25,000 a year

it pays its highest ranking ambassadors. But it got a good bargain in Dillon. . . .

C. Douglas Dillon and his wife possessed the necessary social graces and financial wherewithal. The couple were noted for their fine taste in furnishings, *objets d'art*, paintings, and homes. Their six residences in Washington, New York City, Far Hills, Hobe Sound, Dark Harbor, and Bordeaux, France, were advertisements for the patrician life-style and provided the backdrop for only the most elegant blue-blood gatherings, the kind where multi-million-dollar deals are consummated over cocktails and important charity events are planned over tea. Furthermore, the Dillons had made generous contributions to Harvard, Groton, and Fox-croft and belonged to such aristocratic strongholds as the Knicker-bocker, Links, River, Recess, Century, Racquet, and Pilgrims clubs in New York; and the Metropolitan Club in Washington.

Once in government service, Dillon moved fast as his father had done earlier in the century in business. In 1957, he was appointed Deputy Undersecretary of State for Economic Affairs and under Democratic President Kennedy was named Secretary of the Treasury. By this time, Dillon's solid-gold credentials were such that he transcended petty party politics. He also got an invite from the powerful and influential Council on Foreign Relations and rounded out his résumé with a trusteeship on New York's Metropolitan Museum of Art; today he's the museum's chairman.

In *The Protestant Establishment*, sociologist E. Digby Baltzell of the University of Pennsylvania refers to C. Douglas Dillon as "a patrician Episcopalian who represents not only the finest type of devoted and talented leadership in America but is also an excellent example of the process of aristocratic assimilation in the third generation."

But even C. Douglas Dillon, the reconditioned WASP whose daughter captured a European title by marrying Prince Charles of Luxembourg, had to contend with anti-Semitism at least once during his much-heralded career. Dillon is only one-eighth Jewish but that fact did not escape the membership committee of the caste-conscious Chevy Chase Club of Washington when he applied. Dillon was finally accepted but only with the solemn assurance that his percentage of "ethnic" blood was minimal.

The High Liver

The high livers are the conspicuous consumers of the *nouveau-riche* set. No false modesty about their hard-earned fortune dims their pleasure in the ownership of flashy material possessions. These millionaires revel in their greenbacks like a child romping through a pile of autumn leaves.

As you might expect, the high liver uses his discretionary cash for much more parochial and raucous purposes than does his sophisticated, social-climbing counterpart. In fact, the contrast in their spending habits is startling. While the society striver thinks nothing of dropping millions—quietly, of course—on homes (filled with European antiques) in *the right places* and schools guaranteed to introduce his children to *the right people*, the high liver doesn't give a hoot about that. Hobnobbing with the swells in the big city is not his idea of a good time. He is content living in the town—no matter how unfashionable—where he made his dough and usually sends his kids to local schools, private perhaps. His wife is also a homegrown product. Even though they may live in a big mansion on the outskirts of town, travel in a private jet, and entertain on their very own yacht, they still socialize with the same old friends and behave like the same old "Joe" and "Alice." Everybody who has known them for the last fifty years continues to love them. For a while, anyway.

In 1938, D. J. Witherspoon—"Tex" to his buddies—moved to Omaha from Levelland, Texas, where he and his wife Hillois taught high school during the Depression. They moved with the intention of starting a business. The business was a wholesale notions and novelty operation that eventually blossomed into Pamida, Inc., one of the country's fastest-growing regional discount store chains. In 1969, Witherspoon ventured to Wall Street to meet some of the influential Eastern moneymen he'd heard so much about. In his meetings with them, he reportedly managed to refrain for one of the longest times on record from chewing on his nicotine security blanket, an 11-cent Roi-Tan cigar. His assent to the amenities paid off because he walked away from a public offering of Pamida's stock that year a man worth almost $100 million.

Witherspoon's holdings in Pamida and those of various trusts he's set up for his four children have vacillated considerably since then. From a high of $114 million, his fortune nose-dived to a meager $28 million at one point. (Pamida's 1970–1980 stock price range is 24⅝–2½.) But Witherspoon paid it no mind. "When the stock was increasing in value it didn't make any difference in the way we lived, except for our residence," he shrugged. "And there's no difference in the way we're living now."

Tex is too modest. His increase in buying power has certainly increased his generosity at any rate. His cronies down at the Field Club, a golf course registering near the bottom of the Omaha status scale, like to tell about the time the Witherspoons took several other couples—bridge club acquaintances—on a Caribbean cruise. Witherspoon has also been known to pile his buddies into his Mitsubishi turboprop for spontaneous weekend jaunts to his ranch near Jackson Hole, Wyoming, and to Palm Springs for a quick eighteen holes at the Bermuda Dunes Country Club. With his hunting companions, he's gone on an African safari and a big-game shoot in Canada, where he managed to bag a 642-pound black bear and a four-point buck.

"Witherspoon is as common as an old shoe," a friend told a local newspaper reporter. "You don't have to have a lot of money to be a good friend." Another said, "Witherspoon told me he likes to spend money. That's why he made it."

Witherspoon doesn't like such talk, at least not for public consumption. He describes himself as a simple "cotton picker from Texas" who hates city slickers and "this fishbowl situation we've gotten into. . . . We've gotten so dad-gummed much publicity lately," he complained in 1970. "It's in bad taste. We'd just like to live our own lives and do it our own way."

Witherspoon is particularly sensitive about the stories concerning his "residence." It's this residence, rather than his business savvy or compulsive generosity, that put Witherspoon on the map in Omaha. The house is a fifty-two-room structure equipped with two swimming pools, a bowling alley, a screening room, a huge electric organ, and a surfeit of European *objets d'art*. Witherspoon claimed he built it to please his wife—"I made the mistake of telling her she could have the home she wanted," he once joked. Unfortunately, Hillois didn't live long enough to get much pleasure out of it. When Witherspoon learned Hillois was terminally ill with cancer, he had the construction site floodlighted so crews could work around the clock. They completed it just before she died in

1971. The next stroke of fate was delivered by the tax assessor. In a much-debated ruling, the assessor valued the house at $425,000 because of its "immediate 50 percent functional obsolescence." It was clear he viewed it as a white elephant. He claimed nobody would ever buy it for the $3 million it cost.

According to *FORTUNE* magazine, Pamida is turning a profit despite its hayseed management. In a company profile entitled "Pamida Doesn't Know What It's Doing, But It Sure Makes a Lot of Money" (August 1972), *FORTUNE* accused Pamida's executives of adhering to "the gut-feel school of management."

The story made Witherspoon furious. He let off steam in the Omaha *World-Herald*, explaining that Pamida does, indeed, have a long-range growth strategy: "We're the same company and we're going to stick to the same concepts [we have in the past]—locating in small towns where there's less competition and where the cost of operation is low."

The towns to which Witherspoon refers generally have a population between 5,000 and 20,000; and the stores range in size from 2,000 to 28,000 square feet of selling space and offer up to 14,000 different items on a self-service, cash-and-carry basis. As Witherspoon himself pointed out, the overhead is very low. No one could ever mistake most of Pamida's outlets for anything but strictly discount operations. The stores are a mixed bag of old garages, skating rinks, hardware concerns, theaters, and neighborhood groceries. "No two stores look alike," the *FORTUNE* reporter observed. "Even the signs are often hand-me-downs from former tenants."

Curtis L. Blake, who founded the lucrative Friendly Ice Cream chain with his brother, Prestley, in their hometown of Springfield, Massachusetts, says he contends with the jealousy of old friends every day. He suspects that a schoolmate has grown to hate him through the years merely because of his success. "I'm sure that guy hates my guts because he looks at me and says, 'Geezuz. I was just as smart as him in school and I'm just the same age and I've been in my own business just as long. So why has he got all that dough? He doesn't deserve it!'

"Money does produce a passing parade of friends," Curtis told me ruefully. "I'd say all my present friends are people I've met in the last ten years."

Today, both Blake brothers live high on the hog, at least by local standards, but it's a fairly recent development. Even though the brothers, now in their sixties, coveted automobiles and could have afforded new Cadillacs as far back as 1941, they continued to drive Fords. "The smartest thing my brother and I ever did was pour our early profits back into the business instead of building huge houses and buying expensive cars," Curtis says.

When the brothers borrowed $547.40 from their father, a vice president of Standard Electric Time Corporation, to open a soda shop in 1935, their goal was to make enough money to put Curt through Duke University and Prestley through Trinity College. But both brothers quickly realized they'd stumbled onto a gold mine and skipped any further higher education to reap the rewards. According to Prestley, their "natural Yankee conservatism" was at the root of their reinvestment policy, which has spawned a chain of more than 610 fast-food emporiums located in sixteen states in the Northeast and Midwest.

The Blakes first experienced the resounding crinkle of cool cash in hand in 1968 when they made their first public offering of Friendly Ice Cream stock. Prestley claims estate planning dictated the decision. Since then, they've tested the public waters three more times with secondary stock offerings, netting each brother about $25 million in cash while retaining about 40 percent of the company's stock. In 1978, the Blakes cashed in their chips again and accepted a purchase offer from the Hershey Foods Corp., a company with which they feel spiritually attuned because of its wholesome, all-American image. From this transaction, the brothers shared $65.6 million.

Their life-styles have gradually evolved along with their fortunes. Of the two, Curtis is the more enthusiastic about their newfound wealth. Several years back, he raised his nose from the grindstone long enough to decide he'd deferred his material gratification long enough. He relinquished his Friendly Ice Cream Co. job while still in his fifties, married for a second time, and became a "full-time philanthropist." He travels frequently and devotes an increasing amount of time to his favorite hobby—collecting and tinkering with a fleet of twenty-five mint-condition cars, ranging from the antique to the ultramodern.

"I think being able to buy what I want is terrific," Curtis admits. "I mean, I'm probably the happiest and the luckiest guy in the world."

Prestley prefers the anchor of business responsibilities, but he's also opted to travel more extensively and in style. In 1972, he purchased the 105-foot gaff-rigged schooner *America*, a replica of the famous yacht that captured the first "America's Cup." Since then, Prestley and his second wife—a Japanese woman who is the sister-in-law of the former American ambassador to Japan, Edwin O. Reischauer—have circumnavigated most of the globe, attended by a crew of seven.

Buying lavish homes, however, has never been the Blake brothers' thing. In forty years, they've each lived in three.

Prestley still remembers the time a freckle-faced neighbor kid asked him why he lived in such a small house if he owned all those Friendly Ice Cream stores. The pint-sized critic's rebuke stung: "All of a sudden it struck me that I looked like a scrooge. As it happened, the kid caught me at a time when I had a new house under construction," Prestley recalls. "But I'd say the kid was right. I overstayed my time in that first house by about five years."

His newest house, dubbed "The Admiral Benbow," is his third. It stands on a 100-acre plot in Somers, Massachusetts, and it's surrounded by farmland. Prestley wants to keep it that way. In 1973, he and a neighbor teamed up on a proposal submitted to the Somers Planning and Zoning Commission. It requested a zoning-ordinance amendment designed to protect the neighborhood from such undesirable elements as tract housing, billboards, and pig or poultry farms; and called for ten-acre minimum-lot zoning. The commission chairman called the proposal a "humdinger" and tabled it.

The Concerned Capitalist

There's a reason why capitalism needed the nourishment of Calvinism in the sixteenth century in order to take firm root in Western culture.[1] And in America in the twentieth century, the link between the two "isms" is still unbelievably strong.

The Puritan attitude toward money can be summarized this way: Money-making is next to godliness because it's the inevitable result of hard work, and what could be holier than that? In fact, prosperity is usually a sure sign of your salvation, that God has singled you out, as part of a grand predestination plan, as one of His Elect. But pious moneygrubbing is one thing. Flaunting your material wealth is quite another. While it is vaguely sinful to enjoy your stash (the Silas Marner syndrome), it is unforgivably sinful to do so in public.

As C. Wright Mills observed in *The Power Elite*, vestigial Puritanism helps explain why rich Americans have, down through the decades, "adopted every conceivable type of protective coloration for the essentially irresponsible nature of their power, creating the image of the small-town boy who made good, the 'industrial statesman,' the great inventor who 'provides jobs,' but who, withal, remains just an average guy."

At his death in 1979, Cyrus S. Eaton, the Cleveland industrialist (railroads, steel, utilities, coal, iron), was described as "an ambassador without portfolio." He was also an ambassador without authority. What authority he possessed in Soviet-American affairs derived purely from the fact of his wealth, some $100+ million. And a review of his biography makes it plain how he came to be the country's leading self-proclaimed minister of detente.

As a young man, Eaton aspired to the celestial rewards of the Baptist ministry until his employer one summer convinced him that the earthly rewards of commerce could be put to the service of mankind as well. The employer was John D. Rockefeller, Sr., who told him, "You've got what it takes to be successful in business. And in business you have a great opportunity to benefit mankind."

But Eaton was stubborn and determined and worked his way through McMaster University in Toronto, studying theology anyway. But the senior Rockefeller prevailed in the end. Eaton joined his entourage, learned quickly, and in short order was worth $2 million in his own right.

Because Eaton took substantial risks to get ahead (and sometimes failed), he was considered the buccaneer of the business world. In the 1930s, he began to be viewed as a political maverick as well. Eaton's first break with capitalist orthodoxy came in 1932 when he switched his allegiance from the Republican to the Democratic ticket, the camp where he remained for the rest of his life. Consistent with that move was his willingness to accept trade unionism and sign contracts with labor leaders, much to the disgust of his die-hard fellow industrialists.

As if two strikes against him weren't enough, Eaton became an outright pariah in the 1950s when he began speaking out against the Cold War relations between the U.S.S.R. and the U.S. From 1957 to his death, he was on intimate terms with Communist leaders and frequently exchanged visits with them. Critics in Joseph McCarthy's corner called him the Soviet's favorite capitalist, implying he was soft on Communism and developing a noticeably pink pallor. They also called him to task for his remarks during a 1958 CBS-TV interview with Mike Wallace. (Eaton referred to the Federal Bureau of Investigation as "one of the scores of agencies in the United States engaged in investigating, in snooping, informing, in creeping up on people.")

Eaton counterattacked. He accused American leaders of being "political and economic ostriches" in foreign policy. Moreover, he maintained that nobody was a greater champion of the free enterprise system than he and professed profound devotion to the United States:

"I have a big stake in it," he said. "My treasure is in America. . . . No man is less a Communist than I. I'll match my record as a capitalist against any of my critics. My chief interest is working to help save capitalism and all mankind from nuclear annihilation. We must either learn to live with the Communists or resign ourselves to perish with them."

Eaton's dedication to the cause of world peace did not end with sermons. With the moral support of philosopher Bertrand Russell, he poured millions of his own money into a series of "Pugwash Conferences" [2] which brought together atomic scientists from both sides of the Iron Curtain to discuss nuclear disarmament. The Soviets, at least, were impressed and conferred on him the 1960 Lenin Peace Prize, among other awards. Western politicians balked. Also, it did not go unnoticed on this side of the Atlantic that in succeeding years, members of Eaton's family in conjunction with Rockefeller interests, built a number of hotels in Eastern European Communist bloc countries. But Eaton claimed he did not personally profit from his Soviet stance until 1972 when his railroads hauled American grain as part of the Russian wheat deal. He also sold the Russians some of his prize shorthorn cattle, "But I didn't make anything out of it," he said.

To all appearances, Norton Simon should be a contented man. At seventy-four, he's got glamorous ex-movie star Jennifer Jones for a second wife, a fortune estimated at between $100–200 million to play around with, a picture-book Malibu beach home to enjoy, a fabulous art collection to admire, and a consulting relationship to the company he founded to keep him challenged. Instead, Simon is everything the average self-made man isn't. He's intense, reflective, compulsively private, well read in philosophy, and knowledgeable about art—a true anti-tycoon. With a look of anguish on his craggy face, he says, "In the Dostoevskian sense, I am the suffering man."

To a large extent, Simon's suffering is symbolic. He suffers about all the issues that concern any *bona fide* guilty, white, liberal Republican such as himself: poverty, hunger, injustice, inequality. But in another sense, Simon's suffering is very real and dates back to the fall of 1969 when his favorite son, Robert, committed suicide at the age of thirty-one. The family tragedy transformed Simon into a man with a cause or, I should say, series of causes.

David Shaw, a *Los Angeles Times* reporter, described Simon in 1971 as a man "running frantically from obsession to obsession, resembling nothing so much as a little boy lost in a big department store, scurrying desperately about, banging into shoppers and knocking over lamps, looking for his mother or father or just any familiar face."

Simon's crusades range from the political to the economic. In 1970, at the very last possible moment, he jumped into the Republican primary race against U.S. Senator George Murphy, unloading $2 million in the process of losing. He provided both moral and financial support to maverick U.S. Representative Paul McCloskey in his bid to wrest the 1972 Republican presidential nomination from incumbent Richard Nixon. On the business front, Simon inveighed against the federal guarantees to Lockheed.

But the cause closest to his heart, for obvious reasons, involves the interrelated problems of education, communication, and the alienation of youth. As a long-standing member of the University of California Board of Regents, Simon had the perfect platform for propounding his views. Given his almost religious zeal for psychiatry, it wasn't surprising that he saw merit in the Free Speech Movement on California campuses and said so; and offered his assistance to dissident students at the University of Santa Barbara —all of which embroiled him in a running feud with Governor Ronald Reagan and the more conservative members of the Board of Regents.

"Many educational institutions have become businesses and factories, destroying motivation and giving the kids something to complain about," Simon told them. "We've always had a generation gap. It's nothing new. But at the accelerated pace at which we live and learn today, the gap is wider than ever. Many older people are either unable or unwilling to adapt to the new world. I'd like to do what I can to bridge that gap."

But Simon admits his cosmic crusade—what he calls "the biggest ball game of all"—concerns keeping Ronald Reagan, and all he represents, out of the White House. Simon, for public consumption, has termed Reagan "deceptive, dogmatic, and destructive—potentially the most dangerous man in America." Simon, the kingbreaker, claims what's at stake here is more than just the fiscal stability of the federal government; it's such questions as social progress, human justice, and peace on earth.

California home-builder Eli Broad is another tycoon on the communications-gap bandwagon, but his views are downright mild compared to Simon's. After watching his company, Kaufman & Broad, grow to an industry giant, he decided in the early 1970s it was time for a change:

"My life was very narrow until recently when I very clearly made the decision that I wasn't interested in doing for the next fifteen years what I'd done for the last fifteen. In other words," he confessed, "just continually running a company and having it get larger and larger and hopefully more and more profitable. I started getting interested in other things—including art and education. I started spending more time on political activities."

A man in his mid-forties, Broad became a generous contributor to "political candidates whose philosophies I believe in." He is a director of the National Conference of Christians and Jews, the Los Angeles United Way, the Michigan State University (his alma mater) Development Board, and chairman of the board of trustees of Pitzer College in Claremont, California. Since broadening his horizons, he's deepened his concern about the future of the country —and the plutocratic class to which he now belongs:

"In the last ten or twenty years," he told me, "values have changed among young people. I wouldn't say their outlook has moved all the way from envy to resentment, but from respect for someone who accomplishes a materialistic goal to the view, 'that's nice but it isn't what life is all about.' I think there is also a feeling among young people in government jobs that anyone who's made a lot of money, has done it illegally. Their success is prima facie evidence that they've done something wrong. That's of concern to me. I think the leaders of this country have got to express greater social concern, especially for people who are economically deprived. If not, we are going to have our wealth and personal safety threatened."

NOTES

1. For a fuller explanation of the connection between the soul and the pocketbook see two classic works: *The Protestant Ethic and the Spirit of Capitalism* by Max Weber; and *Religion and the Rise of Capitalism* by R. H. Tawney.

2. Pugwash, Nova Scotia, was Eaton's hometown—really little more than a lobster hamlet—and the site of the first conference. Eaton is buried on his 500-acre Nova Scotia farm, "Deep Cove Farms," in Upper Blandford. Eaton raised purebred cattle there and in later life often walked around his fields talking to his cows and addressing them by name.

THE SEX LIFE OF THE SELF-MADE MAN: A $-RATED ANALYSIS

To the average zillionaire-tycoon, money represents sexual potency. That is an observation of New York psychiatrist Dr. Robert E. Gould, who has counseled several big-buck earners, all of whom equated the size of their bank balance with masculinity. Gould blames American society's distorted value system for this kind of muddled male thinking.

"In our culture money equals success. It also equals masculinity —to the extent that a man is too often measured by his money, by what he is 'worth.' Not by his worth as a human being, but by what he is able to earn, how much he can command on the 'open market.' "

Back when there was still a wild and woolly frontier to conquer, the apotheosis of a he-man was the John Wayne-style hero who used brute strength and raw courage to get ahead. But in real life in the 1980s, says Gould, "all that is left for the middle-class man is the battle for the bulging wallet."

But what kind of man accepts this monetary way of measuring his "masculinity quotient"? According to Gould, it's a man who has "a weak sense of self and who doubts his innate ability to attract women. Because it is hard for such men to face their inadequacies and the anxieties that would follow, they strive for money as a panacea for all their personal ills."

A number of Dr. Gould's colleagues concur. Noted psychiatrist Dr. Theodore I. Rubin once remarked that a woman's reassurance to a man that his sex organs are good-sized seldom allays his doubts. "But business success sometimes helps."

Sexologist Dr. Albert Ellis goes a step further. "Empire builders are often under tremendous pressure to perform well sexually because of women's expectations. In truth, many tycoons have gotten where they are by *not* being tycoons in bed. They have neglected social relations and focused on hard work and have much less experience than some of their low-income friends who started fooling around early, while they were still obsessed with making their first buck. In the real extreme, a guy who knows he's a mediocre lover may try to compensate by becoming a captain of industry."

An analyst who was quoted by Isadore Barmash in *The Self-Made Man* declared flatly that a lot of tycoons have sexual problems. He thinks the cause is the tycoon's over-achievement complex.

"I think these men always expect the best of things for themselves. Being the best, they also have to be sexually great and so they make great demands on themselves. But, in sexual intercourse, as in, say, taking a written examination, you are completely on your own. No one can help. No one can do it for you. The problems that often bring the businessman to the psychiatrist arise when they think that they should be able to function sexually as they do in their offices where they can press buttons that make hundreds and perhaps thousands of people jump."

Magnates would dismiss all this as utter clap-trap, of course. To the very end, John MacArthur was boasting to interviewers, "I used to have a limber back and a stiff front. Now I got a limber front and a stiff back." He told me that his second wife, Catherine, was the greatest, not only because she was a shrewd businesswoman, but also because she never complained when he stayed out all night or didn't show up for a couple of days. Under questioning, he maintained that "what's good for the goose is good for the gander" although he was proud to point out that Catherine never took him up on it.

One anecdote MacArthur liked to tell concerned the time a bunch of his drinking buddies took him to Al Capone's best whorehouse in Chicago. MacArthur remembered the scene vividly. Girls entertained and circulated among the customers in their chemises while others were busy in the "trick rooms" upstairs. MacArthur was a young man at the time and made a deal with his girl: He'd be glad to pay her if she promised to pretend they went through with the transaction. "She was tired anyway," he recalled, "so we sat down and had a cigar together. I never did like the idea of paying for a woman," he told me—the implication being, he never had to!

Self-made men are well aware that their dough attracts women, although most would prefer to think that it's their finer *human* qualities that are drawing them in. Harry Dawes, the main character in Joseph L. Mankiewicz's film *The Barefoot Contessa,* probably expressed it best. He said, "I never met a rich man yet who didn't think he was being loved in spite of his money."

I once asked New Orleans mogul Louie Roussel if he thought women were more attracted to him since he got rich. He said, "I think the publicity I've gotten has made me appear strong. Women are weaklings and they like to have someone strong to look up to. That's my opinion and I gave it to you."

Roussel's low-grade opinion of women is typical. Dr. Alfred E. Messer of Emory University and the Georgia Mental Health Institute's Family Studies Laboratory claims that self-made men often think of women, particularly their wives, the way they think of their money. "She is a jewel, a bauble. He has married her to increase his apparent worth. He wants the world to judge him by the prettiness of this jewel."

This may be true if the tycoon has made his pile first and selected a wife second. But that's seldom the case. In actuality, the compulsive young man beginning his career usually places far greater value on traits such as loyalty and strength than on beauty and sophistication when choosing a helpmate for the long, hard, upward grope. But heaven sustain this unglamorous wife-mother type should her excessively ambitious husband actually arrive at his destination atop Mount Money. Such are the circumstances that usher in mistresses and explode in divorce. If the wife is willing to adopt the role of the comfortable old shoe and keep her mouth shut, she has a chance of hanging in there. But should she insist on confronting her Midas-mate with the sordid truth about his infidelities and refuse to countenance a "utilitarian marital arrangement," she'll probably find herself in the process of being legally replaced.

Studies have been done that show a man's philandering tends to rise with his income. Harry J. Johnson conducted a survey among approximately 6,000 male executives and discovered that only 13.5 percent of the respondents earning less than $20,000 a year had affairs, while 20.2 percent in the $20,000-to-$35,000 bracket were fooling around. In the $35,000-to-$50,000 range, the cheating jumped to 28.7 percent and in the over-$50,000 category, 32 percent were foraging in the fields of extra-marital passion.

A tycoon-mistress relationship is seldom besotted with tenderness and affection, revolving as it inevitably does around the idea of bought-and-paid-for love. The tycoon-buyer often prefers it that way because mercenary motives he can readily understand. Non-monetary motives simply confuse him.

Thomas Wiseman in *The Money Motive* speculates that the self-made man's faith in money over love goes back to his childhood need to control which is characteristic of the anal personality. "Such people are incapable of allowing others freedom of action; typically, they want to determine the tiniest details of the lives of those close to them. They are therefore very suited to keeping mistresses. By paying the rent of the apartment, the maid, and the bills, they can maintain continuous control and scrutiny of the other person's activities. And they have the right—since they are paying."

Wiseman points out that most of these self-made business dynamos have their life meticulously divided up into self-contained compartments. "In each of which there are people who fulfill his needs—and he manages to make it all work by the exercise of monetary control: wife, mistress, prostitutes; each is paid in accordance with her services."

What about the tycoon's sexual practices? As testimony from high-priced hookers such as Xaviera Hollander "bares" out, men with dough seldom take their sex straight. All manner of exotica is the norm rather than the exception.

Even the academic community has looked into the matter. John F. Cuber, a sociology professor at Ohio State University, states his own and his colleagues' view succinctly, if rather dryly, when he says, "The lower-class man has not experienced an expensive call girl and may have never even seen one. The reason is not merely that he doesn't have the money to spend in this way, but rather that he has not learned to need or want the sophisticated and richly embellished sex at which the call girl is adept."

This addiction to expensive sex is fine as long as our tycoon keeps raking it in. But should he experience a major business reversal, his interest in sex—kooky, missionary-style, or otherwise—will probably reverse itself as well. If the reports of mistresses, wives, and shrinks are to be believed, it is indeed true that a tycoon's ego is not the only thing that wilts in such situations.

Dr. Otto Fenichel wrote in 1935 that "men to whom money signifies their potency, experience any loss of money as a castration." Dr. Gould says he's had patients "to whom great losses of money represented such a great loss of self, of ego, and ultimately of masculine image, that life no longer seemed worth living." And Dr. Edmund Bergler claims it's no coincidence that so many of the models and party girls seen in the company of tycoons report their relationships with these men are largely platonic. "Periodically, they are requested to go out on the town and in this way start rumors of sexual prowess—but appearances are all that count."

Thanks to the research of Dr. Robert Rose, a professor at Boston University School of Medicine, there may now be a biological explanation for the magnate's loss of potency during times of monetary stress. The key to the mystery is testosterone, the male take-charge hormone, the one that causes barroom brawls and heart attacks in the executive suite.

Dr. Rose discovered that a rhesus monkey who is *numero uno* in his primate colony also has the highest testosterone level of any of the monkeys. But put this testosterone-titan in a colony where he is unknown and must fight his way to the top and you will have a monkey whose male hormonal level will shrink. Male animals who are defeated in fights also experience this drop in testosterone. Might these findings also apply to human males?

You've no doubt noticed that I've confined my remarks up to this point to the male of the species. Self-made female moneybags are not in abundant supply in our society. Perhaps one reason—feminist explanations aside—is that women do *not* equate money-making prowess with femininity. In fact, it's quite the opposite. While men tend to be unsexed by financial failure, women may be unsexed by financial success. There is another old saying that points up the difference between men and women vis-à-vis money. "A woman tells her age and a man his income only to lie about it." Clearly, women's sensitive areas don't correspond to men's.

An unnamed psychiatrist whom Max Gunther interviewed for *The Very, Very Rich and How They Got That Way*, claims women tend to be more sensible about amassing money than men. "A woman wants enough money to make herself and her family comfortable—enough, perhaps, to enable her to live in luxury. But once she reaches that level of wealth she usually quits striving for more. Many men, on the other hand, go on furiously piling up wealth long after they've got more than they can possibly spend. It's hard to imagine a female Howard Hughes."

THE TYCOON TEST (A QUIZ):
MATCH YOUR PERSONALITY TRAITS
AGAINST AMERICA'S RICHEST
ENTREPRENEURS

12 Be honest with yourself when you answer these questions. After all, you might as well find out now whether you possess the stuff that moguls are made of —or whether you are better suited to reading about the very rich.

1. *I like my current vocation:*
   a) not at all; if I had it to do over, I'd have chosen something entirely different.
   b) all right; I can stand it.
   c) a lot; there are few things I'd rather do.
   d) extremely well; I'm very happy.

2. *Which of the following situations would give me the greatest sense of achievement?*
   a) getting the Good Citizenship Award for selfless volunteer work in my town
   b) landscaping the property around my home to show up all the neighbors
   c) besting an enemy on the golf course, tennis court, or in some other sportsmanlike endeavor
   d) outsmarting a business competitor at the negotiating table

3. *My favorite hobby involves:*
   a) viewing spectator sports
   b) participating in athletic competition
   c) sedentary activities requiring mental acuity and concentration
   d) no hobbies; work is my hobby.

4. *In my value system, which of the following would get top priority?*
   a) wisdom and truth
   b) true friendship and family unity
   c) an exciting, independent, freewheeling life
   d) an overwhelming sense of accomplishment at the end of each day

5. *When I go to a party, I usually:*
   a) find a corner and hide out
   b) wait for people to come to me and introduce themselves
   c) find the most influential person there and monopolize him or her
   d) circulate freely, meeting everyone and passing out my business card

6. *When faced with what appears to be a good business opportunity, I tend to:*
   a) immediately start fantasizing about striking it rich
   b) ask all my friends what they would do
   c) keep my own counsel but give myself a leisurely amount of time to mull it over
   d) quickly investigate all the pros and cons, sleep on it, and then decide

7. *I would characterize myself as:*
   a) a gloomy pessimist
   b) a cockeyed optimist
   c) a born skeptic
   d) a true pragmatist with few innate biases

8. *I identify the most with:*
   a) Walter Mitty
   b) Scrooge
   c) Attila the Hun
   d) a Horatio Alger character

9. *On average, I am sick:*
   a) a month out of every year
   b) a week out of every year
   c) a day out of every year
   d) no days every year

10. *Based on my family's medical history, I am prone to:*
    a) illnesses related to stress (e.g., heart conditions, nervous breakdowns, high blood-pressure, alcoholism)
    b) illnesses with some psychosomatic component (e.g., back trouble, skin inflammations, etc.)
    c) illnesses of a viral or bacterial nature (e.g., measles, pneumonia, smallpox, the common cold)
    d) perfect health

11. *I believe that honesty is:*
    a) always the best policy
    b) sometimes the best policy
    c) seldom the best policy
    d) depends entirely on the circumstances but it's certainly useful to have other people believe I am honest

12. *Given a choice, I prefer to:*
    a) maintain the *status quo*
    b) think long and carefully before making any changes in my life
    c) remain reasonably flexible and open to change
    d) seek constant change because I get bored with routine

13. *Which of the following characterizes how I perceive myself?*
    a) a dewy-eyed romantic
    b) a team player
    c) a hard-nosed business executive
    d) an exuberant supersalesman

14. *As a child, I was:*
    a) a goody-goody who always did what I was told
    b) an average kid who got in trouble occasionally
    c) a mischief-maker who got others to follow my lead
    d) mischievous to the point of delinquency

15. *Which of the following would be most likely to motivate me to immediate action?*
    a) feelings of goodwill toward mankind in general
    b) a promise I made to a dying friend or relative
    c) revenge on someone who did me wrong
    d) the need to make people aware of my existence

16. *Which of the following games appeals to me most?*
    a) darts, requiring good hand-eye coordination

b) backgammon, requiring 70 percent luck and 30 percent skill

c) chess, requiring long-range strategic thinking

d) poker, requiring luck, skill, and the ability to bluff

17. *What degree of luck do I possess?*
   a) none; I'm doomed.
   b) some; but not enough to write home about.
   c) average amount; I win some, I lose some.
   d) a lot; couldn't ask for anything more.

18. *On balance, I would describe my thought processes as:*
   a) unfocused and often mired in trivia, like an unmade jigsaw puzzle
   b) brilliant and theoretical like Albert Einstein's
   c) logical and orderly like a good trial attorney's
   d) spontaneous, flexible, and creative like an Oscar-winning movie director's

19. *My average concentration span is between:*
   a) two minutes and two hours
   b) two and four hours
   c) four and eight hours
   d) almost unlimited if I'm stimulated by what I'm doing

20. *When I have an important problem to solve, I:*
   a) always base my solution on meticulously researched studies and never play hunches—too unscientific
   b) ignore the problem entirely and think about something else for a week before making a decision
   c) convene a committee to brainstorm, thus relying on other people's hunches
   d) immerse myself in the problem, examining all the alternatives (moral, immoral, or otherwise), then turn my mind to other matters for a while until my intuition shouts "Eureka!"

21. *To make a financial killing, I would:*
   a) never do anything immoral even if no one else knew about it
   b) probably do something immoral if I was sure no one else knew about it

---

    c) definitely do something immoral if I was sure no one else knew about it

    d) do something grossly immoral no matter who knew about it as long as there was a reasonable chance I wouldn't land in jail

22. *My body requires:*
    a) 8–10 hours of sleep a night
    b) 6–8 hours of sleep a night
    c) 4–6 hours of sleep a night
    d) less than 4 hours a night

23. *Vacations are:*
    a) a godsend; I couldn't get through the year without one.
    b) something I enjoy, but don't plan my year around.
    c) nothing special; and often more trouble than they're worth.
    d) unbearable; I can't stand sitting around all that time with nothing constructive to do.

24. *I would say my circle of acquaintances is:*
    a) tiny; people don't interest me much.
    b) small; I prefer to have a few intimate friends rather than a string of nodding acquaintances.
    c) moderate-sized; I like to be sociable and mix with my peers.
    d) extremely wide; I hate to be alone and actively cultivate people at all social levels.

25. *What would I do after I made a million?*
    a) retire and spend it
    b) work part time so I can also enjoy my newfound status symbols
    c) delight in exercising power over others
    d) more of the same

Scoring

Give yourself a big fat 0 for every (a) answer; $1,000 for every (b); $10,000 for (c); and $50,000 for (d). Then add them up.

If you make it over that magic $1-million mark, you're definitely mogul material, an entrepreneurial heavyweight. If you made:

$750,000–$1 million .... Consider yourself a light heavyweight.

$500,000–$750,000 ..... A middleweight, my friend.

$100,000–$500,000 ..... A lightweight. Better resign yourself to corporate ladder climbing.

under $100,000 .... A bantamweight in the monetary arena. Better chain yourself down. You might blow away.

HOW THE RICHEST AMERICANS LIVE

IV

EIGHT SURE-FIRE UPPER-CLASS INDICATORS

13

> *In class society everyone lives as a member of a particular class, and every kind of thinking, without exception, is stamped with the brand of a class.*
>
> —Chairman Mao Tse-tung

Communists are not the only people who have noted the pervasive effect that class-consciousness has on our thinking, behavior, and spending patterns. American sociologists are among the first to admit that what Chairman Mao asserts is true. We are a society that has organized itself into a series of hierarchies, with some individuals or groups occupying high places, and others intermediate or low positions. And as individuals, we are acutely aware of our place in the social scheme of things.

In America, there are myriad indicators of social class including family background, wealth, power, education and skill, club memberships, religious and ethnic affiliation, geographic location of your home, etc. But many studies have shown that by far the most important criteria determining class identification are a person's income and occupation. Both are basically economic determinants, underscoring once again Americans' love affair with material values.

How many classes are there in America? That depends on whom you ask. Middle-level Americans tend to divide the whole into three parts: the rich, the poor, and the rest of us. On the other hand, if you ask a poor person, you will get a multilayered definition of "low class." The respondent will always be at least one level above the social sub-basement. No matter how low an American is on the social scale, he will always be able to describe in graphic detail those a notch lower.

Rich people engage in similar social nit-picking at the other end of the class spectrum. They will talk about an upper class consisting of the "old aristocracy"—their class, of course; "the newer-money aristocracy"—acceptable multimillionaires but not old; "the *nouveaux riches*"—those vulgar upstart multimillionaires who are totally *un*acceptable; and "respectable people but nobody" —the professional people comprising the upper-middle-class who seem to be everywhere these days. Like the poor, the rich employ several designations for categories close to themselves in the socio-economic hierarchy and tend to lump together anyone who is socially distant from themselves.

Sociologists claim to have more scientific ways to determine what constitutes the class structure in the United States. They say you should never believe what an American tells you about his social standing because the average American, being inordinately ambitious, will invariably place himself in the social stratum to which he aspires rather than the one he currently occupies. Also, an individual's evaluation of his own status is frequently based on his position in a small group of intimate associates rather than on his position in society as a whole.

The number of distinct classes that sociologists perceive ranges from five up to fifteen, again depending on whom you ask. Richard Coleman and Lee Rainwater in their treatise, *Social Standing in America: New Dimensions of Class*, delineate seven layers. From the top, they consist of the old rich of aristocratic bearing and lineage, the new rich or success elite, the highly educated professional and managerial class, middle Americans with a comfortable standard of living and ordinary aspirations, middle Americans who are just getting along by the skin of their teeth, lower-class Americans who are poor but work for a living, and the nonworking welfare class.

Vance Packard in *The Status Seekers* divided the population thus:

THE DIPLOMA ELITE

I. The Real Upper Class
II. The Semi-Upper Class

THE SUPPORTING CLASSES

III.   The Limited-Success Class
IV.   The Working Class
V.   The Real Lower Class

His definition of "real upper class" is people who probably sit "on the board of directors of local industries, banks, universities, and community chests; who send their daughters to finishing schools and their sons, probably, to a boarding school and, certainly, to a 'good' college. They have heavy investments in local land, industry, banks—they probably inherited much of it—and they can swing a great deal of weight around town when they wish." Packard further notes members of this class would disclaim that their wealth has much bearing on their social pre-eminence. Rather, it is their way of life, their breeding, and cultured good taste that has placed them at the pinnacle of social desirability.

G. William Domhoff, a sociologist who has put the computer to work analyzing upper-class social indicators, claims the American plutocratic peerage consists of people whose parents, siblings, spouse, or in-laws are listed in the Social Register and blue books; attended certain private schools; and belong to certain elite clubs. His definition effectively excludes the *arriviste* since it's not *your* affiliations that count so much as those of your family. And everyone knows it takes, at the very least, two generations with money before a family begins to be accepted by the right people in the right places.

What follows is a round-up of tips, facts, myths, and oddments concerning key patrician indicators: the best addresses around the country, important clubs to join and friends to cultivate, toney schools, Social Register listings worth having, leisure-time activities with the most cachet, "must" churches to attend, names that say "snob," and resorts to frequent.

Much of what you read will undoubtedly surprise you since to the real upper class, "exclusive" by definition means "obscure." The hoi polloi are not supposed to know about such things. However, if you want to rise in the world, you'd *better* know about such things, for as Packard put it:

"Sociologists have found that our home addresses, our friends, our clubs, our values, and even our church affiliations can prove

187

to be 'barriers' if we fail to change them with every attempted move up the ladder."

The Street Where You Live

The whole pressure is for people to live at their own money levels, in groups that will not make them feel either too guilty or too envious. It accounts for the way poor, middle-class or rich neighborhoods spring up and maintain their homogeneity.

—Thomas Wiseman

In upper-income-bracket neighborhoods around the country, there's one obvious item that brands property holders as distinctly U: their beige fiber-glass Abercrombie & Fitch mailboxes with the sportsmanlike bird and animal motifs. These mailboxes carry no name, of course. But the homes themselves—if you can even see them from the road—probably sport a name and for the mailman's edification the street number of each residence is usually posted discreetly somewhere, on a gatepost or stake in the ground perhaps.

This may strike you as an inefficient way to make your whereabouts known. It's supposed to be. The really rich want to keep their whereabouts *un*known to as many people as possible. It's a truism that those who don't know where a wealthy person lives, aren't meant to know.

Every large city and its surrounding suburbs have pockets where an especially heavy concentration of upper-class people live. Sure signs that wealth resides here are large houses, manicured landscaping, and, naturally, the ubiquitous Abercrombie & Fitch mailbox. But there are other geographic and topographic cues.

In many places, nearness to a golf course or country club becomes the measure of eliteness. This is true in Tulsa and some Fairfield County, Connecticut, communities. Needless to say, shrewd realtors make sure they drive any well-heeled house-hunters past the best club in town on the way to the property in question.

If the city has a river or coastline, nearness to the water is often the prime determinant of exclusivity. Examples are the patrician villages on the North Shore of Long Island, Boston's North Shore communities, Chicago's North Lake Shore Drive condominiums, and Minneapolis' Lake Minnetonka addresses.

In hilly and mountainous regions, the local social strata tend to conform to the geological strata. Elevation has always exerted an attraction on the *haut monde*. As a rule of thumb, the higher up the hillside, the richer the resident—for obvious reasons. Better to look down on other people than have them looking down on you. Most would agree that the homes are generally bigger and more expensive in the section of Beverly Hills north of Santa Monica Boulevard where the land starts rising. La Jolla is set on a hill overlooking the sea. So are many of the snootier addresses in and around Los Angeles. Santa Barbara has two prime ribbons of real estate: beachfront and mountainside.

There are marked regional variations when it comes to the amount of acreage accompanying an elegant home. It's ironic that in the Northeast where the population is the most congested, the posh neighborhoods are generally the most countrified. There, demesnes are often twenty and thirty acres with stands of trees and hedges along the property line to ensure privacy. By contrast, in the Sun Belt states where the cities are usually built on flat land encircled by miles of wilderness, such uppity isolation on the part of the rich, no matter how much money they had, would be considered downright antisocial. Southwesterners who are hooked on acreage had best buy a ranch and fly there on weekends.

In many cities today, the desirability of an address is determined by its distance from the downtown business district. Commuting being what it is, this may strike you as self-defeating, but you must remember that top corporate executives often get to and from their offices in limousines and many heirs don't work at all, unless you call sitting on the phone with your stockbroker working. Extracity living for the super-rich was not always the norm, however. Suburbia and exurbia are relatively new phenomena that trace back to the growth of the elite robber-baron suburban estates in the 1880s and '90s followed by the hoi-polloi tract housing boom in the 1920s.

Sociologist E. Digby Baltzell dates the beginning of the real suburban trend to the founding of The Country Club at Brookline, Massachusetts, in 1882, emphasizing that toney clubs and chic addresses have always been inextricably linked in this country, so closely linked, in fact, that whole towns are sometimes operated as private clubs to keep out the riffraff.

Tuxedo Park, New York, is one such private-club community. It was founded by Pierre Lorillard III, of snuff and tobacco lineage, on some 600,000 acres of inherited and purchased land northwest of Manhattan. According to Cleveland Amory, Lorillard was one of the last great snobs. His formula for promoting upper-class exclusivity for Tuxedo Park went as follows:

1) Find out who the leaders of society are and produce the best place for them to live in.
2) Tell nobody else about it so that nobody else will know it's available.
3) Keep it a private club so that other people, even if they do hear about it, can't get in.
4) Keep the place exactly as it was in the beginning so that other people, even if they do hear about it and somehow do manage to get in, won't ever like it anyway.

His plan is nonpareil and is still used successfully by resort developers all over the country. Hobe Sound, Florida, is a good example. Located north of Palm Beach on Jupiter Island in the Atlantic Ocean, this resort is not, strictly speaking, a private-club community. But it might as well be. Hobe Sound is small and intimate, and all the social life revolves around the genteel Jupiter Island Club. Thus, if you own property there and don't belong to the club, you might as well be living in Nome, Alaska. The clique who controls the Jupiter Island Club effectively dictates who moves onto the island. And those people are very WASP and very careful.

Until federal legislation made it illegal, the Grosse Pointe Property Owners Association (composed of 973 families in 1960) had much cruder methods of excluding the unwanted. In league with the local real estate brokers, the Property Owners Association had established a rigid system for screening out undesirables who wanted to buy or build homes in this upper-crust Detroit community, which is actually composed of five towns running along Lake St. Clair east of the city proper.

In most fashionable neighborhoods, multiacre zoning regulations, strict building requirements (e.g., each house has to be different in design from five of its neighbors), and an unwritten gentlemen's agreement are sufficient devices for keeping *them* out. Not so in "Gross" Pointe. There a private investigator was hired to collect data on all prospective buyers with suspicious social credentials. The dick summarized his findings on an extensive three-page questionnaire that covered everything from the buyer's reputation, education, and dress to the status of his occupation and his swarthiness. Prospects were also handicapped on an ethnic and racial basis: Jews had to score a minimum of eighty-five points, Italians seventy-five, Greeks sixty-five, and Poles fifty-five. Blacks and Orientals need not apply at all.

Every once in a while, a minority member with mucho money decides to even the score. Lewis S. Rosenstiel, the late chairman of Schenley Industries, waged his revenge in Greenwich, Connecticut, where he was a summer resident for more than thirty-five years. In a town with four-acre zoning, Rosenstiel wanted to have eighty-three acres of land owned by his Rosenstiel Foundation rezoned so it could be sold in half-acre lots. Rosenstiel's asking price for each lot would be less than $1,000, an absolute steal sure to attract the lower-middle-income buyer in droves. Rosenstiel, champion of integration, maintained his motives were strictly sociological—he wanted to strike a blow against *de facto* economic and racial discrimination. Old-line Greenwich residents believed him and took to their soapboxes at angry zoning board hearings. During the mayhem, Rosenstiel's own ethnic persuasion did not go unnoticed.

It should be apparent that a new-money family's address is a matter of earthshaking proportion to them, especially if the sons are to be admitted into the right schools and the daughters are to come out at the right cotillions. In *The Private World of High Society: Its Rules and Rituals*, Lucy Kavaler described the desperation experienced by the *nouveaux riches* when they relocate:

"Most rising socialites, I find, do not feel that they have unlimited choice as to suburb. Only a few communities are considered acceptable. A family's whole social future can depend on where it moves."

The Fashionable Places to Live In and Around

Atlanta: northwest Buckhead section of the city (Tuxedo Road, Paces Ferry area)

Baltimore: northwest section of city (North Charles Street and Roland Park); Dulaney Valley and Green Spring Valley

Boston: Beacon Hill, Back Bay, Chestnut Hill, Milton, Wellesley,

Brookline, North Shore communities

Chicago: North Lake Shore Drive, Near North Side; Barrington Hills, Flossmoor/Olympia Fields, Hinsdale/Oak Brook, Kenilworth, Lake Forest, Libertyville, and Winnetka

Cleveland: Shaker Heights, Waite Hill

Dallas: northern part of city, University Park, Highland Park

Detroit: Grosse Pointe City, Grosse Pointe Parks, Grosse Pointe Farms, Grosse Pointe Shores, Grosse Pointe Woods, Bloomfield Hills

Houston: River Oaks section

Kansas City: Country Club district; Mission Hills, Kansas

Los Angeles: Beverly Hills, Pasadena, Malibu, Bel-Air, Palos Verdes Peninsula, San Marino, Encino, Brentwood, Hancock Park

Miami: Coral Gables, Coconut Grove, Indian Creek Island, La Gorce Island, Sunset Islands 1 and 2

Minneapolis: Wayzata, Lake Minnetonka

New Orleans: Garden District, Bayou Liberty

New York City: Fifth or Park avenues or an Eastside town house in the 60s, 70s, or 80s; North Shore of Long Island; Southport and Greenwich, Connecticut; northern Westchester County; Far Hills and Princeton, New Jersey

Oklahoma City: Nichols Hills

Philadelphia: Chestnut Hill, Main Line communities

Phoenix: Scottsdale

Pittsburgh: Fox Chapel, Sewickley Heights, Squirrel Hill and Shadyside sections, Schenley Park; Ligonier

San Diego: La Jolla

San Francisco: Nob Hill, Russian Hill, Burlingame, Hillsborough, Woodside, Sausalito; Monterey Peninsula

Tulsa: southeast section of city around the Southern Hills Country Club

Washington, D.C.: Georgetown section, Foxhall Road, Kalorama area; Chevy Chase, Maryland

Wilmington: "château country"

A Friend, Indeed

If you've ever glanced through the Social Register, you've no doubt puzzled over the alphabetical chicken-scratching after people's names. Those impossible-to-decipher abbreviations represent the Elysian Fields of exclusivity—the clubs, schools, and other honors accorded an "in" circle of the nation's aristocratic aborigines.

Ah, this surprises you. You thought club life was dead, the victim of antediluvianism, high property taxes, young scions' lack of respect for tradition, staggering maintenance costs, and discrimination laws.

Not so. According to *New York Times* reporter Frank Prial, who did some nosing around New York's patrician strongholds as recently as 1975, there has been some attrition "but as a group, the famous old clubs are quite hardy for their ages." In Manhattan, the best of them—the Union, Century Association, New York Yacht Club—are more than 100 years old and, despite occasional financial crises, are going strong socially with substantial waiting lists of prospective members.

Private clubs for free, white, adult, male blue bloods, patterned after the English models, first began appearing in this country as early as the eighteenth century. It wasn't long before members realized their clubs' usefulness as places to reflex their male-bonding tendencies; avoid nagging wives, noisy offspring, and the tedium of family life; discuss the larger issues of the day; receive messages from their mistresses; and talk business, maybe even closing a few deals in the process.[1] And that's how mono-male, mono-WASP clubs such as the Somerset (Boston), Knickerbocker (New York), Rittenhouse (Philadelphia), Duquesne (Pittsburgh), Metropolitan (Washington), and St. Cecilia Society (Charleston) became the societal control centers of the elite in this country. True, a small coterie of schools is where ruling-class American males first meet each other.[2] But it's at their clubs where their socioeconomic interests coalesce.

Oligarchy observer Ferdinand Lundberg says clubs serve as a kind of behind-the-scene U.S. *politburo*. "Often a uniform attitude comes suddenly to be expressed in the press from coast to coast on some topic. Never a dissent, never a deviation appears. The source —or sources—of such uniformity, as in the 85-percent press opposition to Roosevelt, is the deliberations of the tycoons and tycoonlets in their clubs."

He points out that, unlike Congress which recesses periodically and has a constant changing of the guard, the clubs are always in session and their members remain until death or disability finally renders them mute. Until that terminus, they can bask in the four freedoms that clubdom affords: freedom of speech against democracy, freedom of worship of aristocracy, freedom from want from tipping, and freedom from fear of women.

The power of clubs—or more accurately, club members' interactions—is awesome. U.S. Presidents and presidential aspirants understand where key clubs fit in the decision-making schema and covet speaking engagements at the Duquesne Club, Economic Club of Detroit, and Bohemian Club, all presidential launching pads of the first order. New corporate board members are also recruited out of the best clubs, underlining the fact that the Old Boy Network is still alive and well and functioning efficiently.

Obviously, you don't gain entry to one of these citadels of exclusivity by knocking on the front door, filling out an application, and plunking down the fee—which in many cases is *not* exorbitant by any means. Your means, in fact, are not the point. It's your antecedents that matter. Anyone who is savvy about the pecking order among the top-drawer men's clubs will find it significant that John D. Rockefeller, the *parvenu*, only made it into New York's Union League Club. His son, John D. Rockefeller, Jr., called the University Club his home away from home. And his grandson, Nelson Rockefeller, was a proud and staunch member of the Old Guard Knickerbocker Club.

The tone of any club is set by whom it excludes. As Cleveland Amory put it: "From the very beginning clubs were formed not primarily to get people in but rather to keep people out." The small and close-knit Philadelphia Assembly, for example, was referred to by one upper-crust commentator as "probably the most compact and inviolable little group of aristocrats in America." The idea of a club is to get your friends in and keep the rabble out. It doesn't always work that way, however. J. P. Morgan was so incensed when the Union Club blackballed one of his friends that he blackballed Unionmen by founding his own club, the Metropolitan, for years known as the "Millionaires' Club on Millionaire's Row," i.e., 1 East Sixtieth Street (on the corner of Fifth Avenue) in Manhattan. Morgan functioned as a "status-lender" to the new club. A powerhouse among the industrial giants of the day, Morgan lent his stature to the new club, making anyone who joined a semi-peer. Morgan, the middling fish at the Union, was a veritable whale at the Metropolitan.

In *Farewell to Fifth Avenue*, a book that rocked New York's gentry when it came out in 1935, Cornelius Vanderbilt, Jr., described exactly how the Union Club polices its membership. One day Vanderbilt found the following cryptic message from the gods in his Union Club mailbox:

"The Chairman of the House Committee is obliged to remind you that the members of this Club must exercise extreme caution when inviting strangers to luncheon in the Club's restaurant. [Note the use of the capital "C."] My attention has been called to the fact that a gentleman brought here by you last week is not the type of person we care to see on these premises."

Vanderbilt did not name the maligned "gentleman" but he did give his curriculum vitae: The man was internationally known and universally admired, according to Vanderbilt. Abroad he was received with pomp and circumstance by prime ministers and nobility alike. To the *nouveaux riches*—what Vanderbilt termed "the Park Avenue set"—he was a hero and prophet. *But* to the old-money peerage—what Vanderbilt termed "the Fifth Avenue set"—he did not belong.

In 1966, J. Paul Getty, who had held the title "richest man in the world" for a while, was denied membership in the exclusive Circolo della Caccia in Rome, Italy. The event was proclaimed in a wire-service news story and Getty was livid. He claimed he didn't mind the blackball since he was pressured into joining anyway by friends—"club members were very insistent that I join and it seemed churlish to refuse." But he was furious about the publicity. "That the affairs of a private club should be made public is unheard of. It just wouldn't happen in England or America. I wouldn't want to belong to a club which made private matters public."

The finest men's clubs in America have a considerable proportion of nonresident members, men who may live 3,000 miles away but use the club whenever they are visiting in that city. In contrast, country clubs and women's clubs are local phenomena.

The growth of country clubs paralleled the growth of the suburbs. The early country clubs were places where the city's elite could repair to enjoy horseback riding, coaching, and other popular sports of the day, most notably golf, a game which Andrew Carnegie dubbed "An indispensable adjunct of high civilization." The Country Club in Brookline, Massachusetts, is often credited with being America's first, but the Myopia Hunt Club in Hamilton, Massachusetts, was actually founded seven years earlier in 1875.

The rise of the country club was also the result, in some measure, of the gradual decline of the great country estates of the Gilded Age. In Great Britain to this day, sprawling English manor houses, with their undulating lawns and parklike settings, provide the backdrop for lordly weekends in the country. Highborn Englishmen and -women are always being invited to such homes for a short holiday even if they don't own one themselves. In the United States, country clubs now fill that role. Indeed, many clubs occupy the mansions and grounds of nineteenth-century American industrialists' estates. Country clubs along Long Island's North Shore once bore such names as Whitney, Vanderbilt, and Burden. Now, bronze plaques on the gateposts say Old Westbury Golf & Country Club, Pine Hollow Country Club, and Woodcrest Club.

There were fewer than twelve country clubs/golf clubs in the United States in the late 1880s, but by 1905, there were more than 1,000. Today, there are some 4,800, with approximately 2 million members (the average country club has 400–600 regular members).

When 2 million people in a country of 220 million people belong to country clubs, it's clear that they're not patronized exclusively by the nation's *crème de la crème*. There are plenty of Nixon's Silent Majority in attendance as well. You might say a country club is an all-purpose sporting club with limited social cachet.

Up to the end of World War II, country clubs were monopolized by white Christians, a reflection of the ethnic and racial composition of the local upper-class neighborhood. After the war, affluent Jewish and middle-class black families began infiltrating the better suburban communities and, as a consequence, a few minorities were admitted on a token basis into the once 100 percent white-Christian clubs. The minority families left pining outside the clubhouse door countered by setting up their own restrictive clubs. A few of the best-known predominantly Jewish country clubs are the Century Country Club and Old Oaks Country Club (Westchester County); Radnor Valley Country Club (Philadelphia Main Line); Woodmont Country Club (Rockville, Maryland); and the Crest View Country Club (Springfield, Massachusetts).

Pedigreed women began forming their own clubs in the early part of the twentieth century, a precursor of and adjunct to the feminist movement. The earliest clubs were the Acorn in Philadelphia, the Chilton in Boston, and the Colony in New York City. The male reaction was typical. None other than Grover Cleveland, ex-President of the United States, spoke out against female clubs in 1905, declaring that a woman's "best and safest club is her home." Newspapers editorialized on the subject, prophesying "everlasting perdition" for the nation at large because of the adventurousness and independence of America's upper-class women. And American clubmen projected that their wives would use clubs for the same illicit purposes they did—to write and receive messages from paramours.

The women's city clubs have managed to maintain their tone utilizing the same methods as the posh men's clubs. The Junior League, a national association of women dedicated, ostensibly, to volunteer work, has not fared as well. The league was founded in 1901 by Miss Mary Harriman (daughter of railroad potentate E. H. Harriman) and Miss Nathalie Henderson, two well-connected young gentlewomen who wanted to put that year's crop of New York City debutantes to work "for the benefit of the poor and the betterment of the city." They decided the College Settlement House on Rivington Street was in dire need of such volunteer labor and The Junior League for the Promotion of Settlement Houses was born. The idea struck a responsive chord and before long there were Junior League chapters in fashionable cities all over the country. The volume diluted the quality, however, and today the Junior League chapters in the older cities have become *déclassée* female assemblages.

If the foregoing discussion of U.S. club life strikes you as shockingly undemocratic and anti-American, consider the findings of noted sociologists. They point out that restrictive clubs are a manifestation of a socioeconomic truism: People prefer to associate with their social equals. An early sociologist, F. H. Giddings, called this tendency among Americans "consciousness of kind." Several studies have been done which underline the fact that people experience undue discomfort and strain when they socialize repeatedly across class barriers. After analyzing the social structure of a Georgia town, Bevode McCall concluded: "The way people choose their friends is a part of the functioning of social class."

A group of Boston Brahmins found this out the hard way when it attempted to solicit donations for the Boston Symphony via a chain letter. Each person who received the letter was supposed to send it on to ten of her friends and, in that way, it was expected that the missives would eventually percolate down to the masses and generate a windfall of dollars. They didn't. Why? Because none of the upper-class women who got the original letter ever circulated it outside her own peer group.

CLOUT CLUBS: STRICTLY FOR GENTLEMEN

Boston
   Somerset Club (founded
      1851)
   Tavern Club
   St. Botolph Club

New York City
   Union Club (founded 1836)
   Knickerbocker Club
   New York Yacht Club
      (founded 1844)
   Brook Club
   The Links (founded 1916)
   Century Association
      (founded 1847)
   Metropolitan Club
   Racquet & Tennis Club
   National Golf Links of
      America (Southampton,
      New York)

Philadelphia
   Philadelphia Club (founded
      1850)
   Rittenhouse Club (founded
      1875)

   Fish House (founded 1732)
   Union League (founded
      1862)
   Locust Club (the "Jewish
      Union League")

Pittsburgh
   Duquesne Club (This business/luncheon club,
      founded in 1873, began
      admitting women in July
      1980. However, its
      membership is expected
      to remain predominantly
      male.)

Baltimore
   Maryland Club (founded
      1857)

Washington, D.C.
   Metropolitan Club (founded
      1863)
   Cosmos Club
   Burning Tree Club
      (Bethesda, Maryland)

Charleston
St. Cecilia Society (founded 1762)

Chicago
Chicago Club
Union League Club
Standard Club (predominantly Jewish)

Minneapolis
Minneapolis Club

New Orleans
Boston Club

Dallas
Idlewild Club

Houston
Petroleum Club
Houston Club

Los Angeles
California Club (founded 1887)
Jonathan Club

San Francisco
Pacific Union Club (founded 1852)
Bohemian Club (founded 1872)

Portland
Arlington Club

CLOUT CLUBS: STRICTLY FOR LADIES

Boston
Chilton Club
Vincent Club
Women's City Club

New York City
Colony Club (founded 1903)
Cosmopolitan Club (founded 1911)

Philadelphia
Acorn Club (founded 1890)
Cosmopolitan Club (founded 1928)

Pittsburgh
Twentieth Century Club

Baltimore
Mt. Vernon Club

Washington, D.C.
Sulgrave Club
Washington Club

Chicago
Fortnightly Club
Friday Club

Los Angeles
Beverly Hills Women's Club

San Francisco
Francisca Club

Seattle
Sunset Club

CLOUT CLUBS: STRICTLY FOR FAMILIES

Boston
The Country Club (founded
1882; Brookline)
Myopia Hunt Club (founded
1875; Hamilton, Massa-
chusetts)

Newport
Bailey's Beach Club
(founded 1893)

Westchester County, New York
Apawamis Club (founded
1890; Rye)
Country Club of West-
chester County (founded
1884)
Century Country Club
(White Plains; predomi-
nantly Jewish)

Long Island, New York
Piping Rock Club (founded
1911; Locust Valley)
Rockaway Hunting Club
(founded 1878; Cedar-
hurst)
Maidstone Club (founded
1891; East Hampton)
Shinnecock Hills Golf Club
(Southampton)

New York City
River Club
Harmonie Club (founded
1852; predominantly
German-Jewish)

New Jersey
Morris County Golf Club
(founded 1894; Convent
Station)

Baltusrol Golf Club
(founded 1895; Spring-
field)

Philadelphia Main Line
Merion Cricket Club
(Haverford)
Philadelphia Country Club
(founded 1890; Glad-
wyne)
Radnor Hunt (Malvern)
Gulph Mills Golf Club
(King of Prussia)
Radnor Valley Country
Club (predominantly
Jewish)

Pittsburgh
Allegheny Country Club
(founded 1898;
Sewickley)
Rolling Rock Club
(Ligonier)

Baltimore
Baltimore Country Club
(founded 1898; Five
Farms)

Washington, D.C.
Chevy Chase Club (founded
1893; Chevy Chase,
Maryland)
Woodmont Country Club
(Rockville, Maryland;
predominantly Jewish)

Atlanta
Piedmont Driving Club
(founded 1887)
Capital City Club (founded
1883)

Palm Beach
Everglades Club (founded 1915)

Miami
Palm Bay Club

Detroit
Country Club of Detroit (founded 1897; Grosse Pointe Farms)

Chicago
Onwentsia Country Club (founded 1895; Lake Forest)
Lakeshore Country Club (founded 1908)

Minneapolis
Minikahda Club
Woodhill Country Club

Dallas
Brook Hollow Golf Club (founded 1920)

Houston
River Oaks Country Club (founded 1922)

San Diego
La Jolla Country Club (founded 1913)

Los Angeles
Los Angeles Country Club (founded 1897)
Hillcrest Country Club (founded 1920; predominantly Jewish)

San Francisco
Burlingame Country Club (founded 1896; Hillsborough)

Portland
Waverley Country Club (founded 1896)

Educating America's Elite

If one had to choose one clue to the national unity of the upper social classes in America today, it would best be the really exclusive boarding school for girls and prep school for boys.

—C. Wright Mills
The Power Elite

You're naive if you think getting your son into an Ivy League college will ensure his acceptance into the Old Boy Network. The old school tie that binds is the one woven in prep school or in one of the snob secret societies at Harvard and Yale. Sure your kid may be plenty brainy, valedictorian of his high school class even. But that's not good enough.

201

If your plan is to elevate your offspring into the upper stratum of society you'd better start when they're still in the crib. You'd better see that they begin their education in a local but fashionable day or country-day school and move on to the right boarding school in the seventh, eighth, or ninth grade. But be prepared. Getting your kid into St. Grottlesex [3] may be the most difficult chore you encounter as a parent.

Why is all this necessary? Because, C. Wright Mills elaborates, "The school—rather than the upper-class family—is the most important agency for transmitting the traditions of the upper social classes, and regulating the admission of new wealth and talent. . . . It is by means of these schools more than any other single agency that the older and the newer families—when their time is due— become members of a self-conscious upper class."

Self-conscious it is! Of the several thousand private schools in this country, barely 100 have any tangible snob appeal. Anyone who looks into the matter can quickly find out which they are. Geographically, the majority of these bastions of privilege are nestled in quiet New England hamlets, although a few of the toniest girls' schools are located in the verdant Virginia countryside. Except in rare cases, admission to this fistful of redoubtable institutions is an automatic open sesame to the best universities, junior-college finishing schools, debutante cotillions, marital alliances, and clubs in later life.

Generally, the sons and daughters of graduates—in short, members of the Old Guard—get preference in admissions. Today, the few places left over usually go to indigent minority students who are courted and given full scholarships to satisfy the tax authorities who have decreed that private schools can lose their nonprofit status if they don't comply with federal antidiscrimination statutes. Finally, any remaining vacancies are filled by the aspiring progeny of the nonminority *nouveaux riches*.

There was a time in the late 1960s when private school administrators, infused with the democratic zeal of the Civil Rights movement, decided to ignore tradition and admit only the "most qualified boy," the M.Q.B. Suddenly, brains supplanted pedigree as the standard of measurement. It was not a wise move. That revolutionary decision not only destroyed the whole idea of the boarding school as the recruitment and training center of the upper class, but wreaked havoc with schools' finances as well.

Historically, certain schools had adopted certain families as their own. It seemed as if there was always a Ford at Hotchkiss, a Mellon at Choate, a Cabot at St. Mark's, a Biddle, Ingersoll, or Pillsbury at St. Paul's. Proof of such families' devotion to their alma maters were the campus buildings bearing the families' name and paid for out of the families' coffers. Now, put yourself in the position of a wealthy father who has just pledged $2 million toward the construction of a new gymnasium at his beloved prep school and, three days later, learns that his only son has just been rejected because his grades aren't good enough. You get the picture. And after a 75-percent drop in alumni benefactions, headmasters also started to get the message. Nepotism was a matter of economic, if not social, necessity. Today, a teen-age Ford would have to be most *un*qualified, indeed, to be spurned by Hotchkiss now that the magnificent Ford Library reposes there.

Headmasters of the junior halls of ivy were experiencing other crucibles as well during this hell-no-we-won't-go era. Like their older counterparts on university campuses, preppies were flouting school dress codes, growing hair down to their shoulders, challenging teachers to defend their conservative political views, experimenting with drugs and getting arrested, seducing any available girls, and staging demonstrations. New England boarding-school discipline, modeled after "public" school strictures in Britain, had always been Gestapolike. Preppies might suffer expulsion for merely being caught smoking—cigarettes. But what were headmasters to do in the late 1960s, expel the whole student body for disorderly conduct, drug peddling, lewd behavior, and criminal mischief? Clearly, the strong-arm tactics used to maintain campus law and order—methods that had worked so well for a century or more— had to go.

A relaxation of rules was not the only thing that changed during this shakedown period. The Mr. Chips-type headmasters were largely replaced with younger, more forward-looking dons. The phrase "prep school," deemed to have a snobby ring, was banned. Forevermore, the likes of Groton, Exeter, and Choate would be known as "independent secondary" schools or "college preparatory" institutions. The curriculum was broadened to include courses considered more relevant to today's society. Chapel attendance at the Episcopal church schools (St. Paul's, St. Mark's, Groton, St. George's, and Kent) was no longer mandatory, and students were issued more weekend passes. And students were allowed to undertake volunteer work in the ghetto areas of the nearest city.

All these alterations were trumpeted as the "New Look." But the most astounding change of all was the transformation of the inviolate boys' school into a coeducational institution. Hotchkiss, among others, began admitting girls in the fall of 1974 and school officials moved quickly in turning the coed idea into a major selling point to prospective parents and students. Headmaster William Olsen declared, "Coeducation is simply better for the kids. It's better for them psychologically, emotionally, and academically." He added that feminism was a historic fact "and its effects are not reversible. Men and women treated equally is the way these kids will live their future lives."

There are still plenty of old-fashioned parents around who rue the new ways on campus, preferring to keep their daughters at home until college or send them to one of the *in loco parentis* girls' schools where essence of WASP is carefully preserved in aspic and the male-female amenities are strictly enforced. The Swiss or English finishing school is another option, but only for girls. Boys, it is felt, should be educated at the top schools on this side of the Atlantic because only here will they meet and mingle with their peers, the future rulers of this country.

But suppose, by some miracle, you do get your son or daughter into one of these exclusive and *expensive* educational preserves— possibly with the help of a society press agent. Your troubles as an ambitious parent may be over but your children's emotional problems may just be starting.

A number of years ago, a Harvard psychologist named Charles C. McArthur did a study of the personalities of Harvard freshmen, noting particularly the difference in outlook between upper-class boys coming from private schools and upper-middle-class boys coming from public high schools. The results were self-evident but startling nonetheless.

Dr. McArthur discovered that public-school boys were oriented toward the future, toward accomplishment. They perceived their fathers as people whom they must surpass occupationally and a Harvard education was a means to that end. In contrast, private-school boys of aristocratic lineage were oriented toward the past, toward *being* rather than *doing*. Their fathers and grandfathers were role models to emulate rather than overcome. To them, Harvard represented the perpetuation of a way of life rather than a means to some vocational end. The "gentleman's C" suited them fine since college grades would have little bearing on their future careers anyway. Mostly, they spent their Harvard years fraternizing with their prep-school buddies in their clubs and competing with other boys on the playing field, squash court, or ski slope.

Thrown into the trust-fund milieu of the privileged prep school, your son may pick up the societal values and behavior patterns of the upper class and in the process form some useful friendships. But he'll never feel really secure there. *His* feelings about life are not *their* feelings. Emotionally and psychologically, he and his patrician peers are miles apart and never the twain shall meet. For your grandson, possibly. For your great-grandson, probably.

POSH PRIVATE SCHOOLS FOR BOYS

Massachusetts
> Eaglebrook School (founded 1922; Deerfield; for younger boys)
> Deerfield Academy (founded 1797; Deerfield)

Rhode Island
> Portsmouth Abbey School (founded 1926; Portsmouth; Catholic)

New York City
> Collegiate School (founded 1738; day students)
> The Browning School (founded 1888; day students)
> The Buckley School (founded 1913; day students)
> St. Bernard's School (founded 1904; day students)

New Jersey
> The Lawrenceville School (founded 1810; Lawrenceville)

Pennsylvania
> The Hill School (founded 1851; Pottstown)
> Shady Side Academy (Pittsburgh)

Virginia
> Episcopal High School (founded 1839; Alexandria)
> St. Christopher's School (founded 1911; Richmond; day students)
> Woodberry Forest School (founded 1889; Woodberry Forest)

Ohio
   University School (founded 1890; Cleveland; day students)

Missouri
   Country Day School (founded 1917; St. Louis)

California
   The Cate School (founded 1910; Carpinteria)
   Robert Louis Stevenson School (founded 1952; Pebble Beach)

U-UNIVERSITIES FOR MEN

Harvard College (Cambridge, Massachusetts)
Brown University (Providence, Rhode Island)
Columbia College (New York City)
Rutgers (New Brunswick, New Jersey)
Washington & Lee University (Lexington, Virginia)
Davidson College (Davidson, North Carolina)
Claremont Men's College (Claremont, California)

POSH PRIVATE SCHOOLS FOR GIRLS

Massachusetts
   Dana Hall School (founded 1881; Wellesley)
   Walnut Hill School (founded 1893; Natick)
   The Winsor School (founded 1886; Boston; day students)
   Foxhollow School (Lenox)

Connecticut
   Miss Porter's School (founded 1843; Farmington)
   The Ethel Walker School (founded 1911; Simsbury)
   Westover (Middlebury)
   The Convent of the Sacred Heart (founded 1848; Greenwich;
      Roman Catholic)

New York State
   The Masters School (founded 1877; Dobbs Ferry)
   Emma Willard School (founded 1814; Troy)

New York City
   The Hewitt School (day students)
   The Brearley School (founded 1884; day students)
   The Chapin School (founded 1901; day students)

The Spence School (founded 1892; day students)
Convent of the Sacred Heart (founded 1881; Roman Catholic)

New Jersey
Kent Place (founded 1894; Summit)

Pennsylvania
The Baldwin School (founded 1888; Bryn Mawr)
The Shipley School (founded 1894; Bryn Mawr)
The Agnes Irwin School (founded 1869; Rosemont)

Maryland
St. Timothy's School (founded 1882; Stevenson)
Garrison Forest School (founded 1910; Garrison)
Oldfields School (founded 1869; Glencoe)

Washington, D.C.
National Cathedral School (founded 1900; day students)

Virginia
Foxcroft School (founded 1914; Middleburg)
Chatham Hall (founded 1894; Chatham)
The Madeira School (founded 1906; Greenway)
St. Catherine's School (Richmond; day students)

South Carolina
Ashley Hall (founded 1909; Charleston)

Missouri
Mary Institute (founded 1859; St. Louis)

Texas
The Hockaday School (founded 1913; Dallas)
St. Mary's Hall (founded 1879; San Antonio)

California
Marlborough School (founded 1889; Los Angeles)
The Westridge School (founded 1913; Pasadena; day students)
The Bishop's Schools (founded 1909; La Jolla)
Santa Catalina School (Monterey; Roman Catholic)

CLASS COLLEGES FOR WOMEN

Colby-Sawyer College (New London, New Hampshire)
Pine Manor Junior College (Chestnut Hill, Massachusetts)
Radcliffe College (Cambridge, Massachusetts)

Wellesley College (Wellesley, Massachusetts)
Mt. Holyoke College (South Hadley, Massachusetts)
Smith College (Northampton, Massachusetts)
Pembroke College (Providence, Rhode Island)
Barnard College (New York City)
Finch College (New York City)
Bennett Junior College (Millbrook, New York)
Bryn Mawr (Bryn Mawr, Pennsylvania)
Goucher College (Towson, Maryland)
Mount Vernon Junior College (Washington, D.C.)
Hollins College (Hollins, Virginia)
Sophie Newcomb College (New Orleans, Louisiana)
Colorado Woman's College (Denver, Colorado)
Scripps College (Claremont, California)
Mills College (Oakland, California)

COED PREP SCHOOLS FOR PATRICIAN ADOLESCENTS

New Hampshire
>   St. Paul's School (founded 1855; Concord)
>   The Phillips Exeter Academy (founded 1781; Exeter; referred to as "Exeter")

Massachusetts
>   St. Mark's School (founded 1865; Southborough)
>   Phillips Academy (founded 1778; Andover; often referred to as "Andover")
>   Middlesex School (founded 1901; Concord)
>   Concord Academy (founded 1922; Concord)
>   Milton Academy (founded 1798; Milton)
>   Groton School (founded 1884; Groton)
>   Northfield Mount Hermon (Northfield founded 1879; Mount Hermon founded 1881; Northfield)

Connecticut
>   Loomis Chaffee School (Loomis founded 1874; Chaffee founded 1872; Windsor)
>   The Hotchkiss School (founded 1891; Lakeville)
>   Kent School (founded 1906; Kent)
>   Choate/Rosemary Hall (founded 1896 and 1890 respectively; Wallingford)
>   The Taft School (founded 1890; Watertown)

Rhode Island
St. George's School (founded 1896; Newport)
Moses Brown School (founded 1785; Providence)

New York
The Dalton School (founded 1916; New York City; day students)
The Hackley School (founded 1899; Tarrytown)

Pennsylvania
Sewickley Academy (Sewickley; day students)

Delaware
St. Andrew's School (founded 1930; Middletown)

Virginia
The Collegiate Schools (founded 1915; Richmond; day students)

Georgia
Westminster Schools (founded 1909; Atlanta)

Michigan
Cranbrook Schools (founded 1920s; Bloomfield Hills)

Indiana
Culver Military Academy (Culver)

Illinois
Lake Forest Academy (founded 1857; Lake Forest)
North Shore Country Day School (founded 1919; Winnetka)
Roycemore School (founded 1915; Evanston; day students)
The Latin School of Chicago (founded 1888; Chicago; day students)

Wisconsin
University School (founded 1851; Milwaukee; day students)

Minnesota
Shattuck/St. Mary's/St. James (Faribault)

Texas
The Kinkaid School (founded 1906; Houston)
Texas Military Institute (founded 1893; San Antonio)

Arizona
Orme School (Mayer; on a working ranch)

California
The Thacher School (founded 1889; Ojai)
Pilgrim School (founded 1953; Los Angeles; day students)
The Head-Royce School (founded 1887; Oakland; day students)
The Katharine Branson School/Mt. Tamalpais School (founded 1920; Ross; day students)

Washington
The Lakeside School (founded 1919; Seattle; day students)

CHIC COED COLLEGES

Bowdoin College (Brunswick, Maine)
Colby College (Waterville, Maine)
Bennington College (Bennington, Vermont)
Dartmouth College (Hanover, New Hampshire)
Massachusetts Institute of Technology (Cambridge, Massachusetts)
Williams College (Williamstown, Massachusetts)
Amherst College (Amherst, Massachusetts)
Trinity College (Hartford, Connecticut)
Wesleyan University (Middletown, Connecticut)
Yale University (New Haven, Connecticut)
Connecticut College (New London, Connecticut)
Colgate University (Hamilton, New York)
Union College (Schenectady, New York)
Skidmore College (Saratoga Springs, New York)
Rensselaer Polytechnic Institute (Troy, New York)
Vassar College (Poughkeepsie, New York)
Sarah Lawrence College (Bronxville, New York)
Princeton University (Princeton, New Jersey)
University of Pennsylvania (Philadelphia, Pennsylvania)
Lehigh University (Bethlehem, Pennsylvania)
Lafayette College (Easton, Pennsylvania)
Swarthmore College (Swarthmore, Pennsylvania)
Johns Hopkins University (Baltimore, Maryland)
Georgetown University (Washington, D.C.)
George Washington University (Washington, D.C.)
University of Virginia (Charlottesville, Virginia)
Duke University (Durham, North Carolina)
Oberlin College (Oberlin, Ohio)

Denison University (Granville, Ohio)
University of Cincinnati (Cincinnati, Ohio)
University of Chicago (Chicago, Illinois)
Northwestern University (Evanston, Illinois)
Carleton College (Northfield, Minnesota)
Tulane University (New Orleans, Louisiana)
Baylor University (Waco, Texas)
University of Texas (Austin, Texas)
Rice University (Houston, Texas)
Colorado College (Colorado Springs, Colorado)
University of Colorado (Boulder, Colorado)
California Institute of Technology (Pasadena, California)
Stanford University (Palo Alto, California)
University of California at Berkeley (Berkeley, California)
Reed College (Portland, Oregon)

Proper Purple Pastimes

How you spend your leisure time is a prime indicator of class affiliation. Sitting in front of a TV set watching football every Saturday and Sunday—with the exception of the Super Bowl—brands you as very middle class. But *playing* touch football on your lawn bespeaks a touch of class.

The rule of thumb is this: A love of spectator sports places a person in a substratospheric position in American society. In contrast, involvement in outdoorsy participative sports is a distinct sign of the snob. However, to qualify as a proper purple pastime, the sport must require an excess of energy and mucho money, two preconditions that automatically exclude motorboating and certain forms of hunting and fishing—the kinds that require the utmost in discomfort pass muster. They also make golf questionable for anyone who isn't past fifty.

The type-casting of games and sports is a relatively recent phenomenon. In fact, until the modern era, leisure time in and of itself reflected one's superior class rating, hence the term "leisure class." Thorstein Veblen made this point graphically in his famous turn-of-the-century opus *The Theory of the Leisure Class.* Veblen emphasized that during the Gilded Age, wealthy people were the only ones who had time for sports. Thus all sports were, by definition, U. That changed in subsequent years when automation gave the average slob more leisure time and the senior business executive less. As a result, leisure lost most of its potency as a status symbol.

A long list of sports has gone the way of suburban real estate. Now even Levittowners have access to tennis courts, golf courses, ski slopes, and racetracks. It's reached the point where there are only three sports left with any real cachet: polo, fox-hunting, and court tennis.

Ballroom dancing is another after-hours activity that plummeted in esteem. It used to be practiced by the Café Society crowd in places such as the Stork Club. Now it's practiced by retired mailmen in such places as Roseland Dance City. The younger generation, in the meantime, has taken up disco dancing. It's the country's greatest social leveler, attracting rich and poor alike and mixing them all up in barns such as Studio 54.

The fashionable prep schools have not been deterred by this alarming turn of events, however. In their curriculum offerings, they continue to maintain that being able to play the right game is as important a part of being a lady or gentleman as using the right fork and speaking with the right accent.

In their survey of New England Episcopal boarding schools for their book *The Power of Their Glory*, Kit and Frederica Konolige remarked on this special approach to preppie pedagogy. They observed that the church schools instill certain vaguely defined aristocratic qualities in their students, first and foremost, by sending them out on the playing field. "At the church schools as they developed, muscles were as important, not only as Christianity but as the cut of one's clothes." Success at sports guaranteed social success at these schools.

They're probably right, for you simply don't graduate from a school such as Andover unless you are thoroughly proficient in hockey, lacrosse, rugby, crew, tennis, and squash. Compare this line-up with the usual public high school phys-ed fare: There the "in" sports are football, wrestling, basketball, baseball, track, and possibly swimming. For girls, it's cheerleading. Now I ask you, have you ever heard of a debutante who was a cheerleader?

No, for proper young ladies, riding is the premier sport. Lately, a number of posh girls' schools are turning it into a vocation. Foxcroft offers a course of study leading to a "Stable Diploma" and Bennett Junior College in Millbrook, New York, has instituted a three-year program leading to a certificate in horsemanship. Students take classes in the care and knowledge of the horse, theory of stable management, theory of equitation, and the theory of teaching. The third year consists of an internship at the Bennett riding academy or at some other approved off-campus stable.

Bennett's dean said the program was developed "in response to requests by many of our present and prospective students who wish to pursue careers in the field of horsemanship. Our surveys show that more than half the students at the college said the stress on riding was an important factor in their choosing Bennett."

William Woods College, a women's school in Fulton, Missouri, has gone Bennett one better. When Woods introduced an equitation minor, its enrollment doubled. Woods topped that with a four-year major leading to a B.S. degree in Equestrian Studies.

What do graduates do with their equine knowledge? Some showcase their skill as members of the United States Equestrian Team in the Olympics. Others teach, go into blacksmithing, or design and sell riding clothes. A few manage horse farms, stables, or dude ranches. But the really lucky ones marry a Whitney or a Vanderbilt and spend the rest of their days haggling over expensive thoroughbred horseflesh—that is, when they're not off somewhere riding to hounds.

Perhaps Stephen Birmingham gave the best summation of the patrician recreational situation circa 1980. He said, rather whimsically, "Society fathers expect their sons to have learned, by the time of their maturity, to ride and respect horseflesh, to handle a firearm or a trout rod, to sail a boat, and to be kind to pedigreed dogs. Girls are expected only to be able to ride."

The Snob Index of Aristocratic Recreation

We have rated the traditional patrician sports by their current social cachet:

Exclusively Upper-Class
    polo   court tennis
    fox-hunting

Infiltrated by Arrivistes
    yachting
    thoroughbred horse-racing   dog breeding

Hopelessly Bourgeois
  skiing   croquet
  tennis   squash
  golf

No Class Affiliation
  auto racing   flying
  motorcycling   trout (or salmon) fishing

The Little Black Book

The little black book with the orange lettering isn't so little any-more. Once a compact 4¾ by 6¼ inches, it's now 8¾ inches square.

But the physical size of the Social Register is nothing compared to the major change made in its scope in 1977—it went national. Every since the Social Register was started by a profit-minded New Jersey farmer named Louis Keller in 1887, it had had separate editions for various "society center" cities. At its peak in 1925, it had editions in twenty-one cities, but the number gradually dwindled to a steady twelve: Boston, New York, Baltimore, Washington, Philadelphia, Pittsburgh, Buffalo, Cleveland, Cincinnati-Dayton, Chicago, St. Louis, and San Francisco.

"What! Lump us together with the rest of the country!" New Yorkers especially considered the sweeping change a low blow. The New York edition was the oldest and generally ranked—at least by New Yorkers—the most prestigious. How prestigious any of the editions ever were, however, is still a matter of weighty social conjecture.

The standard line tossed out by socialites is that the Social Register is "just a glorified telephone book. It's handy because it's distinctly more wieldy than the local Bell System directory." What they fail to point out is that their Register listing was probably the source of some of their best invitations last year. For the Social Register is, without a doubt, the chief reference work of social secretaries planning elegant gatherings, invitations committees of major balls and benefits, the mothers of debutantes compiling party lists, private-school administrators weighing admissions decisions, society editors of newspapers deciding how much play to give an engagement announcement, and charity fund-raisers seeking donations, as well as all manner of other annoying solicitors.

When questioned closely, most socialites admit that being *in* the Register doesn't count for much since the old New York edition alone once contained as many as 30,000 names. (The number of listings tends to ebb and flow with the economy.) But as Louis Auchincloss expressed it, "The Social Register has gotten so enormous that it looks rather peculiar if you're *not* in it."

True, for social climbers, a Register listing offers documentary evidence of their arrival, a kind of coming-out event. How does one pull it off?

Basically, you get in because you have a lot of friends who are already in, "subscribers," they're called. Although the listing procedure sounds objective enough, don't be fooled. First, you must get a subscriber to write a nomination letter in your behalf. It should be addressed to the Social Register Association's New York headquarters at 381 Park Avenue South or to the lone association correspondent in each of the twelve Social-Register cities. Your friend in court, so to speak, should give specifics about you and your life-style: your family lineage (skip this part if your father was a carpenter); the schools you, your spouse, and your children have attended; your offsprings' names and ages; your occupation; your clubs, board memberships, affiliations, and anything else that looks good on paper. The powers that be in the Social Register Association—no one knows who they are or how they operate—will review your friend's request and, if you pass initial muster, send you an application. Your completed application must be accompanied by five more letters of recommendation from five more subscribers, all claiming they know you well and want you included. The Association's mysterious Advisory Board will then scrutinize the entire package in order to determine if your blood is really blue or just an off-color shade of green.

If you're deemed fit, congratulations. Your family's pedigree will be printed on pumpkin-colored paper in "the book," and you will be given the opportunity to purchase its winter and summer editions at the going rate of $35.00. Unless you suddenly develop a social clubfoot which you proceed to stick in your mouth in front of the wrong people (particularly the news media), you will be sent an application form each year updating your listing.

The only way to get into the Social Register without going

through these elaborate machinations is to be born into it or marry into it.

One thing the Social Register is *not* is a reliable guide to society's inner circle. Some of the best names simply aren't there. At times, the Social Register seems a more reliable guide to its outer edges —those upper-middle-class squares who keep their noses clean, their marriages intact, and their good names out of the newspapers.

Indeed, notoriety appears to be the quickest way to get sacked. In the past, notoriety has included marrying someone in show biz or getting a divorce. Stephen "Laddie" Sanford was dropped for marrying actress Mary Duncan who retaliated by becoming the "queen of Palm Beach society." The esteemed broker William C. Langley got similar treatment when he married singer Jane Pickens. And, in a move on a par with insulting the American flag, Charles Alden Black got dumped for marrying little Miss Shirley Temple.[4] On the other hand, the late great stage personalities Ruth Draper and Cornelia Otis Skinner were never *out* of the Social Register. Ditto Jane Wyatt and Dina Merrill.

There seems neither rhyme nor reason to the Register's posture on divorce. Some divorced people stay in, some get booted out. After their divorces, Brenda Frazier, Eleanor Seale Whitney (her ex-spouse C. V. Whitney was dropped even though Eleanor's marriage was what got *her* in), and the late Margaret McKim Vanderbilt Baker Amory (née Margaret Emerson) remained in. On the other side of the fence, Barbara Hutton, Doris Duke, Gloria Vanderbilt, Mr. and Mrs. William Paley, Winston Guest, Tommy Manville, and John Marquand were abandoned.

Although public sins are supposed to signal automatic exclusion, Ann Eden Crowell remained in after she accidentally shot and killed her husband William Woodward, a real shocker since she was an ex-model. Subscribers who have eloped with chauffeurs have also remained in, proving once and for all that those nameless mortals who pass judgment on the manners, morals, and marriages of the upper crust do so on a completely arbitrary basis.

The two most famous blue bloods to actually demand exclusion were Alfred Gwynne Vanderbilt and John Hay Whitney, who asserted that the Register's secret admissions criteria represented a "travesty on democracy." There are some Jewish folk included but not many.[5]

The twelve Social Register Association cities are not the only places in the nation that maintain some sort of society list. Other cities with locally compiled and published directories are the Hamptons, Washington, D.C., Palm Beach, Detroit, Indianapolis, Minneapolis, Kansas City, New Orleans, Dallas, Houston, Denver, Portland, and Seattle.[6] Los Angeles has two; the *Southwest Blue Book* is the more discerning. In its more than seventy-five years, it has listed very few movie personages. The sixty-five-year-old *Los Angeles Blue Book* is more democratic, thus less authoritative. A real social coup is a listing in both.

The American Social Register may not be *Burke's Peerage*, but it's all the rich have. One High Society critic has ventured that the popularity of the Register is the result of one simple fact: A listing can't be bought, unlike all the other possessions and status symbols in our society. When too many people get high incomes, the things that money can buy are no longer the most coveted.

Cracking Society's Code

It takes a good deal of practice before one becomes proficient in the fine art of reading a Social Register listing—without consulting the indexes in the back of the book, that is. Allow me to give you Lesson No. 1.

A typical Social Register listing appears as follows:

> Manhattan Mr. and Mrs. Midas III (Abelsworth—Elizabeth H. Bishop) Kni. Ny. Ngl. Pcn. Cly. Hort. Ncd. Pr. Cl '45; Juniors—Misses Sarah Hadley and Edith Bishop Abelsworth. Master Christopher Farhnam Manhattan. 1 Sutton Place, N.Y.C. 10022. 555-4890.

Translation: Mr. Midas Manhattan III is married to a woman who was born Elizabeth H. Bishop and who was married previously to a man named Abelsworth. Mr. M. is now a member of the Knickerbocker Club, New York Yacht Club, National Golf Links of America, and Pacific Union Club; while Mrs. M. is a member of the Colony Club, the New York Horticultural Society and the National Society of Colonial Dames in the State of New York. Their country club is Piping Rock. Mr. M. graduated from Columbia University in 1945 (the alma maters of wives aren't listed). Mrs. M. has two daughters, named Sarah Hadley Abelsworth and Edith Bishop Abelsworth, by her previous marriage. The

Manhattans have a son, Christopher Farhnam. The family resides at 1 Sutton Place in New York City, zip code 10022, and their phone number is 555-4890.

To Which God Do You Pray?

Among the upper classes, God most certainly is not dead. On the contrary, He comes in very handy as a social-climbing device.

In the United States, the religion of the aristocrat is the Episcopalian. Indeed, the stereotype of the WASP (White Anglo-Saxon Protestant) is sometimes spelled, more accurately, WASPE (White Anglo-Saxon Protestant Episcopal).

Kit and Frederica Konolige did an exhaustive study of typical U-Episcopalians, whom they dubbed "Episcocrats," for their book *The Power of Their Glory*. They concluded: "What has made them [Episcocrats] so important to the country is that their set of attitudes and mores, fertilized by a distinctly Anglophiliac and Episcopal atmosphere of feeling, has been adopted by non-Episcopalians as the standard for upper-class conduct."

The appeal of the Episcopal Church to wealthy Americans seems to stem from its close kinship ties with the Anglican Church, the establishment Church of England. Historically, the American elite has been mesmerized by all things English, especially the appurtenances of the peerage. Aesthetically, as well, there is little dispute that the rituals and costumes of the Episcopal liturgy and the churches' stained–glass-and-stone architecture reflect an unmistakable aura of dignity and breeding. Unlike the feeling engendered in a lower-class revivalist worship service—the feeling that life will be better in the celestial hereafter—the residual emotion following an Episcopal service is that life is A-OK as it is.

There's a joke told by self-deprecating Episcopalian clergymen that illustrates the point. A newcomer to heaven is curious why certain antechambers are filled with boisterous, boozing, dancing people while one of the rooms a little farther on is deathly still. St. Peter the tour-guide explains that the noisy rooms are filled with Methodists, Baptists, and Presbyterians who are enjoying themselves for the first time after a pretty straitlaced stretch on earth. The quiet room, on the other hand, is filled with Episcopalians. "They drank, laughed, and danced on earth," St. Peter says. "They don't need to repeat that performance here."

A 1976 demographic study of Episcopalians done by pollster George Gallup, a leading Episcopalian himself, removed any doubt that the Episcopal religion was the religion of the elite. The study revealed that about 3 percent of the population, when asked, identify themselves as Episcopalians. This does not mean they go to church. In fact, Gallup found that Episcopalians attend church *less* frequently than any other Christian sect. Furthermore, Episcopalians consider any pious stirrings they may feel as strictly a private matter. They do not talk about their religion or recite to anyone the glorious details of any "born again" experiences— if they have them. You might say Episcocrats maintain an aloof, stiff-upper-lip stance toward their church, another British affectation.

Gallup also discovered that 48 percent of all Episcopalians had incomes exceeding $20,000 a year, in many cases by a lot. However, their bank balance does not seem to have much bearing on their generosity when the collection plate is passed around. The National Council of Churches' list of per-member contributions by denomination always shows Episcopalians near the bottom.

Except for Jews, Episcopalians are the most urban religious group in the nation and tend to concentrate their forces in the big Eastern cities. Adventurers and frontiersmen they are not and never were. When the other young men were going West in droves all through the nineteenth century, Episcocrat youth were staying home, preferring to live and die within spitting distance of their moldering pre-Revolutionary War ancestors.

The Episcopal Church is also heavily white. No surprise here. However, it's significant that the handful of blacks who have emerged as national leaders tend to be Episcopal, among them ex-Massachusetts Senator Edward Brooke; Andrew Brimmer, the first black member of the Federal Reserve Board; and John Walker, the bishop of Washington, who was the first black master at St. Paul's School. But mingling with the run-of-the-mill minority has never been a favorite Episcocrat pastime and some wealthy Episcopalian parishes have ducked the problem by establishing branches or mission churches in the poorer neighborhoods.

The Gallup poll shows that 45 percent of all Episcopalians have gone to college and that 43 percent are engaged in a profession or business. In 1976, *FORTUNE* magazine reported a similar statistic: Fully 20 percent of the chief executive officers of *FOR-*

TUNE 500 companies are Episcopal. Politically, the Episcopal Church is easily the most heavily Republican religion in the country. Thirty-eight percent told Gallup they were GOP adherents, while only 27 percent favored the Democrats.

Jews were the only religious group that challenged the Episcocrat stranglehold in almost every statistical category covered by the Gallup study. While Episcopalians still have more money than Jews, more Jews go to college. Gallup found a higher concentration of Jews in business and the professions and an even greater percentage of Jews than Episcopalians living in the Eastern metropolises.

Within the Jewish subculture, there is also a social pecking order. Sociologists have studied and trumpeted their findings until it's almost become a cliché to say that upper-class Jews are Reform, those a little lower on the status ladder are Conservative, and the rest of the hoi polloi are Orthodox.

I don't want to leave you with the mistaken impression that all wealthy Protestants are Episcopal. A number are Presbyterians, second only to Episcopalianism in tone. As you move into New England, the Presbyterians are transformed into Congregationalists. The upper-class intellectuals are Unitarian, also New England based. It's one of the tiniest sects in the country but outranks all others in the number of eminent Americans who have claimed it as their own.

Since the ascension of John F. Kennedy, the Roman Catholic Church, in a society sense, has gained more respect—and a lot more attention. Now, Rev. Andrew Greeley, a priest-sociologist working at the University of Chicago's National Opinion Research Center, has challenged the traditional profile of American Catholicism as working class (i.e., predominantly blue-collar, lower-middle class). His surveys show that Catholics, outside the South, have higher income and educational levels than any Protestant sect, including Episcopalian. If his findings are valid, Catholics are second only to Jews in those statistical categories.

Whether Catholics have, indeed, moved up the socioeconomic ladder as much as Greeley contends is a matter for the pollsters to decide. However, one thing is indisputable: Some Catholics still consider themselves better than other Catholics and would rather not mix at mass.

Because Catholic parishes are organized along geographic lines, wealthy Catholics have tended to carve out enclaves in fashionable Protestant neighborhoods and petition the church hierarchy for a local church. If they're unsuccessful, they have to attend mass in some adjacent ethnic neighborhood. In such situations, there is frequently some very *un*-Christian elbowing that goes on and the parish priest is at a loss to organize auxiliary church activities everybody will attend.

Actually, the religious preferences of U.S. Presidents say it all. We've had ten Episcopalians, six Presbyterians, four Methodists, four Unitarians (five if you count Thomas Jefferson who was born into the Episcopal Church but later declared himself a deist with Unitarian leanings), three Baptists, two Disciples of Christ, two Quakers, two Dutch Reformed, one Congregationalist, and one Roman Catholic.

Classy Kirks

Wealthy American dynasties usually have one special church they call their own. It's the church where scions are baptized, wed, and eulogized—although there is seldom any regular Sunday-worship-service attendance that takes place there between familial events.

The Rockefellers lay claim to two churches, the nondenominational Riverside Church in upper Manhattan and the more intimate Union Church of Pocantico Hills, New York. (Neither of these churches is Baptist, which is the traditional Rockefeller-family religion.)

The "Mellon church" in Pittsburgh is the East Liberty Presbyterian Church, the church where all important family events are blessed, even though a number of Mellons claim they're really Episcopalians. The Pews are staunch members of the Ardmore Presbyterian Church outside Philadelphia. J. Howard Pew was a prominent and outspoken lay leader in the United Presbyterian Church hierarchy.

The Whitney clan has worshipped for generations in the 200-seat Christ Episcopal Church in Manhasset, Long Island. The *nouveau-riche* Hunt family of Dallas gathers at the Highland Park Presbyterian Church, although they, too, are historically Baptist.

The Huguenot du Ponts have the most picturesque kirk. Christ Church Christiana Hundred is several miles outside Wilmington and the bucolic country cemetery behind it contains every important du Pont who ever lived on this side of the Atlantic— with the notable exception of Alfred I. du Pont. One corner is even reserved for the dynasty's faithful servants.

Drawing their congregations from a number of eminent and moneyed families are the five cardinal Episcopal churches in America: St. Thomas' on Fifth Avenue, St. James' on Madison Avenue, and St. Bartholomew's on Park Avenue in New York City, Trinity on Copley Square in Boston, and St. John's on Lafayette Square in Washington, D.C.

What's in a Name?

A rose by any other name would smell as sweet? The rich do not agree, Mr. Shakespeare. On the subject of names, they have very definite and very traditional ideas.

Aristocratic WASPs observe time-honored customs in their naming patterns. The most important: If you get hold of a good name, recycle it. That's why all the old-money family trees contain the same names generation after generation. The Vanderbilt family has had at least five Cornelius Vanderbilts, the moniker of the founder. The Rockefellers, to date, have had four adult John D.s with another one waiting in the wings. The Houghtons, the New York State glass dynasty, have had several Amorys, Arthurs, and Alansons. And, to complicate matters even further, up in Corning, the Arthurs have all been Arthur Amorys.

It makes you wonder, of course, how other family members keep them straight. Philadelphia's Pew family, a resourceful bunch, have worked out a system which they use when addressing each other. All family members who share the same name have been assigned their own special occupational or geographical appellation. George Pew, for example, is referred to as "Aero Commander George"; he was once the head of an airplane manufacturing concern. Another George Pew, a seventy-year-old distant cousin of "Aero Commander George," is known as "Portland George." You guessed it, he lives in Portland, Maine. But the quintessential family name has always been Joseph Newton Pew. At one time, there were at least five of them above ground. The problem was partially solved by using various forms of the same name. There was a Joseph N. Pew and a J. Newton Pew, and a Joseph N. Pew 3d (also known as "Joe-three-I's"). The Joseph Newton Pew father-son combination, both residing in Chester, Pennsylvania, finally solved their mutual identification problem by becoming known as "Chester Joe" and "Banker Joe."

Outside the immediate family, duplicate names aren't as big an issue since each living specimen bearing the name has his own numeral tacked on to the end, a practice borrowed from the royalty of Europe. High Society commentators still haven't resolved the question of which numerical form is more chic—the Roman numeral as in P.A.B. Widener III, or the ordinal as in John D. Rockefeller 3d.

When they resolve that one, perhaps they'll move on to the debate concerning the psychological consequences of nominal ancestor worship. Most psychologists disparage the custom of naming offspring after the famous—in many cases infamous—family fortune builder. They say it places far too great a burden on so-designated descendants. Dr. George H. Pollock of the Institute for Psychoanalysis in Chicago says: "Man does wish to have a link with his ancestors and a child can feel proud to have a relative's name. On the other hand, we all need to be individuated and parents should not deprive a child of that experience." A Case Western Reserve University study made the claim that three times as many "Jr.s" receive psychiatric treatment than other males more casually named. Professor Leonard R. N. Ashley of Brooklyn College says being named after a well-known or living relative makes a child's life more stressful since he has to *uphold* the name.

John D. Rockefeller IV, who ought to know, disagrees. Until he was twenty-one, he was known as plain old "John Rockefeller" —"Jay" for short. Then *he* decided that he wanted to go all the way and add the middle initial "D." and the Roman numeral "IV." Why did he do it? "I was challenged and motivated by the name and its traditions," he says. "I've never had anything but positive reactions to carrying it and, above all, I'm comfortable with being a person within that name." His son also bears the name and Jay is leaving him the same option of adding a "D." and "V" at some later date.

Adlai Stevenson III, the Illinois senator, expresses similar sentiments. "My father left me a good name. [For the word "good," substitute "unblemished."] No father could do more, and I will try to leave a good name to my son." Stevenson III swears he's never experienced any emotional stress or feelings of competition with his father, the deceased U.S. presidential contender. "No," he insists, "not even when my powers as an orator were measured against his. And Adlai IV, alias Adlai the Next, shows no signs of emotional stress, either."

Johns Hopkins sociologist Alice Rossi studied upper-class naming patterns and discovered that boys are more apt to be named after forebears than are girls. Moreover, firstborn children get names of kin more often than do their brothers and sisters. Of the group surveyed, 78 percent of the firstborn sons but only 20 percent of the fourth-born daughters were named for relatives. Shades of primogeniture. From all this, Rossi arrived at the rather obvious conclusion that sons "are of special symbolic significance to the temporal continuity of the family" because their names remain the same no matter whom they marry.

The other appellation habit of the upper class is to give its children family surnames as first and middle names. The end result can be an extremely arch moniker that does double duty as an onomastic pedigree. Some examples: Courtney Iddleson Aldrich, Winthrop Percival Talmadge, and Wendell Blaine Rand. The latter can at least draw consolation from her feminine nickname "Wendy." Yes, even girls get hit by this custom, especially Southern women. The classic is Commodore Vanderbilt's Alabama-born second wife, née Miss Frank C. Crawford.

In addition to regional differences in nomenclative mores, there are ethnic and religious ones as well. Jews, for instance, abide by a religious proscription against giving progeny the names of *living* relatives. (Have you ever run across a Morris Goldfarb, Jr., or a Manfred Orentreich 4th?) Roman Catholics name their children after saints, which doesn't preclude the adoption of the Protestant U practice of recycling names. Take the Kennedy family. So far, there's been a Joseph P. Kennedy, Sr., a Joseph P. Kennedy, Jr., and an emerging powerhouse, Joseph P. Kennedy 3d.

They say names conjure up instant pictures. This is certainly true in the case of Henry Ford II's only son, Edsel. Consider what it's like for that poor fellow, going through life with the same name as one of his family's worst commercial failures. But since Edsel, Jr. (he was named in honor of his grandfather) was born first and the car came and went second, we know one thing at any rate. His parents had no malicious intent.

Special Spas for Special People

The herd instinct plays an important role in the seasonal migratory tendencies of the wealthy. Whether planning a winter or summer holiday, the purebred rich beat a well-worn path to about thirty trendy watering holes, all triple-A rated socially. These are the same places most of them have been visiting for years, proving once again that the rich simply don't take chances. Their destinations are always places where they know exactly whom they'll meet and what to expect.

The winter and summer vacation circuits of the well-to-do contain two distinct kinds of refuges—the resort and the retreat. The resort is a very self-conscious gathering spot, a place to see and be seen. In these gossip-column venues, events of social import are frequently staged: charity balls, elaborate home entertaining, coming-out parties, and weddings. The retreat is just the opposite: a place where one goes to escape all that. Of course, the only kind of rich people who want to escape all that are the top-of-the-pile plutocrats, the old-money patricians whose security is bound up in their trust funds and family trees.

A third category is the spa where mineral springs for drinking and bathing provide the magnet. Today, they are passé, frequented only by the regal remnants of an earlier era.

The most resplendent winter clout clusters accumulate from Thanksgiving through Easter over:

Aiken, South Carolina (for the horsey set)

Aspen and Vail, Colorado (Midwestern and Texas skiers)

Caribbean: St. Barts (Rockefellers, Rothschilds, and Michelins)
    Lyford Cay on New Providence Island (Radziwills, Paleys, Heinzes, McMahons, and Mellons)
    Harbour Island
    Great Harbour Cay
    Peter Island

Gstaad, Switzerland (skiers from the international celebrity set)

Hobe Sound, Florida (Eastern establishment: Reed, Harriman, Lamont, Drexel, Whitney, Mellon, Doubleday, and Dillon)

Naples, Florida (Midwesterners: Fleishmann, Uihlein, Magins, Briggs, Benedum, Buhl, and Norris)

Palm Beach (Midwesterners, Texans, Oklahomans, and Northeasterners)

Palm Springs and Palm Desert, California (predominantly Western money plus the Firestones, Annenbergs, and Fords)

Pinehurst, South Carolina (for golf nuts from all over)

St. Moritz, Switzerland (Greeks, Middle Eastern oil money, and other Jet Set types)

Squaw Valley, California (for California ski weekends)

Sun Valley, Idaho (most chic resort for those who like to celebrate Christmas on skis: New Yorkers, Hollywood stars, Jet Set)

From June through Labor Day, society can be found rattling its string of pearls in the following places:

Bermuda (Eastern elite)

Cape Cod/Oysterville-Hyannisport area (the best from Boston, Pittsburgh, and New York)

Côte d'Azur (Mary Lasker, Harding and Mary Lawrence, the Lauders, and Farkases)

Deauville, France

Fishers Island, New York (mostly New Yorkers and a few du Ponts)

The Hamptons, Long Island, New York (New Yorkers: Murrays, Pattersons, Fords, Newhouses, Biddle Dukes, and Phippses)

Lake Tahoe, California-Nevada/western shore (San Franciscans)

Mackinac Island, Michigan (Midwesterners)

Maine coastline and islands (Philadelphia Main Liners, New Yorkers, Boston Brahmins, Minneapolis clan)

Martha's Vineyard and Nantucket Island (New Yorkers, Bostonians, Philadelphians, Washingtonians, Baltimorians, and Chicagoans)

Monterey Peninsula (San Franciscans)

Newport, Rhode Island (Philadelphia and New York crowd)

Rehoboth Beach, Delaware (St. Louis, Washington, Baltimore, and Philadelphia set)

Santa Barbara, California (the best Californians from all over)

Saratoga Springs, New York (for the racing crowd in August: Whitneys, Vanderbilts, Paysons, Phippses, and Wideners)

Watch Hill, Rhode Island (local smart set plus New Yorkers, Philadelphians, Pittsburghers, Cincinnatians, and Washingtonians)

It is no longer *de rigueur* that the wealthy own their own homes in these places. An extremely enterprising woman named Claire Packman has made it fashionable to rent. Working out of a posh East Fifty-seventh Street office under the imprimatur At Home Abroad, Inc., Ms. Packman has introduced more than 5,000 well-heeled Americans to the pleasures of vacationing in somebody else's villa. Mary Lasker, among others, makes a habit of it. Sites of Ms. Packman's luxe villas, manors, châteaux, and apartments range from far-off Tunisia and Nairobi to the ever-popular French Riviera and Avignon countryside.

High-Society Ghost Towns

In a bygone era, these were the "in" resorts of the very elegant and the very rich. No longer. Today, their best hotels either gone or ramshackled and their image turned to honky-tonk, these has-been resorts are completely overrun by the wrong people:

Bar Harbor, Maine	Cape May, New Jersey
Nahant, Massachusetts	Hot Springs, Virginia
Lenox (in the Berkshires), Massachusetts	White Sulphur Springs, West Virginia
Tuxedo Park, New York	Fernandina Beach, Florida
Long Branch, New Jersey	Reno, Nevada

What hastened their demise as society centers? Cleveland Amory, author of *The Last Resorts*, ascribes it to "a sort of Gresham's Law of Resorts—i.e., that bad millionaires drive good millionaires out of circulation." According to this theory, the evolution of a fashionable resort proceeds in this manner:

Writers and artists in search of pleasing vistas and solitude usually find the place and they're followed by professors, clergymen, and other so-called solid people with long vacations and little money. Eventually, the "nice millionaires," concerned about introducing their children to the simple life, move in. Once that happens, of course, it's the beginning of the end since "naughty *nouveaux-riches* millionaires," wishing to rub elbows with the "nice millionaires," are sure to start buying up all the available real estate. On it, they invariably build lavish "cottages" and fancy clubs; and start entertaining in a manner that's anathema to the original settlers. The simple life is utterly destroyed. The end result is trouble.

Profiles of the Super-Rich with Upper-Class Credentials in Five U.S. Cities

MR. & MRS. PROPER BOSTON BRAHMIN

Address:	Beacon Hill, Boston
His Profession:	attorney
Religion:	Unitarian
Clubs:	(his) Somerset, Harvard Club, Nantucket Yacht Club, Rittenhouse (Philadelphia)
	(hers) Chilton
	(theirs) Myopia Hunt Club (Hamilton, Massachusetts); Jupiter Island Club (Hobe Sound, Florida)
Children's Schools:	Winsor, Foxhollow School, Radcliffe; The Brimmer and May School, St. Mark's, Harvard
Canine:	Old English sheepdog named Berwick
Cars:	1972 Oldsmobile station wagon; Audi 4000
Her Favorite Store:	Filene's basement; Shreve, Crump & Low (jeweler)
Her Favorite Decorator:	"they're a waste of money"
Her Favorite Fat Farm:	"unnecessary"
Their Favorite Restaurants:	The Ritz Carlton's dining room; Maison Robert; Locke Ober
Other Homes:	North Haven, Maine; Hobe Sound, Florida

Winter Skiing:	Sugarbush, Vermont, or Franconia Notch, New Hampshire
Favorite Spot for a Week-end Away from Home:	200-year-old Jared Coffin House (Nantucket Island, Massachusetts)
Family Shrink:	Dr. Vernon Mark, Harvard University
Plastic Surgeon:	"We don't believe in such nonsense."
Rehabilitation/"Dry Dock":	Silver Hill (New Canaan, Connecticut)
Super-Status Symbol:	own their own island

MR. & MRS. MIDAS MANHATTAN III

Address:	Sutton Place, New York City
His Profession:	investment banker
Religion:	Episcopal
Clubs:	(his) Knickerbocker; New York Yacht Club; National Golf Links of America (Southampton); Pacific Union (San Francisco); also a member of the Council on Foreign Relations
	(hers) Colony; Vassar Club; New York Horticultural Society; National Society of Colonial Dames in the State of New York
	(theirs) Piping Rock Club
Children's Schools:	Brearley, Miss Porter's, Finch College; Trinity, St. George's, Yale
Canines:	pair of pugs named Sandow and Mandrake
Cars:	TVR 2500M; Mercedes-Benz 450 SEL
Her Favorite Store:	Bergdorf Goodman; Cache-Cache and Tiffany's (for gifts)
Her Favorite Decorator:	Parish-Hadley, Inc.
Her Favorite Fat Farm:	Bircher Benner Clinic (Zurich, Switzerland); Palm-Aire (Pompano Beach, Florida)

229

Their Favorite Restaurants: La Grenouille (for lunch); La Côte Basque; Le Club; El Morocco

Other Homes: Fishers Island, New York; Aiken, South Carolina; Lyford Cay (Bahamas)

Winter Skiing: St. Moritz, Switzerland, or Sun Valley, Idaho

Favorite Spot for a Weekend Away from Home: Hotel Du Cap (Antibes, France)

Family Shrink: Dr. Michael Stone, New York State Psychiatric Institute

Plastic Surgeon: Dr. Ivo Pitanguy (Rio de Janeiro)

Rehabilitation/"Dry Dock": The Palm Beach Institute (Palm Beach, Florida)

Super-Status Symbol: a swimming pool in their penthouse apartment

MR. & MRS. CHICAGO CHIC-WATER

Address: Lake Forest, Illinois

His Profession: industrialist

Religion: Roman Catholic

Clubs: (his) Chicago Club; The Links (New York City); Metropolitan (Washington, D.C.); Knights of Malta (hers) Fortnightly (theirs) Onwentsia Country Club

Children's Schools: Foxcroft, Bennett Junior College; Lake Forest Academy, Hotchkiss, Yale

Canine: Airedale named Honneger

Cars: Lincoln Continental Mark VI; 1978 Mercury station wagon; Volkswagen Rabbit

Her Favorite Store: Carson Pirie Scott

Her Favorite Decorator: Richard Himmel

Her Favorite Fat Farm: Maine Chance (Phoenix, Arizona)

Their Favorite Restaurants: Chez Paul; Cape Cod Room of the Drake Hotel; Pump Room at the Ambassador East Hotel; The Bakery

Other Homes:	Naples, Florida; Mackinac Island, Michigan
Winter Skiing:	Aspen, Colorado
Favorite Spot for a Week-end Away from Home:	Camelback Inn (Arizona)
Family Shrink:	Dr. Roy Grinker, Jr., Chicago Institute of Psychoanalysis
Rehabilitation/"Dry Dock":	Hazelton (Center City, Minnesota)
Super-Status Symbol:	own an ocean-going yacht

MR. & MRS. TEX "GUSHER" TYCOON

Address:	Highland Park section, Dallas
His Profession:	oil wildcatter
Religion:	Methodist
Clubs:	(his) Idlewild Club; Petroleum Club; Boston Club (New Orleans); Seminole Golf Club (Palm Beach); New York Athletic Club (New York City)
	(hers) Dallas Garden Club; Daughters of the Republic of Texas
	(theirs) Brook Hollow Golf Club; Bath & Tennis Club (Palm Beach)
Children's Schools:	Hockaday, Rice University; Missouri Military Academy, Baylor University
Canines:	Afghan Hound named Beauregard and a Shih-tzu named Missy
Cars:	1980 Cadillac Seville; Buick Riviera; Jaguar XJ12L
Her Favorite Store:	Neiman-Marcus; Grace Jones dress shop (Salado, Texas)
Her Favorite Decorator:	John Astin Perkins
Her Favorite Fat Farm:	The Greenhouse (Arlington, Texas); Maine Chance (Phoenix, Arizona)
Their Favorite Restaurants:	Brennan's; Ewalds Continental Cuisine; Ports O' Call; Doubles (New York City)
Other Homes:	Palm Beach, Florida; New York City duplex penthouse apartment

Winter Skiing:	Vail, Colorado
Favorite Spot for a Week- end Away from Home:	Las Hadas (Manzanillo, Mexico)
Family Shrink:	Dr. Howard Crutcher
Attorney:	Richard "Racehorse" Haynes
Rehabilitation/"Dry Dock":	The Meadows (Wickenburg, Arizona)
Super-Status Symbol:	own their own football team

MR. & MRS. BARNEY "BIG BUCKS" BELAIRSKY

Address:	Bel-Air, California
His Occupation:	entrepreneur with diversified interests
Religion:	Jewish (Reform)
Clubs:	(his) Jonathan Club; Union League (New York City) (hers) Beverly Hills Women's Club. Also, fundraising for the City of Hope Hospital (theirs) Hillcrest Country Club; California Yacht Club (Marina Del Rey); Thunderbird Country Club (Palm Springs)
Children's Schools:	Marlborough, University of California at Berkeley; Robert Louis Stevenson, Stanford University
Canine:	pedigreed toy poodle named Renee
Cars:	Rolls-Royce Silver Shadow II; Lamborghini Jarma; Ford Econoline van
Her Favorite Store:	I. Magnin; Georgio's; Fred Joaillier (for jewelry)
Her Favorite Decorator:	William Haines, Inc.
Her Favorite Fat Farm:	La Costa (Carlsbad, California); The Golden Door (Escondido, California)
Their Favorite Restaurants:	Chasen's; The Bistro; Melvyn's (Palm Springs)
Other Homes:	Palm Springs, California; Colorado ranch

Winter Skiing: Lake Tahoe, California, or Steamboat Springs, Colorado

Favorite Spot for a Weekend Away from Home: Mauna Kea Beach Hotel (Kamuela, Hawaii)

Family Shrink: Dr. Burton N. Wixen

Plastic Surgeon: Dr. Mar McGregor (San Francisco)

Rehabilitation/"Dry Dock": Las Encinas (Pasadena, California)

Super-Status Symbol: Learjet with a private airstrip on their ranch

NOTES

1. A lot of important business transactions throughout the nation's history have been consummated in prestige clubs, although the stuffier clubmen tend to disparage the practice, money being too filthy a commodity to discuss outside an office. Such an antiquated attitude certainly did not hamper Charles Schwab, the turn-of-the-century industrialist, at the nineteenth hole at St. Andrews Golf Club in Yonkers where he succeeded in persuading Andrew Carnegie to sell out to J. P. Morgan, the decision that led to the creation of U.S. Steel.

The status of the club and the size of the business deal are closely intertwined. *FORTUNE* magazine commented, "At the Metropolitan or the Union League or the University, you might do a $10,000 deal, but you'd use the Knickerbocker or the Union or the Racquet for $100,000, and then for $1 million you'd have to move on to the Brook or the Links."

2. Gentlemen get the club habit in college, at Yale, Harvard, and Princeton, that is. At Harvard, the top clubs—really secret societies—are Porcellian, Fly, and A.D. At Yale, it's Skull and Bones (Bones) and Scroll and Key (Keys). And at Princeton, it's the eating clubs: Cottage, Ivy, Tiger Inn, and Cap and Gown. Getting into one of these collegiate bastions paves the way for men seeking membership in the best clubs for themselves and their families in later life.

3. St. Grottlesex is an acronym for the prep school junior Ivy League. It includes such New England schools as St. Paul's, St. Mark's, St. George's, Groton, Kent, and Middlesex.

4. Other Registerites who were kicked out for show-biz alliances were Dorothy Benjamin when she married Enrico Caruso, Ellin Mackay when she married Irving Berlin, Elliot Roosevelt when he married Faye Emerson, Anthony Bliss when he married Jo Ann Sayers, Polly Lauder (niece of Andrew Carnegie) when she married Gene Tunney, and Marjorie Oelrichs when she married Eddy Duchin.

233

5. A few prominent Jewish people who have appeared in the Social Register over the years are Bernard Baruch, Ralph M. Strassburger, Adele Lewisohn Lehman (Mrs. Arthur Lehman), John Schiff, and Iphigene Ochs Sulzberger (Mrs. Arthur Hays Sulzberger).

6. Society lists are not popular in Deep South cities. Why? As one Charleston matron put it, "Here we know who's who without being told."

THE SILLIEST PARTIES OF
THE PAST CENTURY

14 It's a good thing Mrs. Stuyvesant Fish was a charter member of Gotham's Old Guard or her madcap antics would have gotten her drummed out of High Society. As it was, she and her homosexual social advisor, Harry Lehr, trod a fine line separating the well-executed joke from the blatant insult. For "Mame," as they called her, had an uncanny knack for exposing the foibles of robber-baron society through her parties. In fact, her "vaudevilles," as she termed them, bore a closer resemblance to morality plays than carefree Gay Nineties wingdings.

Mrs. Fish burst onto the social scene like a skyrocket about the time Caroline Astor, of Four Hundred fame, was petering out. Mrs. Astor, a traditionalist in matters social, did not approve of "Mrs. Fishwife's" soirées for the "circus set," especially the notion of providing entertainment for one's guests after dinner. "Mrs. Astor never has bridge-whist after *her* dinners," her social secretary explained. "Following the old custom, Mrs. Astor relies upon the conversation of her guests to provide the entertainment."

In actuality, Mrs. Fish's innovations were far more sweeping than bridge-whist. After lengthy conferences with Lehr, she shortened the time spent at table. In the nineteenth century, it was customary to serve eight or ten courses, keeping the guests weighted to their chairs for a good three hours. Mrs. Fish shortened the dining time to fifty minutes. During those fifty minutes, she insisted that everyone dispense with the "Mr." and "Mrs." form of address and call one another by their first names. Moreover, most of those assembled around Mrs. Fish's table would never see the inside of the rival Mrs. Astor's dining room since they were people of achievement—explorers, architects, poets, musicians, writers, inventors—rather than people of pedigree. Finally, Mrs. Fish dispensed with receiving-line folderol completely at the beginning of the evening and added entertainment at the end—she had to. With dinner over by 8:30 P.M. what else was left to do?

It was her divertissements that earned Mrs. Fish her outrageous reputation. Her most infamous evening was dubbed "the monkey dinner." It was a spoof on Americans' boot-licking attitude toward titled Europeans. Elegant invitations went out to the *crème de la crème* of Newport society to attend a dinner in honor of Prince del Drago, who was making his premier visit to these shores from far-off Corsica. True to form, the nabobery of Newport were dying for an introduction. They got it. Into Mrs. Fish's salon ambled "Prince del Drago," a bewildered monkey attired in full evening dress. But the monkey got his reward. He was seated at the head of the table, as befits all guests of honor, and was fed alternately by Harry Lehr and Mame. One newspaper editor charged, "Now the monkey and the swell must be accepted as interchangeable types."

Mrs. Fish never topped that one, but she tried. In 1913, she held a "Mother Goose Ball" which required all comers to costume themselves as nursery rhyme characters. In attendance were the Cow That Jumped over the Moon, Humpty Dumpty, Mistress Mary Quite Contrary, Little Jack Horner, and Bo Peep. Just when everyone had gotten into the spirit of the thing, Mrs. Fish stopped the music and read a satiric poem honoring Mrs. Isaac Goose and poking fun at a number of her guests.

Guest participation was always the hallmark of a Fish affair. At one party, guests were required to talk baby talk to each other all evening. On many other occasions, Mrs. Fish had written minstrel and vaudeville-type sketches that guests were asked to perform, sometimes in pickaninny dialect. At a Mardi Gras ball, guests were treated to a ballet performance, with lights lowered, while servant boys dressed as kittens passed out party favors to the women. The favors were live mice and the ladies' reactions were the *real* entertainment.

But even sophisticated silliness is wearying and Mrs. Fish could be "gallantly rude," as her biographer put it, when she'd had enough. One night she commanded the orchestra to keep playing

"Home Sweet Home" until every last guest got the message. "I'm so tired of being hypocritically polite," she said.

Parties where the theme of the evening was developed to its extreme were all the rage during this period. In 1903, utility tycoon Cornelius K. G. Billings held a stag party that required guests to literally ride for their supper. To celebrate his election to the presidency of the New York Equestrian Club, Mr. Billings invited thirty-one fellow members to a dinner in his Riverside Drive mansion. At least Mr. Billings put the word out to the press that the event would take place there. In reality, it took place miles downtown in Sherry's restaurant where the guests arrived *sans* paparazzi.

Billings' friends were served a first course of champagne, oysters, and caviar on a lower floor and were then asked to assemble in the restaurant's fourth-floor ballroom for the main courses. The catch was they had to finish the meal on horseback. Sure enough, Billings had thirty-one of his best steeds—plus two more for himself and New York's former Mayor Richard Grant—grouped in a circle awaiting their riders. Mounted on each horse's back was an impromptu table, a flat two-foot-long surface draped with a gold tablecloth. Waiters dressed as grooms scurried back and forth serving the remaining six courses. It consisted of caviar, soup, trout, lamb, guinea hen, and peaches flambé. Simultaneously, the horses were chomping away on fresh oats, and stableboys were on hand, armed with elegant dustpans, to take care of any emergencies. Over cigars and coffee, guests were treated to the proverbial stag show—in this case, twelve scantily clad showgirls and, for levity, James Lederer and his Watermelon Party. At the door, the departing gentlemen were given tokens of Mr. Billings' appreciation—a solid-gold matchbox, an inscribed cigar case, and a handsome sterling silver dinner menu in the shape of a horseshoe. Not to be outdone, one of the horses proffered his own memento: a wrecked elevator.

By the 1930s, the mantle of outrageous entertaining had fallen on a new *enfante terrible* of Publi-ciety, a word Cleveland Amory coined to combine the idea of publicity with "what people used to think of, in happier days, as Society." Amory was referring to the opportunistic ambiance of Café Society, the milieu in which Elsa Maxwell practiced her craft.

Her profession—if you could call it that—was journalism, a

surprising one considering her lack of book-learning. Her father, an insurance agent hailing from Keokuk, Iowa, didn't believe in formal education; thus, his daughter never graduated from grammar school. Actually, Miss Maxwell's career had been progressive, moving from that of pianist in a nickelodeon, to vaudeville accompanist, business partner in two Paris nightclubs, press agent with the Monte Carlo account, aspiring actress, and finally daily columnist and lecturer. In between, she radiated gaiety—"I've always been like a little girl on Christmas morning," she once said—and made a lot of friends and enemies among the rich and noteworthy.[1]

She also gave a lot of parties. Other people's homes were borrowed for these occasions. The theme and execution of some of these gatherings made one wonder if old Mrs. Stuyvesant Fish hadn't returned to earth in a new incarnation.

One of her finer endeavors was a come-as-your-opposite affair. Guests were exhorted to impersonate their antithesis. Ina Claire came as a bishop. George Gershwin came as Groucho Marx. Mrs. Vincent Astor came as a low-caste woman. But Cole Porter was the most honest. He came as a football player. As usual, Maxwell donned men's garb, this time that of then-President Herbert Hoover. Before the event, Mrs. Cornelius Vanderbilt's social secretary had phoned to inquire whether her employer could drop in at some point during the evening with a few friends and watch. Like social arbiters before her, Elsa knew precisely how to level her enemies, employing the least amount of words and the most amount of bite. "Tell Mrs. Vanderbilt," said Maxwell, "the party is restricted to my friends. You may add that I do not include *her* among them."

Maxwell's come-as-you-were party was more risqué. Her sixty guests were commanded to appear exactly the way they'd looked at the moment they had opened the invitation. To ensure the maximum diversity of attire, Maxwell had the invitations hand delivered at odd hours. Thus, she ended up with a half dozen women in slips (it was the Roaring Twenties so it was fashionable to behave scandalously with little provocation), one lady carried her underpants, Bébé Bérard had a telephone attached to his ear, and another man had his face covered with shaving cream.

Elsa's barnyard party was perhaps the most cockeyed. Guests came as farming figures. Cecil Beaton was a scarecrow. Serge Obolensky was a Russian peasant, what else? And Mrs. Ogden S.

Mills came as a farmhand, dressed in overalls, and wearing a tiara. The incongruous event got totally out of hand when the real cows imported for the occasion started defecating like real cows and a real Ohio hog caller ran into the room leading a passel of real, squealing pigs. It's a wonder the management of the Waldorf allowed it.

NOTES

1. While Café Society was closing ranks protectively behind Wallis Simpson, the newly mitered Duchess of Windsor, Elsa Maxwell was continuously aiming barbs at her in print. Her basic complaint against the duchess was that "she's not interested in anything except herself," a charge that might have been made about Maxwell. When pressed to the wall, she once admitted "I just don't like her." The two ladies eventually came to a truce, but the odor of their enmity was never completely dispelled.

STATELY STATUS SYMBOLS

15 In olden times—and in fairy tales—kings and queens were expected to live opulently, acting out their subjects' fantasies on a grandiose scale. Lacking royalty in most corners of the world today, we depend on rich people—the modern version of royalty—to fulfill this function. You might say ostentation has become the duty of the rich.

Unfortunately, throughout American history only the *nouveaux riches* have been willing to cooperate and flaunt their meretricious life-style for the amusement and enjoyment of the rest of us. Our nineteenth-century industrialists were the ultimate *parvenus* in this regard. The robber barons may have raped the country and thrived on sweat-shop labor, but they certainly met their obligations as purveyors of the American Dream. They had a real flair for the theatrical and eagerly transformed their private lives into pageants for the peasantry. Old-money Americans have never been so obliging. In contrast, they've always endeavored to keep their considerable consumption out of the newspapers. They consider secrecy the duty of their class.

Times change. Since the Depression, the *nouveaux riches* are starting to see the wisdom of old-money reticence. Thieves, kidnappers, IRS agents, and political radicals are too much with us. It's reached the point where it's hard to get even your average self-made man to preen a little. With the exception of Texans, most contemporary wealth-holders are no longer willing to invite the public into their rose garden to admire their possessions.

Even so, it's hard to hide the trappings of wealth. Their glitter is blinding. Herewith is a survey of the present-day ruling class' panoply of swank status symbols, that top-of-the-line tinsel only rich people can afford.

Homes

Just about the first thing most people do when they come into money is build or buy a big house. The urge seems instinctive. Actually, it's sociological. A huge home is a power symbol. It's part of the millionaire facade, a necessary implement if one is to keep the power building in momentum.

During the period between the Civil War and World War I, a new-money millionaire wouldn't dream of settling into someone else's leftover digs, no matter how splendid. In that era, all mansions were made to order. They had to be because your house was a personal advertisement. It proclaimed your newfound status. Not only must it look more magnificent than the mansion next door, but at the same time it had to embody all your grandest illusions about your importance in the world plus your dopiest private whims. It was a tall order, but talented architects such as Stanford White and Richard Morris Hunt met the challenge. In the process, architects became the darlings of the turn-of-the-century society set, a role that's filled today by chi-chi fashion designers and popular artists.

The Vanderbilts were the country's premier mansion-builders. The name "Vanderbilt" is practically synonymous with large estates. In town, their ducal residences lined Manhattan's Fifth Avenue and, their country *dashas* appeared up and down the Eastern Seaboard in such places as Newport, Rhode Island ("The Breakers" and "Marble House"); on the Hudson River in Hyde Park, New York; and in the hills of Madison, New Jersey.

One of the most ornate was the French Renaissance château built by George Washington Vanderbilt II, the Commodore's grandson. "Biltmore" was set on 130,000 acres in the foothills of the Smoky Mountains in Asheville, North Carolina. Images of Versailles and Fontainebleau floated through visitors' minds as they traveled up the three-mile drive from the gate to the main house, which contained 250 rooms. When it was built in 1895, the cost was estimated at between $6 million and $7 million. To replace such a structure today might cost as much as $60 million, one reason why such structures aren't replaced.

241

The impulse behind the Vanderbilt *palazzo* production was social elevation. Their homes were social-climbing vehicles pure and simple. They were purposely built to look like European palaces to convey the impression that the Vanderbilts were on a par with ancient nobility. The ploy worked. More than one Vanderbilt lass hooked a titled European, thereafter becoming known as the Duchess of Marlborough or the Countess Széchényi.

Other wealthy families have staked their claim in one city or town and retained their allegiance to that place from one generation to the next. The Mellon dynasty is still centered in Pittsburgh and Ligonier, Pennsylvania, even though a few loners such as Paul Mellon prefer to reside elsewhere. For two centuries, the du Ponts have clustered around Wilmington, Delaware, and passed down ownership of the large châteaux that dot the Brandywine River valley there.

The Rockefellers' residential pattern is even closer-knit. The Rockefeller compound known as Pocantico Hills lies due east of Tarrytown, New York, in the Sleepy Hollow region made famous by Washington Irving in his fable about Ichabod Crane. The Rockefeller estate is completely surrounded by a high stone wall and encompasses more than 4,000 acres of rolling terrain. Each of John D. Rockefeller, Sr.'s five grandchildren had a house there, although they maintained homes in other places as well. The main house, called "Kykuit," is a fifty-room granite monstrosity, modified Georgian in design, said to cost $2 million to build. Many smaller homes are also scattered about the estate, the whole affair requiring a staff of 350 gardeners, maintenance men, chamber maids, parlor maids, cooks, butlers, and the like.

The Kennedys have also adopted the compound idea for their clump of summer homes at Hyannisport, Massachusetts. And anyone looking for a Phipps need only wander around Old Westbury and Brookville, Long Island, for a while. When you want to locate a Kleberg, the King Ranch near Corpus Christi, Texas, is the place to go.

A few fortune builders have carried the notion of family togetherness and social distance to extremes and bought an island. Island ownership may be the ultimate status symbol. After all, what could be more exclusive and rarified than a private kingdom in the middle of the sea? Gardiners Island, off the eastern tip of Long Island, probably has the longest history of ownership in the same family. It was granted to Lion Gardiner, a military engineer, in 1639 for services rendered to the Crown. Today, those same 3,300 acres are presided over by Robert David Lion Gardiner, the sixteenth Lord of the Manor, and you don't go there except by invitation.

More public was the pleasure island of the late William Wrigley, Jr., the Chicago chewing-gum potentate. For $2 million, he purchased Santa Catalina Island off the coast of southern California and poured another $2 million into the erection of a grand hotel, golf course, tennis courts, theater and dance pavilion, and an airplane landing strip. For those who preferred to sail over, Wrigley shelled out yet another $1 million for a steamer line that ran between Santa Catalina and the mainland.

In his heyday, J. P. Morgan owned East Island off the North Shore of Long Island near Glen Cove and had an elaborate country manse with extensive gardens erected on the site. Sapelo Island, off the coast of Georgia, was once owned by Howard E. Coffin, the Hudson Motors millionaire; and Naushon Island near Martha's Vineyard is the summer gathering place for the Boston Brahmin Forbes clan. More recently, Mr. and Mrs. Lester Norris (Mrs. Norris is the niece of John Bet-a-Million Gates and a large stockholder in Texaco) secured their dream—five miles of unbroken beach in the Gulf of Mexico. Their island, Keewaydin, is off the coast of Naples, Florida, and at current real estate values, their beach property alone would sell for more than $1,000 a front foot.

Today, those rich people who still opt to build their own homes do so on a much smaller scale than their plutocratic forebears. Wealthy city dwellers seldom do it at all. Why bother when there are so many deluxe cooperative and condominium apartments available?

There's a catch here, however. Perilous social shoal waters must be charted carefully before you buy into a building because whatever status attaches to the building soon attaches to you, the new occupant. For instance, 740 Park Avenue in Manhattan is generally known as the building where "it only takes money to get in." Saul Steinberg of the Reliance Group; David Mahoney of Norton Simon; the Bronfmans of Seagrams; and Mrs. Enid Haupt, sister of Walter Annenberg, live there among others. On the other hand, 1 Sutton Place, 1 Beekman Place, 960 Fifth Avenue, and

834 Fifth Avenue can't be beat since residents get to rub elbows with such people as the Douglas Dillons, the Winthrop Aldriches, the C. V. Whitneys, and the Laurance Rockefellers.

The rich may have recovered from that excessive mansion-building phase of yesteryear, but they've never completely adopted ordinary bourgeois living arrangements either. Geraldine Rockefeller Dodge, the niece of old John D., and her husband, Marcellus Hartley Dodge, the Remington Arms Co. heir, maintained "his" and "her" residences across the fields from each other for most of their married life. They set up housekeeping together in a spooky-looking baronial manse in Madison, New Jersey, a wedding present from Mrs. Dodge's father, William Rockefeller. It was an extremely dark, rambling place—lots of mahogany—and Mr. Dodge never felt comfortable there. He much preferred the cheerier little house that was set on top of a hill nearby and had once been part of a Fresh Air Camp for underprivileged children. That's where he moved, although the couple had a son and continued on cordial, if not passionate, terms for the rest of their lives.

Art Collections

Grand homes require grand decor. And what could be more grand than a multimillion-dollar art collection?

One of the greatest American collectors, Pittsburgh financier Andrew Mellon, used to say that the austere portraits by Gainsborough, Romney, and Reynolds that lined his dining-room walls "make excellent company when I dine alone." For the rich, material possessions often serve to alleviate loneliness. But artwork does this and more. For rags-to-riches millionaires, paintings and sculpture give the proud possessors a much-sought-after aura of civility, an aura they may not deserve, mind you. For those among the rich with true aesthetic sensibilities, owning selective artworks is a primary experience in their lives, one of their few real joys. And for those with more money than they know what to spend it on, art is often touted as "a good investment."

Our American multimillionaires spend lavishly on art. In 1968, *FORTUNE* magazine identified at least ten who owned collections valued at $20 million or more. Some wealthy collectors have even arranged for their private collections to get nonprofit status as museums—private museums. Viewing is by invitation only. Other collections never surface at all until the owner suddenly bequeaths his treasures to some unsuspecting *public* art museum.

The Virginia Museum of Fine Arts in Richmond got one of these surprises in 1947 when Lillian Thomas Pratt (Mrs. John Lee Pratt), the wife of an early General Motors vice president, transferred a king's ransom worth of Fabergé *objets d'art* to the institution in her will. She gave the museum little indication of what was coming, except for an aside delivered to a museum official at a Fredericksburg, Virginia, garden party in 1942. "You ought to know," she whispered conspiratorially, "that I have a collection of art. I don't feel at liberty to tell you what it is, but the Virginia Museum will get everything." The museum got 523 of the jeweled miniatures created by Peter Carl Fabergé for the imperial czars of Russia, including five of the famous Fabergé Easter eggs out of a total production of fifty-six to fifty-eight. The collection has been appraised but museum spokesmen will say only that it is "priceless in value."

Today, our most notable living collectors are probably various members of the Rockefeller clan; Dr. Armand Hammer, the medical doctor-turned-oil corporation head whose family owns the Hammer Galleries; Norton Simon, the ex-conglometeer and controversial savior of the Pasadena Museum of Modern Art where he has consolidated his Old Masters art holdings to the dismay of the museum's former trustees; Patrick Lannan, the majority stockholder of MacMillan, Inc., with the "private" museum of the avant-garde in his Palm Beach home; Walter Chrysler, Jr., the auto heir and creator of the wide-ranging Chrysler Museum in Norfolk, Virginia; Nathan Cummings, the Chicago food entrepreneur and chief donator of art centers to major universities; Paul Mellon, son of Andrew, and The National Gallery's overseer of last resort; the Charles Wrightsmans, whose Oklahoma oil money propelled the couple to Palm Beach where they find Old Masters the best backdrop for their French furnishings and decor; DeWitt and Lila Acheson Wallace, the *Reader's Digest* duo who have surrounded themselves with fine Impressionist and post-Impressionist paintings; ditto Mary Lasker, widow of the advertising ace Albert D.; and Malcolm Forbes, the self-styled showman of *Forbes* magazine and Fabergé Easter egg fame. Of course, there are always those super-rich with super-bourgeois taste; for instance, Mrs. H. L. Hunt who collects Boehm birds. She's been known to serve her guests dinner using place settings of limited edition plates, the kind other people keep in their breakfronts.

Yachts

As status symbols, nothing afloat today under private ownership can compare to the magnificent steam yachts that plied the seas between 1860 and World War I. Back then, a vessel didn't even get the designation "yacht" unless it measured at least 200 feet from bow to stern. Currently, you can count on one hand the number of privately owned "yachts" that meet that criterion.

The first palatial pleasure vessels began appearing in English waters in the 1830s. By the 1860s, the oceangoing cruise was an established custom among European gentility and becoming a tempting idea to budding American titans. By the 1890s, the Americans had burst onto the yachting scene in a big way, determined to pilot the best, most admired craft under sail. "Best" back then meant most beautiful and, indeed, the famous yachts of the day were far more awe-inspiring than anything that's come off the ways since.

Even yachts' names were more graceful then. During those golden summers in Newport, the harbor always had at anchor at least five of the fabulous American fleet, majestic pleasure ships bearing such appellations as the *Alva* (the 285-foot, $500,000 yacht of William Kissam Vanderbilt) and the *North Star* (the Commodore's personal flagship). There was the *Nourmahal* (meaning "light of the harem" and owned by William Astor); *Noma* (the pride of the tinplate Leedses from Indiana, the name deriving from Mrs. Leeds' given name Nonnie May); *Sultana* (meaning "wife, or mistress, of the Sultan," owned by the Philadelphia Drexels); *Josephine* (P.A.B. Widener's lass); *Lysistrata* (the possession of New York *Herald* newspaper heir-hellion James Gordon Bennett, Jr.), and the regal *Corsair* (J. P. Morgan's joy).

Once those in the exalted yachting fraternity hit upon a pleasing maritime moniker, it became like a brand name, to be recycled throughout eternity in much the same manner as plutocrats recycle forebears' names. J. P. Morgan owned four successive *Corsair*s; the last went on the rocks off Acapulco in 1946. The Philadelphia Cadwaladers commissioned three *Savarona*s, but the 408-foot *Savarona III* was a Depression baby; the family was forced to charter her until 1938 when she was finally sold to the Turkish government as a training ship. The patrician Brown family of Providence still kids about being known as the Bolero Browns, *Bolero* being their famous racing yacht that went through several incarnations. And the Benson Fords have had more than one *Onika.*

By 1913, there were 500 American-owned steam yachts under commission, all measuring more than 100 feet; eighty-one were longer than 200 feet; and twenty-nine exceeded 300 feet. World War I didn't end all wars, but it certainly ended the parade of princely pleasure craft coming off the ways. Practically all large private yachts saw service as convoy vessels and picket boats during the war and most never returned to their earlier status. A few large private cruising yachts were built during the 1920s but the Depression put a stop to even that. The days of the floating resort were over. In the 1935 edition of *Lloyd's Register of American Yachts,* there were still listed more than fifteen U.S. pleasure vessels, both steam and diesel, 200-plus feet in length. In the 1974 edition, the number was down to two—Charles Revson's 257-foot *Ultima II* and William J. Levitt's 237-foot *La Belle Simone.*

In 1975, *Town & Country* asked the editorial question, "The Big Yachts—Are They an Endangered Species?" The author, M. Phillip Copp, answered "yes." They are the victims of progressive income taxes, more frenetic life-styles, and—in his opinion— bad taste. After the Depression, he maintains, no more beauties were built. The post-Depression yachts "looked as though they were by *Clorox Bottle* out of *Cookie Cutter;* and most of them were, and are, under 200 feet long."

You can see this lineup of uglies—what Copp calls "stinkpots" —docked along Florida's Gold Coast during the winter months. The average size is less than 100 feet and crews seldom number more than four. They bear names such as *Black Hawk* (Arthur Wirtz's 123-foot entry); *The A & Eagle* (owned by Anheuser-Busch for the use of the company's founding Busch family); and *Buckpasser* (which shares the name with a famous thoroughbred, also owned by Ogden Phipps; this 99-foot vessel was designed specifically to accommodate Phipps' helicopter which comes and goes from a 19-square-foot landing pad on the upper deck).

Although maintenance costs are staggering, most $125,000-and-up yachts seem to appreciate in value, but that's small consolation to the financially strapped owner who can't get up the thousands in cash they eat up each year. However, according to those who ought to know, there are some signs that the trend to smaller yachts is reversing itself. Melville Spencer, present owner-operator of the Spencer Boat Company in West Palm Beach, says: "Big yachts are coming back in favor again. The trend is now to the 70- to 110-foot models. People want comfortable boats for living and long-range cruising . . . and they want modern conveniences aboard like washers and dryers, which take space."

Private Railroad Cars

Vehicular status symbols fade in and out in keeping with the latest technology. Before the advent of the ubiquitous auto, riding around in a private railroad car was considered the lap of luxury, leading Mrs. August Belmont, *doyenne* of Victorian society, to quip, "A private [railway] car is not an acquired taste—one takes to it at once."

In the late nineteenth century, it was *de rigueur* for any millionaire who aspired to be a big shot to own his own railroad car, and preferably his own railroad. At the very least, Mr. Moneybags had to build a railway spur from the main line onto his vast country acreage. William Randolph Hearst had one that penetrated "San Simeon." So did John D. Rockefeller, Sr., on his Pocantico Hills estate. Farther up the Hudson in Rhinebeck, Vincent Astor had an entire small-gauge steam railroad with five chugging locomotives on his spread; and Henry Huntington had a similar set-up on his New York estate. I won't bore you with the list of turn-of-the-century magnates who owned private cars; it would be like listing the wealthy Americans who own Rolls-Royces today.

Although this form of private luxury may seem an anachronism, it's persisted to the present day. Joan Whitney Payson (Mrs. Charles Shipman Payson) had a private car called *Adios II* and used it to travel to and from her five homes until her dying day, which was October 4, 1975. The car had three bedrooms, a bar, lounge, and at various times a Goya, Cézanne, and Matisse hanging on the walls.

In 1954, August A. Busch, Jr., the St. Louis beer baron, paid the Wabash Railroad $4.3 million for a deluxe railway car that contains four bedrooms, a dining section and kitchen, two baths, and quarters for two attendants. Strictly speaking, the car is owned by Anheuser-Busch, but then so are all the Busch family toys from its baseball team (the St. Louis Cardinals) to its yacht and Busch gardens.

The most recent multimillionaire with a craving for railroad nostalgia is Ray Kroc, the hamburger maven, who purchased a forty-three-year-old car in 1968 for $63,000. He frankly admitted he didn't know what he was going to do with it but he was sure of one thing—he was *not* going to turn it into a hamburger stand.

Cars

In modern America, the airplane and automobile have supplanted the private railway car as modes of deluxe locomotion. As status symbols, they're center stage right now. The right car, especially, will not only transport its owner around the nation in comfort, it could also transport him or her vertically up the status ladder.

But expensive automobiles are tricky status indicators and should not be flashed around indiscriminately. The rule of thumb is the right car for the right place. Using your Rolls-Royce to run errands in Palm Beach is a common practice. But tooling around Allentown, Pennsylvania, in a Rolls would probably make you the butt of jokes for months. This is one reason why wealthy car nuts who live among the *bourgeoisie* go out of their way to make it known that they are "car collectors"—lends an aura of respectability—and not just conspicuous "car consumers."

Curtis Blake, a founder of the Friendly Ice Cream chain, lives in West Hartford, Connecticut, with a second wife, her children, and about twenty-five new and used cars ranging from old Stutz Bearcats and Duesenbergs to current model Mercedes and Rolls. Avoiding the label "show-off" has not been easy for Blake since many of his envious neighbors, who knew him back when, are still scratching their heads trying to figure out why he's rich and they're not. Blake did it by turning his private obsession with cars into an amusing, albeit harmless, public spectacle. He is regularly pictured on the front page of the local newspaper behind the wheel of one of his prized specimens on the way to and from some antique car convention. He managed to create audible ripples of laughter among the populace awhile back when he and his first wife made the grand tour of Europe in his very own tin lizzy— average speed: 20 miles per hour.

In places such as New York City, Palm Beach, and certain Sun Belt cities—places where there are high concentrations of new money—a luxe car owner isn't as likely to give the illusion of a bandit squandering his spoils. In fact, in a community such as Palm Beach, a very wealthy man who does not pump a sizable sum into a classy conveyance may be viewed as either a cheapskate or one of those old-money reverse snobs.

In Palm Beach, the top-of-the-line car is still the Rolls-Royce. Arlette Gordon (Mrs. Robert Gordon), whose husband made his pile through fortuitous real estate investments in Boston, voiced the popular sentiment: "We moved to Palm Beach to live a little," she explained. "Although we completely renewed our life-style, I didn't feel I had achieved the ultimate in luxury until Bob bought me that Rolls convertible. When I sank into the leather seat, my feet on the lamb's-wool carpet, I knew I was really living at last." [1]

That testimonial was *not* part of a Rolls-Royce advertisement. It was a spontaneous expression of how the upscale crowd feels about being seen in the car with the Spirit of Ecstasy on the hood.[2] Myth and substance converge in a Rolls, a combination of expert marketing since the first one was driven out of the factory in 1904, and true quality. Most auto manufacturers rely on planned obsolescence to keep sales up. The Rolls-Royce Motor Company of Crewe, England, has staked its impeccable reputation on planned durability. Owners still justify the $85,000 it costs for the basic Silver Shadow II model by quoting its resale value—often far more than the manufacturer's list price.[3] The car is a genuine investment, evidenced by the fact that at least half the Rolls ever built are still running.[4] As F. Henry Royce put it, "The quality will remain when the price is forgotten."

As a status symbol, the Rolls is not exactly what you'd call subtle. It's a showy way of showing off. The up-and-coming man is a big owner, and *he* includes everyone from rock stars who consider Rolls camp to self-made industrialists who consider them just the thing for projecting a gentlemanly image.

Rocky Aoki, owner of the Benihana chain of Japanese steak houses, is one of the few Rolls owners with nerve enough to express his reservations. "Very unreliable car. Very costly to maintain. I pay mechanic $20,000 a year, but I like style of Rolls. I don't care about engine. One time I buy car from Sheik of Bahrain. Engine blew up." Despite his discontentment, he still owns a quartet of Rolls-Royces—a 1938 Sedan de Ville, a 1959 Silver Wraith, a 1971 Silver Shadow, and a two-tone Phantom 5—that's down from eight. Overall, he admits, the car can't be beat for snob appeal. "Big car really eye-catching," he nods.

Rolls-Royce craftsmanship has been known to create some knotty problems for their owners. Trink Wakeman, the International Harvester heiress, will never forget the time she found a mound of sawdust under her rare 1929 Phaeton. "I realized immediately it was termites," she said. "The coach, you see, is built on a wooden base. I called the exterminator right away and had it tented."

Private Aircraft

In the 1930s, they were called "air yachts" and they were the ultimate toy among the blue-serge suit set. In 1937, a twin-engine Grumman amphibian air yacht cost $47,000 and carried six passengers. A number of Wall Street tycoons owned them and used them daily to commute back and forth from their Long Island estates to their offices.

Today, there are more than 2,000 airports for small jet traffic in the United States, but most of the jets you'll see there are owned by corporations rather than individuals. In 1977, the Federal Aviation Administration underscored this point. Of the total U.S. small jet population, 1,376 were business-owned and only 64 were privately owned. Among the individual owners were Walter Annenberg, Arnold Palmer, Burt Firestone, Jack Dreyfus, Barron Hilton, Norton Simon, Gloria and Loel Guinness, Paul Mellon, F. Lee Bailey, John W. Galbreath, and Henry Ford.

The reason why fewer and fewer individuals, no matter how rich, own planes—at least under their own names—is the cost. The purchase price of a small jet will run you anywhere from $890,000 for the ubiquitous Learjet to $5 million for Lockheed's JetStar II (Elvis Presley owned one). And annual operating expenses will probably exceed $250,000 by a wider and wider margin as the gas shortage deepens. On the larger jets the operating cost is closer to $1,000 an hour. Obviously, from a tax standpoint, it's much more sensible to let your company own a plane and write it off as a business necessity.

Another alternative is to charter a jet when you need it. Executive Jet Aviation of Columbus, Ohio, has the corner on this market and, if its management is to be believed, the market is not only lucrative but also extremely high toned. Bruce Sundlun, EJA's president, claims: "The old money flies with us; the new money buys its own airplanes." He may be telling the truth. Executive Jet Aviation planes are always booked solid for such ruling-class events as the Kentucky Derby and America's Cup races. Douglas Dillon, William A. M. Burden, and Mr. and Mrs. Charles Munn are steady customers—all four insist on Falcon jets, which seat ten and require a crew of three. The Munns don't bat an eye about the $10,000 they shell out regularly to commute between their San Francisco and Hobe Sound homes. Ditto EJA's other sherry-sipping Jet Setters.

While the private plane may not be the *ne plus ultra* of status symbols because of its new-money bizjet aura, a private landing strip on one's estate is quite rarified. Paul Mellon has several as do a number of the du Pont clan. The only other aeronautical status symbol that quite compares is to get a scale model of your plane hung from the ceiling over the bar at the "21" Club in New York.

Jewelry

The problem with jewelry as a status symbol is if you flaunt it, you may lose it. On the other hand, if you keep it where the insurance company recommends—in some dark bank vault—what's the sense of having it?

Anna Thomson Dodge, widow of auto tycoon Horace E. Dodge, Sr., grappled with this problem all her life. "I probably have more genuine pieces of jewelry and wear less than anyone I know," she sighed. As to her favorite baubles, she felt diamonds were "cold" but she liked emeralds well enough. But at the very top of her list were pearls—"a lady's gem, always correct." When her daughter Delphine entered ladyhood, Mrs. Dodge presented her with an $800,000 pearl necklace that was once the property of Catherine II of Russia.

Many of the gems now owned by American aristocrats once belonged to the famed monarchs of Europe. Before Marjorie Merriweather Post gave the Smithsonian most of her jewelry, she frequently appeared on formal occasions wearing the pear-shaped diamond earrings that were found sewn into Marie Antoinette's pockets when she was seized at Varennes and a diamond necklace Napoleon had given to Empress Marie Louise. At balls, she often wore a diamond tiara set with turquoises, another sparkler that had belonged to Marie Louise.

As a plutocratic collectible, fine jewelry has three things going for it: its scarcity, its portability, and its investment value. Anything that gets one-of-a-kind billing holds immediate interest for the rich. Crown jewels fall into this category. The fact that gems can be worn on one's person is another attraction. They are status symbols that can truly be possessed. Third, a brilliant ornament is practically guaranteed to appreciate in value at a tremendous rate, barring a worldwide depression or other economic catastrophe. For example, the big fat 34-carat emerald ring that Enid Annenberg Haupt bought in 1968 for $265,000, she sold in 1972 for $385,000—that's a tidy profit of $120,000 in four years. Elizabeth Taylor held on to her 69.42-carat pear-shaped diamond for a full decade then finally sold it for $2.5 million. Richard Burton had paid $1.1 million for it, giving the bauble an appreciation rate of 127 percent during a ten-year period. (Taylor's asking price of $4 million had to be scaled down considerably.)

Unfortunately, precious gems are sometimes a risky spiritual investment. Some stones have been known to carry a curse. Evalyn Walsh McLean's lifelong series of misfortunes were often laid to her possession of the infamous bad luck charm, the Hope Diamond.

Evalyn Walsh was the spoiled-rotten daughter of a strike-it-rich Colorado gold miner who wasted no time moving his family to Washington, D.C., in 1898 to begin scaling the social pyramid. In 1909, she married Edward Beale McLean, scion of the Cincinnati *Enquirer* newspaper family, and they set out on a honeymoon trip that has never been matched for utter greed, wastefulness, and dissipation. (Ned McLean was a heavy drinker and Evalyn was a morphine addict.) When they returned to the States two months later, they were $200,000 poorer but Evalyn had in tow the world-famous, 92½-carat pear-shaped diamond called the Star of the East. Her appetite for priceless trinkets was not satisfied until some years later, however, when she acquired the inimical Hope

Diamond, reportedly wrenched from the forehead of an Indian idol centuries earlier. The gem's track record was one of blood and destruction. Louis XVI bought it for his wife Marie Antoinette and everyone knows what became of them. Then the diamond disappeared for a while and reappeared in 1830 reduced in size from its original 66 carats. Several interim owners, including English Lord Francis Pelham Clinton Hope, had similar reversals of luck, and the pattern didn't change when Evalyn Walsh McLean became its owner.

She purchased it from the Paris jeweler Pierre Cartier for a mere $40,000 and later refused an offer of $2 million for it. Although her friends insisted she chuck it, Mrs. McLean steadfastly maintained that her blue diamond had nothing whatsoever to do with the tragedy that surrounded her. She and her husband were divorced, and he later died in a mental institution. Her only daughter died young of an overdose of sleeping pills and her son Vinson was killed in a car accident, a boy of eight. And her other son Ned met a relatively early death of a heart attack while incarcerated in a Towson, Maryland, sanitarium where he had spent the last eight years of his life.

But Evalyn herself endured, becoming one of Washington's greatest hostesses—"Lady Bountiful." Not only did she sleep with the Hope Diamond under her pillow every night, but she also frequently displayed it, along with the Star of the East and six diamond bracelets, as part of her costume at her lavish parties. At these affairs, she retained an entourage of up to fifteen private detectives to follow her around and circulate among her guests in quest of any suspicious characters. When she finally died in 1947, she had gone through most of her fortune. New York jeweler Harry Winston purchased the Hope Diamond from her estate but when he found no takers, he donated it to the Smithsonian Institution, its present resting place.

NOTES

1. In Palm Beach, once a Rolls owner always a Rolls owner. It's a select club and owners plan social events based on their common bond. In 1973, the James Hunt Barker Galleries planned an elegant invitation-only party around an exhibition of twenty paintings of Rolls-Royces by the Australian artist Melborne Brindle. The cream of Palm Beach society—all Rolls own-

ers—was there. The paintings depicted the Silver Ghost model Rolls-Royces built between the years 1907 and 1914. Guests were asked to choose the car painting they wanted to be photographed with and dress in appropriate period clothing. Among those arriving in their Rolls-Royces that evening were Princess Evangeline Zalstem-Zalessky, who posed next to the painting "Self-Driving Phaeton with Dickey Seat"; Mr. and Mrs. Harold P. Whitmore, who chose "The Silver Ghost Used by H.R.H. Queen Mary"; A. Atwater Kent, Jr., who admired "Five Seater Touring Car"; and Mr. and Mrs. Frank McMahon who chose "Tulip Backed Limousine," a car which was considered the ultimate in luxury during its time since the crimson-colored interior was outfitted with a crystal-cut bud vase intended to be filled with the flowers of the season.

2. Artistic types have even waxed eloquent on the subject of the Rolls-Royce. Writer Michael Arlen once wrote that riding around in one puts life in a new perspective. Another author, Jan Morris, said she'll never forget her first cruise in a Rolls. "I felt—you must not laugh at me—I felt like Botticelli's Venus emerging from her shell, so pearly was the ambience, so sensual the breath of the wind as we swept along, so gentle the tick of the engine, so gaily but majestically did the silver Spirit of Ecstasy, the perennial mascot of Rolls-Royces, dance on the radiator before me. . . . It was purely its quality that gave me that unforgettable *frisson*, coupled of course with the idea of it."

3. In January 1979, Rolls-Royce Motors applied to the British Prices Commission for a retail price hike, based partially on the argument that a higher manufacturer's list price was needed to keep the car out of the hands of speculators. It seems that soaring demand for Rolls was creating a situation where a new $57,000 Silver Shadow could be resold immediately for $20,000+ more. "All sorts of people order a car they don't intend to keep," explained the company's managing director David Plastow. "We are asking our retailers to help because of their knowledge of the man, if he's got a car already, and that sort of thing." The new price established was $77,600. In 1980, the price rose again—to $85,000. The highest-priced model hit $156,000.

4. The Rolls is the closest thing you can get to a car with a pedigree. Every Rolls-Royce ever built has its own loose-leaf binder, entitled "History Book." In it, the company records everything and every owner the car has throughout its life.

16

Beastly Occasions: Doggie Birthday Parties and a Canine Fashion Show

One of the first pet parties on record was the canine dinner given by turn-of-the-century hostess Mrs. Stuyvesant Fish. The affair featured 100 dogs owned by Mrs. Fish's best friends. The canines were seated at Mrs. Fish's baronial banquet table while their owners stood behind the chairs and served. The menu consisted of stewed liver and rice, fricassee of bones, and shredded dog biscuits. While Mrs. Fish and her friends considered it a great lark, the press and public were not amused, especially about the $15,000 diamond collar one of the dogs wore.

It may have been the first such event on record, but it certainly wasn't the last. In 1971, a thirteen-year-old Yorkshire terrier named Mop was similarly fêted in Palm Beach. Mop's mistress, Countess Margaret (Migi) Willaumetz, arranged the surprise birthday event—a lawn party, naturally—and invited twenty of the town's most elegant pooches. Among them were B. Ann Thompson's Yorkshire Juliet, a brace of Danes named Medusa and Leda who lived next door, Mrs. Lucius P. Ordway's English Lucas terrier Pamela, Mrs. Stephen Sanford's dog Duke, and Jimmy Barker's six Cavalier King Charles spaniels.

The event got full-page treatment in the *Palm Beach Daily News*, commonly called "the Shiny Sheet" because of its high-grade paper guaranteed not to smudge milady's fingers when she's reading in bed. The flavor of the reportage deserves preservation: "Considering the formidable size of the canine group," reporter Helen Adams wrote, "there were no, shall we say, contretemps. Behavior was circumspect and impeccable. (That's breeding for you.) Chic breeds in evidence ranged from Labrador to pug to Lhasa to dachshund, but nary a poodle in sight. It wouldn't do among the BP to have an out-of-style BD."

Two years later Mrs. Michele Bertotti, a divorced New York art collector, gave a birthday party for her black Schipperke Fellow because "he's so sick." She explained that Fellow had a heart condition, had suffered two strokes, and had to take pills twelve days out of every month for the rest of his life. The party for his ninth birthday was to cheer him up.

The owners of the Animal Gourmet, a dog delicatessen on Manhattan's chic East Side, were delighted Mrs. Bertotti had chosen their store for the event since the party was written up on the family/style page of *The New York Times*. The two owners wore tuxedos for the affair and served the canine guests appetizers of liver-paté canapes and shrimp on morsels of rye bread; an entrée of beef ragout, steak tartare, and Swedish meatballs; and the birthday cake—a liver-and-dog-meal concoction with a yellow, green, and white frosting of whipped powdered milk. Dinner was served on a low doggie banquet table with a large floral centerpiece which one of the dogs mistook for a fire hydrant. The cost was "about $65" but did not include the champagne Mrs. Bertotti served to her human guests. (One owner confessed she had once tried some of the Animal Gourmet's chicken supreme. "You know," she said, "it was better than the chicken I had the other night at El Morocco.")

The birthday boy's gifts included a bottle of Horlick's Malted Milk Tablets, several rubber toys, and an autographed picture (paw prints, of course) from two of his canine guests. Behavior at the affair was generally decorous, although Mimi Gladys kept eating everyone else's food and Pouffy got frosting all over her furry face.

When the word "decadent" was used to describe the event, Lex Whatley, owner of two dachshunds, came to the defense. "Lord," he said, "I think if the Fords, Carnegies, and Mellons can spend anywhere from $60,000 to $100,000 to bring their daughters out, then one woman can certainly give a little birthday party for her dog." Larry Apodaca, owner of a fuzzy white bichon frisé, added, "This is a way of doing something nice for poor little animals, with no political implications one way or the other. After all, dogs are so loyal, faithful, and honest, and how often do you find that anymore?"

Certainly *haute couture* designers will never forget the time they were asked to make dog-shaped copies of their designs for a fashion show benefitting the Animal Medical Center in New York. The eminent Jo Hughes of Bergdorf Goodman produced the fashion show-luncheon and her black-and-white Shih-tzu Tony was the canine guest of honor. (During the show, he wore a jeweled crown by Kenneth Lane, a Sarmi red velvet cape trimmed in ermine tails, and sat on a miniature throne.)

On the runway, pets attired like their owners paraded up and down while various and sundry socialites in the audience looked on. Among the pedigreed pets modeling were Randolph, Mr. and Mrs. Alexander Liberman's St. Bernard; Chino and Chula, Mrs. Andrew Goodman's Shih-tzus; Mei-Sin, Mrs. Joseph Thomas' Pekingese; Samantha, Mrs. Edwin Russell's Old English sheepdog; and Baron Charlie Von Knapitsch, the Baroness Von Knapitsch's poodle.

THE SEVEN MOST GENEROUS
AMERICAN MULTIMILLIONAIRES

17 Although there are some genuine humanitarians among the ranks of the super-rich, a soft heart is not the prime impulse driving your average philanthropist to give millions away to charitable causes. In fact, some of our better-known benefactors—what *Town & Country* magazine calls "Super Santas"—are hard-hearted businessmen with little or no interest in bettering the lot of mankind. Their primary interest all their lives has been in bettering the lot of their bank account and if philanthropy helps them do that, so be it.

An in-depth survey of the country's foremost philanthropists and their foundations reveals a wide-ranging pattern of motivations, running from the utterly selfish and aggrandizing to the purely altruistic. They include:

- *the desire to take maximum advantage of the income tax laws* which allow you to deduct as much as 50 percent of your income each year for charitable contributions and up to 30 percent of your gross adjusted income for "in-kind" giving (stocks, artworks, etc.). BENEFIT: You get to decide where to park your excess cash instead of leaving it up to the government.

- *the pay-out of "conscience money"* to make you feel better about the slimy tactics you used to get rich—what Edmund Burke termed "the useful fruit of a late penitence." BENEFIT: A sense of relief and emotional well-being and, if you are religious, the hope that St. Peter will stamp your ticket at the Pearly Gates.

- *enlightened self-interest*, the type of thinking that led to-bacco tycoon James Buchanan Duke to insist that 32 percent of his foundation's income go toward the building and support of hospitals in North and South Carolina with the explanation, "People ought to be healthy. If they ain't healthy they can't work, and if they don't work they ain't healthy. And if they can't work there ain't no profit in them."

- *the lack of any heirs*—or at least any *acceptable* heirs—making the establishment of a foundation or charitable trust practically the only alternative. BENEFIT: Keeping most of your millions out of the coffers of the federal government.

- *the satiety of an "edifice complex,"* or the conspicuous construction of public monuments with your name emblazoned over the portal. BENEFIT: Resounding immortality.

- *the transformation of one's public image from that of a rapacious capitalist to an avuncular Kris Kringle.* This type of philanthropic public relations campaign was waged successfully by such robber barons as Andrew Carnegie, John D. Rockefeller, Sr., and Andrew Mellon.[1] BENEFIT: Making life easier for your offspring.

- *offering a palliative to the mob to avert violence.* Rockefeller, Sr., listened hard when Baptist Minister Frederick T. Gates advised him to distribute his fortune faster than it grows or "it will crush you and your children and your children's children." Heeding Gates' dire prediction, Rockefeller gave away more money in his lifetime than any of his contemporaries—some $531 million. BENEFIT: Personal safety.

- *the purchase of social prestige and honorary degrees.* Uneducated entrepreneurs are the most likely victims of this fund-raising ploy—you give our school $10 million, and we'll give you an honorary degree even though you never made it through the eighth grade. BENEFIT: Ego inflation.

- *a bid to escape the loneliness of riches and buy love*, which seldom works.

- *the underwriting of pet projects.* This often leads to the establishment of such kooky philanthropic entities as the Dr. Coles Trust Fund for Ice Cream for the Pupils of South Plains and Fanwood (New Jersey) and the Dorr Foundation which finances the painting of white lines along the edges of roads to promote safe night driving. BENEFIT: Negligible.

- *the longing to associate with a new crowd of people.* Andrew Carnegie craved acceptance from scholars and international statesmen and created his Endowment for International Peace to further that ambition. Cleveland industrialist Cyrus Eaton had a similar dream and set up his Pugwash Conferences which brought together scientists, philosophers, and other heavyweight thinkers from the East and West to discuss world peace. BENEFIT: Escaping capitalist shop talk for a while.

- *the desire to do good and bring the populace around to your way of thinking.* This ideological umbrella shelters everyone from the ultra-right-wing H. L. Hunt and the Pew family to the hard-line liberal Rosenwalds and Stewart Mott. BENEFIT: The furtherance of truth, justice, and public morality, of course.

- *an unremitting urge to foster scientific progress and alleviate human suffering.* The health, social welfare, and technological grants of the Rockefeller Foundation fall into this category as do the medical benefactions of Mary Lasker (Mrs. Albert Lasker). The benefits, for once, are truly substantial.

- *regional chauvinism,* or an eagerness to promote one's birthplace. GM executive Charles Mott poured his millions into his hometown of Flint, Michigan. The Fleischman Foundation is fixated on the Lake Tahoe, Nevada, region. And the Moody Foundation supports Southwestern concerns only. BENEFIT: demi-god status among the locals.

- *a quest for the aesthetic ideal.* Many cash-rich culture patrons are aesthetically poverty stricken. But not all. The late Martha Baird Rockefeller, John D., Jr.'s second wife, was an accomplished musician herself who derived exquisite pleasure from developing the talent of others through her Martha Baird Rockefeller Fund for Music, Inc. Peggy Guggenheim had finely tuned visual sensibilities and lent her support to emerging artists. William Paley, via his CBS Foundation, assists young film makers in their careers. BENEFIT: Personal satisfaction as well as good PR.

One thing that does *not* figure into the philanthropic equation is the notion of self-sacrifice. Among the American rich, no St. Francis of Assisi has ever appeared. Americans may spread some of their wealth around a bit, but they don't dump it all on others during their lifetime and live as paupers. Those who do live as paupers do so because of some neurotic notion that they *can* take it with them.

If I had to pick one motivation that runs through all munificent gestures on the part of wealthy Americans, I would say it's sheer, unadulterated hatred of the federal government and its lackey tax collectors.

Paul Mellon, seventy-four, Upperville, Virginia

Estimated personal worth: $500 million–$1 billion
Estimated total benefactions to date: $250 million

With Paul Mellon, it's hard to determine where his personal benefactions leave off and his family's begin. Under the Mellon banner are a number of philanthropic conduits, including the Andrew W. Mellon Foundation (formed by a merger of the Avalon and Old Dominion foundations); A. W. Mellon Educational & Charitable Trust (liquidated in 1980 with twenty-eight grants totaling $25 million); and the Bollingen Foundation. Paul Mellon is a principal trustee in all of them. What one can say with some assurance is that the Mellon family has given away more than $700 million to universities, art museums, historical societies, wild-life sanctuaries, and mental-health programs since World War II. (The *Wall Street Journal* places the family's aggregate fortune at around $5 billion.)

Mellon has taken as his life's work the goal of "spending my fortune sensibly. . . . Giving large sums of money away is a soul-searching problem since you can cause as much damage with it as you may do good." Indeed, minding his charities takes up the lion's share of his time. Among those charities are the National Gallery of Art in Washington, his father's posthumous glory; and Yale University, his alma mater. The National Gallery is at least $120 million richer because of Paul and his late sister Ailsa's generosity, and Yale is at least $15 million better off.

One of Paul Mellon's most celebrated monuments is the $10-million Yale Center for British Art, designed by Louis Kahn. Completed in 1977, it houses the largest concentration of British paintings (1,800), drawings and watercolors (7,000), prints (5,000), and rare books (16,000) from the Elizabethan period to the mid-nineteenth century found anywhere outside England. The collection is probably worth substantially more than $35 million and took Mellon twenty years to amass.

Henry Crown, eighty-five, Chicago, Illinois

Estimated personal worth: $200–$300 million
Estimated total benefactions to date: $100 million

Henry Crown claims his goal since 1945 has been to end up with less money at the end of each year than he had in the beginning. "I don't need it," says the modest financier-turned-philanthropist. "It's needed more elsewhere—philanthropy, charitable funds, other members of my family."

While various nonprofit institutions have gotten Crown's cash in abundance, his family has gotten that and more. His parents, brothers, first wife, and sons have all seen their names chiseled in marble all over the country. Crown allowed his own name to appear only once. It's on a gallery in the Art Institute in Chicago. In contrast, Henry's father, Arie, has his name emblazoned on a theater in McCormick Place, a city swimming pool, a Talmud Torah Hebrew day school, an auditorium at the Chicago Loop Synagogue, and a Cook County forest. To his mother's credit is the Ida Crown Jewish Academy on the North Side of Chicago. The Illinois Institute of Technology has an S. R. Crown Hall, honoring Henry's late elder brother. Another brother, Herman, has his name headlined on a Roosevelt University building. Northwestern University's administration center is named for Henry's first wife, Rebecca, and Henry's late son, Robert, is immortalized by a law library at Stanford and a sailing center at the U.S. Naval Academy.

There are other institutions that have benefitted from Crown's largesse, often with less visible results. They include the Chicago

Symphony, Chicago Historical Society, various students in need of scholarship aid, the Jewish United Fund, Israeli causes, and such universities as Brandeis, Notre Dame, Loyola, De Pauw, and Hebrew University in Israel. All told, some 300 schools, hospitals, synagogues, churches, arts institutions, and sundry charities have been touched by Crown's magnanimity.

Crown has not walked away empty-handed, however. Besides experiencing the satisfaction of giving, he's been the recipient of more than five honorary degrees.

E. Claiborne Robins, seventy-one, Richmond, Virginia

Estimated personal worth: $100–$200 million
Estimated total benefactions to date: $75 million

One stroke of eleemosynary luck has been known to transform an educational backwater into a respected institution. Pharmaceutical heir E. Claiborne Robins has worked that miracle for the University of Richmond, a hometown Baptist-affiliated school that has graduated three generations of the Robins family.

After giving the school a few million here and a few million there over a fifteen-year period, Robins—a university trustee—pulled out all the philanthropic stops in 1969. At the commencement exercises that year, the university president announced that Robins had pledged an unrestricted gift of $50 million in A. H. Robins Co. stock, $40 million outright, and $10 million in a matching grant. The audience was stupefied since the bonanza was five times the school's total endowment.

Admittedly, it is one of the greatest demonstrations of educational magnanimity this country has ever seen, at least during a benefactor's lifetime. Bequests of this size are more common in wills. But Robins must have known what he was doing because his family has subsequently gotten a hefty return on the investment in terms of prestige.

Six months after the donation was announced, Robins' three grown children joined him on the board of trustees. Four years later, Mrs. E. Claiborne Robins received an honorary degree of doctor of humanities. The name "Robins" is also plastered all over the school; among other things there's a Robins Memorial Field and a $10 million Robins Athletic Center, fitting since the Robins clan is extremely sports oriented.

Robins has also showered other local causes with cash, but in $1,000 doses rather than $1-million portions. Virginia Commonwealth University, where Robins went to pharmacy school, came the closest to duplicating the University of Richmond's luck. In 1973, it got $3 million to help build a $17-million allied health professions building on its Medical College of Virginia campus.

W. Clement Stone, seventy-nine, Chicago, Illinois

Estimated personal worth: $100–$200 million
Estimated total benefactions to date: $75 million

Word of mouth has amplified W. Clement Stone's magnanimity even beyond its proportions. And the principal mouths creating this impression are those of W. Clement Stone and his PR man.

In 1973, the Combined International Corp. vice president for public relations told me that the W. Clement and Jessie V. Stone Foundation had given away $73 million since 1958. Stone himself underlined the message with effusive quips about the healing power of money, how it widens the possessor's horizons and allows him or her to do good in the world.

However, one wonders exactly what Stone lists on his scorecard under the heading "Philanthropy." Does he put the $5 million he shelled out to Richard Nixon in that column, for instance? Or the dough he spent supplying S. I. Hayakawa with PR counsel during the student uprising at San Francisco State? (Stone said he did it because he approved of the strong stand acting-president Hayakawa was taking against the demonstrators.)

As charity cases, these two are certainly open to question. But not all of Stone's beneficiaries have been as controversial. His favorite charity is probably the Boys' Clubs of America, the catalyst that brought Stone and Nixon together in 1964. He has also helped finance various mental health, youth welfare, religious, and educational organizations.

The Stone Foundation has a unique mode of operation. Most foundations are supported by the annual income from a large endowment. The Stone Foundation, on the other hand, depends on yearly contributions from Stone himself. Stone's practice has been to make charitable contributions in cash by borrowing money, then later selling a large block of Combined International Corp. stock to pay back the debts.

That *modus operandi* caught up with him in 1974, however, when Stone found himself strapped for cash. That year Stone had less than $200,000 available for grants, compared to almost $9 million handed out in the foundation's peak year of 1971. His solution: to donate organizational and consulting services to worthy charities instead of cash.

DeWitt and Lila Acheson Wallace, both ninety-two, Chappaqua, New York

Estimated personal worth: $200–$300 million
His estimated total benefactions to date: $15 million
Her estimated total benefactions to date: $30 million
Their estimated total benefactions to date: $25 million

Sometimes it seems as if *Reader's Digest* cofounders DeWitt and Lila Acheson Wallace are in a race with each other to see who can give away the most money. As Mrs. Wallace jokingly puts it, "We steal from each other," a reference to the fact that their assets are held jointly. The childless couple claim they give about 105 percent of their taxable income to charity these days.

DeWitt Wallace's philanthropic loyalty has remained relatively constant throughout the years. His principal charity was Macalester College in St. Paul, the Presbyterian school that Wallace attended and his father presided over as dean and president in the early part of this century. However, in 1971 there were reports that Wallace was "rethinking all my commitments" and had trimmed back his usual donation of $1.2 million a year to $584,438. At the time, Paul H. Davis, Wallace's representative on Macalester's board of trustees, said he thought the school was "too affluent" and "extravagant" already and would benefit from a period of austerity. Typically, all Wallace's statements to the press on the matter were delivered through spokesmen and the ultimate outcome was never made public.

In contrast, Mrs. Wallace's largesse is diversified, and she seems to enjoy the publicity surrounding each benefaction. Some say the Metropolitan Museum of Art in Manhattan is her principal beneficiary, and that statement goes unchallenged since the amounts she contributed for the restoration and maintenance of the museum's Great Hall and redesign of the Egyptian galleries have never been disclosed. What is a matter of public record is Mrs.

Wallace's $9-million contribution to the Juilliard School; almost $1 million to the Metropolitan Opera for four new productions; $5 million to the New York Zoological Society; $1.1 million to Egypt-related causes; $1 million to her alma mater, the University of Oregon; $1 million to the White Plains, New York, YWCA; and more than $100,000 to the Martha Graham Dance Company.

With all these gifts, Mrs. Wallace seems to have gotten value for her money and in two cases she got her name preserved in marble for posterity. The Juilliard School houses the Lila Acheson Wallace Library, which displays her name, and the Bronx Zoo's bird house bears a similar inscription. Whether Mrs. Wallace got her $8 million worth out of the restoration of "Boscobel," the 1805 home of Loyalist landowner States Morris Dyckman, is another matter. Initially, she donated $750,000 to help restore the Hudson River valley mansion and fill it with authentic period furnishings. But that's where the restorers went wrong. The contents were not authentic enough to satisfy Mrs. Wallace and she eventually agreed to put up the dough to see the errors corrected. The curator of the American wing of the Metropolitan was brought in as a consultant to see that the mistakes weren't repeated. Many millions of dollars later, Mrs. Wallace's philanthropic folly was ready for viewing, described in its promotional literature as "one of the grandest expressions extant of the New York Federal style of domestic architecture. . . . You'll find our 1800s mansion truly re-restored and even more magnificent than before."

Edith Rosenwald Stern (Mrs. Edgar Bloom Stern), eighty-six, New Orleans, Louisiana

Estimated personal worth: $200–$300 million
Estimated total benefactions to date: $50 million

Nobody has ever placed a dollar value on the philanthropy of dowager Edith Rosenwald Stern, so the above figure is purely a guess. However, anybody who has ever come into contact with Mrs. Stern and her late husband has been struck by the couple's well-developed sense of social responsibility.

Mrs. Stern's philanthropic instincts are hereditary. Her father, Julius Rosenwald, was one of the founders of Sears Roebuck Co., the world's largest retailer; and gave away about $63 million before his death in 1932. Black and civil rights causes got the major portion of his gifts.

Mrs. Stern and her husband continued the family tradition of supporting black causes, but in the Southern city of New Orleans, that can be dangerous. Through the years, the couple received threats and hate mail for their trouble, but the growth and prestige of Dillard University, which prospered with their largesse, is one of their rewards. Tulane and Harvard universities have also received sizable donations.

Mrs. Stern has expressed her philanthropic nonconformity in other ways as well. In the not-so-distant past, New Orleans had such a sloppy voter registration system that elections could easily be rigged by shady politicians. It was so bad that Mrs. Stern recalls, "You could register a dog, an old cat, and all your dead relatives and then cast a vote for them if you wanted." Mrs. Stern became the cofounder and chief financial supporter of the volunteer Voter Registration League, which has since been incorporated into the city government. (Mrs. Stern's electoral remodeling campaign made her most unpopular, to put it mildly, with the Long family factions in Louisiana.) In the same vein, the Stern Family Fund has made grants to the Governmental Affairs Institute in Washington and Mrs. Stern's son, Philip—a writer who lives in New York City—is an outspoken advocate of tax reform, the type of reform that would not appear to be in the best interests of a wealthy heir such as he.

But social and political causes aren't Mrs. Stern's only concern. Without her, New Orleans probably would not have a symphony orchestra. In 1974, the Women's Committee of the New Orleans Philharmonic expressed its gratitude by giving a ball in her honor. The gardens of her home "Longue Vue" are open to the public, and Mrs. Stern would like to see her estate preserved by the New Orleans Museum of Art after her death—an endowment for maintenance to be provided by her estate, of course. "The museum wants it," she sighed, "but the neighbors don't. It's very frustrating."

(Mrs. Stern died on September 11, 1980, in her suite at the Pontchartrain Hotel, New Orleans, after a long illness. She was eighty-five years old.)

John Hay Whitney, seventy-seven, New York, New York

Estimated personal worth: $200–$300 million
Estimated total benefactions to date: $50 million

John Hay Whitney claims that eighteen days as a prisoner of war during World War II made him aware of the fundamental fault in America's educational system. When German interrogators asked him why the United States was fighting, he always answered, "For freedom." But he was shocked when his fellow American prisoners never gave a moral or ideological reason. Then and there he resolved to give up his former life as a playboy-sportsman and embrace the role of the concerned capitalist-philanthropist.

This resolve was helped along by the fact that he was simultaneously coming into a $40-million inheritance ($20 million from a trust established by his father Payne Whitney and $20+ million from his mother Helen Hay Whitney's will). After the war, he took $10 million of this windfall and established the John Hay Whitney Foundation to help everyone from disadvantaged minorities to high-school teachers make the best use of their talents through further study. For his high-visibility benefactions, he captured seven honorary degrees from prestigious universities and in 1955 was elected to his alma mater's governing body, the Yale Corporation. It may have been the smartest fund-raising move Yale University ever made, for Whitney showered the school with some $30 million in gifts throughout the next twenty-five years. As a member of the board of governors of New York Hospital-Cornell Medical Center, Whitney also gave that esteemed institution $5 million.

The liberal bent of the foregoing largesse served a dual purpose, placing in bas-relief Jock Whitney's image as a prominent member of what President Eisenhower called "the military-industrial complex." Whitney served as U.S. Ambassador to the Court of St. James's in Britain from 1957 to 1961 and apparently never completely severed his ties with the *sub rosa* activities of the American diplomatic community. In 1967, an exposé in *The New York Times* revealed that the John Hay Whitney Trust for Charitable Purposes had been used as a conduit for CIA funds. Whitney rose above the allegation by refusing to acknowledge it.

Indian Givers

Robert Brinkley Smithers' experience with the administrators who run his alcoholic treatment facility in New York has convinced him to revise the Golden Rule. The Smithers' version: He who has the gold makes the rules.

The seventy-three-year-old Smithers' gold came to him through inheritance. His father was a cofounder of IBM. In 1971, he decided to give $10 million of that gold "as needed" to Roosevelt Hospital to establish an alcoholism recovery program. Smithers' letter of intent went on to say, "it is understood that detailed project plans and staff appointments must have my approval."

Eight years later, Smithers announced that he would not cough up the $5 million still owing on his pledge because the wrong kind of people were being treated at the Smithers Center in Roosevelt Hospital and at the posh forty-four-bed rehab unit, housed in the former Billy Rose mansion in Manhattan's fashionable upper East Side.

Smithers expressed his displeasure on the front page of *The New York Times*. Smithers, a reformed alcoholic himself, explained that the group he wanted to reach with his donation, "are people from my walk of life, plus employed alcoholics"—not the Hispanics, blacks, and other minorities who had been showing up on the doorstep of the Smithers Center practically since its inception.

"Rich people have more problems than poor people," he maintains, "especially the women. The children grow up and leave; they have servants; they have no strong hobbies. So they have drinks at lunch; play bridge; have some more drinks. Then their husband gets home from work and they have a couple of cocktails with him. These poor women drink themselves into addiction. I've seen this firsthand. . . . You take a Park Avenue dowager rubbing shoulders and eating with people she considers below her—she just wouldn't stay in that kind of treatment program."

The chief spokesperson for the opposition is Dr. LeClair Bissell, the fifty-three-year-old psychiatrist and recovered alcoholic who heads the Smithers Center. Dr. Bissell claims she understood that Smithers wanted "an upper-class, lily-white Protestant population" in his center but "he was immediately told by me and others that this is the 1970s and New York City, and we do not set out to run a racist establishment. Besides, philosophically I think it's good for a variety of people to be in treatment together." Smithers, on the other hand, claims Bissell and her staff went against his wishes because they were afraid they couldn't fill up the center without accepting Medicaid people.

This was not "Brink" Smithers' first foray into the world of big-league philanthropy. Since 1952, he has earmarked more than $8 million of his own money for alcoholism research and treatment, in addition to more than $7 million contributed through the Christopher D. Smithers Foundation, established in memory of his father. He's been called "the sugar daddy to the whole alcoholism field."

At last report, it was a standoff with Smithers refusing to budge on the remaining $5 million "unless they sue me." So far, they haven't.

Not all administrators of eleemosynary institutions are as willing to acquiesce when a fat cat reneges on a pledge. When Joan Whitney Payson (Mrs. Charles Shipman Payson) died in October 1975, it took the Metropolitan Museum of Art in New York less than three years to sue her estate for the $1.5-million balance still owing on a total pledge of $5 million. In this case, Mrs. Payson hadn't even put her intentions in writing but had made them known during a casual conversation with the museum's president, fellow plutocrat C. Douglas Dillon.

The Payson-estate lawyers refused to pay, basing this position on two arguments: 1) Mrs. Payson had not signed a pledge, thus the estate was not legally obligated to lay out the rest of the money; and 2) the museum's claim had already been satisfied by the $4.3 million worth of paintings it received in accordance with a provision in her will.

The latter argument did not cut ice with the judge. He agreed with the museum's contention that the painting bequest in Mrs. Payson's will and her verbal pledge of cash made four years before she died were two entirely different matters. Thus, the estate owed the money. But the judge did not close the file on the case without chastising museum officials for their sloppy fund-raising techniques. "These proceedings would not have been necessary if the Metropolitan Museum had followed reasonable prudent business methods and had the decedent sign a simple pledge form," he said. The museum had no pledge forms, according to Dillon.

Three officials of Elmira College in New York State got more than a tongue-lashing from the New Jersey Supreme Court judges when the school lost its legal fight to collect the $1.75 million art collection of the senile-but-still-breathing Geraldine Rockefeller

Dodge in a similar case in the mid-1960s. The school got a public-relations black eye that haunted it for years, for the high court's opinion was nothing short of a devastating indictment of the college's fund-raising techniques, characterized as psychological arm-twisting of the worst order.

The chief villains of the piece were Dr. J. Ralph Murray, Elmira College's president, and Harold W. McGraw, then a vice president of McGraw-Hill Publishing Co. and member of the school's board of trustees. Perry Shoemaker, president of the bankrupt Jersey Central Railroad and former trustee, didn't come out looking too good either.

"The sins of the able are no less sins when committed in what they believe to be a worthy cause," the court declared in its opinion. "McGraw's pressure and manipulation of her [Mrs. Dodge] to achieve their ends, even after the alleged gift was made and when patently he knew she was waning mentally, leave his credibility seriously doubtful. His reckless and misleading statements to her about advantages, including possible tax advantages she would receive by signing the proffered letter, demonstrate that he and Dr. Murray considered that the end justified the means employed, however inequitable their nature."

The lawyers representing the Dodge interests—specifically Mrs. Dodge's legal guardians, The Fidelity Union Trust Co. of Newark and Peter C. Netland of Madison, New Jersey—claimed that the wooing of the aging dowager began as early as 1955 and moved into high gear in 1958 when Elmira's board of trustees voted to give her an honorary degree. Perry Shoemaker's Jersey Central provided the private railroad car that transported Mrs. Dodge to Elmira, New York, in 1960 to accept the honor. By this time, symptoms of Mrs. Dodge's "impending mental dissolution" were apparent to everyone, most notably Elmira College officials.

The lawyers contended that the cultivation campaign was stepped up "to the point of virtual bombardment" after Mrs. Dodge's trusted friend and longtime business advisor died that year. By the spring of 1961, the collaborators had her primed for the kill and presented her with the draft of a letter which made it clear that she would retain possession of her beloved art objects—sculptures, porcelains, and paintings—during her lifetime and release specific items as she saw fit. However, the letter she finally signed a month later did not say anything of the kind. Rather it read:

"By this letter I wish to confirm the arrangement I discussed with you concerning my entire collection of paintings, pictures, jade, bronze and various objets d'art located in my home at 61st Street and Fifth Avenue in New York City and my New Jersey residence at Giralda Farms in Madison, New Jersey, and in storage in various places in New York City and elsewhere.

"I wish to present and hereby do present and convey title to all of these items as a gift to Elmira College. It is to be understood, however, that I may retain possession of such items as long as I am able to enjoy them."

In June 1963, Mrs. Dodge was declared mentally incompetent because of arteriosclerosis, and her husband was made her guardian; he died six months later. School officials immediately construed incompetent to mean Mrs. Dodge could no longer enjoy her precious art objects and began demanding the benefaction in full. Later, Mrs. Dodge's nurses testified in court that although Mrs. Dodge seldom recognized people and seemed unaware of her surroundings, she did occasionally admire specific artworks and ask to fondle them. Furthermore, a stipulation in Mr. Dodge's will made it clear that his executors could not dispose of his property if doing so would in any way disturb the environment that his wife was accustomed to. Mr. Dodge apparently felt a disruption in his wife's life-style in her feeble state might cause her mental or physical harm.

The college's case was not as compelling. The school's lawyers contended that Mrs. Dodge agreed in September 1958 to give her collection to the college "as soon as she could no longer enjoy it." On the strength of that verbal promise, the college purchased a large mansion called "Strathmont" in Elmira to house the collection and proposed renaming it the "Geraldine R. Dodge Center." Meanwhile, the board of trustees had voted Mrs. Dodge an honorary degree and, during the awards ceremony, described her as a "splendid woman. . . . Her deep and active concern for mankind and the wide diversity of her worthwhile interests will be an inspiration to the entire Elmira College community." (In court, Elmira's attorneys pictured her as being in competition with her husband who had received an honorary degree from Columbia University,

Edward Ball, the administrator of the rich and powerful and increasingly noncharitable Alfred I. du Pont estate headquartered in Jacksonville, Florida. TIMES-UNION & JACKSONVILLE JOURNAL (1973)

his alma mater, a few years earlier. Supposedly, Mrs. Dodge was overheard to remark after receiving the honor, "Now, Hartley has nothing on me.")

Between 1958 and 1960, Mrs. Dodge gave the school $200,000 of a $250,000 pledge toward the purchase price of the mansion; and delivered 216 porcelains valued at $50,000 and a collection of bronzes valued at $70,000. Then the benefactions stopped and that's when school officials began pushing for the written agreement which they got on May 16, 1961. However, the high-pressure atmosphere in which the letter was signed was the evidence that eventually did the college in. The Supreme Court ruled:

"She [Mrs. Dodge] was lonely and had few friends; she was aged and unquestionably deteriorating in mental vigor; she was without her longtime advisor during this critical period, as they [Murray, McGraw, and Shoemaker] knew; she had an unusual family life [her husband lived by himself on an adjoining estate] and no companionship from relatives. As events proved, she was an open door to the superficial manifestations of friendship and blandishments of able men.

"In the stream of almost weekly reports from McGraw to the other two men—marked 'personal and confidential'—relating to his many luncheon and dinner meetings with her, the singleness of their donation-seeking purpose is grossly apparent. We rarely find a kind word or a note of solicitude about her as a person, unless a reference to the fact which had drawn them to her, that she was civic-minded and had done a great deal of good with her money can be so considered."

The Miserly Midas

"Eleemosynary" is one word that's not likely to pass from the lips of Edward Ball even though he is the senior trustee of a major charitable foundation. In fact, the whole idea of charity—of "handouts"—is anathema to this feisty, ninety-three-year-old administrator of the Alfred I. du Pont estate, headquartered in Jacksonville, Florida.

In 1977, the State of Delaware—the deceased du Pont's home territory—finally got around to something it had been threatening for years. Delaware authorities slapped Ball with a $50-million lawsuit for failing to carry out the provisions of the late chemical heir's will, which made the Nemours Foundation and its offshoot, the Alfred I. du Pont Institute Children's Hospital near Wilmington, the estate's sole beneficiary. The suit, which is expected to drag on for five to ten years, contends that Ball disregarded the deceased's intent and set himself up as the estate's principal beneficiary for the last forty-five years.

Ball has prospered handsomely since the death of his brother-in-law in 1935, but not through embezzlement; nobody has ever accused him of that. Rather, he's accused of diverting the estate's assets into highly profitable business ventures, schemes that made Ball a multimillionaire in his own right while the handicapped children and geriatrics who were supposed to benefit did not—at least not in sufficient degree.

Ball is living proof that "the rugged individualist," glorified in American folklore, has not passed completely from the national scene as yet. While Ball's critics, who are legion, ascribe his good fortune to flagrant disregard of the law and sheer tightfistedness, Ball claims hard work was his only mentor. In truth, Alfred I. du Pont was his real mentor.

Horatio Alger would have loved Ball's success story. Descended from a "first family of Virginia" (FFV), a royal distinction in Southern climes, Ball was raised on a farm in Tidewater, Virginia, the son of a Confederate cavalry captain and country lawyer of modest means. As soon as Ball could, he dropped out of grammar school to make money, an occupation he found infinitely more appealing than book learnin'. Thereafter, he industriously peddled everything from law books to furniture until luck finally clouted him over the head. In 1921, his only sister, Jessie, a public-school principal, married the rich and influential Alfred I. du Pont of Delaware. The couple never had any children but du Pont grew increasingly fond of his young brother-in-law and eventually hired him as his personal aide-de-camp.

Du Pont immediately singled out pugnacity as Ball's predominant trait. "Ed is a little pigheaded," du Pont wrote in a letter to his father-in-law, "so it is necessary to bat him over the head with a club occasionally. But he is a fine, loyal, hard worker, as tenacious as a bulldog on a tramp's pants—all qualities appealing strongly to me."

When du Pont died, he left $27 million to a charitable trust with Ball named one of its four trustees. Seizing the opportunity, Ball quickly elbowed out the opposition, consolidated his control, and over the years has increased the trust's holdings and value many times over until it is reputedly worth between $1 billion and $2 billion today. In the bargain, he made himself a tidy $20-million bundle on the side, proving once again that money is easy enough to make if you've got some to start with.

During the last two decades, Ball's strangle-hold over the estate, which now controls the St. Joe Paper Co., two railroads, a sugar concern, and more than 1 million acres of prime Florida and Georgia timberland, has engendered considerable controversy. A proponent of the lock-'em-out-starve-'em-out theory of labor relations, Ball hired scabs to break the strike against the Florida East Coast Railway, one of the estate's assets; and kept it operating for nine years from 1963 to 1972, defying the combined might of the federal government and eleven railroad unions. Later, he got around the legal decree ordering the du Pont estate to divest itself of its bank chain by selling a majority interest to the Charter Company, a conglomerate headed by Ball's closest business ally, Raymond K. Mason.

Throughout his long business career, Ball has steadfastly reserved the major share of his enmity for the government. Ball, as did his robber-baron predecessors, believes that any government which interferes with what he wants to do is too much government. Next on his list are labor unions. You might say Ball still operates as if the twentieth century never dawned, the reason he can't be moved by ordinary modern business logic.

Ensconced in his vintage-1920 office in Jacksonville, this five-foot-four-inch Southern autocrat brushes aside the criticism of the world with a chuckle. "If it means to belong to the twentieth century, you've got to jump through a hoop every time some union or government official holds one up, then it's true, I don't belong in this century." Ball flaunts his peppery image. "A reporter once wrote that I'm about as feeble as an adolescent wildcat with a Roman candle tied to his tail. That's very complimentary, I'd say." His favorite toast, before he downs his usual bourbon and ginger ale, is "Confusion to the enemy."

Ball is a wily horse trader who never comes out on the short end of any deal, romantic or otherwise. He claims his short-lived marriage many years ago was "one of my least fortunate ventures," although he was shrewd enough to hedge his bets even then. The unfortunate woman signed a premarital agreement limiting her share of his personal fortune to a mere $250,000 in the event of divorce.

So far, his run-ins with the Delaware du Pont interests have left him equally unscathed. The first sally was heaved in March 1974 when the Wilmington newspaper, then owned by the du Pont family, charged Ball with running the Alfred I. du Pont trust like a rapacious business enterprise, more concerned with turning a profit than in supporting the Delaware charities in the style to which they had become accustomed during Alfred and Jessie's lifetimes.

NOTES

1. Carnegie erased his ruthless reputation as a slave-driving steel manufacturer by endowing public libraries across the land. Rockefeller, who looked like a dried prune by the time he finally kicked the bucket at the grand old age of ninety-eight, devoted the last half of his life to reversing his bad-guy persona, becoming instead the doddering old man who gave away dimes to the kiddies. And Andrew Mellon, the Pittsburgh plutocrat, used art philanthropy in the form of the National Gallery to blot out the rumor that he had single-handedly caused the Depression when as Secretary of the Treasury under Harding, Coolidge, and Hoover, he openly promoted the interests of his class by reducing the taxes paid by rich people (those earning more than $66,000 a year) and corporations from a maximum of 73 percent to a meager 33 percent. The orgy of speculation that followed, so the theory goes, led ultimately to the stock market crash.

SOLID-GOLD HEADACHES

V

WHEN IS AN ASSET A LIABILITY?
WHEN IT'S A FIFTY-ROOM HOUSE

18   Architectural Albatrosses: What Are They Now?

Like his fellow tycoons of the Gilded Age, Henry Morrison Flagler felt compelled to build himself a gargantuan house with the spoils from his Standard Oil and Florida East Coast Railway fortune. Thus, around 1902, a massive seventy-three-room edifice appeared on the shores of Lake Worth in Palm Beach, Florida. The structure was sort of a Spanish-inspired temple with huge Doric columns that made the front entrance look more like a public building than a private home. Ostensibly a wedding gift for his third wife, it cost Flagler $2.5 million to build, but he never felt entirely comfortable there and always avoided the institutional-looking portico, using the side entrance whenever he came and went. In his dotage, he finally confided to a friend, "I wish I could swap it for a little shack."

If a robber baron felt that way about his baronial residence, how do you think the heirs feel about these edificial white elephants? I'll tell you how most of them feel—like disposing of the monsters as soon as possible. The palazzo life-style is no longer in vogue even if the heirs could afford the taxes, upkeep, and find competent domestics to staff them.

Herewith is a survey of famous yesteryear mansions and their current status:

"The Breakers" is the most famous of the Newport, Rhode Island, summer "cottages" by the sea built in the 1880s and '90s. It was built by Cornelius Vanderbilt II, the grandson of the founding father, Commodore Vanderbilt. For sheer size and showmanship, "The Breakers" is rivaled only by two other Vanderbilt homes—"Marble House," also in Newport; and "Biltmore" in Asheville, North Carolina. These homes were constructed by Cornelius II's brothers, William K. and George Washington Vanderbilt, respectively. DR. JEFFREY R. SMITH

When theatrical producer Billy Rose lived in this mansion at Madison Avenue and 93 Street in Manhattan, he never dreamed it would one day house recovering alcoholics. Today, it's the forty-four–bed rehabilitation unit of The Smithers Center, affiliated with Roosevelt Hospital. JACQUELINE THOMPSON

MANSION (*name and description*)	FAMOUS RICH OWNER	ITS DISPOSITION
"The Breakers" in Newport, Rhode Island. Designed by Richard Morris Hunt, it's the grandest of the resort's cottages, often cited for its "frigid splendor."	Cornelius Vanderbilt II, grandson of the Commodore, built and furnished it at a cost of about $10 million.	Gladys Vanderbilt (Countess Laszlo Széchényi) was the last family member to live there. She eventually leased it to the Newport Preservation Society for $1 per year. It's now open to the public for tours.
Billy Rose mansion at Madison Avenue and Ninety-third Street in New York City.	This town house's most famous inhabitant was theatrical entrepreneur Billy Rose.	In the early 1970s, this residence became part of the Smithers Alcoholic Rehabilitation Center. It can house up to forty-four recovering alcoholics—rich, recovering alcoholics who can afford the steep fee of $3,000 for the twenty-eight-day program.
"Falaise" in Sand's Point, Long Island. A twenty-six-room home designed in the style of a Norman manor house.	The late Harry F. Guggenheim, industrialist and philanthropist, laid claim to this edifice.	Guggenheim's will stipulated that his Guggenheim Foundation was to maintain the house as a private museum in perpetuity. Today, many of Guggenheim's retinue of servants still keep the place in occupied order even though nobody lives there. Eight people may view it at any one time for $2.00 a head.

MANSION (*name and description*)	FAMOUS RICH OWNER	ITS DISPOSITION
"Caumsett" in Lloyd Harbor, Long Island. This fifty-six-room Georgian superstructure is set on 1,426 acres of unspoiled land.	Marshall Field 3d, the Chicago department store heir, purchased the property in 1925. When he died in 1956, his estate was the largest parcel of undeveloped North Shore land left on Long Island.	The property was the focus of a heated controversy in the early 1960s when real estate developers wanted to subdivide the land into 700 two-acre plots. Next Robert Moses tried to get it for a recreation area and the Long Island terminus for a bridge to span the sound. Instead, Field's widow sold the land to the government for $4.3 million, making a substantial donation in the bargain since it was worth $15 million. Queens College uses the house as an environmental study center and teaching facility while the grounds have been operated as a state park—with limited public access—ever since.

"Eagle's Nest" was one of the homes of William K. Vanderbilt II who used it about thirty days out of every year. This Spanish-Moroccan–style villa overlooks the Northport, Long Island, harbor. Among the buildings that are currently open to the public under the auspices of Suffolk County are the main house, a planetarium, and a separate museum of marine life, once Mr. Vanderbilt's private museum. JACQUELINE THOMPSON

MANSION (name and description)	FAMOUS RICH OWNER	ITS DISPOSITION
"Eagle's Nest" in Centerport, Long Island. This Spanish-Moroccan-style villa sits on forty-three acres overlooking Northport Harbor. In its heyday it required a staff of thirty-five, including five men just to maintain the seven-hole golf course.	William K. Vanderbilt II, a fourth-generation heir, built this home then used it one month out of each year.	When Vanderbilt died in 1944, he willed the estate to Suffolk County, which has operated it as a museum since 1949.
"Winterthur" near Wilmington, Delaware. This 1,000-acre estate was built in 1839.	The estate was developed by Mr. and Mrs. James Antoine Bidermann, the great-uncle and -aunt of Henry Francis du Pont, its last individual owner. He made it his home from 1927 to 1951.	In 1951, H. F. du Pont turned it over to a nonprofit charitable foundation to run as a museum and horticultural attraction; it has sixty acres of gardens and a house full of priceless antiques.
"Dumbarton Oaks" in Washington, D.C. This sixteen-acre preserve is situated at the highest point of Georgetown. Its gardens and fountains are replicas of seventeenth- and eighteenth-century European gardens.	Mr. and Mrs. Robert Woods Bliss purchased the estate in 1920. Mrs. Bliss was the heiress to the Fletcher's Castoria fortune.	In 1940, the Bliss family gave the estate to Harvard University and four years later it was used for the famous diplomatic summit that resulted in the United Nations. It is now the home for the Harvard Center for Byzantine Studies. The gardens and the Byzantine Collection and pre-Columbian museum are open to the public.

"Bassett Hall" is the manor house of a 585-acre former tobacco plantation near Williamsburg, Virginia. John D. Rockefeller, Jr., and his first wife, Abby Aldrich, purchased the estate and completed the restoration of the eighteenth-century house in 1936. "Bassett Hall" provided the perfect backdrop for Abby's valuable collection of early American folk art. Under the aegis of the Colonial Williamsburg Foundation, the house—looking as it did when the Rockefellers lived there—will soon be open to the public. NYT Pictures/Gene Maggio

"Dumbarton Oaks" is a name etched in every American history textbook, for this Washington, D.C., estate was the 1944 convening point for the Allied envoys who drew up the initial plans for the United Nations. After a succession of wealthy owners, the sixteen-acre estate was deeded to Harvard University in 1940 by Mr. and Mrs. Robert Wood Bliss. (Mrs. Bliss is the Fletcher's Castoria heiress.) The deceased benefactors are buried in "Dumbarton Oaks'" rose garden. NYT PICTURES/D. GORTON

MANSION (*name and description*)	FAMOUS RICH OWNER	ITS DISPOSITION
"Bassett Hall" outside Williamsburg, Virginia. This 585-acre plantation boasts a two-story eighteenth-century manor house, gardens, and ten outbuildings.	Mr. and Mrs. John D. Rockefeller, Jr., purchased it in 1927, restored it to its pristine eighteenth-century splendor, and filled it with first-rate examples of American antique furniture and folk art. After the first Mrs. Rockefeller's death, Rockefeller lived on there until his own death in 1960 when the property passed to his son, John D. Rockefeller 3d.	Upon Rockefeller 3d's death in 1978, all his heirs disclaimed interest in the property. Thus, it was given to Colonial Williamsburg, the historic town that adjoins the land.
Cumberland Island, part of the Golden Isles, in the Atlantic off southern Georgia. This 24,000-acre unspoiled preserve has five mansions, plus some 300 auxiliary buildings. The major residence is called "Dungeness." The others are "The Cottage," "Grey Field," "Stafford," and "Plum Orchard." The buildings alone are worth an estimated $1.5 million. It required 600+ servants to maintain them in the early days of the twentieth century.	Thomas Carnegie, the brother of steel magnate Andrew Carnegie, purchased the island in the late 1880s. Under the will of Carnegie's widow, Lucy, who died in 1916, all but 1,500 acres were held in trust for her eight children and had to be kept unchanged throughout their lifetimes. Lucy's children didn't use the island much and balked at the $150,000 it took yearly just to keep the houses in minimal repair.	The grandchildren of Thomas and Lucy Carnegie started selling their holdings in the island to the National Parks Foundation in 1970 to forestall commercial development. By the end of 1970, the government had title to 75 percent of Cumberland and planned to turn it into the nation's eighth National Seashore sometime in the future. (The island has eighteen miles of beaches and is valued at between $10 million and $13 million.)

MANSION (*name and description*)	FAMOUS RICH OWNER	ITS DISPOSITION
"Mar-A-Lago" in Palm Beach, Florida. A Moorish palace of fifty rooms on Lake Worth surrounded by seventeen acres. "Mar-A-Lago" is Spanish for "sea-to-lake," an apt name since the property stretches from Lake Worth almost to the Atlantic Ocean—South Ocean Boulevard intervenes.	Marjorie Merriweather Post had this pleasure dome constructed in 1927 (cost $8 million) as her winter residence.	When Post died in 1973, she willed the property to the National Park Service to be used by the President and visiting heads of state. It was soon discovered that for security reasons it couldn't be used for that purpose because the property is situated directly under an important airplane flight pattern, making it a cinch for anyone wishing to drop a bomb to do so. Furthermore, the trust fund income that is supposed to cover the costs of maintenance is woefully inadequate, requiring the government to make up the difference. The Palm Beach Civic Assn. wants the empty structure returned to the Post heirs so it will again start generating property tax revenues which are considerable. Its future is still in limbo.

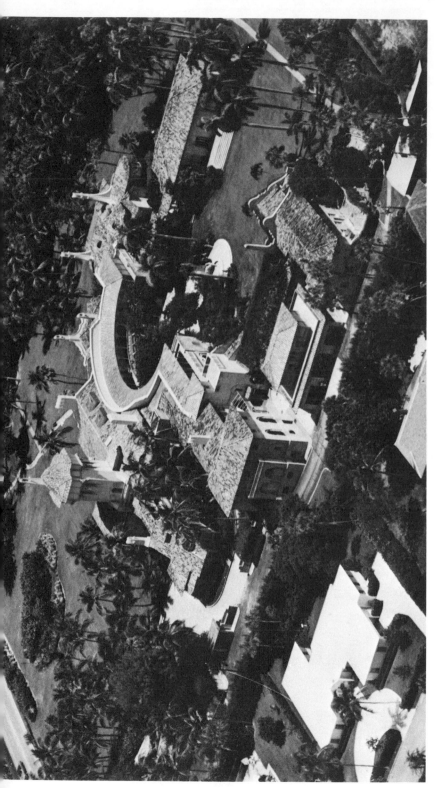

The current status of "Mar-A-Lago," the late Marjorie Merriweather Post's Moorish pleasure palace in Palm Beach, is that of federal government white elephant. When Mrs. Post died in 1973, she left the seventeen-acre estate to the National Park Service to maintain as a retreat for U.S. Presidents. But that idea was scrapped the moment it was discovered that the property was situated directly under an important airplane flight pattern, making it a perfect target for mad bombers. BERT & RICHARD MORGAN

"Ca' d' Zan"—John Ringling's imitation of the aristocratic Doge's Palace in Venice—metamorphosed into the plebeian Ringling Museum when it passed to the State of Florida upon Ringling's death. John Ringling, one of the five Ringling brothers who started their circus careers as lowly comics and musicians, claimed he would have been happier with "just a little bit of a place," but his wife, Mable, a former circus dancer, had other ideas. The result was this $2-million, thirty-room edifice on Sarasota Bay. MONKMEYER PRESS SERVICE

The Edsel B. Ford mansion on Lake St. Clair in Grosse Pointe Shores, Michigan, was off limits to the prying eyes of the public until its mistress, Eleanor Clay Ford (Mrs. Edsel B. Ford) departed this earth in 1976 at age eighty. This strong-willed daughter-in-law of Henry Ford, Sr., had spent her last years investigating how other great plutocrats' homes were being en-shrined and was determined that hers be among them. To that end, her will established a $15-million fund to maintain the mansion "for the benefit of the public. . . . I believe my residence is such a property that it should be preserved," she wrote. DETROIT NEWS

MANSION (*name and description*)	FAMOUS RICH OWNER	ITS DISPOSITION
"Ca' d' Zan" in Sarasota, Florida. This thirty-room mansion is an imitation of the Doge's Palace. In the Venetian vernacular, its name means "House of John."	John Ringling, one of the five brothers who went into the circus business, built this extravagant home to please his wife, Mable, a former circus dancer.	Ringling willed his home to the State of Florida. It is now called the Ringling Museum and is open to the public.
Edsel Ford mansion in Grosse Pointe Shores, Michigan. This sixty-room mansion and acreage lines the shore of Lake St. Clair.	When Eleanor Clay Ford (Mrs. Edsel B. Ford) died in 1976, her will provided $15 million to maintain her home "for the benefit of the public." This strong-willed daughter-in-law of Henry Ford, Sr., said further, "I believe my residence is such a property that it should be preserved."	After her heirs got first crack at the contents, what was left plus the house is being transformed into a historical and cultural center.

PUBLICITY CAN BE LETHAL: SEVEN REASONS WHY HIGH VISIBILITY AND WEALTH DON'T MIX

19 J. Paul Getty claimed the loss of privacy was the biggest liability of being rich. "One feels one is a target," he said. "You feel apologetic when you walk down the street. The nice thing about England [where Getty spent his latter years] is that people don't bother you much."

In the United States, the rich feel plenty bothered, beleaguered, and besmirched. The late billionaire John MacArthur told me, "Nobody enjoys being rich anymore because of all the people who are jealous and envious of you. They hate you, plain and simple."

Just how much the American upper class is on the defensive became clear when I wrote to selected wealth-holders asking for interviews for this book. I wrote to 107 people, introducing myself and declaring my journalistic intentions in as benign a manner as possible. I said the book was about "what people choose to do with their lives when they've got great wealth at their disposal" and "how being recognized as a wealthy individual has changed your life and the way other people view you." For the reluctant heirs and heiresses, I softened the blow even further. I wrote: "I realize that you are not accustomed to getting personal publicity and I expect you think people like me are one of the liabilities of wealth. However, let me assure you that I am interested neither in your financial affairs nor the details of your private life. Quite simply, I would like to elicit your personal reflections on the pleasures and problems of inheriting a prominent name and substantial sum of money."

This approach got me an audience, telephonically or in person, with 30 percent of the people I contacted. However, some got on the phone with me specifically to tell me the book was a rotten idea.

Ray Kroc, famous for his hamburgers and infamous for his outbursts, exploded: "That's a bad subject! That's a *very* bad subject! I don't want to be on any list. It doesn't mean anything anyway. I'm the same guy I was before I made my money. . . . Anybody can write a book, you know. I've got a book about me coming out in the fall. It's called *Grinding It Out*. It's about the important things—what you have to sacrifice to get ahead in this country. In America," he aphorized, "if you are successful, you are rich," then added in a lower voice ". . . unless you inherit a lot of money, of course." End of interview.

John S. Pillsbury, Jr., heir to the Minneapolis-based pastry fortune, said: "I suppose this book is really going to be rather gossipy although you imply in your letter it is going to be some kind of sociological treatise. Well, I can tell you in one word what I want—*anonymity*. Of course, here in Minneapolis, I carry a trade name so that is not entirely possible. On the other hand, I'm not Nelson Rockefeller who forfeited his right to privacy when he became a politician."

I made the observation that self-made men were generally more willing to be interviewed than people from older families. Pillsbury sniffed, "I'm glad you said that and not me."

Charles Francis Adams, a direct descendant of two U.S. Presidents and reigning member of one of Boston's first families, sent me a curt note which read: "Since I am not at a level that is currently accepted as 'wealthy,' I fear an interview would be fruitless."

Often my wealthy subjects put me through a screening process before agreeing to a meeting. Richard Mellon Scaife, one of Nixon's most extravagant boosters, required a résumé, copies of my articles, and a chat with his lawyer who explained that a new smear book about Paul Mellon had the Mellon clan on the defensive. "It is making it harder for journalists to get interviews right now," he said. "At the best of times, we have a real security problem."

Ed Daly of World Airways in Oakland, California, wanted a list of people I'd already met and called up John MacArthur in Palm Beach Shores, Florida, to check me out. MacArthur told him, "She's legit." MacArthur, in contrast, had relied on sheer instinct. When I had telephoned him to find out his reaction to my request, he claimed he'd never received any letter, forcing me to ad lib an introduction. My letter was in front of him the whole time. S. Prestley Blake, the Friendly Ice Cream man, asked me straight out, "Are you sure this whole project isn't just a way to find a rich husband?"

Paranoid? Yes, the rich are paranoid. One obscure Chicago Midas was right up front about his fear. "Although I'm flattered by your interest," he wrote, "I have not been pleased with the aftermath of some publicity that appeared in *FORTUNE* magazine listing my net worth erroneously. In general, I live in a small town and have children who go to the public schools. I am therefore not anxious for them to be set apart from their peers. The current kidnapping of the Hearst girl is another reason for wanting to avoid personal publicity. My children have felt threatened and I don't want this kind of publicity."

In some cities, the local media are surprisingly sheepish about piercing the veil of secrecy enshrouding their rich residents. Indeed, they help keep the veil intact. My fruitless attempts to gain access to certain newspaper libraries spotlighted this unfortunate fact. The assistant managing editor of the *Houston Post* put it the most bluntly: "We must protect our relationship with these people. We don't want to be a middle man."

Such complicity was most evident in smaller cities where a few established families predominate. Alienate them and newspaper advertising revenues will suddenly shrink—the rich work in mysterious ways—and the philanthropic faucet will abruptly dry up. In Winston-Salem, North Carolina, where the Reynolds tobacco kin reign supreme, the newspaper librarian advised me to forget about getting any photos of family members. Whenever the newspaper publishes any pictures they don't like, they either call up and ask that they not be run again or come into the office personally and fetch the negatives. The pictures never appear again. A journalist tried to do a biography of the family once but gave up when the whole town clammed up.

In larger cities where it's harder to keep the lid on the press, the rich use another tactic—they buy the media, keeping in mind the adage of the late A. J. Liebling: "Freedom of the press belongs to the man who owns one."

In those cities with a tradition of hard-hitting, no-sacred-cows investigative reporting, the crumbling clippings in the newspaper office morgues were a revelation to me. I discovered there was a

correlation between the rich people who had most adamantly refused to see me and those who have had the worst misadventures
because of their wealth. The evils ranged from petty burglaries
and constant hate mail to attempted murder and extortion. The
larger the fortune, the more monstrous the mayhem—all of which
explains why many rich folk hire press agents to keep their names
out of the newspaper and a person such as Doris Duke always
travels under an assumed name. "It avoids trouble," she says, "and
keeps people from paying any more attention to me than anyone
else."

Reason #1: IRS Audits

You've heard of clipping bureaus, those hole-in-the-wall outfits
that employ batteries of flunkies to scan newspapers and magazines
for references to specified subjects. Well, the Internal Revenue
Service has heard of them too. It retains clipping services. The subject it wants researched: rich Americans, especially stories that
highlight their estimated net worth or tangible assets (homes, cars,
yachts, expensive hobbies, art collections, etc.). The IRS finds this
information excellent grist for the audit mill and smart plutocrats
know it.

When *Playboy* magazine asked Malcolm Forbes, the owner/
publisher of *Forbes* magazine, to reveal how much he was worth,
he tried to brush off the query with an evasive, "Plenty! And hap-
pily, more so almost every day." When pressed, Forbes finally
admitted his reluctance to name a figure: "I really don't want to
be on the record saying that I'm worth some far-out amount because I can assure you the people who collect death taxes will
read this article and stick it into their dossiers. They'll come around
later and want to know why my estate lawyers claim I died practically penniless. It would leave me with what you might call a
credibility gap."

The war between the bottomless-bank-account crowd and the
tax authorities is as old as the republic. Before the government got
into the income-tax-assessment business in 1913, it focused its
scrutiny on the landed gentry. Those who owned property paid the
local government for the privilege each year. And even back in
1897, revenue agents were reading the newspapers for tip-offs.
That was the year that Mr. and Mrs. Bradley Martin, an ambitious

couple with more money than discretion, threw the "party of the century" at the Waldorf Hotel (cost: about $125,000) and had the assessment on their New York City real estate doubled as a result of the publicity. Incensed, they relocated to England to escape such "blatant ingratitude."

The IRS goes to incredible lengths to ensnare its prey. In 1968 and 1969, for example, it was concerned about fat cats who were stashing money away in numbered Swiss bank accounts. To locate account holders, the IRS enlisted the aid of another federal agency, the Post Office. The IRS obtained the postal meter numbers used by various Swiss banks by writing to those banks about opening accounts and noting the meter numbers on the replies. Next, it used high-speed copiers in New York's main post office to copy the fronts of all airmail letters arriving from Switzerland in plain envelopes. (Swiss bank account holders receive their monthly statements in plain brown envelopes, natch!) By comparing the copied meter numbers from the letters with those of the target Swiss banks, the IRS compiled its little list of several hundred probable U.S. income tax cheats. One hundred fifty of them got audited.

Reason #2: Irate Stockholders

When you were reading through the list of the country's richest self-made moguls, did you happen to notice how many of them head privately held companies? A lot. There's a reason.

Closely held companies are fiefdoms, usually controlled by one head honcho, or that person and his immediate family. The head honcho of a privately held company is a dictator. His decisions are law since there are no outside stockholders looking over his shoulder or Securities and Exchange Commission strictures to gum up the works as happens at publicly held corporations. The majority stockholder of a privately held company reigns supreme.

Given the obstinate, uncompromising character of your average fat-cat entrepreneur, private corporate ownership is the only way to go.

But although remaining a private corporate entity may rid a company's owner of stockholder interference, it does not circumvent all governmental watchdoggery. John MacArthur, sole owner of Bankers Life & Casualty Company of Chicago, constantly battled with government agents, for the gimmicky promotional ideas that attracted customers—running newspaper ads for mail-order insurance with dollar-a-month premiums, offering free gifts to new customers, direct-mail solicitations for new business—also invited investigations by numerous regulatory agencies. At various times, authorities alleged that MacArthur ignored reserve requirements in order to channel the company assets into the quest for fresh business, sold policies so broadly worded that they gave little or no coverage, misled consumers in advertisements, and used the mails to defraud. But despite the myriad investigations, lawsuits, and publicity campaigns against it, the MacArthur insurance machine steamrolled on, and MacArthur continued to maintain that no governmental meddling into his affairs could compare to the self-righteous, proprietary kind of interference he would have to brook from stockholders if his company went public. He'd take government agents over nosy stockholders any day.

S. Prestley Blake and his brother Curtis, the founders of the Friendly Ice Cream chain, didn't go public until 1968. Since then, they've been more careful about the kind of personal publicity they submit to, cognizant that one slip made by a journalist at a typewriter can cause them horrendous headaches. It's already happened at least once.

Sailing magazine did a big photo spread on Prestley's 105-foot schooner *America*, a replica of the famous yacht that captured the first America's Cup Race, and incorrectly identified the vessel as the property of the Friendly Ice Cream Co. When Prestley saw the error, he hit the roof. "I was really upset," he recalls. "I immediately wrote a letter to the editor setting the record straight. If the reporter had only taken the time to look up the *America* in *Lloyd's Register*, he would have seen it is owned by me personally. Instead, that seemingly small error could set the IRS to wondering why the Friendly Ice Cream Co. needs a yacht like that and get the shareholders thinking, 'Why should we support a plaything for Mr. Blake?' "

In 1978, dissident Ford Motor Co. shareholders stopped musing and filed a $50-million suit against Henry Ford II, the company's chairman, accusing him, among other things, of diverting corporate funds for his personal use. The complaint charged that Mr. Ford used company money to buy and furnish a duplex cooperative apartment in the Carlyle Hotel in New York City and to buy two other apartments in London intended for the exclusive use of him and his family. The suit was eventually settled for about $130,000, but that did not erase from Ford's mind the nagging question, "If I'd maintained a less flamboyant image, could I have avoided these accusations?" Maybe Ford will discover the answer as he retires into obscurity in 1980.

Reason #3: Annoying Solicitations

I agree with Ben Whitaker, author of *The Philanthropoids*:

"It is impossible not to feel some sympathy with the rich for that combination of snobbish dislike for the way they made their wealth plus the sycophantic importuning to which they are subject."

For most rich people, seldom a day goes by that they aren't on the receiving end of some kind of monetary appeal, veiled or straightforward. John D. Rockefeller, Sr., was "hunted like a wild animal" by petitioners at his office, his home, his church, on his walks, everywhere he went, according to Rockefeller's philanthropic advisor, the Rev. Frederick T. Gates. When Gates suggested golf as a way to relax and make some new friends, Rockefeller replied wearily, "I have made experiments, and nearly always the result is the same. Around the ninth hole out comes some proposition, charitable or financial." When Rockefeller played golf, he preferred a solitary game on his private course at Pocantico Hills.

The practice of hounding millionaires for handouts continues to this day. J. Paul Getty said he received up to 1,500 begging letters a month from absolute strangers, the total amount requested often exceeding $5 million. On one memorable day in the early 1960s, a single mail delivery brought requests for no less than $28 million! "I feel I'm a target," Getty confessed. "I worry about people recognizing me and I feel apologetic."

How many of these mail-order mendicants scored with Getty? None. "Naturally, I send nothing to these people," Getty said. "I make my contributions only to organized, legitimate charities. I've tried to make this clear in many press interviews and public statements. That's why I don't understand this continuing avalanche of personal appeals."

Of course, the continuing avalanche of personal publicity was Getty's main problem, but naively he never made the connection.

One crafty old codger who has managed to shut off the solicitation spigot is Ed Ball, the tightfisted administrator of the Alfred I. du Pont estate in Jacksonville, Florida. The letters trailed off years ago as the news got around about his response.

"People used to write in and tell me their desires to do this, that, and the other," Ball recalls. "A good many of them wanted me to finance their education and they'd pay me back in the sweet by and by. Well, I'd always tell 'em if they want an education, that's fine. Earn it!"

S. Prestley Blake has no quarrel with the *content* of the appeals he gets. It's the *form* they take that annoys him. "People aren't realistic," he complains. "I'm not going to send a person or organization I've never heard of a check for $5,000 out of the clear blue. Fund raisers should know something about me, about my interests, before they approach me cold turkey. I have to have some sort of special tie, some special reason for giving to a cause. If I had a child who was deaf, for instance, obviously I'd be an easy mark for a deaf institution."

Blake doesn't dismiss all noninstitutional sob stories outright, as do most of his peers. But he admits it's harder to get money out of him for an individual. He did lay out $500 once to put a needy local kid through summer camp, largely because the matter was handled delicately and personally. "I'd never have done it if the request came across my desk in a pile with all the others," Blake says. "In this case, an interested party made an appointment and came over to see me in my office. I didn't know him but he lived in my town so it gave substantiation to the story. I sent the kid to camp for the summer and never heard any more about it."

John MacArthur was another Midas inundated by letters from supplicants. I know. I wrote an article about him in 1977 that appeared in *Parade* magazine and I received more than fifty pleading missives to forward to him. They ranged from the worst kind of unctuous appeal to the bombastically threatening.

MacArthur claimed he never read the "bushel baskets full of letters—some very worthy, others on the ridiculous side"—that poured into his office daily. He had his clerical help weed through the pile and pick out anything that looked particularly interesting or legitimate. Then he and his wife would personally handle those. If they did give out any dough, MacArthur always demanded anonymity, contending that philanthropic good deeds were not something he cared to boast about. "Charitable giving is for three types," he maintained. "Those who believe in God, those who want to be remembered when they're gone, and those who want to impress somebody. I'm an atheist, I hope people forget me, and if I want to impress anyone, I'll paste the annual statement on the wall."

Public announcements about a rich person's generosity merely breed more requests for more money. Rockefeller, Sr.'s aides claimed that publicity about a bequest to a university or church would often bring as many as 50,000 appeals in the next month's mail. It also makes prices go up when a rich person does his or her own bidding at an auction or negotiates for secretarial or domestic help or buys something in a store. Bobo Rockefeller, the ex-wife of the late Winthrop Rockefeller, once observed that she could almost feel the prices rising when she walked into a store. Her name may have been her credit card but it also seemed to give merchants, doctors, and other professionals a license to steal.

Although most rich people don't like it, they get inured to being overcharged and find ways to shelter themselves from the out-stretched palms of strangers. But one thing many of them never get used to is having the empty pockets of friends turned inside out in front of their eyes.

"I have no trouble dealing with solicitations from strangers," says Herman Lay, the man who lent his name to a brand of potato chips. "Those appeals are impersonal and no matter how sad the story, I would never break down because once I did, I know I would be flooded with similar requests. Word gets around fast.

"The thing that bothers me is when friends are in trouble and need a loan. That's a tough one because you know when you make the loan that it probably won't be paid back."

Reason #4: Thefts and Insurance Problems

In the good old days, mansion burglars never bothered filching anything they couldn't fit in a suitcase. Massive antique furniture and oversized paintings didn't interest them. Too heavy and bulky to get out the window and too hard to fence once you did. Gems, silver pieces, and furs—those were the ideal booty of the burglar.

No longer. As art prices have escalated in the last decade so have thieves' desire to trade in that commodity. In 1978, the art market rang up a robust $5 billion in sales in the U.S. alone and

that same year, the art pilfering problem reached epidemic proportions. In this country, crooks made off with nearly $50 million
in stolen art, up an estimated 35 percent in two years. And in
Europe, police reported that the purloined-art market was thriving
and growing faster than any other form of larceny.

Wealthy individual collectors, museums, and art galleries are
all victims of this crime—on both the losing and receiving end.
In addition to having their proud possessions stolen, frequently
unsuspecting collectors end up buying a questionable work of art
without doing a thorough search of its pedigree. And when the
FBI shows up on their doorstep nine months later to cart off the
stolen object, they lose everything—the work itself and the money
they paid for it. They may also be asked to prove their innocence,
since police know that works of art are sometimes stolen to order
for connoisseurs. Museum curators and ethical gallery-owners are
less likely to get caught with stolen goods because they have become extremely cautious about their purchases.

Reflective of this new aesthetic crime wave is the boom in the
art insurance business. Art owners have gotten so wary that some
take out mini-term policies lasting only hours merely to cover the
transport of an art object from one place to another. For instance,
when Rembrandt's "Aristotle Contemplating the Bust of Homer"
was moved from the Parke-Bernet Galleries on Madison Avenue
in New York to the Metropolitan Museum of Art seven blocks
away, a short-term policy of $2.3 million went into effect for less
than an hour. A syndicate of seven insurers shared the risk.

Collectors who don't want trouble with their insurance company avoid all publicity about their artistic possessions and scrupu-
lously ban photographers from their premises. The smart owner,
however, has his own set of photos of all his important art objects
so if any are stolen, they can be identified more easily by the authorities. Unfortunately, most don't. Charles Koczka of U.S. Customs says that a typical theft report reads, "Missing: picture of cow
in pasture. Very valuable." With that kind of info to go on, it's
not surprising that only about 5 percent of all stolen artworks is
recovered.

With wealthy collectors paying out hefty amounts in insurance
premiums these days, it was only a matter of time before a few of
the shrewder owners figured out they might be able to make a
profit by getting robbed. That allegation was made against a Dallas

Robbery Roster

WHO got robbed	of WHAT	WHEN	WHERE	HOW
Joseph Hirshhorn	six paintings worth $500,000 (one Thomas Eakins, one Edward Hopper, two Winslow Homers, and two Adolphe Monticellis)	March 9, 1974	Greenwich, Connecticut, estate	The Hirshhorns were in Florida when the robbery took place. Three men were arrested for the theft and the paintings were recovered unharmed.
Mr. and Mrs. C. V. Whitney	$780,000 worth of jewelry	August 6, 1967	Saratoga Springs, New York, home	The cat burglars missed the $175,000 worth of gems Mrs. Whitney wore to dinner that night.
Clare Boothe Luce (Mrs. Henry Luce)	jewelry valued at $20,000–$35,000	November 1, 1948	the Luces' hotel suite at the Waldorf-Astoria	Burglary occurred while Mr. and Mrs. Luce were sleeping in an adjoining room.
Samuel I. Newhouse, Jr.	art works valued at $43,000, including $6,000 in silver flatware	June 1974	Newhouse's East Side Manhattan town house	The Newhouses were away for the weekend when the burglar forced his way into their home. The thief was not terribly knowledgeable about art. He overlooked Newhouse's most valuable works.

WHO got robbed	of WHAT	WHEN	WHERE	HOW
Mrs. Elizabeth Fondaras	$300,000 in necklaces, rings, and other jewelry	January 23, 1975	her ten-room cooperative apartment on Fifth Avenue in New York City	The four intruders confronted her as she returned home from a charity ball, blindfolded her, her maid, and the doorman and killed her barking French poodle as they ransacked the wall safe in her bedroom closet. The loss was not insured. This was the third time Mrs. Fondaras has been victimized by thieves.
Mr. and Mrs. Thomas Kempner and their houseguest, Angelika Lazansky	almost $2 million in jewelry	November 21, 1975	Park Avenue duplex in New York City	The thief got caught when he tried to ransom the rocks for $17,000 a few weeks later. His original asking price was $33,000 but Kempner, in a series of telephone conversations, got him to knock off $16,000.
Alyce Kaiser (Mrs. Henry J. Kaiser)	$500,000 diamond necklace	March 7, 1978	lobby of her United Nations Plaza apartment building	Mrs. Kaiser was returning home alone from a party for Elizabeth Taylor at Studio 54 when a man followed her across the lobby of her building. When they reached the elevator bank, he pulled a gun and yanked the necklace off her throat and fled. He didn't bother with the ermine coat and other expensive stones she was wearing that night.

WHO got robbed	of WHAT	WHEN	WHERE	HOW
John S. Samuels 3d	small-sized valuables (mostly jewelry and silverware) worth about $500,000	weekend of January 5, 1979	East Side town house in New York City	Thieves forced their way into the town house through a basement door and ransacked its contents while Samuels and his family were away for the weekend.
Mr. and Mrs. Joseph Lauder	$1 million in jewelry and $2,000 in cash	October 16, 1979	East Side Manhattan town house	One of the three thieves came to the side entrance around 5:30 P.M. He was dressed like a chauffeur and claimed he was there to pick up Mrs. Lauder (Estée Lauder of the cosmetics firm bearing her name). When he was challenged by the Lauders' real chauffeur, the bogus chauffeur was joined by his two armed accomplices. At gunpoint, they forced Mrs. Lauder to direct them to her valuables, then tied up Mrs. Lauder, the Lauders' chauffeur, two maids, and an unidentified man. Mr. Lauder returned a half hour later and called the police.
Mr. and Mrs. William S. Paley	$190,000 in jewelry	March 1963	North Hills, Long Island estate "Kiluna Farms"	The thieves entered the house by way of a second-floor sun deck outside Mrs. Paley's bedroom. The intruders were described as "expert safecrackers" because they opened the small floor safe in Mrs. Paley's powder room by dialing rather than blasting it open.

WHO got robbed	of WHAT	WHEN	WHERE	HOW
Winston F. C. Guest	art objects, jewelry, and silver worth $100,000	Thanksgiving week-end 1974	Old Westbury, Long Island estate	Three months after the burglary, a sharp-eyed official at Sotheby Parke Bernet Galleries spotted a number of the stolen items in a consignment of goods being readied for auction. The F.B.I. fingered a disgruntled former employee of the Guests as the perpetrator.
Mr. and Mrs. John H. Culbertson (Mrs. Culbertson is the daughter of the late Allan P. Kirby)	jewelry worth $80,000–$90,000; furs worth about $1,000; firearms worth $1,000, including a rare Remington over-and-under 12-gauge shotgun; $200 in cash; and assorted cameras and electronic equipment	January 19, 1961	their two-story brick colonial home in New Vernon, New Jersey	The heist took place between 11:10 A.M. and 3 P.M. while Mrs. Culbertson was out visiting. The burglars were thorough. They had ransacked every room. The Culbertsons had lived there for only five weeks. Their previous home burned down.
Mrs. John A. Roebling	at least $160,000 in jewelry and $4,000 in cash	November 1968	"Boulderwood," her Bernardsville, New Jersey, estate	Four men assaulted the gardener before forcing their way into the thirty-room house. At gunpoint, they tied up Mrs. Roebling, her sister, and the housekeeper and searched the house for valuables. After they left, the housekeeper eventually chewed her way through her bonds and called the police.

WHO got robbed	of WHAT	WHEN	WHERE	HOW
Mr. and Mrs. William Coxe Wright (She is the former Charlotte K. Dorrance, daughter of the Campbell Soup Co. founder)	$531,000 in jewelry, silver, furs, clothing, and cash	April 3, 1965	"Ravenscliff," their 300-acre estate in St. Davids, Pennsylvania	While the couple were in Bermuda celebrating his birthday, four armed, masked men entered through the solarium at 3:30 A.M., bound and gagged six servants and a watchman, using cords from the draperies. They rifled the house, then made their getaway in the watchman's car. A maid freed herself two hours later and called the police. A series of rewards was offered totaling $75,000. In 1957, two bronze eagles, each weighing 450 pounds and valued at $3,000, were stolen from the estate's gateposts. In 1964, a watchman surprised a burglar on the estate.
J. Patrick Lannan	—	February 1974	Palm Beach home, "Four Winds"	The attempt to filch some of Lannan's famous modern art collection was aborted when the butler confronted the two ski-masked men on the patio. They fled into the ocean in Lannan's front yard and their accomplice took off in a twenty-two-foot motorboat. Several hours later, the police apprehended the suspects but the butler couldn't identify them.

310

August A. Busch, Jr.	March 23, 1953	a horse and Sicilian donkey	"Grant's Farm," Busch's baronial homestead near St. Louis	Five boys, ages eight through twelve, kept the Busch's stable manager at bay with a loaded pistol as they attempted to make off with the animals. The donkey refused to cooperate, however, and the group managed to cover only a half mile in two hours. Police released them in the custody of their parents.
William Herbert Hunt (son of H. L. Hunt)	January 1956	$15,000 in cash	Hunt's Dallas home	The break-in occurred while the Hunts were away during the Christmas holidays. The money—all in $100 denominations—was pilfered from a chest in a walk-in bedroom closet. A single $1,000 bill was left behind as well as the pistol lying on top of the money. Two weeks after the burglary, the money was returned in the mail.
Julian Hammer (son of Armand Hammer)	October 1974	destroyed property (i.e., slashed paintings, overturned furniture, scrawled on the walls, and scattered clothing about)	Pacific Palisades, California, home	Hammer and his daughter returned home to find a twenty-one-year-old man and his female accomplice—a former Hammer housekeeper—ransacking the place for loot. The intruder grabbed Hammer and held one of Hammer's own guns to his head. Meanwhile, Casey Hammer ran to a neighbor's home and called the police. After a tense few hours, the gunman was talked into surrendering and the couple was booked on suspicion of armed robbery.

widow by her insurance company, Lloyd's of London. In a civil suit Lloyd's contended that the art, antiques, jewelry, and cash taken from the woman's home was actually removed with her consent as part of a gigantic swindle. Lloyd's refused to pay a cent of the claim, alleging the break-in was staged to help cover outstanding debts.

Reason #5: Extortion Attempts

On the lethality scale, extortion falls somewhere between annoying solicitations and outright kidnapping. The extortion attempts on record against the rich are generally the ones that haven't worked because the extortionist had no real information to sell or relied on threats that were rebuffed. We'll never know about extortion and blackmail schemes that *have* worked.

One of the most brazen and hard-working blackmailers in the early part of this century was the infamous Colonel William D'Alton Mann, the editor of a weekly scandal sheet called *Town Topics*. It chronicled the sordid transgressions of staid Victorian Knickerbocracy, sins that ran the gamut from sexual philandering to gambling losses, cheating at cards, social *faux pas*, and High Society feuds. Mann paid an unofficial battery of stringers for his information. His backstairs informants included disgruntled butlers, valets, maids, coachmen, and cooks in the best homes as well as bellhops, chambermaids, and desk clerks from hotels all over town.

But the money Mann paid out for information was nothing compared to the money he took in for silence. Mann had an instinct for sizing up people's weaknesses and strengths and could estimate within a few dollars exactly how much an embarrassing piece of information would be worth to the subject in question. His clientele consisted of the most notable figures of the day, among them William Kissam Vanderbilt who was $25,000 poorer once Mann got through with him; William C. Whitney who paid to the tune of $10,000; Thomas Fortune Ryan, also $10,000; Collis P. Huntington, $5,000; and even the esteemed J. P. Morgan, $2,500.

The following abortive extortion attempts are just a sample dating from the last twenty-five years. The victims, in every case, were very wealthy people:

  • In 1957, a man who had been posing as an heir to the Coors beer fortune for twenty years was finally nabbed by the FBI in Cheyenne, Wyoming. The fifty-seven-year-old Adolph Hecker had added the middle name "Coors" to his own and had worked an elaborate confidence game on unsuspecting victims. He would solicit money from strangers by promising them he would reward them richly once he came into his huge inheritance from the Coors family mother lode. The money advanced him was being used to pay his legal expenses in his fight to claim what was rightfully his. A real Coors scion, Adolph Coors III, said he had never heard of Hecker.

• John Peipert, age sixty-five, signed his extortion notes "Viet Cong guerrilla." The receiver was Jack Eckerd, the Tampa drugstore tycoon and two-time Florida gubernatorial candidate. The letters threatened violence against Eckerd, his family, some of his stores, employees, and customers if a $240,000 "loan" was not forthcoming. FBI agents finally nailed Peipert after a high-speed car chase around midnight on May 7, 1973.

• Mr. and Mrs. Randolph A. Hearst, the parents of the kidnapped Patty Hearst, during those trying months of 1974 and 1975 also had to deal with bogus kidnappers. In September 1974, Nile D. Marx, an out-of-work taxicab driver from Indiana, was convicted of trying to extort $100,000 from the Hearsts and sentenced to from five years to life in prison. His wife, Shirley Ann, was an alleged accomplice in the crime of impersonating the real kidnappers of Patty Hearst.

A year later Richard Kravanja, a thirty-five-year-old Brooklyn, Ohio, native, pleaded guilty to attempting to extort $250,000 from the Hearsts, again posing as their daughter's captor. He was sentenced to three years' imprisonment.

Reason #6: Kidnapping

It may just be that 1974 will go down in history as the Year of the Kidnapper. The spectacular snatching of Patricia Campbell Hearst, granddaughter of the yellow-journalism king William Randolph Hearst, in February of that year pried the lid off Pandora's Box. Within seven weeks after Ms. Hearst's abduction in California, no fewer than twelve other kidnappings had occurred—plus countless threats of the same.

The rash of kidnaps underscored something that criminal psychologists have contended all along: publicity about kidnapping and extortion breeds more kidnapping and extortion. According to Dr. David Hubbard, there are at least a million people in the United States who are capable of committing this wrenching act. Hubbard says, "These people have complex emotional problems and imaginations. They're essentially losers or failures whose personal lives are in such despair that they'll do anything to attract a great deal of attention. All they need is to be exposed to the germ of the idea 'kidnapping' and they become affected. This crime is as contagious as the flu."

A similar opinion is expressed by Dr. Domeena Renshaw, professor of psychiatry at Chicago's Loyola Medical School: "The simplest explanation for the rash of kidnappings is mimicry. These people are searching for attention and they get it in the headlines of newspapers and the limelight of television."

Los Angeles psychiatrist Dr. Barbra Beavens claims, "Kidnappers feel they've achieved a kind of social status that separates them from ordinary criminals"—a notion that conflicts with views expressed by a number of convicts in the slammer for other crimes. Kidnappers are universally treated as vermin by other criminals as well as the general public. One ex-convict explained why:

"Kidnapping is the 'amateur night' of crime. I mean, you rob a store or beat somebody up, you might not make everybody happy, but at least people know what you're doing and why you're doing it. The kidnapper is different. He's got to be desperate and sick to start with, and that makes him vulnerable. Then he puts himself in the worst heat there is, with the whole country looking for him and people figuring that they'll be heroes if they shoot him. Even a genius couldn't find a way out."

A genius wouldn't try it because he'd be smart enough to calculate the odds—which are against any kidnapper's succeeding. Modern technology is such that it becomes easier and easier every day for police to detect such things as fingerprints on ransom notes or to trace phone calls from telephone booths or to analyze voices from telephone tape recordings. Then there's the almost insoluble problem for the kidnapper of claiming the ransom money without walking into a trap. Even if he negotiates that one, the money in all likelihood is "hot" and laundering it may net him less than 10 cents on the dollar. It may even be treated with a substance that makes it radioactive, a dead giveaway when passed over Geiger counters. According to one loan shark experienced in these matters, "The only safe thing you can do with ransom money is eat it."

The FBI says that in 95 percent of the kidnapping cases it's handled throughout the years, the victims have been returned, the kidnappers arrested, and most of the ransom retrieved. And in 1974—the year of the big snatch—there were ninety-six convictions of kidnappers in federal courts with some of the accused drawing life sentences for their heinous misdeeds.

What were the rich—the potential prey—doing in 1973 through 1975 while all these seizures were occurring? Hiring bodyguards, buying Doberman pinschers, and installing expensive alarm systems in their homes, just to name three things. Such security-agency firms as Pinkerton's and Burns International Services reported being flooded with inquiries about personal-protection measures during this period. And the president of Guardsmark, Inc., a Memphis-based company, said many wealthy families were specifically requesting the services of female agents who could pose as their children's governess or nursemaid.

For a while, having one's own bodyguard became such an "in" status symbol that a Palm Beach charity offered a week's personal protection as first prize in a raffle. And for the first time in their flamboyant lives, some socialites were actually ducking reporters in their efforts to lay low. Bonnie Swearingen, the wife of Standard Oil of Indiana's chairman, claimed she contacted all the society editors in Chicago, where the couple lives, and asked them *please* to stop running her photograph. "I just think that a low profile is best in times like these," she told a *Wall Street Journal* reporter.

The rampant paranoia also made ransom insurance a popular item. Generally, kidnap policies are individually written, tailored to the precise needs of the fortune-holder. Most of this insurance is carried by corporations because they can deduct the outrageously high premiums—$20,000 to $250,000 a year for coverage of $1 million to $20 million in ransom demands—as a business expense and cover a number of board members and senior executives on the same policy. Lloyd's of London has offered this type of insurance for years, but by 1974 a number of American insurers had also gotten into the act. The American Underwriters Corporation of Detroit even ran newspaper ads in upscale communities for such policies, referring to kidnapping euphemistically as "this unfortunate reality of our times"; while the California Union Insurance Co. was marketing a policy that paid for rewards for information leading to the arrest and conviction of kidnappers. Most insurance companies would not reveal any details about their kidnapping policies, except to say that the insurance was cancelable if any of the insured parties blabbed about it.

But even an uninsured plutocrat who got snatched had an out. In 1974, at the peak of the kidnapping spree, the IRS quietly announced that ransom payments could be claimed as income tax deductions. Kidnap ransoms were considered theft losses and could be claimed as such on the regular schedule of itemized deductions. However, the IRS also made it plain that as a casualty loss, the first $100 of the ransom couldn't be deducted and that insurance reimbursements, if there were any, must be subtracted from the total sum.

Holding fat cats for ransom is a relatively modern phenomenon in American history. In a tome called *Ransom Kidnapping in America*, Ernest Kahlar Alix says that the crime was first committed in 1874 but did not become a common occurrence until the World War I era, 1912–1917. After that, it went through various periods of dormancy and resurgence, reaching a climax in the early 1930s.

The mere mention of the word "kidnapping" elicits a range of responses from its most likely victims—the rich. George H. Weyerhaeuser, who was held captive for a week as a child, maintains a philosophical attitude, probably figuring fate would never have the audacity to strike his family twice. "You live a thousand deaths if you worry constantly about the things that might befall your children," he told a reporter in 1965. "My own motto has been 'trust your hopes and not your fears.' "

When I asked several wealthy people how they felt about kidnapping during the height of the craze in 1974, their answers weren't as sanguine. The one exception was the optimistic Atlanta tycoon, J. B. Fuqua. He said, "I don't think that's a real problem. It runs in cycles. A new cycle has just been nipped in the bud." The date of the interview was July 23, 1974.

Louie Roussel, the New Orleans oil ace and financier, exploded: "I want to tell you somethin'. I'm scared of nothin', not even the devil himself . . . so I mean, ah . . . I don't worry about that.

If ever anything would happen to me, you can bet it's going to be a damned good scrap, I can tell you that much."

Recent Kidnappings of the Very Rich

1972: Greek authorities arrested two gangs of kidnappers— one Greek, the other West German—on charges of plotting to seize *John F. Kennedy, Jr.*, the stepson of shipping magnate Aristotle Onassis, and hold him for ransom.

1972: Dallas socialite *Amanda Mayhew Dealey* (Mrs. Joe Dealey, Jr.), the daughter-in-law of the president of the *Dallas Morning News*, was freed by her kidnappers after her family paid $250,000 in ransom. The abductors were counting their take when police arrived at their apartment to arrest them.

1973: *J. Paul Getty III*, the adolescent grandson of the oil billionaire, was kept in captivity in Europe for nearly six months while his abductors negotiated a $2.9-million ransom. To strengthen their negotiating position, Getty's captors cut off his right ear—an old Calabrian bandit custom—and mailed it to a newspaper in Rome. Italian authorities later arrested eight members of a Mafia-style gang and charged them with the crime. Two were convicted and given jail terms of sixteen and eight years.

1974: In the kidnapping of the decade, publishing heiress *Patty Hearst* was seized by the radical Symbionese Liberation Army and held captive for more than a year, during which time she allegedly embraced a new *persona*, that of "urban guerrilla." Whether she had made common cause with her abductors out of fear or political convictions became a major issue in her trial for bank robbery. She was found guilty and served time in prison before receiving a pardon from no less than President Gerald Ford.

317

1974: A kidnapping threat against "all children of Kennedy blood"—which turned out to be a false alarm—resulted in six of Robert Kennedy's eleven children and the son of Patricia Kennedy Lawford being protected by the Secret Service for about a week. Muckraker Jack Anderson estimated the fiasco—"based upon a third-hand tip from a police informant in the Boston area"—cost the taxpayers about $126,000.

1975: After the Seagrams liquor company family paid out the $2.3-million ransom for the release of twenty-one-year-old *Samuel Bronfman 2d,* it didn't take police long to arrest a former New York City fireman and a limousine-service operator and charge them with the crime. The two countered by claiming the heir himself had engineered the abduction. That story didn't wash and both were convicted and sentenced to lengthy terms in jail.

Reason #7: Sabotage and Murder Attempts

Walking around sporting a name such as "Rockefeller" is downright dangerous. The original Rockefeller knew it and got so paranoid and remote in his later years that even his only son took to communicating with him by interoffice memos. When the old man acquired his 4,180-acre estate at Pocantico Hills, he'd wanted to ring it with barbed wire, but Rockefeller, Jr., finally prevailed upon him to settle for a mighty iron fence. And then the old man wondered why the locals in Tarrytown could never get used to calling him "Neighbor John," his preferred form of address.

Rockefeller, Sr.'s great-grandchildren feel equally hounded, if not more so. At the 1974 annual "cousins meeting," personal security was topic A of discussion. Sure enough, a year later, powerful bombs blasted two branches of the Rockefeller-controlled Chase Manhattan Bank in Puerto Rico. Local police said it was an apparent protest against the vacation visit of then-U.S. Vice President Nelson Rockefeller, who was staying with his family at the Dorado Beach Hotel, thirty-five miles away from the sites of the explosions. Asked for a comment, Nelson shrugged, "What can I do about it? Go and help clean up the broken windows?"

Henry J. Kaiser's nemesis also missed his mark when he tried to sabotage two high-powered racing speedboats owned by the Oakland industrialist. The tampering was discovered by Kaiser's aides a half hour before Kaiser himself was to have piloted one of the 160-mile-an-hour craft in the 1952 Lake Tahoe Gold Cup Race. A local constable, Harry Johanssen, ventured that the sawed propeller shaft, stuffed carburetor and gasoline-soaked hull were the work of a crank—probably somebody angry about all the noise the Kaiser boats had been making in preparation for the races. "There have been many complaints from residents about the noise," Johanssen said. "Some people have been getting pretty cranky."

Henry J. couldn't have disagreed more. "This was a murderous attempt on my life," possibly by Communists, Kaiser declared. "Pouring gasoline in a boat is just plain, cold murder as far as I'm concerned."

No one was hurt in the incident but other members of the ruling class haven't been as lucky. Donald Newhouse, scion of the Newhouse newspaper clan, was filing a key at his basement workbench in Portland, Oregon, the night of October 16, 1960, when a shot tore through the window and pierced his lower right hip and thigh. When his wife found him, collapsed and bleeding, he was muttering, "I don't know how it could have happened." Police figured it out quickly enough when Newhouse told them about the labor union turmoil at *The Oregonian* where he was production manager; and about the threat hurled at him by a picket outside the newspaper's office: "You're going to get it," the man had sneered. "You'll go to heaven soon." Newhouse was the chief architect of a plan that enabled the newspaper to continue publishing using scab labor after the company had been struck eleven months earlier.

Mr. and Mrs. Harry Helmsley also lived to tell the tale about a gas-masked intruder of indeterminate gender who stabbed them both in their Palm Beach Towers penthouse apartment one terrifying night in November 1973.

"We were awakened by someone in our bedroom leaning over

my wife," he said. Mrs. Helmsley started screaming and the couple managed to knock the intruder down. "When we chased her or him—I'm not sure whether it was a man or woman—we got stabbed. My wife got stabbed in the chest and I got stabbed in the arm. The person fled and I called the switchboard, and the girl got me an ambulance."

Nothing had been stolen from the apartment, and there was no indication of forced entry. Police later found a twelve-inch knife from the Helmsleys' kitchen on the grounds outside the luxurious building and closed the investigation two months later after they'd turned up neither a motive nor a suspect.

Peter Hilton, the thirty-eight-year-old nephew of hotelier Conrad Hilton, wasn't as fortunate. William Freeman, a man whom Hilton had testified against in a shoplifting case, barged into the super-market where Hilton was working as a cashier in April 1974 and pumped five successive bullets into the heir in full view of more than a dozen shoppers. Freeman immediately surrendered himself to a store security guard, and Hilton was pronounced dead on arrival at South Miami Hospital.

How the Rich Maintain a Low Profile

When a wealthy person takes out an insurance policy on his multi-million-dollar collection of old masters or kidnap insurance to cover ransom demands, the insurance company that writes the policy may make a few demands of its own. Especially in the case of kidnap coverage, the insurer may insist that the insured main-tains an "invisible" profile.

How is that done? An identity blackout means an erasure of all clues that could help a potential burglar or body snatcher seize his booty. It calls for de-listing from the local telephone book; the uprooting of signs on the lawn; the disappearancce of names— both family surnames and estate monikers—from the mailbox, gatepost, or portico; and the removal of gold-plated monograms and initials from the doors and license plates of cars and the sterns of yachts. It also means a little less communication with the local society editor and no more gossipy little items about the family's travel and entertainment plans in the newspaper. The less the public knows about the insured the better.

In Palm Beach, where affluence is a way of life, the city fathers laid out the streets with the security problem uppermost in their minds. Cul-de-sacs and circles were used profusely in the town's design to cut down on through traffic. And many residents went one step farther by growing twelve- and fifteen-foot high hedges that completely encircle their property. In Palm Beach, they don't bother with "No Trespassing" signs. It's understood.

About thirty miles up Route 1 in Hobe Sound—where the quiet WASP money lives—thick tropical foliage serves as a coverall. Indeed, a drive down the main road of Jupiter Island might leave you thinking the place has yet to be discovered by modern man. In 1970, the local workmen and mailmen finally protested. At their insistence, the likes of the Harrimans, Searles, and Paysons finally agreed to post either their names or house numbers in the driveway.

TAX WRANGLES OF THE RICH

20 Audits are the bane of every taxpayer's existence. But according to several studies, traditionally they've been considerably more worrisome for the middle class than for the rich.

In 1974, two *Philadelphia Inquirer* reporters analyzed the tax treatment of the rich, the *bourgeoisie*, and the poor. Their conclusion: The IRS attempts to squeeze the last penny out of minor miscreants while it often settles with plutocrats for a fraction of the amount in dispute. In a typical case, the failure of a wealthy person to pay $200,000 in taxes might be tied up in the courts for five years and result in a compromise payment of $80,000. But a $15,000-a-year wage slave would probably lose the argument over $500 more in taxes while he's sitting at the auditor's desk and have to pay up within the next year. The *Inquirer* reporters also claimed that the tax laws were so favorable to the rich that they actually encouraged upper-class nonpayment.

Around the same time, a federally sponsored study of the tax system revealed a similar disparity. The study found relatively more audits were made on citizens in lower income brackets than on those in higher; and that the treatment of the American taxpayer by the IRS was frequently "whimsical, inconsistent, unpredictable and highly personal." For example, in 1974 the study reported that 3.6 percent of the returns in the low-income group with itemized deductions were examined while only 2.4 percent of those in the $10,000 to $50,000 group were subject to audits.

Finally, the study disclosed that even when the affluent are audited, the larger the IRS's initial claim against the alleged

evader, the smaller the percentage of the assessment that is ulti-
mately recovered. The reason was the intervention of lawyers.
Wealthy taxpayers let batteries of attorneys fight their tax battles.
The rest of us usually go it alone.

How true are all these assertions? Very true, if my own informal case study of fifteen upper-tax-bracket millionaires is representative. Using this sample, I contend fat cats have won their
battles with the tax authorities during the last fifty years far more
frequently than they have lost them. And when they do lose, the
blow is softened because U-evaders seldom end up paying the
full amount of the initial IRS claim.

Take the case of Andrew Mellon, the Pittsburgh industrialist
and U.S. Secretary of the Treasury under Harding, Coolidge, and
Hoover. In 1934, after he'd returned to private life, Mellon's
1931 income tax return came under scrutiny. The Treasury Department's Internal Revenue arm was seeking to recover approximately $3 million in tax, interest, and penalties. One of the points
of contention was the allowable deductions for the enormously
valuable paintings Mellon had given to the tax-exempt A. W.
Mellon Charitable and Educational Trust.

Mellon denounced the IRS's vigilance as "political persecution"
—it was true that FDR's New Dealers held Mellon in low repute—
and fought the claim through all the available appeals procedures.
He never seemed concerned about the outcome, however, and once
remarked that the series of exhaustive hearings on the matter had
their positive aspects. "It gives me lots of time to think about other
things," he told a reporter. Sure enough, Mellon was exonerated
of the tax charges four months after he died in 1937.

Lessing J. Rosenwald, the Kirby family, John Olin, and John
Cuneo fared almost as well when their tax returns were declared
deficient by thousands of dollars. After a protracted controversy
over his 1937 return, Sears Roebuck heir Rosenwald was awarded
$28,173.29 in refunds and $4,694.69 in credits against subsequent
taxes. The nit-picking Treasury Department still said he owed a
penny but didn't press him for it.

When the two nieces of financier Allan P. Kirby won a $2.6-
million tax refund in 1957, the press hailed it as perhaps the largest
rebate individual claimants ever got out of the government. The dispute concerned the evaluation of certain securities held by the estate
of the two women's father who had died in 1945.

In 1962, Mr. and Mrs. John M. Olin of Alton, Illinois, and Olin Mathieson lineage, agreed to pay $12,101 to settle the argument over their 1957 and 1958 taxes. The amount was substantially less than the $45,797 the government originally demanded. And in 1964, John Cuneo boasted to a U.S. Tax Court that he never sought outside tax counsel for his complex personal and corporate affairs. He was countering an IRS charge that he had practiced "very sophisticated tax avoidance planning" in lowering his tax bill by $7,963,091 for the years 1954–1957. A year later, the Tax Court sustained most of Cuneo's deductions and the Chicago printing magnate had to ante up only another $33,343.

On the other hand, a few big fortune-holders have gotten trounced. In 1938, Barbara Hutton—then known as Countess Haugwitz-Reventlow—agreed to pay another $20,068 in back taxes for the year 1933 to settle a deficiency claim of $25,108. And Baltimore oilman Jacob Blaustein lost his tax appeals and eventually had to transfer $1,145,000 from his coffers into those of the IRS. But do not weep for Blaustein. He had the use of that sum for the nine years it took to settle the case.

With more sophisticated computer programming, the IRS now maintains that the disparate tax treatment of the rich and the poor no longer exists in this country. By 1979, the IRS was claiming that taxpayers with less than $10,000 in adjusted gross income and who don't itemize, stand only a 1-in-200 chance of being called down to their local tax office for an unpleasant little chat. In contrast, a citizen with $50,000+ in income who itemizes, stands a risk of 1 out of 10—and possibly even higher if his or her deductions and sources of income are unusually complicated. In the case of rich taxpayers, what an eagle-eyed IRS agent examines are the gray areas, such things as hidden gains from the sales of stock or property; and the failure to report income from tax shelters that are no longer considered tax shelters because of a change in the law.

Of course, there's another far more insidious and inequitable way influential private citizens get around the tax laws. They arrange to have a special provision inserted into a tax bill, a very special little loophole that applies only to them. If you've never heard of this practice before, don't be surprised. You aren't supposed to hear about these individualized exemptions. When the public does, it's usually because some Congressman or Senator is being asked to justify his involvement in the scheme, for preferential language can't make its way into a tax bill unless somebody in a high place puts it there.

Senator John J. Williams, the Delaware Republican, was accused of slipping a bill through Congress in 1964 that permitted a special tax deduction for the loss of Irénée du Pont's $2-million Cuban estate "Xanadu." The estate had been expropriated by the Castro government in 1961 and turned into a nautical school for boys. H. Ross Perot, the Texas superpatriot, is another tycoon fingered for getting a special tax benefit included in a 1975 revenue bill. For that one, Georgia Democrat Phil Landrum plus nine other members of the Ways and Means Committee took the rap.

The practice is as old as the sixteenth amendment to the U.S. Constitution. In 1976, *The New York Times* exposed it in a front-page article headlined, "TAX BREAKS FOR THE FEW HINGE ON ACCESS TO POWER." The article named names and gave facts and figures, contending that every big tax bill contains a number of narrowly drawn provisions designed to benefit a small group of people or companies—what Senator Edward M. Kennedy, Democrat of Massachusetts, calls "one-eyed, bearded, man-with-a-limp" provisions. Kennedy, the son of one of the Prohibition era's most infamous wheeler-dealers, was also quoted as saying, "The method by which these special interest provisions make their way into tax legislation is a scandal and a disgrace, an embarrassment to the Finance Committee and every member of the Senate."

Do not come away from this essay with the mistaken idea that every tycoon with $50 million in his pocket knows how to pull the right strings to make one of these provisions materialize. Not true. It's clear that New Orleans wildcatter Louie Roussel doesn't know how or his opinion of the IRS and other federal agencies would be far less negative. He contends that federal bureaus and bureaucrats have gone out of their way to make his life miserable for a number of years now.

"Don't get me wrong," he said to me. "I don't mind payin' taxes because I love this country. But I want to tell you one thing: When an individual can come in and announce, 'I don't like the way you have this. I want you to change this and change that. And we're gonna assess you X numbers of dollars'—all this poppycock. It's a bad tax system when it works that way. It's just to try to make people scared that they did somethin' wrong. Now, me. I'm not a compromiser. When they start that on me, I fight it all the way."

Artful Dodger Awards (for tax avoidance)

Every informed tax lawyer knows of individuals with very high incomes whose actual tax payments are on the same level as those of restaurant employees or mechanics or others who service their affluent style of life.

—Stanley S. Surrey, former Assistant
U.S. Treasury Secretary for tax policy

How about the millionaires who don't pay any taxes at all? Every year, this country produces a passel of them. For obvious reasons, they would rather *not* see their names in the newspapers for accomplishing such a feat, and the Treasury Department meekly obliges.

However, the Treasury Department does release statistics on the number of top-drawer taxpayers who escape the ubiquitous web of federal taxation each year. Treasury officials call it the "zero taxpayers' list."

The number of tax shirkers has remained relatively steady each year. This is happening despite the fact that our esteemed federal lawmakers actually passed legislation in 1969 (effective 1970) designed to eliminate the possibility of zero federal taxes for wealthy individuals. Called the "minimum tax law," it supposedly guaranteed that virtually everyone with high income would pay some federal tax, even if it were a negligible amount. Clearly, the law contained the usual loopholes because several hundred rich people still slipped through unscathed by the tax collector in subsequent years.

How do they do it?

First of all, the source of most rich people's income is capital gains which are taxed at a lower rate than income from salaries and wages. But why, you may ask, should some rich heir, who has probably never earned a dime in his life, be taxed less for making a profit on his appreciated property than the guy who works like crazy just to bring home a $15,000 salary each year? That is just one of the many conflicts and anomalies inherent in our tax system. Here are some others: How about the buyer of a municipal bond (most can only be purchased in huge denominations placing them off limits to the middle-class investor) who earns dividends on it but pays no tax while the holder of a $500 United States savings bond pays all the way? Or the high-class speculator in the stock market who gets a reduced rate on his winnings, while the low-life horse-track bettor pays full rate on his? Or the apartment tenant who pays in his rent his portion of the real-estate taxes and interest on the building's mortgage while the landlord is the one who takes the deduction on his tax return.

Sure, it's unfair. Even the defenders of the system admit that. According to Mr. Surrey, their arguments in defense of provisions favoring wealthy individuals and corporations are never framed in terms of proper tax structure or tax equity. They're stated in terms of incentives and assistance for this or that industry or activity or hardship—in short, the preservation of the *status quo*.

As to the exact mechanics of 100 percent tax avoidance, the following devices, utilized in various creative combinations, are the most common:

- *borrowing to the hilt "for investment purposes" then deducting the huge interest payments on the loans.* This one was the specialty of the late and unlamented Howard Hughes.

- *plunking all one's income into municipal bonds and living off the tax-free dividends.* The late Mrs. Horace Dodge, the auto maker's widow, perfected this art.

- *the old oil-depletion-allowance ploy favored by Southwestern oil wildcatters.* The notorious conservative H. L. Hunt and his son Nelson Bunker Hunt have employed this one and catapulted themselves onto the "zero taxpayers' list" for several years running.

- *applying against one's U.S. tax liability the enormous tax credits one gets for paying taxes to foreign governments.* Rich people with homes dotting the globe love this one.

- *the "unlimited charitable deductions" provision, entitling those extremely generous Americans who gave away more*

than 90 percent of their gross adjusted income to charity
for at least eight of the ten previous years to deduct all
such contributions "without limit" in succeeding years.

That last device is enough to make a philanthropist out of Silas
Marner. It made one out of Nelson Rockefeller who paid zero
taxes for several years via this unlimited-deduction privilege. His
brother, John D. Rockefeller 3d, eschewed the opportunity, however, implying it was immoral.

"I believe all individuals who are able should pay some reasonable tax, including those who have become entitled to the unlimited-deduction privilege," he told the House Ways and Means
Committee during tax-reform hearings in 1969. "In my own
case," he said, "although I have qualified for the unlimited-deduction privilege during every year since 1961, I have deliberately
paid a tax of between 5 percent and 10 percent of my adjusted
gross income each of those years."

Committeemen apparently agreed with him. In 1973, Congress
voted to close this loophole once and for all. Today, no one—
rich or poor—can deduct more than 30 percent to 50 percent
for charitable contributions.

Seeking Shelter: The Five Favorite Tax Dodges of the Filthy Rich

Did you know that our government, by way of the tax system,
subsidizes the rich?

It does this through a series of special tax benefits written into
the U.S. tax code. Because of the nature of these benefits, only
the affluent can make use of them when they itemize on their
tax returns.[1]

There are various euphemisms for these special benefits. The
U.S. Treasury Department prefers to obscure the issue as much
as possible with the phrase "tax expenditures." "Tax subsidies"
is the term dearest to the hearts of crusading tax-reformers while
"tax shelters" is bandied about by tax attorneys and accountants.
But perhaps the word that describes it best, a word we're all
familiar with, is just plain "loopholes."

It is by way of these loopholes that some public-be-damned
plutocrats avoid paying any taxes whatsoever some years. Although a multimillionaire's net worth may be in the $500-million

U.S. TAX SHIRKERS [1]

Year	Number of Americans with adjusted gross incomes of more than $100,000 who paid no federal taxes	Number of Americans with adjusted gross incomes of more than $200,000 who paid no federal taxes	Number of Americans with adjusted gross incomes of more than $1 million who paid no federal taxes
1958	81	n.a.[2]	8
1966	367	n.a.	18
1967	399	n.a.	23
1969	n.a.	300	56[3]
1971	276	112	n.a.
1972	402	108	6
1973	n.a.	164	7
1974	n.a.	244	5
1975	n.a.	230	n.a.

[1] otherwise known as the "zero taxpayers' list"
[2] not available
[3] The only other tax bracket with a higher percentage of nontaxpayers in 1969 was those under $5,000.

range, he may show up in Internal Revenue statistics as a low-income individual because his *taxable* income—which, of course, is only a fraction of his actual personal net worth—has been skillfully reduced to rock-bottom level by the clever manipulation of tax-expenditure benefits on his tax returns.

In 1974, the House Ways and Means Committee finally got curious about the extent to which well-heeled Americans were actually benefitting from loopholes and commissioned a study of the tax returns of twenty high-income individuals. The examination showed clearly the injustice of our tax laws. While a few of the twenty paid very high taxes because they did not make excessive use of deductions and exclusions, most paid very low taxes and two paid no tax at all on incomes of more than $500,000. One person tried valiantly to escape all tax by claiming $900,000 in tax-shelter losses; and another paid only $25,000 in tax, even though his income exceeded $2 million. The twenty returns demonstrated a widespread use of capital-gains deductions, charitable donations, gifts of appreciated property to nonprofit institutions, tax shelters, etc.

What follows is a survey of the five favorite loopholes that millionaires crawl through every April 15.

Tax Dodge #1: Donations of Appreciated Personal Property

As more than one cynical observer has pointed out, it is monetarily far more beneficial for wealthy Americans to give than to receive, given our U.S. tax laws. "No one should assume that philanthropy is necessarily good for the economy," commented the late multimillion-dollar Mormon, Marriner Eccles. "Much philanthropy today is merely a tax dodge, with no other motivation."

Lest you doubt this premise, let me give you an illustration. In 1969, Congress passed a law barring income-tax deductions for the donation of scholarly, donor-created material to libraries and other archives. By 1974, the handwriting was on the walls of libraries all over the country: no tax deduction, no papers. A Library of Congress spokesman stated the problem succinctly. "We haven't had one significant collection given to us since the 1969 act." The library's manuscript division received twenty collections in 1968, seventeen in 1969, eight in 1970, and none during the next three years.

The prospects weren't much brighter elsewhere. The Association of Research Libraries made a survey three years after the law took effect. Some of its findings: Forty persons had made regular contributions to the University of California at Los Angeles before 1969; none had since. Ninety percent of the gifts to Columbia University and 75 percent of the gifts to Syracuse University had ceased. Cornell received twenty gifts in 1968, seven in 1970. Two large donations expected by New York University were stalled. And authors who had always contributed their manuscripts to Harvard suddenly stopped.

So much for the high-minded philanthropic stirrings in the breasts of U.S. taxpayers. Even the motives of such a major American philanthropist as the late Andrew Mellon have been called into question. Critics contend the Pittsburgh industrialist had never been a particularly generous man, so he probably decided to donate his $50-million art collection to the nation in the form of the then-unbuilt National Gallery of Art in Washington, D.C., for two seemingly more plausible reasons: 1) The benefaction made good business sense. By announcing the donation in 1936, a year before his death, he obtained a tax deduction of many millions of dollars during his lifetime, while simultaneously lowering the value of his estate and, in turn, his estate tax assessment. 2) The gift ensured some measure of immortality for Andrew and, indeed, the whole Mellon clan.

There's no doubt that the tax deductions materializing from the donation of paintings, sculpture, and other collectibles as well as yachts, homes, and securities to charitable institutions are a great boon to the upper-income-bracket set. The tax advantage comes about as follows:

In 1976, Mr. Mortimer Moneybags decides he needs deductions totaling $500,000 to reduce his tax bite for the year to a bare minimum. Happily, he owns one of the world's great white elephants, a 250-foot yacht willed to him by his grandfather, the famous financier J. P. Moneybags I. Since he already donated his $125,000 collection of rare duck-decoys to the Eastern Shore Hunters' Museum in 1962, and his $250,000 London town house to the U.S. government to use as consular quarters in 1968, and his $320,000 Tiffany glass collection to the Fine Arts Museum of Podunk in 1971, Mortimer's tax advisor thinks it's time to go for the big break and unload his floating heirloom onto some cooperative nonprofit institution.

But first Mortimer has to find a cooperative yacht appraiser who is willing to place the vessel's value at $500,000 or more. That turns out to be easy since most yacht appraisers are also yacht brokers who are smart enough to realize they could be in line for a handsome sales commission if they follow the transaction to its ultimate conclusion.

Mr. Moneybags gets his $500,000 appraisal—so what if it is a little inflated?—and takes it to the president of his old prep school. After very little discussion, the headmaster decides the gift is an excellent idea and agrees to report the yacht donation to the IRS as worth $500,000.

At this point, the shrewd appraiser/ship broker moves in and talks the school officials into letting him unload the vessel for them onto the highest bidder. Unfortunately, the bids aren't very high and the broken-down vessel's true market value now becomes apparent. Even mustering his best used-car-salesman spiel, the yacht broker can't get any sucker to bid more than $150,000 for the antique. No matter. The school still ends up $150,000 richer, less the sales commission. And Mr. Mortimer Moneybags and his tax attorney feel, once again, they've pulled off a real coup.

Mr. Moneybags' 1976 adjusted gross income, mostly from his trust-fund proceeds and capital-gains sources, amounts to $1 million. But the law says he can apply a charitable deduction, such as a yacht donation to an educational institution, against 50 percent of that adjusted gross income, in his case $500,000. Conveniently, the "just value" of the yacht gift is $500,000. So Moneybags takes a $500,000 deduction, pulling his taxable income down to $500,000, his tax (70 percent in that bracket) to $350,000, and—presto!—our millionaire has just saved himself $350,000 additional in taxes.

Fine, if you can get away with such a scheme. But since 1968, IRS sleuths have been cracking down and disallowing all or part of the hefty deductions claimed by many rich folk who have donated their personal property to charity.

The crackdown on yacht-donation ripoffs has centered on abuses in south Florida and the audits were carried out by the IRS's Joint Compliance Program. In 1976, the IRS announced the outcome of its examination of some twenty yacht donors in the Palm Beach area and the results, to say the least, bordered on the scandalous. Of one claimed $275,000 deduction, $100,000 was disallowed.

Another deduction of $90,000 was reduced to $43,000. A third deduction of $25,000 was knocked down to $9,800. The pattern was the same throughout all twenty audits.

In truth, you don't have to be particularly smart to figure out that something is amiss when a forty-six-foot ketch, which is donated at an appraised value of $62,000, sinks because of its rotted hull as it is being towed to the recipient. The IRS reported that example as well as the case of a fifty-three-foot custom motor yacht, built in 1938, which was donated to a foundation at an appraisal of $158,000. Two months later, the foundation sold it for $21,000.

Donations of artworks, a more common type of deduction, are also coming under heavier scrutiny. Since 1968, the IRS—using its own staff and an outside panel of art experts—has reviewed deductions for more than $250 million of donated and inherited art and recommended adjustments, in the government's favor, of some $75 million. Caught in the probe were such distinguished philanthropists as Dr. Armand Hammer and Edna Lacy. The IRS landed on Hammer for the $321,500 value he had placed on six paintings (one a Rubens work, "Venus Wounded by a Thorn") he gave the University of Southern California and a Frederic Remington sculpture ("The Bronco Buster") he donated to the Lyndon Baines Johnson Library in Austin, Texas. The IRS's advisory panel of art experts cut their value to $109,500, leaving Hammer with a tax bill of $154,000 additional. Mrs. Lacy, the chairman of Lacy Diversified Industries, donated a Kerman Oriental rug to the State Department in 1973. She deducted $128,333.33—the average of the three appraisals she got on the carpet—but the IRS balked, claiming $16,000 was closer to the mark. "It seems obvious the IRS isn't interested in fair market value," grouses Mrs. Lacy, "but in compromise, in shaking down the taxpayer."

Tax Dodge #2: Funneling Assets into Trusts and Foundations

In perhaps the plutocracy's last show of deference to the common-weal,[2] thirty of the wealthiest Americans voluntarily disclosed their estimated incomes and income taxes to the public in a *New York Times* article published on March 13, 1918. Although the prevailing prewar tax rate was 1 percent levied against incomes exceeding $20,000,[3] World War I was raging and the megabuck boys were determined to show their patriotism. For the year 1918, John

D. Rockefeller, Sr., expected to rake in a whopping $60 million and pay the government $38.4 million, followed by Henry Clay Frick's $11.25 million on which he would pay $7.1 million. Next came Andrew Carnegie's $10-million income and $6.4-million tax; George F. Baker and William Rockefeller's $7.5-million income and $4.8-million tax bill each; and so on.

No such mass ruling-class confession has occurred since. However, even if it had, the public would have been astounded at the sudden impoverished state of the country's "zillionaires." For after a 1917 change in the tax laws, it became much more profitable for fat cats to park their excess cash and securities in trust funds and foundations than to leave them lying around in bank accounts and personal stock portfolios. And they did so en masse. By 1921, the Internal Revenue Service reported that the highest personal income for the year was a lowly $3 million. Clearly, the majority of the assets of the aristocracy had gone underground. They've been hidden there ever since.

From the point of view of a greedy capitalist, trusts and foundations [4] have everything going for them. As financial entities, their assets are exempt from income, capital-gains and estate taxes. In the case of trusts, they represent a way for fortune-holders to transfer funds to their designated heirs and avoid gift taxes during their lifetime and estate taxes upon their death. In the case of charitable foundations, it's a way to retain control of a large sum without having to pay taxes on it. The money, tax free, is always available when a handsome-looking proposition—stock in the latest *wunderkind* company, underwriting a new culture center with your family's name plastered all over it, etc.—comes along.

Furthermore, until the 1969 tax reform act put a stop to the more blatant shenanigans, a foundation was a terrific way to carve out an all-expenses-paid life-style for yourself. Consider the example of the ingenious millionaire who set up a foundation, donated his home to it, made himself head trustee and executive director, and thenceforth paid for all his travel (in search of causes worthy of beneficence, of course) and household expenses out of the foundation's coffers. Other "philanthropists" have been known to put their research foundation's tax-exempt laboratories to work devising new technological solutions that their company—a commercial venture all the way—will then use to turn a handsome profit.

Clever! Then there's the old lease-back scheme in which a property is sold to a foundation, thus making it off limits to the tax collector; and immediately leased back to the seller at an extremely low figure. Or how about the "business-development" device in which a growth-minded tycoon uses his foundation to donate money to the pet charities of his clients and potential clients, thereby putting himself in line for future business favors. Then there are the foundations that are hardly foundations at all except for the piece of paper declaring them such in some tax attorney's file cabinet. The objective here is to give away zilch and at the same time pay no taxes on the foundation's stated assets.

Finally, there's the private-museum racket. Doris Duke has her Southeastern Asian Art and Culture Foundation, the repository for her many artworks collected from Thailand and Burma. Patrick Lannan's museum is in his Palm Beach home where he houses his valuable *avant-garde* art collection. But the most infamous private museum of all remains suburban Philadelphia's Barnes Collection, which despite its nonprofit status, kept the public out from 1927 until 1951 when the Pennsylvania Supreme Court finally ruled: "If the Barnes art gallery is to be open only to a selected restricted few, it is not a public institution and the foundation is not entitled to tax exemption as a public charity. This proposition is incontestable." Thereafter, the public was admitted from September through June, from 9:30 A.M. to 4:30 P.M. on Fridays and Saturdays; and from 1 P.M. to 4:30 P.M. on Sundays. Advance reservations are advisable since attendance is limited to 100 people a day. It's still not exactly an open sesame, but at least the general public now stands half a chance of viewing one of the world's finest collections of paintings by Renoir, Matisse, and Cézanne.

Tax authorities tend to take a rather dim view of foundations, particularly when they are used to evade estate taxes, as occurred in Andrew Mellon's case. Just before the financier kicked off in 1937, he diverted a huge sum into the A. W. Mellon Educational and Charitable Trust, under the trusteeship of his son, Paul, and son-in-law, David K. Bruce. In the August 29, 1937, edition of the *Herald Tribune*, federal and state revenue agents were depicted as the dupes of Mellon's financial savvy. The donation, it read, "came at a time when officials of the United States Treasury . . . were expecting a windfall in taxes from the Mellon estate. So did the tax collectors in Harrisburg, where already eager functionaries had announced that the Mellon estate was expected to yield at least $28 million for the State of Pennsylvania."

Mellon's legerdemain is the perfect illustration to support one eleemosynary executive's definition of a foundation: "It's a pile of money totally beyond the reach of the tax collector—and of anyone else we don't like."

Tax authorities, however, got some measure of revenge by way of the Tax Reform Act of 1969, which critics nicknamed the Accountants' and Lawyers' Relief Act because of its awesome complexity. The Act represented a stunning defeat for the foundation lobby. The lobby did manage to stave off a proposal that would have made all foundations self-liquidating within forty years after their inception.

Tax Dodge #3: Pro Sports Franchises

Any adult who yearns to own his own sports franchise is probably either an unregenerate fan, someone craving instant celebrityhood, or someone in search of a tax shelter—or perhaps all three.

It's amazing how the chance to invest in pro sports seems to turn otherwise-hardheaded businessmen into goo. When Cleveland shipbuilder George Steinbrenner, via a fifteen-man syndicate, purchased the New York Yankees from CBS in 1972, he gushed to a reporter: "God, if you'd told me when I was a little boy that I'd have a chance to own the Yankees, I'd never have worked but just waited, holding my breath until the day came!"

Boring businessmen often see ownership of a sports team as a way to carve out a new image for themselves. Joe Smoe, the toilet-seat king whom nobody outside Dubuque has ever heard of, buys the Raleigh Raccoons and suddenly he's a celebrity on a regional, if not a national, scale.

But according to a 1974 *U.S. News & World Report* study, it's the booming appreciation in the value of big-league franchises, the prospects of TV income, plus the enormous tax advantages that lure most centimillionaire owners. "The huge loopholes in the tax laws which permit owners to write off players' contracts—the same way farmers depreciate breeding cattle—have made ownership of a pro team a choice financial plum," says expert Roger Noll, the author of the Brookings Institution tome *Government and the*

Sports Business. "The principal source of income from the owner-ship of a pro team is the reduction of taxes from other income."

About the stupidest thing you could do is buy a pro sports franchise with the idea of getting rich off it, for only high-tax-bracket individuals stand to profit from the situation when the color of the ink in their team's accounting ledger turns red—as it inevitably does. If the owners aren't members of the bottomless-bank-account crowd when this happens, the red they see may be their own blood.

Here's how the tax advantage works:

There are three basic provisions of the tax laws that benefit team owners. In sports, the concept of *depreciation* can be applied to the players under contract. They are considered assets that eventually wear out just as the machinery in a manufacturing plant. Before a 1975 court ruling which modified the advantages some-what,[5] a person could spend $11 million on a team and for tax purposes claim that $1 million was the sum paid for the franchise itself while $10 million went toward player contracts. That $1 million–$10 million allocation makes a big difference. A franchise right can't be depreciated (i.e., deducted over a certain period) because it it assumed to have an indefinite useful life. Not so with players. In this case, the $10-million stock of players can be depreciated over a five-year period so that $2 million is deducted each year from whatever income would be subject to tax. And after using up his depreciation privilege in the fifth year, the opportunistic owner may start looking around for a buyer who, once he purchases the team, can replay the same tax scenario for the next five years. Thus, a merry-go-round situation is created in which it becomes practical to rotate team ownership every five years.

Secondly, there's the *write-off* provision that permits a team owner to subtract the losses from his sports ventures from the profits he makes as owner of the XYZ Manufacturing Co. To get maximum mileage out of this provision, sports-team ownership should be a secondary business for the owner.[6] His serious business interests—the ones from which he is determined to show a profit—should lie elsewhere: in oil wells or pharmaceuticals or insurance.

Finally, if the owner manages to sell his franchise for more than he paid for it—which is not a sure bet these days [7]—his profit is taxed at the lower *capital-gains* rate.

These are the tax advantages of sports-franchise ownership. However, one should not overlook certain other benefits that the professional sports industry enjoys. In the words of one critic, "professional sports leagues are taxpayer-subsidized, self-regulating monopolies." There's more than a grain of truth in this charge. Each of the major professional leagues is protected by one or more anti-trust exemptions without being burdened with the usual *quid pro quo* of government regulation, although there was once talk in Washington about setting up a sports regulatory agency. In addition, the vast majority of teams are housed in arenas underwritten by John Q. Public. For instance, twenty-six out of twenty-eight National Football League teams call some publicly financed stadium home. What other industry has its place of business built and maintained by private citizens?

But all good things must come to an end and there are definite signs that the free ride is almost over for the team owners what with the IRS pressing its suit in appeals courts, and lawmakers considering a similar legislative crackdown, not to mention the revolt in the locker room. Furthermore, while it may be true that owners tend to exaggerate their expenses and create *paper* rather than *real* losses, it is also true that expenses are rising at an almost prohibitive pace.

For the owners, a shakedown is in the offing. The hit-and-run owners are finally heading for the showers, leaving only those diehard, true-blue, sports-nut owners with money to burn and that irresistible urge to field a winning team.

Tax Dodge #4: Corporate Ownership of Assets Used for Personal Pleasure

As have many captains of industry, Malcolm Forbes has perfected the art of the overlap. As the sole stockholder of Forbes, Inc., the publishing firm, Forbes has managed to meld his flamboyant personal life-style into a flamboyant corporate life-style that is largely tax-deductible. His business is his pleasure and his pleasure is his business. It's a neat trick if you can convince the IRS of its validity.

If Forbes ever got audited for excessive business expenses,[8] he'd merely explain to the revenue agent, as patiently as possible, how business is conducted at the top. After all, how would a lowly bureaucrat know? Forbes would point out that the lavish parties he stages aboard spanking-white yachts and in elegant Manhattan town houses, and the personal publicity he courts by way of such oddball hobbies as ballooning—these are devices, mere devices to stimulate interest and business for his corporate entity, *Forbes* magazine. He isn't indulging in sybaritic luxury for its own sake. Oh, no! He's just entertaining clients and potential clients—and readers and potential readers—in the manner he finds most effective.

There, the "Infernal Revenue Service" [9] couldn't argue. *Forbes*, "the capitalist tool," has been enormously successful at beating out the competition (*Business Week, FORTUNE*, and the news weeklies) for advertising. In January 1976, Phil Dougherty, the *New York Times* advertising-industry reporter, did a column on Malcolm and his magazine, pointing out that *Forbes'* ad pages had increased a whopping 86 percent in the last decade compared to *FORTUNE's* decline of 30 percent and *Business Week's* decline of 29 percent. During the same period, *Forbes'* circulation went up 60 percent.

The remainder of the column was devoted to a description of Forbes, Inc.'s assets and how Malcolm Forbes, head honcho, uses them to "maintain that top-of-mind awareness with decision makers." Those assets include: ten opulent plots of real estate scattered around the globe, ranging from Christopher Wren's Old Battersea House in London and the 300-acre Château de Balleroy in Normandy, France, to a 4.7-square-mile island in the Fiji Group; a 117-foot yacht, based in Manhattan, named *Highlander* (which burned to its waterline in 1980); a gold-painted, twenty-three-seat DC-9 dubbed *The Capitalist Tool*; a fabulous collection of old masters and French Impressionist paintings; possibly the world's largest privately owned collection of Fabergé jewelry and miniatures; a collection of presidential autographs; a collection of toy soldiers housed in his Tangier palace; a museum of ballooning on his Normandy spread; and a motorcycle distributorship near his main residence in Far Hills, New Jersey.

As if to convince the IRS of his probity, Forbes rotates his frequent business soirées. While his yacht, moored at the Seventy-ninth Street Boat Basin, was used to entertain advertising clients at least three days a week from spring through fall, his homes have been the site of even more elaborate entertainments. *Forbes* magazine's 100th anniversary bash was conducted under a series of tents on the grounds of "Timberfields," his forty-acre horse-country abode in New Jersey. His palace in Tangier was used to celebrate the launching of an Arabic edition of *Forbes* with thirty-five West German ad executives flown in for the occasion. And Old Battersea House is used regularly to wine and dine English and Irish executives. There are a lot of anecdotes told about Malcolm Forbes and almost all of them end with Forbes delivering the same line: "Enjoy yourselves, gentlemen. You're deductible!"

Not only is Malcolm something of a male Perle Mesta with the tax savvy of an Andrew Mellon, he appears to have the blood of P. T. Barnum coursing through his veins as well. "Malcolm the Magnificent"—*Town & Country*'s tag line for him—doesn't deny it. Perhaps no man alive has a better knack for turning a diversion into a tax-deductible publicity stunt.

For example, when Forbes developed a sudden passion for ballooning in 1972, Forbes, Inc., immediately spawned a new division, the Balloon Ascension Division. "It seemed a natural extension of the hot-air business we're in," Forbes joked. He didn't joke about his willingness to pump dough into his new hobby-turned-tax-deduction, however. With undue dispatch, he commissioned the nation's foremost balloon designer to create an elegant blue-and-gold sphere with the word "Forbes" splashed across it, sort of an aerial advertisement for the magazine. Of course, it also doubled as the vehicle Malcolm could pilot in the balloon races he began entering —and winning. In less than a year and a half after his first balloon flight, he managed to set six new world records and gather an enormous amount of free print and television publicity. Unfortunately, the bubble burst when Forbes poured $1.2 million into preparations for a Charles Lindbergh-like Atlantic crossing, only to have a pre-flight accident not only abort the launch but almost kill him in the bargain.

Even if the IRS was willing to view Forbes' balloon adventures as a legitimate commercial venture, Forbes' insurance company was not. Forbes would have made another stab at the Atlantic flight if his life-insurance underwriters hadn't so rudely intervened.

"I had hoped to make a second attempt once I was out of owning and running my business," Forbes explained, "but now, my life-insurance policies all have a clause in them saying they are inoperable if I die ballooning across any large bodies of water."

Forbes purposely carries many millions of dollars of insurance on his life so the policies will pay the huge inheritance taxes on his estate when he dies. Here's one case where Malcolm's shrewd, long-range tax planning has cramped his short-range style. With Malcolm Forbes, the reverse is usually the case. His serendipitous enthusiasms dictate the color of the ink and the composition of his tax returns for years to come.

Tax Dodge #5: Thoroughbred Horse Breeding

Thoroughbred racing and breeding—otherwise known as the Sport of Kings—has *très cachet*, so it would undoubtedly attract the rich whether or not it carried with it certain tax advantages. Fortunately for the wealthy, the equine business does carry with it some tax benefits, although they've been greatly reduced in the last decade.

Horseracing remained strictly a sport in this country until 1927 when George D. Widener and his uncle Joseph E. Widener won a tax case allowing them to deduct about $403,000 in racing-stable losses from their taxable incomes for the years 1919 and 1922. The Wideners contended that losses and expenses related to running breeding stables should be deductible since, as coupon-clipping scions, they considered their main occupation to be managing their horse operations. The U.S. Board of Tax Appeals agreed with them and two years later, the Federal Court of Appeals in Philadelphia upheld that decision. Henceforth, the Wideners and their peers could treat their equestrian activities as a business when addressing the IRS.

Thus began the epoch of the thoroughbred tax shelter. For the next forty-five years, George Widener continued to refer to his vocation as "the sport of the business of racing" and he and other turf *aficionados* walked around with self-satisfied smiles on their faces every April 15. And by the 1950s, some plutocrats had tax-evasion-via-equitation worked out to an art form.

Until 1969, the law stated that if losses on such things as horse-breeding farms were more than $50,000 a year for five years, then the amount in excess of the $50,000 could no longer be treated like a business loss since the taxpayer was obviously indulging in a hobby. The ingenious heir Murray McDonnell found a perfectly legal way around this obstruction. For a number of years he had been operating his Water Mill Farms—his Southampton, New York, ocean-front breeding farm—in the red. In order to make the stud business worth his while, at least from a tax point of view, Murray and his sister Anne (Henry Ford II's first wife) worked out a convenient little arrangement whereby they sold the farm back and forth to each other every four years. This kept the farm's liabilities tax-deductible no matter who owned it at the time. Murray would realize the tax benefits for four years, then Anne would, then Murray again, and so forth.

Everything was ducky for the horsey set until 1969 when the law was changed. A thoroughbred owner had to show a profit for at least two out of every seven years in order to qualify for business-related tax deductions. This put a slight crimp in some owners' style—Murray and Anne had to rethink their arrangement, for instance—but where there's a strong will to avoid paying taxes, there are still ways. Owners of several horses can make sure they show a profit for the requisite number of years by concentrating their horse sales in those years, for example. And selling a half-way-decent thoroughbred for a stupendous price is no problem these days.

Overseas buyers have been bidding up the price of yearlings to dizzying heights (an increase of more than 25 percent annually) since about 1973 for three reasons: First, American horses have clearly become the best in the world; second, the decline in the value of the dollar makes any type of U.S.-based investment attractive; and third, inflation has bred a craving for tangible commodities, and horseflesh is tangible. So are the profits to be made syndicating a winning four-year-old stud if you are lucky enough to own a champion the likes of a Secretariat or Seattle Slew or Alydar. But how long this speculative mania will last is anybody's guess.

"Lately, I've been having this recurring dream," confesses John Finney, the head of perhaps the finest thoroughbred brokerage firm, Fasig-Tipton. "I'm standing in front of a crowd and instead of horses, I'm auctioning off tulip bulbs." [10]

NOTES

1. The extent to which "tax expenditures," otherwise known as "loopholes," favor the upper-income brackets became clear in 1972 statistics compiled by Stanley S. Surrey, a Harvard Law School professor and former

assistant secretary for tax policy at the Treasury Department. "On the average," he writes, "an individual at the $3,000 to $5,000 level received $10 in tax-expenditure assistance; in the $25,000 to $50,000 bracket, $1,358; in the $100,000 to $500,000 bracket, $29,264; and in the $1-million bracket, $725,000."

2. The disclosure was a savvy public-relations move. American soldiers were dying on battlefields abroad and the American aristocracy wanted to prove it too was doing its bit for the war effort.

3. A pundit once described the early income tax laws as the art of so plucking the goose as to obtain the largest amount of feathers with the least possible amount of hissing.

4. Don't expect to be able to distinguish a trust from a foundation by its name. The following are all foundations despite the disparate nouns employed to describe them: Duke Endowment, Carnegie Corporation, Rockefeller Brothers Fund, Pew Memorial Trust, Whitney Benefits, the Classen Legacy of Denmark, Bishop Estate, Youth, Inc., and the American Academy in Rome.

5. In a 1975 U.S. District Court ruling involving an Atlanta Falcons tax dispute, Judge Frank A. Hooper lowered the amount of depreciation an owner is allowed to take on player contracts from about 90 percent to less than 50 percent. The ruling is being appealed, but if it is ultimately allowed to stand, the value of pro sports franchises are expected to plummet. James Quirk, an economics professor at California Institute of Technology in Pasadena, has estimated that the depreciation angle has doubled the value of major-league teams since the pro-sports boom began in the early 1960s. If the depreciation allowance is banned as the IRS would like, Quirk thinks the average NFL team would be worth about $11 million instead of the current $20 million (in the 1974 market). He opines that baseball clubs would drop from an average of $9 million to about $5 million.

In a related development, the tax laws have also been reinterpreted, depriving an owner retroactively of his depreciation write-offs if he sells his team before five years have elapsed.

6. In the third of a series of 1974 *New York Times* articles on "The Changing Face of U.S. Sports," Leonard Koppett said: "Of the 120 major league teams on the scene right now (in eight leagues in four sports), no more than a dozen are owned by anyone whose principal business is running that team."

7. According to *Forbes* magazine (February 15, 1975), a group of Newport Beach, California, cronies, led by a boyish-looking tax lawyer named Gary Davidson, was largely responsible for the boom-and-bust atmosphere in pro athletics in the late 1960s and early 1970s. Beginning with basketball in 1967, they huckstered the franchise concept from one sport to another. Many of the investors who took the bait lost their shirts. Davidson's biggest disaster was his World Football League. During its first season in 1974, the

WFL's twelve teams lost an estimated $11 million—$22 million before the WFL itself sunk completely into well-deserved oblivion a couple years later.

8. In a *Playboy* magazine interview, April 1979 issue, Forbes admitted the IRS has some doubts about his myriad business-related deductions each year. "Don't *ever* think the IRS is out to make it easy on the rich," he told the interviewer. "It's my experience that those guys are out to get you for every nickel they can. They go over my returns every year with a fine-tooth comb. It's a constant battle in big business, even small business, and it's reached the point where the amount of time spent in figuring out how to best structure your business, given the complexity of the tax laws, is probably greater than that spent in conducting basic business."

9. The late billionaire John D. MacArthur's favorite term for the IRS.

10. Finney refers to one of the greatest boom-and-bust episodes in economic history. It occurred in Holland in the early part of the seventeenth century and is now referred to jocularly as "tulipmania." In brief, a craving for a rare type of tulip bulb swept over the land, causing speculators to mortgage practically everything they owned to pay for these bulbs which in many cases hadn't even left the ground yet. One day the market suddenly collapsed and with it went many of the speculators. The stock-market crash of October 29, 1929, was a reprise of the same basic theme.

FORTUNE HUNTER'S ALMANAC:
ELIGIBLE MULTIMILLIONAIRES
WORTH KNOWING

21 These days a sixth sense about gold diggers is bred into most heirs and heiresses from the moment they are introduced to their first playmate of the opposite sex. This was not true earlier in this century when entrée into the ranks of nobility was the premier objective of most *nouveau-riche* parents.

Barbara Hutton, the dime-store heiress, could have written the book on fortune hunters. She married six of them (Cary Grant excluded). In return, she got three opportunities to put the word "Princess" in front of her name, and one chance each for the titles "Countess" and "Baroness." But she paid for the privilege many times over in wrenching heartache and disillusionment.

After a particularly sour marriage to Lithuanian Prince Igor Troubetzkoy, her fourth husband, she told a reporter: "You can't believe the depths to which some people will stoop for money. People have blackmailed me all my life and I never did anything to deserve it. I always make the mistake of believing people are like they appear to be. Yet it turns out I'm always wrong."

To avoid this emotional and monetary devastation, most well-to-do parents these days advise their offspring to "stick to our own kind" in choosing a mate. Unfortunately, that admonition became harder to police once prep schools and the halls of ivy began admitting students based on merit rather than pedigree. Today, highborn children have more opportunities to mingle with those strange human weeds from the wrong side of Fifth Avenue. And parents run a greater risk of watching their darling little ones succumb to the charms of pulchritude and the reality of propinquity.

Anachronistic as it may seem, upper-class parents to this day do not think that romantic love (i.e., sexual attraction) is a sound basis for a marital alliance.[1] It's the basis for an affair and that's about it. No, a prospective mate's antecedents and bank balance are far more important factors than the cut of his or her jib. While the middle class may think of marriage in terms of enriching the family's gene pool, the sherry-sipping set thinks of it in far different terms: Will this match replenish the family's financial reserves and add to the luster of our name? *That* is what might be termed the dynastic point of view.

That viewpoint has served the ruling class well. Take the Rockefellers, for example. Seldom have they married outside the pecuniary circle. As Ferdinand Lundberg concluded in his 1939 study of *America's 60 Families*: "The wealthiest Americans, with few exceptions, are already joined by a multiplicity of family ties, just as they are joined by interlocking directorates and mutual participations in economic and social undertakings. . . . The rich families with which the Rockefellers have interlocked in turn have been interlocked by marriages with other wealthy families, so that one can trace an almost unbroken line of biological relationships from the Rockefellers through one-half of the wealthiest sixty families of the nation."

In light of the genealogical proof supporting Lundberg's contention, it might be more accurate to refer to the American upper *class* as the American upper *caste*. "Intermarriage within the upper class defies simple description," writes G. William Domhoff, another academic who has done exhaustive research on the American plutocracy. "It does not go too far to say that everyone is related to everyone else, and sometimes many times over."

When nubile heirs and heiresses do go outside their own set for a mate, only two choices are considered at all acceptable: Intellectuals are considered a safe bet because of their presumed contempt for material values. Likewise, an exceptionally bright, well-educated member of the upper middle class might pass muster if his or her father is a professional man, especially one of stature. Take the three daughters of the eminent Boston brain surgeon Dr. Harvey V. Cushing. Mary (Minnie) married Vincent Astor and replaced him with the affluent and well-connected painter James Fosburgh. Betsy's first husband was James Roosevelt, the son of President Franklin D. Roosevelt; her second and current is John Hay Whitney. Barbara (Babe) bagged the very rich, very social Stanley G. Mortimer, Jr., the first time around. She followed up that coup with an even greater coup in strictly financial terms—her 1947 marriage to the up-and-coming broadcasting tycoon William S. Paley.

The list of unacceptable choices is long. For heiresses, the most common misalliances seem to occur with chauffeurs, butlers, horse trainers and stable hands, cowboys, ski instructors, and ambitious young men on the way up in daddy's company. (The cowboys and ski instructors make the list because rich women seeking quickie divorces tend to congregate on dude ranches in and around Reno and on the ski slopes of Sun Valley.)

Wealthy men dipping down into the proletariat for wives tend to hitch up with models, actresses, stewardesses, maids, social secretaries, and their own executive secretary in the office, while those invalided souls past seventy often succumb to the maternal charms of their middle-aged nurses (e.g., Henry J. Kaiser, William McKnight, and Charles Shipman Payson). When I asked octogenarian John D. MacArthur what he thought of this phenomenon, he opined, "I think it's ridiculous when a loaded old man takes up with a young working woman. You and I both know that the only thing she could possibly be after is what's in his pockets, not what's in his pants!"

Another self-made man in his sixties spoke to me about his courtship and second marriage to a struggling divorcée and mother several years his junior. He admitted he was suspicious of her motives while they were dating but says he finally popped the question when it occurred to him that becoming a stepfather to her three children was a way of "turning the clock back" and making him feel younger.

"After our third break-up, I began to see that, if nothing else, she needed emotional support with those children. Now that we're married, she's so grateful that I can give her financial and emotional support with those kids that she cries sometimes. I admit I was cynical about women and never thought a man of my age and in my position could find love. Now I know she loves me—

at least I *feel* she loves me . . . Well, anyway, even if she doesn't love me, she's making a good show of it and that comes down to the same thing in the end."

Here's a Little List

For those of you intent on adding some extra zeros after your net worth, I have compiled a little list of eligible multimillionaires. But let me warn you: Fortune-hunting has its pitfalls. Fortunes usually look better on paper than they are in reality. The big bucks are frequently locked up in trust funds under heavy guard of dour-faced fiduciaries. Even if the mound takes the form of relatively liquid securities, you may still be out of luck because you can't sell off a goodly chunk without wrecking daddy's hold over the family business, heaven forbid! And when daddy finally ascends to that great boardroom in the sky, the long arm of the IRS will seize the lion's share of the visible assets with little left over for squandering.

For the male of the fortune-hunting species, there is an even greater risk. Daddy just may take a liking to you as the son he never had and install you in the office next to his in the family business, in which case, you will be expected to work as hard as he does. In short, you'll get two, at most three, days off every year.

PREY	ESTIMATED PERSONAL WORTH (millions)	AMMUNITION
Josephine Abercrombie, fifty-five (Houston)	$200–$300	Josephine is the only child of the late James S. Abercrombie who founded the Cameron Iron Works, a manufacturer of heavy equipment for oil drilling. Her parents both died in 1975, leaving her control of about 60 percent of the company's stock.
		Her first husband was a dashing Argentinian named Fernando Segura. They shared a passionate interest in ranching and horses. Her second husband, Tony Bryan, rose to the presidency of Cameron but departed after their divorce. She has resumed her maiden name.
Caroline Leonetti Ahmanson, sixty-three (Los Angeles)	$5–$10	Caroline Leonetti is the second wife and widow of savings-and-loan tycoon Howard Ahmanson who plastered his name across a number of important Los Angeles cultural institutions before he died in 1968. Most of his $300-million estate was left to a charitable foundation to perpetuate his memory in the cultural world.
		Ms. Leonetti—her professional name—continues to head her own charm/modeling school and lives in a magnificent English Tudor mansion in Hancock Park.

PREY	ESTIMATED PERSONAL WORTH (millions)	AMMUNITION
Muffie Bancroft Amory, late 20s (New York)	$1–$5	Muffie's ancestral roots are solid gold. Her great-grandmother was the Knickerbocker dowager Elsie Woodward of the banking clan. Her mother is descended from the Standard Oil Bedfords and is now the Duchess d'Uzès. Muffie hasn't let her divorce from Minot Amory get her down. She has modeled for *Town & Country* and the high fashion magazines and could accurately list her vocation as "celebrity endorsee." The competition for her hand is stiff.
Wallis Annenberg, forty-two (Los Angeles)	$20–$30	As the sole surviving child—except for two stepsisters—of the Philadelphia publisher Walter Annenberg (whose net worth is conservatively placed at $200–$300 million), she can look forward to a windfall when he dies. She is divorced from a neurosurgeon and the mother of four. She is a trustee of the University of Southern California and collects rare antiques as a hobby. She lives in Beverly Hills.

PREY	ESTIMATED PERSONAL WORTH (millions)	AMMUNITION
Gloria Vanderbilt Cooper, fifty-seven (New York)	$5–$10	This great-great-granddaughter of Commodore Vanderbilt already has four husbands and the same number of sons to her credit. If you can't visualize what Gloria looks like, start paying more attention to those blue-jean commercials on TV. Gloria is the skinny, black-haired lady who looks a little like a vampiress and coos ". . . *my* jeans really hug your derrière!" Gloria Vanderbilt also has her signature on other around-the-home products, among them wallpaper and linen designs. If you want to make time with Gloria, best praise her work and accept the fact that it comes first in her life. Also, keep in mind something she said recently: "I am shy in my relationships with most people. I mean, I'm terrified of rejection. If someone is interested in me, they must be the first to make the effort."
Cordelia Scaife May Duggan, fifty-three (Pittsburgh)	$200–$300	The important name here is Scaife. If you live in Pittsburgh, you know what it signifies: "Scaife" spelled M-E-L-L-O-N means *MONEY*. Cordelia's mother, Sarah Mellon, was the sister of Richard King Mellon and the niece of Treasury Secretary Andrew Mellon.

PREY	ESTIMATED PERSONAL WORTH (millions)	AMMUNITION
		This frumpy heiress has been married twice. Her second mate was Robert Duggan, the Pittsburgh district attorney who ended it all the day before his indictment for tax evasion. Cordelia spends much of her time traveling abroad. When she's in the States, she lives like a recluse in her Ligonier, Pennsylvania, home aptly named "Cold Comfort." This childless heiress' generosity centers on population control and family-planning philanthropies.
Jane Engelhard, sixty+ (Far Hills, New Jersey)	$200–$300	This convent-bred gentlewoman is the widow of minerals tycoon Charles "Goldfinger" Engelhard. Her late husband turned Catholic at her urging and no doubt her next spouse will have to make the same concession.
		Jane Engelhard is a charter member of the Jet Set. She numbers Lady Bird Johnson and Jackie Onassis among her close friends. She has one stepdaughter from her previous marriage to a Dutch banker and four daughters by Engelhard and spends the majority of her time in two of her many homes—her 172-acre estate "Cragwood" in the horsey section of New Jersey; and "Pamplemousse," her Boca Grande, Florida, residence.

PREY	ESTIMATED PERSONAL WORTH (millions)	AMMUNITION
Anne Ford Uzielli, thirty-eight (New York)	$25+	New York Governor Hugh Carey is her constant companion but the rumors of a pending marriage never seem to materialize. Ms. Ford—Henry Ford II's daughter—was once hitched to the Italian stockbroker Giancarlo Uzielli and they have one son, Alessandro. Unlike her sister and closest pal, Charlotte, Anne has little interest in working for a living and seems content with the role of mother/heiress/best-dressed-list matron. (Some say the reason she and Carey have *not* tied the knot is because her pretty party-girl image does not sit well with the voters.)
Katherine Graham, sixty-four (Washington, D.C.)	$100–$150	This lady became a household word during her newspaper's (*Washington Post*) Watergate crusade in 1973 and 1974. If she's had any serious beaus since the suicide of her husband, Philip Graham, in 1963, the news has never reached the gossip columns. Her job as chairman of the expanding Washington Post Co. seems to consume all of her energy. Currently, she is intent on seeing her thirty-five-year-old son, Donald, assume the top spot in the company her father, financier Eugene Meyer, bought in 1933. "Kay" also has three other children, the most visible being the New York socialite writer Lally Weymouth.

PREY	ESTIMATED PERSONAL WORTH (millions)	AMMUNITION
Hugh Hefner, fifty-five (Los Angeles)	$20+	Hugh Hefner, head of the Playboy bunny empire, is another fat cat who has suffered severe business reverses since 1974. When the heat got too intense—among other problems, the feds probed the use of narcotics at the Chicago and Beverly Hills Playboy mansions—Hefner finally decided it was time to start delegating some of his authority since he obviously had more genius for picking centerfold subjects than for managing a diversified corporation. Thus, the job of tidying up the empire fell to Derick J. Daniels, who was named president, and Hef's twenty-nine-year-old daughter, Christie, who was made a vice president and the company's chief spokeswoman. Hef's son prefers to stay out of the limelight; he's a free-lance photographer.
Ruth June Hunt, thirties (Dallas)	$30–$50	Ruth is one of the ten legitimate children of the late oil billionaire H. L. Hunt, who reputedly had several illegitimate offspring as well. She is heavily involved in born-again Christian activities. Her talent as a gospel-style crooner was substantial enough to land her a record contract and USO/Defense Department sponsorship for an entertainment tour of Vietnam.

354

PREY	ESTIMATED PERSONAL WORTH (millions)	AMMUNITION
Patricia Kennedy Lawford, fifty-seven (New York)	$5–$10	Doesn't everyone know her story? She's the daughter of venture capitalist Joseph P. Kennedy, the sister of assassinated President John F. Kennedy, the ex-wife of actor Peter Lawford, and the mother of four children.
Robert Murchison, twenty-seven (Dallas)	$5–$10	Robert is the son of Clint Murchison, Jr., owner of the Dallas Cowboys football team, and the grandson of the famed oil wildcatter. He was educated in the East at Lawrenceville and Yale and returned to his hometown to follow the family tradition: He lists his vocation as "independent oil and gas operator." Once or twice a year Robert invites some friends to accompany him to his family's island in the Bahamas called Spanish Key. If you get invited, you'd better enjoy sports, particularly tennis, jogging, and fishing. Robert does most of his skiing in Telluride, Colorado.
Jacqueline Kennedy Onassis, fifty-two (New York)	$20–$30	I won't repeat this lady's bio. I will repeat what *Esquire* magazine's society columnist Taki wrote about her recently: "Both Jackie and Lee [Radziwill, her sister] were taught at a

PREY	ESTIMATED PERSONAL WORTH (millions)	AMMUNITION
		very early age that the root of all evil is poverty. And they listened well, although Jackie obviously was more attentive. . . . Here is a woman as avaricious as the Aga Khan, as extravagant as the shah's sisters, and as acquisitive as Elizabeth Taylor during her Burton days."
Abby Rockefeller, thirty-eight (Boston)	$10–$15	Abby is one of the six children of David Rockefeller, head of the Chase Manhattan Bank. You may not want to tangle with this spirited heiress whose views are radical to say the least. "Love between a man and woman," she has said, "is debilitating and counterrevolutionary."
		Despite her upbringing—Miss Chapin's School, Milton, cello major at the New England Conservatory—she is an ardent feminist/Marxist/environmentalist. The last involvement led her to buy a farm in New Hampshire and the U.S. distribution rights for the clivus multrum, a toilet compost system developed in Sweden.

PREY	ESTIMATED PERSONAL WORTH (millions)	AMMUNITION
David Rockefeller, Jr., forty (Boston and New York)	$10–$15	"Young David"—as he's referred to by his father David Rockefeller, Sr.'s generation—is still trying to find himself. Although music is one of his passions, he bowed to his father's wishes and majored in economics at Harvard, attended Harvard Law School, and did a year's worth of graduate work in economics at Cambridge University. He's an accomplished baritone and trained musician, but he's never had the nerve to view music as his profession, instead accepting his father's judgment that it's a mere hobby. He did, however, hold the post of assistant general manager of the Boston Symphony for several years. Now, he lectures in support of arts education in America and tends to family business. His marriage in 1968 to Sydney Roberts ended in divorce.
Margaretta (Happy) Rockefeller, fifty-five (New York)	$50+	Happy Rockefeller gave up a lot—namely, the custody of her four children by former husband Dr. James Slater Murphy—when she married then-New York Governor Nelson Rockefeller

357

PREY	ESTIMATED PERSONAL WORTH (millions)	AMMUNITION
		in 1963. Thus, it was only fair that she inherit a goodly chunk of Rockefeller's assets upon his death in 1979. Of course, Happy had some assets of her own thanks to her grandfather who bequeathed her $8 million in his will in 1931. Granddaddy was in the rope business and Happy learned the social graces growing up in Philadelphia's Main Line.
Lorinda Payson de Roulet, fifty (New York)	$10+	"Linda" is the widow of Vincent de Roulet, former ambassador to Jamaica. When her mother, Joan Whitney Payson, died in 1975, her controlling interest in the New York Mets baseball club passed to her husband, Charles Shipman Payson, who retained 54 percent of the club's shares and gave 33 percent to his four living children. Linda asked to be named chairman of the club and attempted unsuccessfully to turn it around with the help of her two daughters. In 1980, the old man sold the team to the Doubleday Publishing Co. for $21 million cash.

NOTES

1. Mrs. Madeline Gilbert, the granddaughter of Rockefeller, Sr., is an exception. When asked how she had counseled her six children about prospective marriage partners, she said she always told them to wed for love. On the subject of gold diggers, she maintained, "They're very intuitive about that. This sort of thing tends to reveal itself, don't you think?"

THE ELUSIVE SEARCH
FOR IMMORTALITY

TWO MONUMENTAL EGO TRIPS OF AMERICAN MULTIMILLIONAIRES

22 *The subconscious fear of death is the one constant in everyone's life, regardless of their station. Whether we realize it or not, death influences just about every decision we make and every action we take.*

> —Thomas T. Frantz of the
> Life and Death Transitions
> Center

Death is one indignity even the rich can't avoid.

When this shattering realization hits an aging Croesus, some extremely uncomfortable soul-searching generally follows: How will posterity remember me? Will I be depicted as a money grubbing philistine or a beneficent Samaritan? Will my grandchildren be welcomed into the best circles or reviled as vulgar *parvenus*?

Many multimillionaires have undergone miraculous transformations as a result of such introspective interludes. In their memoirs, some have even alluded to that "crucial turning point" in their lives when they first envisioned their surname etched in granite over the portal of some prestigious institution or fantasized about future generations of schoolchildren awed by their good deeds in the history books.

Traditionally, plutocratic reveries of this sort have produced concrete results ranging from William Randolph Hearst's San Simeon to Andrew Mellon's National Gallery of Art. But fortune-holders with a less visual imagination and more highly developed social conscience have also been known to dump millions into less tangible endeavors—grand misguided schemes such as Henry Ford's

"Freedom Ship" and the du Pont dynasty's support for the ultra-conservative American Liberty League. Of course, there will always be those vintage supermillionaires who find their solace in ancestor worship. Their genealogical quest for respectability inevitably culminates in a semi-fictitious family saga Sir Walter Scott couldn't equal.

By the foregoing I do not mean to imply a rich person's generosity is always tainted by an ulterior motive or that the upper class hasn't made important social and cultural contributions throughout our nation's history. Indeed, it would be grossly unfair to characterize all of our current American philanthropists as either selfish immortality-seekers or shrewd tax-evaders, for many are altruistic for all the right reasons.

However, a fine line separates the truly magnanimous gesture from the monomaniacal ego trip, and the two fabulously wealthy individuals profiled in these pages appear to have crossed it. They are examples of seemingly public-spirited citizens who eventually became far more obsessed with their own subconscious drives than with solutions to the rest of humanity's problems.

By Love Obsessed

To honor a beloved wife, Shah Jehan, the fifth Mogul of India, summoned the ancient world's most renowned architects to design the "loveliest building on earth." The outcome was the Taj Mahal.

In modern times, Johnson & Johnson pharmaceutical heir, the eighty-five-year-old J. Seward Johnson, attempted similar architectural feats each time he married—with less notable results certainly. His first wife merited a $350,000 copy of an English castle, while his second wife, who craved a pastoral existence, got a large, stately, clapboard farmhouse in Oldwick, New Jersey.

But for his third wife, Barbara, a Communist refugee forty years his junior, Johnson spared no expense. Unfortunately, by most aesthetes' standards, Johnson's most recent effort, situated in Princeton, New Jersey, looks more like a medieval fortress—its bronze casement windows are bullet-proof—than an advertisement for love, even if it did subtract $21+ million from Johnson's $350-million bank account. But no matter. Barbara is pleased. She ought to be. Her last-minute changes added more than $5 million to the price tag.

J. Seward Johnson, the Johnson & Johnson pharmaceutical heir, spent $21 million over four and one half years building this fortress-mansion in Princeton, New Jersey. He dubbed it "Jasna Polana" in honor of his Polish-born third wife. TOM DUNHAM

Unlike her predecessors, Barbara Johnson's origins are shrouded in mystery. (Some say she met her husband while serving as a domestic on his household staff.) One thing is indisputable, however: She's a woman of great artistic ambition, if not accomplishment. To her, her wedding gift—dubbed "Jasna Polana" after her homeland—represents the fulfillment of all the dreams she harbored as a starving young art student in Poland.

The manifestation of those dreams is a forty-room Irish-Georgian edifice that was finally completed in 1976 after four and a half years of agony for all concerned. The house contains all manner of extravagance, including bathrooms with heated marble floors; gold-plated, heated towel racks; and tubs made of single slabs of Italian marble. In addition to the main house, the 140-acre estate also contains an indoor tennis court which doubles as a lawn-bowling green; a glass-enclosed swimming pool; an orchid house; an amphitheater; a reflecting pool; an herb garden; and a custom-made, air-conditioned doghouse with a kitchenette and an ornate bronze staircase leading outside. The whole works is surrounded by a one-mile-long wall of hand-cut stone.

If the place sounds ridiculously palatial in an age when most wealthy people are desperately trying to divest themselves of such assets, there is a logical explanation. The Johnsons are packing the main house with art treasures the value of which is already rumored to exceed $50 million; and after their deaths, the couple hope to transform the estate into a great art museum bearing their name. By all accounts, the estate is hopelessly institutional already.

There is a final ironic footnote to this tale:

"Jasna Polana"—which means "Bright Glade"—was the Russian country home of Count Leo Tolstoy who labored alongside the peasants in the fields because he believed men should renounce their "appetite for greed" and "the corrupt and artificial civilization" built by the rich.

Collecting Kudos

"Medici from Brooklyn" is the subtitle of a recent biography of Joseph H. Hirshhorn, the rags-to-riches minerals and securities tycoon. It's a reference to Hirshhorn's notorious art collection and his Latvian-immigrant origins. Grace Glueck, art critic of *The New York Times*, says she would prefer a title that more accurately

Joseph H. Hirshhorn, the self-made minerals and securities ty-coon, has his name etched in big letters on the portico of this art museum, part of the Smithsonian Institution in Washington, D.C. The Hirshhorn Museum—variously referred to as a bomb shelter, stone bagel, oil barrel, and armory—houses his 6,000-piece mixed bag of an art collection appraised at $60 million to $100 million. DENNIS BRACK/BLACK STAR captures the spirit of the man, something such as "Joe Hirshhorn and His Big Collection."

Glueck's dig is hardly the first potshot taken at Hirshhorn since 1966 when he talked President Lyndon Johnson into accepting his renowned collection of twentieth-century masterpieces *provided* the federal government build a suitable structure to house the collection, a structure with his name etched in big letters on the portico. The donation has been dubbed everything from a "bid for immortality" to "a shrewd deal in which the megalomaniac Hirshhorn emerged the winner." Art critic Aline Saarinen said, "Joe took the U.S. Government like it's never been taken" and John Brademas, Congressman from Indiana, summed up the feeling of many of his colleagues when he said, "There was something unseemly and in rather bad taste in the way the Hirshhorn decision has been jammed down our throats."

Hirshhorn attributed the opposition to raw anti-Semitism. "I'm a Jew," he says. "There's a lot of people who don't like the idea of the name Hirshhorn on the Capitol Mall. Do I mean that? Absolutely, Hirshhorn Mall. I like the sound of it."

Controversy has surrounded every aspect of the project. Its site is still a sore point with some. The Joseph H. Hirshhorn Museum and Sculpture Garden of the Smithsonian Institution is located on Washington, D.C.'s Mall where traditionally the monuments are named only for the giants of American history, the George Washingtons, Thomas Jeffersons, and Abraham Lincolns. The architect of the $16-million edifice—$15.3 million paid for by the feds and $1 million paid for by Hirshhorn—is another source of jibes. Architecture critic Ada Louise Huxtable has likened the windowless concrete cylinder to a doughnut; ". . . it totally lacks the essential factors of aesthetic strength and provocative vitality that make genuine 'brutalism' a positive and rewarding style. This is born-dead, neo-penitentiary modern. . . . Its mass is not so much aggressive or overpowering as merely leaden." Less eloquent critics labeled it simply a bunker, bomb shelter, stone bagel, oil barrel, and an armory.

Finally, there's the 6,000-piece collection appraised at $60 million–$100 million. Hirshhorn assembled his collection over a period of forty years and admits he liked the *game* of collecting— socializing with artists and their High Society patrons, roaming around galleries, and driving hard bargains. When he was struck with strong spontaneous urges to own paintings or sculptures, he usually bought in bulk. According to the critics, the collection reflects his eclectic taste and inconsistent whims. It's not all great, but it's not all bad either.

But the real crux of the issue is how "Joe's place"—as the museum is more popularly known around Washington—fares with the public. Pretty well, apparently. Its attendance record compares favorably with New York's Museum of Modern Art, the Whitney, and the Guggenheim. The Hirshhorn's guest register contains numerous "Ahhhs," hundreds of "WOWs," and one rhapsodic "a song of civilization."

THE BIG PAYOFF: THE SPOILS
RESERVED FOR THE VERY RICH

23 Have you ever come away from a university commencement feeling like a fool because you'd never heard of the handful of "distinguished" people who were awarded honorary degrees that day? Made you resolve to start reading *Time* magazine more thoroughly, I'll bet.

Don't feel so bad. There's no reason why you should know anything about the majority of the so-called distinguished people who collect honorary degrees in this country on a regular basis. The truth is, the only distinguishing feature about most of them is the size of their portfolios. It's certainly not the magnitude of their talent, which is virtually nonexistent in most cases.

Honorary degrees are essentially a fund-raising ploy and rich people know it. They play along with the pretense for one reason only—they like the attention. And they know that the average American takes such awards ceremonies at face value—especially if there are a few ringers in the line-up (i.e., honest-to-God distinguished citizens such as a Margaret Mead or a Jonas Salk). Later, when the school's prexie asks for a few million, the newly degreed plutocrat shells out willingly, remembering the compliment the school paid him by valuing his supposed accomplishments on the same par with people of true achievement.

There are wealthy people who resist such blandishments or, even worse, go along with the ruse and then refuse financial aid. John MacArthur was one of them. When money was at stake, he prided himself on his ability to smell a rat before it emerged from its hole. He loved to tell about the various fund-raising appeals he thwarted. A Midwestern college once approached him for three successive years about awarding him an honorary degree. (Mac-

Arthur quit school after the eighth grade.)

"It's the oldest extortion scheme in the book," MacArthur chuckled, "but I finally went along with it just so they'd stop pestering me." How much did he donate? ". . . not one quarter."

MacArthur, like many of his fat-cat peers, viewed political campaign contributions in the same light. He claimed he abruptly dismissed Nixon's CREEP fund raisers by telling them: "Nixon's got too much money already from what I hear. Anyway, I'm supporting a local dog and cat hospital and that takes precedence over Nixon any day. Besides, what do I want to be an ambassador for?"

Curtis Blake, a cofounder of the Friendly Ice Cream chain, refers to honorary degrees as "a cheap shot for getting money." He would much prefer that a college president invite him to lunch and level with him about the school's monetary needs. "At least that way it's direct. Everybody's got their cards on the table."

Another wealthy man I interviewed told about the time the college he had attended for one year voted to give him an honorary doctor of laws degree. "When I opened the letter, my first thought was, 'This is going to cost me a lot of money.' But then I got to thinking. You see, I never graduated, and the school has a policy that when a nongraduate has been out twenty-five years, they look at his record to see if he merits a degree based on accomplishment. In my case, twenty-five years came and went and nothing happened. I felt sort of bad about it.

"So my first thought when I got that letter was, 'All they want now is for me to buy a degree with my money.' And then I said to myself, 'If you take that attitude you are going to become a cynical old man. You should just accept it gracefully.' So I did."

Clearly, the *quid pro quo* aspect of honorary degrees, ambassadorships, Papal honors, and other types of awards bothers some rich people more than others. More commonly, rich people cheerfully accept the prizes that are handed out and the solicitations that inevitably follow—or precede—the honor with a kind of stoic good grace. They see all these veiled forms of fund raising as part of their lot in life, a burden to be borne with equanimity if not enjoyment.

The following members of the carriage trade—some deceased— are recipients of honorary degrees. The figure after their name indicates the number of degrees. If anything, my figures are conservative. Many of these people collect degrees so prolifically that it's hard to keep up.

The Honorary Degree Honor Roll
(Multiple Awardees Only)

Walter Annenberg (6)
Jacob Blaustein (8)
Herman Brown (2)
John Nicholas Brown (3)
Godfrey L. Cabot (4)
Mrs. Andrew Carnegie (2)
John F. Connelly (1, plus a Knighthood in the Order of St. Gregory [1])
Lammot du Pont Copeland (4)
John F. Cuneo (1, plus various Papal honors)
Arthur Vining Davis (2, plus the Chinese Government Order of Jade)
Mrs. Alfred I. du Pont (9)
Frank Gannett (4); degrees were also awarded to his wife and son)
William T. Grant (2)
Mrs. Clifford Heinz (6)
Bob Hope (3 degrees and over 800 awards)

Amory Houghton (6)
Arthur A. Houghton, Jr. (10)
Roy Arthur Hunt (3)
Henry J. Kaiser (9)
Joseph P. Kennedy (8 from British universities; Knight of Malta [1])
Charles F. Kettering (30)
Peter Kiewit (4)
Dr. Edwin Land (13)
Eli Lilly (10)
Richard King Mellon (many)
James S. McDonnell, Jr. (many)
John Olin (many)
Marjorie Merriweather Post (3)
W. Clement Stone (many)
George W. Strake (4 Papal decorations from Pope Pius XII [1])
Mrs. Arthur H. Sulzberger (2)
Juan Terry Trippe (many)

Fat-Cat Ambassadors

If the general public didn't know about the causal link between political campaign contributions and ambassadorships before the Watergate debacle, it certainly did afterwards. The Nixon administration scandals produced a string of revelations about how fat-cat contributors get to fill such prestigious posts as ambassador to the Court of St. James's (Great Britain) without any previous diplomatic experience. The Watergate probe also produced testimony that was extremely embarrassing to several wealthy ambassador-aspirants and forced Herbert Kalmbach, Nixon's personal attorney and CREEP fund raiser, to plead guilty to a misdemeanor charge of offering an ambassadorship in Europe to J. Fife Symington, Jr., in return for a $100,000 campaign contribution. (Symington coughed up the contribution but never got the appointment.)

Of course, Nixon denied authorizing any such *quid pro quo,* declaring "ambassadorships cannot be purchased." But the evidence—and statements made by those in the know about such matters—contradicted him.

Vincent de Roulet, the son-in-law of Joan (Whitney) Payson, was another $100,000+ Republican contributor. He was already U.S. ambassador to Jamaica, hardly a diplomatic plum, and his pledge was ostensibly to help him gain a more attractive embassy.

When de Roulet was questioned about his contribution he said, "I don't see how anybody could make the statement [that the contribution and a hoped-for transfer were unrelated]. But I never said to him [Kalmbach] 'I gave you $100,000, now where the hell's my post?'"

C. V. Whitney gave $250,000 to CREEP and reportedly made it plain that he wanted to serve as ambassador to Spain, where he owns substantial real estate. The sum was eventually returned in full and he was told his name was being "dropped from consideration due to age."

Walter Annenberg (Triangle Publications heir), Arthur K. Watson (IBM heir), Leonard K. Firestone (tire company heir), and Ruth L. Farkas (wife of the founder of Alexander's department store chain) fared better.

Annenberg was a personal friend of Nixon besides being a heavy Republican contributor for years. Appointing Annenberg to the premier diplomatic post of ambassador to the Court of St. James's was one of Nixon's first acts when he assumed the Presidency in 1969. Annenberg subsequently donated another $254,000 to Republican campaign coffers between 1969 and 1972.

The Watson appointment turned out to be something of an embarrassment for all concerned—not only because he "bought" his ambassadorship to France in return for his $303,000 worth of donations, but also because of an airplane incident that cost him the job.

Watson, a Francophile by inclination, went to France in 1970. Two years later, he was forced to resign when the press got hold of a story about his abusive conduct toward a stewardess on a flight from Paris to Washington. Reporters claimed he was drunk but Watson denied it. "The most one could say," Watson told U.S. Representative Wayne Hays (D-Ohio) who was investigating the incident, "is that I was exceedingly and, I think, uncharacteristically rude." According to Jack Anderson, Watson "kept shouting for more scotch, grabbing the stewardesses and trying to stuff money down the fronts of their blouses. He finally passed out," after trying to "buy" one of the stewardesses for his teen-age son.

The flap finally proved too detrimental to Watson's image as ambassador and he resigned, claiming the Paris climate aggravated his asthma condition. (In 1974, Watson fell and hit his head at his home in New Canaan, Connecticut. He died a few days later at age fifty-five.)

Dr. Ruth Farkas and her husband had contributed $300,000 to Nixon's re-election campaign and she became U.S. ambassador to Luxembourg soon after Nixon started his second term. She lasted until May 1976 and weathered the storm over her "political" appointment with dignity. Leonard K. Firestone, named ambassador to Belgium for his $115,100 in 1974, resigned a year later to run his three-hundred-acre winery north of Santa Barbara.

Nixon was hardly the first U.S. President to hold out ambassadorships as prizes to the largest donors. Nixon's campaign aides just did it more openly. Herbert Alexander, the director of the Citizens Research Foundation and considered one of the most knowledgeable people in the country on the subject of campaign financing, said: "I don't think it [the practice of rewarding contributors with ambassadorial appointments] was quite as blatant before Nixon. The Democrats had their share of it, but it certainly wasn't as high a price tag."

Franklin D. Roosevelt was the first President accused of "selling" embassy posts. Among his envoys were financier Joseph P. Kennedy who contributed $25,000, lent $50,000, and raised $100,000 to help get FDR elected in 1932. (FDR's total campaign budget was only $2.2 million.) Six years later Kennedy got his reward—the coveted British ambassadorship. Another early and heavy contributor, department store head Jesse Straus, became U.S. ambassador to France.

President Dwight Eisenhower continued the tradition. Amory Houghton, the Corning Glass heir, donated $9,000 and went to France while John Hay Whitney came up with $47,100 and went to England.

It should be said that the American political system of picking envoys is not all bad. The system has turned up some top-flight ambassadors—as well as a few duds. Even spokesmen for the American Foreign Service Association, made up of career diplomats who generally oppose fat-cat appointees whom they consider unqualified, have occasionally nodded approval.

"Some of the greatest ambassadors we've ever had, like Averell Harriman and David Bruce, were political appointees," said Robert Cleveland, chairman of the Foreign Service Association's professional affairs committee. "We just feel if a President is going to name a politico, it should be a first-rate person."

In truth, the size of a fat cat's contribution is not the only reason to name him or her an ambassador. Another good reason also concerns money—how much a wealthy envoy is willing to dig down in his own pocket to finance his sojourn abroad. The federal government has always made niggardly provisions for its embassies. The budget allotted for the American embassy in a place such as Costa Rica may be sufficient. But the budgets for embassies in sophisticated and expensive countries in Europe, for instance, are never large enough to cover the entertainment expenses let alone other necessities.

So no matter what people thought of Walter Annenberg's performance as ambassador to Britain, they couldn't sneer at the $1 million he put up to refurbish Winfield House, the U.S. embassy in London. (The U.S. government contributed a mere $50,000.) Annenberg also spent between $200,000 and $250,000 beyond his government allowance of $25,000 in each of his five and a half years there.

True, rich ambassadors are able to write off these extra costs against their income taxes, but not unless they've got a huge income to start with. Annenberg and his ilk do and consider their ambassadorial appointment "the greatest honor of my life."

NOTES

1. Catholic honors reserved for big contributors to the Church.

THE PERILS OF SOCIAL
CLIMBING—AND HOW IT'S ACCOMPLISHED

24 It happens to a lot of so-called self-made men. They devote 90 percent of their time and energy to clawing their way up in the business world, stock up a huge pile of million-dollar chips, and one day wake up wondering why they bothered. Now that they're rich, they're dissatisfied. "Why am I working so hard?" they ask themselves, especially when they notice that other people—who are less rich but more *social*—are having more fun.

Suddenly, those old middle-class values of industriousness, hard work, and thrift seem outmoded while status, glamour, and material possessions seem all important. It's this radical shift in perspective that has propelled many an aging workaholic tycoon out of the executive suite and onto the dance floor . . . or out of an old-shoe marriage and into a more fashionable "society" match . . . or off of the corporate board of directors and onto the local symphony's board of trustees . . . or out of an obsession with stocks and bonds and into an obsession with art and other newfound pleasures.

Our tycoon has been bitten by the bug of status striving.

What are he and his childhood-sweetheart wife striving for? Acceptance by that segment of society that systematically excludes them, the segment at the apex of the social pyramid populated by old-money aristocrats. Of course, no well-bred upper-class American ever admits that such undemocratic divisions as classes exist in this country. But while they continue to deny that there is such a thing as "High Society," they work to keep it intact and inviolate generation after generation. "And on this firm foundation of paradox," says Stephen Birmingham, "society exists."

How will Mr. and Mrs. Arriviste accomplish this great leap upward? The first thing they will do is deny they're even trying to move upward.

In the Robber Baron era when fortunes were made overnight, social climbing was a game that was practiced openly, with some *nouveaux riches* men getting as caught up in it as their wives. Many an aspiring nineteenth-century tycoon spared no expense to raise his family's standing, even to the point of hiring a "social guide" (a highborn man or woman who was long on lineage and short on cash) to launch the family into the exclusive world of High Society. Before that was accomplished, the social guide had usually gone through millions of his employer's money hiring diction coaches, French teachers, dancing and riding instructors, hairdressers, dressmakers, and tailors to whip the family into shape for the onslaught.

Some of the same things happen today but few would ever admit it. The modern version of the social guide is the society press agent. They also direct their clients to the "right" exercise salons or hairdressing establishments or dress shops, restaurants, and churches. But the most important service they provide is introductions to the "right" people.

How is the aspirant introduced to the Old Guard? "The classic way is to get the client on important committees of the right charities, the good balls, the theater benefits," says Lee Bond of the oh-so-social Rasponi Associates. "People active in the chic charities are well on the way to being accepted socially."

In the process of being transformed into socialites, a tycoon and his wife usually gain a new set of manners, opinions, and interests, but they inevitably lose just as much. "At every step," writes Osborn Elliott in *Men at the Top,* the self-made man "leaves something behind—his parents, perhaps; his friends and old associates, his old neighborhood, his church, his club, his Thursday-night bowling team. For most of the men who hit the top, such parting is neither sorrowful nor sweet, but simply a fact of life."

Social observer Vance Packard calls the resolute striver "a lonely man making his way on a slippery slope"; and points out that the upward striver is often resented and rejected by the group he is leaving. "However, if an upward striver does succeed and goes on to become a conspicuous success, his old associates left behind forget their old resentment and brag fondly of having known him when."

Even for those social climbers who eventually achieve success and the tacit support of old friends, there are still problems. Sociologists and psychiatrists who have studied the upwardly mobile report an increase in emotional and physical disorders. Jurgen Ruesch, a psychiatrist affiliated with the University of California, for example, has concluded that the social climbers turn up in "unusually large numbers" among patients suffering psychosomatic ailments. He hypothesizes that strivers frequently encounter new social situations beyond their emotional capacity, and the resulting strain manifests itself in bodily ailments.

There is another alternative for the tycoon who feels restless: Reject society before it rejects you. This was the stance adopted by John MacArthur and his second wife, Catherine.

While MacArthur lived the last twenty years of his life just north of ultraexclusive Palm Beach, he was seldom invited to PB's classy affairs. When asked about this apparent rejection, he always replied—a mite too heatedly—that he couldn't care less. On the other hand, he made sure the "snobs" knew about it whenever he got invited anywhere big. The Palm Beach newspaper, for instance, carried MacArthur's unadulterated review of President Gerald Ford's state dinner for visiting Queen Elizabeth to which MacArthur had escorted his widowed sister-in-law Helen Hayes:

"I wasn't going to go because I thought I'd be bored," he told a reporter. "Besides, I'm busy. But when I found out only 200 people in the entire country had been invited, I thought I'd better get me a monkey suit and go on up there. After all, it's my first free meal at the White House.

"The star of the show was Betty Ford. She just shone. And I wouldn't dare quote what she whispered to me. But I guess I should say something nice about the queen so I'll say she had a beautiful headdress. I never saw so many diamonds in one pile. Yes, she certainly was beautiful . . . from the head up. I thought her husband was the butler until somebody tipped me off he was the prince."

As much as MacArthur and other outspoken and crude "men of monetary achievement" might deny it, they—as do all the rest of us—feel a shiver of excitement when a liveried butler admits them to a Main Line Philadelphia mansion with a marble hall and sweeping staircase. Or they get invited to dine in a rarified men's club with mahogany wainscotting and Gilbert Stuart portraits of the venerable founders.

For those who choose to climb, perhaps the healthiest attitude to adopt is that of society chronicler Stephen Birmingham:

"Social climbing is like a game. You play it by climbing the walls and crossing the little squares between, one after another. Progress is slow and arduous, and often you must rely on guesswork. Through it all, your goal is *Real* Society, and as you approach its fringes, the going becomes harder. . . ."

Social Climbing: THE MARRIAGE ROUTE

An ample helping of Old Family and less money on one side, can usually be brilliantly matched with a smaller amount of family, and more money, on the other.

—Stephen Birmingham

"Marrying up" is a classic way to advance socially.

In the Gilded Age, it was generally the female who supplied the infusion of new capital and the male who supplied the lineage in a marital alliance, although occasionally the roles were reversed.

August Belmont, né August Schönberg, is an example. He arrived on these shores in 1837—a Jew masquerading as a Gentile, a German masquerading as "a Frenchman, I think"—with the financial backing of the House of Rothschild and the inner determination to become a social potentate. Playing by nineteenth-century society's rigid rules, he eventually succeeded. Since dueling was an established social elevation device, for instance, Mr. Belmont slapped the esteemed Mr. Edward Heyward of Charleston across the face with his gloves, thereby establishing himself with the public as a man on a par socially with his opponent. But his *pièce de résistance* was his marriage to Caroline Slidell Perry, the daughter of Commodore Matthew Perry and niece of the naval commander, Oliver Hazard Perry. Some said he chose her as carefully and objectively as he chose his dinner companions, his dueling partners, the stocks in his portfolio, his name, and his religion.

Nothing's changed. Lower-crust multimillionaires are still choosing their upper-crust mates with the same mix of cynicism and opportunism that Belmont displayed a century ago. They say, for example, that Josephine Hartford, the A&P heiress and sister of Huntington Hartford, always had a hankering to be accepted by Europe's *ancien régime*. After all, her mother had bagged a real Italian prince and sported the title Princess Pignatelli, and seldom is competition more fierce than that between a socialite mother and her daughter.

The fourth time around, Josephine achieved her goal. In 1950, she married a *bona fide* English gentleman, John (Ivar) Bryce. Although his income couldn't match her legendary $500-million inheritance, he was no pauper either. He had gone to the right schools, had the right friends among the peerage, his father was a major in the Coldstream Guards, and his mother was Lady Phillimore.

The match lasted a good fifteen years and Josephine could never complain that she hadn't gotten her money's worth. During their marriage, she had hobnobbed with English royalty, dabbled in the world of British film making, and bred and raced horses with a vengeance.

When a union such as this one doesn't last, nobody really cares. It's the *fact* of the marriage that counts, not its longevity. For, as Ferdinand Lundberg pointed out in *The Rich and the Super-Rich*: "The Europeans, mostly impoverished noblemen, have only in a few cases brought an increase in fortune to their American partners. The chief assets of the Europeans have been hereditary titles, leisure-class manners, perhaps a shabby estate or two, and passports into the world of snobbery."

As the following list indicates, title-hunting Americans were mostly of the feminine gender. There's a good reason for this: When a wealthy American male marries a titled European female, the title is *not* shared.

American Heiress	*Titled Person(s) She Married*
Louise Van Alen	Prince Alexis Mdivani; Prince Serge Mdivani
Ava Alice Muriel Astor	Prince Serge Obolensky
Margaret (Peggy) Bedford	Prince Charles d'Arenberg
Ethel Field	Lord Earl Beatty
May Goelet	Duke of Roxburghe
Anna Gould	Count Boni de Castellane; Duc de Talleyrand

American Heiress	*Tilted Person(s) She Married*
Ella Haggin	Count Festeils De Toina
Lilian Warren Hammersley	Duke of Marlborough
Alice Heine	Prince of Monaco
Clara Huntington	Prince Hatzfeldt-Wildenburg
Barbara Hutton	Prince Alexis Mdivani; Count Court Haugwitz-Reventlow; Prince Igor Troubetzkoy; Baron Gottfried von Cramm; Prince Doan Vinh Na Champassak
Grace Kelly	Prince Rainier of Monaco
Estelle Manville	Count Folke Bernadotte
Helen Morton	Duc de Valeccay
Millicent Rogers	Count von Salm
Anita Stewart	Prince de Braganza
Margaret Rockefeller Strong	Marquis George de Cuevas
Alice Thaw	Earl of Yarmouth
Consuelo Vanderbilt	Duke of Marlborough
Gladys Vanderbilt	Count Lâszló Széchényi
Pauline Whitney	Sir Almeric Paget
Consuelo Yznaga	Duke of Manchester

Social Climbing: THE CULTURE-PATRONAGE ROUTE

Nowadays, the culture scene has opened up for the same pressing reason charity boards did—the need for funds. Again, the comers have a chance to make it with a fat wallet, or at least with the knack for getting at someone else's fat wallet.

> —Patricia Moore
> "A Social-Climber's Guide to Making It Big in the Big City," *Chicagoan* (October 1973)

Ms. Moore was referring to the maneuvering in the uppermost reaches of Chicago society where her article may be true. There, a person such as Ray Kroc may be able to buy his way into society by handing the hoity-toity Ravinia Festival $250,000 to wipe out its 1972 deficit and offering it a matching grant of $1 million the following year. But in New York—the center of the American cultural scene—social climbing via the arts isn't that easy. Sheer millions will get you nowhere, at least at the Metropolitan Opera which is still the country's premier citadel of civility.

Opera as an art form has long been society's favorite because of its exorbitant expense, lavish ritual, and European derivation; hence, its intrinsic snob appeal. Some say nineteenth-century society was particularly fond of opera because it gave them a place to digest their meal between dinner and a ball, a place where they could continue to gossip while the curtain was up, confident that the singing would drown out their chatter. Opera, with its elaborate conventions, was also less taxing intellectually than the theater and easier to drop in on than a symphony concert where conductors rued the disturbance.

Until 1883, the Academy of Music on Fourteenth Street in Manhattan was the seat of Old Guard opera attendance. There, the eighteen boxes were passed down from one generation to another by such old-line Knickerbocracy names as Schermerhorn, Livingston, Bayard, and Beekman, and the business affairs of the institution were managed by none other than Pierre Lorillard, August Belmont, and Robert L. Cutting. But up-and-comers such as Alva Vanderbilt, the Commodore's daughter-in-law, were determined to have their night at the opera too and had to build a rival opera house—the Metropolitan on Broadway between Thirty-ninth and Fortieth streets—in order to do it.

In the process of raising money for the new structure, which turned out to be enormously costly, determined social climbers such as Alva approached new and old money alike for contributions. As the project gained momentum and it became clear that the ancient Academy of Music's days were numbered, such *grandes dames* as Caroline Astor—*the* Mrs. Astor—rushed forward with their generous donations which automatically secured them a box in the Met's Diamond Horseshoe. Thus, according to Lloyd Morris in *Incredible New York*, the new Metropolitan Opera House that opened on the night of October 22, 1883, with a performance of *Faust* in Italian, "represented the passing of social power into new hands, the final defeat of the city's aristocracy by the great capitalists who were the masters of banks, railroads, vast industries."

Today, the Metropolitan Opera House is located farther uptown at Lincoln Center for the Performing Arts and if anything, its social patina has gained luster through the years. The Met's board of directors is fifty-one strong and many of its members boast ancestral ties to the institution.

Take Mr. Francis Goelet, possibly the board's most influential member. The Met's red-carpeted grand staircase is named for his father in recognition of a $500,000 gift from the elder Goelet's widow and children. Other legacy members are Anthony Bliss, the Met's executive director, whose father, Cornelius, was board chairman from 1938 to 1946; Mrs. William Francis Gibbs, whose father also served for many years; and Mrs. John Barry Ryan, whose father was financier Otto Kahn, an important mover and shaker in the Met's history. He came on the board at the turn of the century, worked to put the company on a solid business footing and, because of his Jewish heritage, was not invited to own a box in the Diamond Horseshoe until 1917. He accepted the box graciously but never used it and continued to sit in the Director's Box, where he had always sat.

To this day, there are few Jews on the Met's board. (The self-made Leon Hess is one.) In fact, the board is about as lily-white WASP as any organization could ever be in this day and age. Some complain it's an exclusive club, peopled by Wall Street lawyers, investment bankers, brokers, industrialists, and a few oilmen who went to certain schools (Choate, St. Paul's, Phillips Exeter, Yale, Harvard, and Princeton); belong to certain clubs (Knickerbocker, Links, Metropolitan, Racquet and Tennis, and Century); and sit on the boards of the most fashionable foundations and charities.

Clearly, entrée to the board is not just a matter of donating heavily. If it were, the composition of the board would be far different. William Rockefeller, grandnephew of John D. Rockefeller, Sr., and the current board president, claims that a skill or talent not already represented on the board might help a candidate gain entry; and a willingness to contribute at least $10,000 or $15,000 a year could also be considered a qualification.

But generally, he claims, "we try to get people on the board who either have some talent or can produce if sparked. I'm constantly looking around when I'm in the opera house to see if I can notice anyone who might be helpful to us. People accuse us of being elitist, but I don't like to use those words." As for himself—

"I grew up knowing opera as a responsibility. I used to drive down from Yale and drive back the same night after a performance. I was asked to come on the board of the Opera Guild when I graduated from law school at twenty-eight. Langdon Van Norden came on about the same time—we were the youngsters."

One striver who did not have the Met in his bloodline and therefore had to turn elsewhere for surcease from obscurity is the *nouveau-riche* but well-educated (Texas A&M, Harvard Law School) John S. Samuels 3d. The son of a Texas postman, the fortyish clean-cut-looking Samuels didn't let any crabgrass mar his personal landscape once he found himself with a wad of million-dollar bills in his pocket, money that he made trafficking in coal, graphite, carbon products, insurance, and securities. His ascent in the New York arts community was fast. In 1975, he became one of eight members of the new board of governors of City Center, charged with overhauling the financial and administrative affairs of the City Ballet, the New York City Opera, and the City Center theater on Fifty-fifth Street. Within months, Samuels was elected chairman of the newly autonomous boards of the ballet and opera companies, City Center, and the Vivian Beaumont Theatre at Lincoln Center.

Samuels' motives are transparent even though he claims, "I seem to have a need to be involved in the creative process. The arts seem to allow me to function better." In describing how he came to buy Marietta Peabody Tree's old town house on East Seventy-ninth Street, or Mrs. Junius Morgan's (daughter-in-law of J. P. Morgan) estate in Glen Cove, Long Island, or the du Ponts' manse in Southampton, or the three-story Southern Gothic house in Galveston that he now refers to as the family homestead, Samuels frequently tells a revealing personal anecdote. For example, Samuels admits he attended all the blue-chip charity events in New York at first and just watched. He says it quickened his interest in anthropology.

"I studied New York. I grasped it. Later, when I had a flat in England [it was in the famous Albany, off Piccadilly], I found that London was more complicated, more subtle." His brush with the British also turned him into an unmitigated Anglophile which shows in everything from his taste in clothes to his snobby habit of referring to his peers as "old boys."

The size of Samuels' donations to the arts are a mystery (reportedly in the high five figures), although whatever they were in the past, they are sure to be less in the near future. By 1979, Samuels found himself caught up in what is euphemistically known as a "cash squeeze" and unable to pay some of his bills. At the same time, his wife Ellen left him after twenty-two years of marriage and it was further revealed that he was not an infallible business brain, after all. His personal worth probably fell far short of the $200–$300 million *FORTUNE* estimated he had. But with his usual patrician aplomb, Samuels brushed off any allegations of mismanagement: "I expect people to understand that I'm not an endless supply of cash," he said, "whatever my asset value."

In early 1980, Samuels announced that he planned to step down as the chairman of the board of the ballet and the opera, although he intended to stay on as chairman at City Center and the Vivian Beaumont Theatre. The announcement came amid speculation that Samuels was being forced out of the two chairmanships because, according to *The New York Times,* his aggressive personality "rubbed a number of his colleagues the wrong way."

In the meantime, arts critic John Corry of *The New York Times* summed up the prevailing feelings about the man: "In the arts world, there is one theory that Mr. Samuels is The Great Gatsby, and another that he is really the cultural philanthropist Otto Kahn. In Galveston, however, his family calls him Bubba."

Social Climbing: THE CHARITY BALL ROUTE

When the elegant private dance, held in the ballroom of one's very own mansion, passed out of existence as a routine twentieth-century social function, the charity ball appeared to take its place.

As an arena for social climbing, the charity ball—or "dancing for a disease"—holds far more promise for the striver than the private ball ever did. Because of an ever-escalating need for funds, the Old Guard boards of today's charitable organizations can't afford to operate with the same closed-door policy as a society hostess/social arbiter of yesteryear. Thus, a representative sprinkling of wealthy newcomers is allowed in to help raise money each year and if that means letting down the social barriers a little, so be it. In contrast, Mrs. Caroline Astor of 400 fame didn't *need* the Vanderbilts for anything, so nineteenth-century social climbing was a much more cutthroat and devious proposition.

However, of all the contemporary routes to social acceptance, the charity-ball avenue—in terms of sheer hard work—is one of the roughest. Signing on to a charity-ball committee is a lot like volunteering your services for a political candidate: No one can substitute for you. No matter how much money you have and how many surrogates normally do your dirty work for you, *you*—not your social secretary or maid—are the one who is expected to lick the envelopes and solicit your friends for freebie gifts and underwriting grants. The only people who get credit for work and don't actually do any are those blockbuster socialites with box-office appeal, so to speak, who merely lend their names to the endeavor in order to suck the social climbers in.

Obviously, arrivistes must pick their charity carefully. Not all good causes carry social cachet. In Chicago, for instance, the top charity functions benefit a handful of hospitals (Passavant, Presbyterian-St. Luke's, Children's Memorial, and, in Jewish circles, Michael Reese) and welfare institutions (Chicago Commons and Hull House settlements, Illinois Children's Home and Aid Society, Chicago Boys Clubs, and the Cradle adoption home). The list varies in every city. Indeed, in some places, it's the culturally oriented causes—art museums, opera companies, and orchestras—rather than the welfare-oriented causes that provide the best opportunity for social claim jumping.

Choosing a charity can be a problem, as Lucy Kavaler pointed out in *The Private World of High Society: Its Rules & Rituals.* Since the object of working on a ball committee is to get to know those who have already arrived socially, it's important to know who really works for a charity and who just lends their name to the letterhead. A good deal of sleuthing—and possibly the aid of a society publicist—may be required to find out.

In large cities, the most prestigious charities may be the least publicized. And keep in mind that a charitable event with a guest list of 500 people is bound to be more exclusive than a huge ball to which 2,000 to 3,000 are invited. In small cities or the suburbs, on the other hand, the social topography is usually more distinct since there are only a few charitable causes extant. The choice may be limited to one major hospital or old-age home or the fund-raising committees of the United Fund, Community Chest, or heart, cancer, or arthritis foundations.

But no matter where they're located, the prestige charities all have one thing in common: You don't just walk in off the street and announce your willingness to serve. A chic charity adheres to the "Don't call us, we'll call you" policy of recruitment. Here's where a good address and sending your toddlers to the best private nursery and country day schools help. If your neighbors or the parents of your children's schoolmates constitute the local establishment, you shouldn't have too much trouble wangling an invitation to work for a ball committee. Don't be concerned if the local charity does not mount a ball. Committees for other types of fund-raising events—fashion shows, art auctions, dog shows—are almost as good.

Why is the charity ball such a good showcase for the aspirant? Because it provides the perfect stage for displaying all the requisite upper-class status symbols: money, clothes, jewelry, friends. Furthermore, how much money you raise is seen as the indicator of how much clout you have in the community.

"Charity balls are excellent places to find out what other people have and to show what you've got," said William Wright in his exposé of New York's fashionable April in Paris Ball, a book called simply *Ball*. "There are many ways to do the latter. You can take a table, which at the April in Paris would cost you $1,750 for a table of ten. Then you can show what you've got by wearing it. Or, if what you want to show can't very well be worn into the ballroom—a medium-sized Cézanne, for example—then you can throw open your home for a pre-ball cocktail party. . . . The ball world is a world of status symbols: the invited and the uninvited, the well-seated at dinner and the badly seated, the generous donors, the mere ticket-buyers, and the hangers-on."

There is one problem with charity extravaganzas as social-climbing devices, however. If you don't choose your event with care, you may end up hobnobbing with no one fancier than yourself. Many old-line gentlewomen have dropped out of the charity-ball scene.

"I gave up charity balls years ago," said Mrs. William Woodward, a *doyenne* of New York society. "They are a crashing bore. You came, but you didn't know twenty people in the room. All those funny little people you'd never seen before. Charity balls may still have a function for people who've come into money recently, but as far as society goes, they are dead, for the most part."

It is true that many of the big names associated with charity balls these days are ex-showgirls, models, etc. who had the good fortune to marry the scions of old families. They find volunteer work useful for validating their own social credentials. Into this category fall Eleanor Searle and Mary Lou Schroeder, wives Nos. 3 and 4 of C. V. Whitney, a third-generation Whitney and a fifth-generation Vanderbilt; Dru Mallory who married H. J. "Jack" Heinz II, grandson of the pickle company's founder; Gloria Rubio, today Mrs. Loel Guinness, a woman married to a man who reportedly inherited $200 million from his father in 1947; Gregg Sherwood Dodge Moran, once the wife of auto heir Horace Dodge, Jr.; Mary Hartline, widow of Woolworth Donahue, the dime store scion and cousin of Barbara Hutton; Mildred Brown, once married to restaurant heir George Schrafft before becoming "Brownie" McLean, wife of Jock of newspaper and gold-mine lineage; and the current queen of Palm Beach society, Mrs. Stephen "Laddie" Sanford, the former Mary Duncan, an actress, and now the wife of a carpet heir.

The Tale of an Oyster
by Cole Porter

> Down by the sea lived a lonesome oyster,
> Ev'ry day getting sadder and moister,
> He found his home life awf'lly wet,
> And longed to travel with the upper set.
> Poor little oyster.
> Fate was kind to that oyster we know,
> When one day the chef from the Park Casino
> Saw that oyster lying there,
> And said, "I'll put you on my bill of fare."
> Lucky little oyster.
> See him on his silver platter,
> Watching the queens of fashion chatter.
> Hearing the wives of millionaires
> Discuss their marriages and their love affairs.
> Thrilled little oyster.
> See that bi-valve social climber
> Feeding the rich Mrs. Hoggenheimer,
> Think of his joy as he gaily glides
> Down to the middle of her gilded insides.

THE PERILS OF SOCIAL CLIMBING—AND HOW IT'S ACCOMPLISHED

Proud little oyster.
After lunch Mrs. H. complains,
And says to her hostess, "I've got such pains.
I came to town on my yacht today,
But I think I'd better hurry back to Oyster Bay."
Scared little oyster.
Off they go thru the troubled tide,
The yacht rolling madly from side to side,
They're tossed about till that poor young oyster
Finds that it's time he should quit his cloister.
Up comes the oyster.
Back once more where he started from.
He murmured, "I haven't a single qualm,
For I've had a taste of society
And society has had a taste of me."
Wise little oyster.

A Checklist of Basic Social-Climbing Requirements

—lots of money and a liberal attitude about squandering it
—gutsy, extroverted personality without appearing pushy
—steely determination
—skin the thickness of armadillo plates
—good looks or the ability to make the most of what you've got
—a hefty clothes budget and a knack for dressing in a distinctive manner
—pleasant manners and knowledge of etiquette
—self-deprecating wit, as opposed to the comedian's flair for monopolizing the conversation
—an appreciation of gossip and how to use it to telling effect *without* seeming malicious
—good memory for names
—ability to hold your liquor
—a laissez-faire attitude about other people's moral codes, or lack thereof
—smattering of knowledge, superficial though it may be, of a variety of subjects—particularly the latest fads and art trends
—a residence in keeping with your occupation (e.g., if you're a banker, an antique-filled mansion in the suburbs or a large apartment in the city would be appropriate; if you're passing

yourself off as a painter, a loft in SoHo or a converted barn in the country is essential.)
—familiarity with current status symbols even if you don't sport them yourself
—facility with at least two of the following: tennis, court tennis, squash, skiing, backgammon, bridge, yachting, horsemanship (riding, breeding, and/or racing), fox hunting, polo, horticulture, dog breeding, billiards (no, *not* pool, you idiot!)

WILLING IT:

RICH PEOPLE'S LEGACIES

25 Ever wonder where the moola goes when the big bucks bow out? Herewith, an overview of how the richest Americans have disposed of their assets via wills since 1950.

DECEASED	DATE AND MANNER OF DEATH	AGGREGATE AMOUNT OF ESTATE (if known)	WHO BENEFITTED MOST
Vincent Astor, sixty-seven (New York) heir to a real estate fortune	February 3, 1959 heart attack	$127 million	His widow, Mrs. Brooke Russell Astor—$2 million plus residual trust fund Twenty-five other individual bequests, including one to his first wife (none to his second) totaling $827,500 Vincent Astor Foundation—one-half gross estate Federal inheritance tax—$198,552 New York State tax—$27,876 Footnote: his half-brother, John Jacob Astor 3d, challenged the will and settled out of court for $200,000.
Alice B. Atwood, eighty-five (Chicago) granddaughter of the founder of Texas' King Ranch	December 11, 1965 natural causes	$10 million	Chicago policeman Michael J. De Bella, who had befriended the elderly spinster, was named her sole beneficiary. She specifically disinherited her two brothers and one sister. The estate remained in litigation for four years as executors pressed charges against Miss Atwood's longtime attorney, Thomas

DECEASED	DATE AND MANNER OF DEATH	AGGREGATE AMOUNT OF ESTATE (if known)	WHO BENEFITTED MOST
Bernard Baruch, ninety-four (New York) Wall Street financier	June 20, 1965 heart attack	in excess of $1 million	His son, retired naval officer Capt. Bernard M. Baruch, Jr.—lifetime income plus $600,000 trust fund His daughter, Renee (Mrs. H. Robert) Samstag—lifetime income Two nieces—income from two $100,000 trusts Nurse, Miss Elizabeth Navarro— $200,000 outright and lifetime income from a $200,000 trust fund Thirty-one other monetary bequests to four godchildren, friends, employees, and organizations totaling $537,000 City College's Baruch School of Business and Public Administration—two-thirds

Hart Fisher, who finally agreed to return $3 million–$5 million to the estates of two Atwood heirs. Mr. Fisher died six months after the settlement was reached.

DECEASED	DATE AND MANNER OF DEATH	AGGREGATE AMOUNT OF ESTATE (if known)	WHO BENEFITTED MOST
William H. Benton, seventy-two (Southport, Connecticut, and New York) owner and publisher of *Encyclopaedia Britannica*; founder, Benton & Bowles ad agency; U.S. Senator	March 18, 1973 pneumonia	not available; fortune during his lifetime set at $150–200 million	His widow Helen—real and personal property of unnamed value His four children—ditto Six cousins—$10,000 each Friend Walter Schleiter—$25,000 Employees—bequests ranging from $5,000 to $50,000 William Benton Foundation—remainder Footnote: The second paragraph of his will read, "Under protest by me, but at the insistence of lawyers, this will is overwritten in legal gobbledygook of the kind I deplore. . . ." of the rest of the estate and one-sixth each to the departments of Rehabilitation and Physical Medicine at Bellevue Hospital and at Columbia University.

DECEASED	DATE AND MANNER OF DEATH	AGGREGATE AMOUNT OF ESTATE (if known)	WHO BENEFITTED MOST
Ailsa Mellon Bruce, sixty-six (New York and Syossett, Long Island) inheritance; daughter of Andrew Mellon	August 25, 1969	$571 million	Andrew W. Mellon Foundation—bulk of her estate National Gallery of Art—her art collection Her three orphaned grandchildren—her jewelry or an equivalent amount in cash; otherwise, her will stated that they "are amply provided for from other sources." Thirty+ employees—pensions New York State—Since about $557 million of her estate went to charitable and public institutions, the federal and state tax authorities claimed only approximately $7 million.
Godfrey L. Cabot, 101 (Boston) heir; founder of the Cabot Corp., an international chemicals manufacturer	November 2, 1962 died in his sleep	not available; during his lifetime, his wealth was estimated at $75–100 million	He was survived by four of his five children, fourteen grandchildren, and twenty-nine great-grandchildren who have now increased in number to more than thirty-two. His daughter, Eleanor Cabot Bradley, claims his descendants would be wealthier today if he hadn't

DECEASED	DATE AND MANNER OF DEATH	AGGREGATE AMOUNT OF ESTATE (if known)	WHO BENEFITTED MOST
Bing Crosby, seventy-four (Los Angeles) singer and entertainer	October 14, 1977 heart attack	not available because he had established a "living trust" four months before he died to guarantee privacy. The trust provided for his seven children by his two marriages. The remainder of the estate was distributed via a will.	postponed planning his estate in the hope that the Republicans would abolish the inheritance tax. His widow, Kathryn Grant Crosby—$150,000 Gonzaga High School and Gonzaga University—$50,000 each St. Aloysius Catholic Church, Spokane—$5,000 A sister, cousin, four nieces, and four business associates—bequests ranging from $5,000 to $25,000
Irénée Du Pont, eighty-six (Wilmington) inheritance; executive, Du Pont Co.	December 19, 1963 natural causes	$40 million	Seven daughters and one son—eight equal trust funds In 1971, Ralph Nader's Raiders accused two Delaware officials of railroading a special tax provision through Congress that benefitted du Pont heirs by allow-

DECEASED	DATE AND MANNER OF DEATH	AGGREGATE AMOUNT OF ESTATE (if known)	WHO BENEFITTED MOST
			ing them to write off as a tax loss their father's multimillion-dollar Cuban estate "Xanadu" which was confiscated by the Castro government in 1961.
Cyrus S. Eaton, ninety-five (Cleveland and Nova Scotia) industrialist —railroads, iron, steel, and coal— under the banner of Chessie Systems.	May 9, 1979 natural causes	not available; wealth estimated at $100+ million during his lifetime	He was survived by his second wife, Anne Kinder Jones Eaton, who received the bulk of the estate; two sons, Cyrus, Jr., and Dr. MacPherson Eaton; three daughters; a stepdaughter; fifteen grandchildren, among them reporter Fox Butterfield of *The New York Times*; and ten great-grandchildren. Two of his children predeceased him.
Benson Ford, fifty-nine (Grosse Pointe) inheritance, grandson of Henry Ford, Sr.; executive, Ford Motor Co.	July 27, 1978 heart attack aboard his yacht docked in the Cheboygan River in Michigan	$100 million, mostly in Ford Motor Co. stock	His widow, Edith McNaughton Ford— his real estate, cars, jewelry, artworks, and one-half his total estate His two children, Lynn (Mrs. Paul D.) Alandt and Benson, Jr.—$7.5 million each under a family trust fund. Son

DECEASED	DATE AND MANNER OF DEATH	AGGREGATE AMOUNT OF ESTATE (if known)	WHO BENEFITTED MOST
			Benson is engaged in a protracted legal battle contesting the will and the trust it creates. He maintains that neither instrument specifically provides for him to control any of his father's Ford Co. stock because the trust gives control of the shares to his mother (who died in August 1980) and then, successively, to his uncles, Henry Ford II and William Clay Ford. Charging "breach of fiduciary duty," Benson seeks $200+ million in punitive and other damages from various family members and their representatives. Inheritance taxes—$35 million Henry Ford Hospital—$500,000
Childs Frick, eighty-one (Roslyn, Long Island) inheritance; son of Henry Clay Frick; paleontologist and trustee of the American Museum of Natural History	May 9, 1965 heart attack	not available; his sister, Helen Clay Frick, is still alive and reputedly worth $150–200 million	He left a son, Dr. Henry Clay Frick 2nd; two daughters, Mrs. I. Townsend Burden, Jr., and Mrs. J. F. Symington, Jr.; and fifteen grandchildren. American Museum of Natural History—fossil collection valued at about $6.5 million and about $3.5 million to build a Childs Frick wing.

DECEASED	DATE AND MANNER OF DEATH	AGGREGATE AMOUNT OF ESTATE (if known)	WHO BENEFITTED MOST
J. Paul Getty, eighty-three (London) inheritance; executive, Getty Oil Co.	June 6, 1976 heart failure	$1.7 billion, mostly in Getty Oil Co. stock	J. Paul Getty Museum in Malibu—$750+ million yielding about $50 million annually plus his personal art collection Twelve women friends—individual bequests ranging from $100 a month for life to $826,500 plus $1,167 a month for life. One of the women, Rosabell Burch, who was Getty's live-in companion for the last fifteen years of his life, sued for a larger share of the estate and settled for $150,000, about twice what she was willed. One of his five former wives, Louise Lynch Getty—$55,000 a year for life His three surviving sons, Jean Ronald Getty, J. Paul, Jr., and Gordon Peter Getty; his sixteen grandchildren; and one great-grandchild—undisclosed amounts if any. Sons Gordon and Ronald received more than $1 million each in executors' fees. Son J. Paul, Jr., and

DECEASED	DATE AND MANNER OF DEATH	AGGREGATE AMOUNT OF ESTATE (if known)	WHO BENEFITTED MOST
			his son, J. Paul III, and any of their progeny were specifically excluded from succeeding at any time to positions in the family trust. His oldest grandchild, Anne Catherine Getty, contested the will, claiming the bulk of the estate should have gone to a family trust rather than to the J. Paul Getty Museum. She lost. His mausoleum to be constructed on the grounds of his museum—$50,000 to cover building costs and $150,000 for perpetual maintenance. Estate taxes—$10 million
Leo Goodwin III, twenties (Fort Lauderdale) inheritance; grandson of the GEICO founder	June 1, 1977 drug overdose	$2.7 million	Two women, both claiming Leo III as the father of their daughters, are suing the estate. His estate is entangled with that of his father who died six months after him.

DECEASED	DATE AND MANNER OF DEATH	AGGREGATE AMOUNT OF ESTATE (if known)	WHO BENEFITTED MOST
Millicent Willson Hearst (Mrs. William Randolph Hearst, Sr.), ninety-two (New York) inheritance	December 5, 1974 natural causes	$2.5 million	Her son, William Randolph, Jr., and his progeny—trust fund comprising one-third of her estate. Her son, David Whitmire Hearst, and his progeny—same Her son, Randolph Apperson Hearst, and his progeny—same
Conrad Hilton, ninety-one (Los Angeles) founder, Hilton Hotels Corp.	January 3, 1979 pneumonia	$100 million, including 28 percent of the stock of Hilton Hotels Corp.	His son, Barron Hilton—$750,000 and the option to buy his father's shares of the company His son, Eric—$300,000 His daughter, Constance Francesca Hilton—$100,000. She contested the will, contending that her father had renounced her because he was guilt-ridden over having married her mother, Zsa Zsa Gabor, without having his first marriage annulled by the Catholic Church. She lost.

401

DECEASED	DATE AND MANNER OF DEATH	AGGREGATE AMOUNT OF ESTATE (if known)	WHO BENEFITTED MOST
Howard Hughes, seventy (residence? anybody's guess) inheritance; executive, Summa Corp., holding company/ conglomerate	April 5, 1976 kidney failure brought on by massive doses of aspirin over a long period of time, according to his personal physician	conflicting amounts ranging from $169 million to $1 billion	In effect, Hughes died intestate since none of the many wills which surfaced after his death could be authenticated. In addition to intra-family scrabbles over the estate, three states—Texas, California, and Nevada—claim him as a resident, and Delaware and Louisiana retain jurisdiction over portions of the estate. A cousin and the estate's executor, William R. Lummis, contends Hughes was a resident of Nevada which has no inheritance tax. Attorneys litigating the dispute—$3.5 million in fees for 1978 alone. Federal inheritance tax—at least 78 percent of the estate's value.

Charitable foundation—bulk of estate (His surviving wife, Mary Frances Kelly Hilton, received nothing under the will because Hilton had provided for her amply in a premarital agreement.)

DECEASED	DATE AND MANNER OF DEATH	AGGREGATE AMOUNT OF ESTATE (if known)	WHO BENEFITTED MOST
H. L. Hunt, eighty-five (Dallas) independent oil operator	November 29, 1974 viral infection	not available; wealth during his lifetime estimated at $500 million to $1 billion	His widow and second wife, Ruth Ray Hunt—all his Hunt Oil Co. stock in trust and their home and surrounding real estate His five sons and five daughters—other stock and property as outright bequests as well as funds accruing to them through both the Loyal and Reliance trusts, established many years before his death. Hunt's Louisiana real estate interests were divided into fourteen parts, with his six older children receiving one-fourteenth each in an outright bequest. The four younger children by his second wife each receive a one-fourteenth interest in the Louisiana property through the Loyal Trust. The remaining four-fourteenths go to the Reliance Trust. His son-in-law, Al G. Hill—all his Tenable Oil Co. stock

DECEASED	DATE AND MANNER OF DEATH	AGGREGATE AMOUNT OF ESTATE (if known)	WHO BENEFITTED MOST
			Six grandchildren, the sons and daughters of Mrs. Al G. Hill and Lamar Hunt—residuary estate
			In 1978, a former Atlanta socialite who claimed she was married to Hunt for nine years from 1925 to 1934, sued the estate for half the money Hunt earned during their alleged marriage. She also claimed "Franklin Hunt," the name under which Hunt courted and married her, was the father of her four children. The woman, Frania Tye Lee, dropped her suit and accepted an out-of-court settlement of an undisclosed amount. Rumor placed it at $7.5 million, half of the $15 million Hunt was worth when they parted.
			Hunt's will also contained a provision disinheriting anyone who challenged it.
Joseph P. Kennedy, eighty-one (Boston and Palm Beach) financier and real estate entrepreneur	November 18, 1969	not available; fortune during his lifetime estimated at $300–500 million	Joseph P. Kennedy, Jr., Foundation devoted to research in mental retardation —bulk of estate
			His widow, Rose Fitzgerald Kennedy—$500,000 in cash plus real estate in

DECEASED	DATE AND MANNER OF DEATH	AGGREGATE AMOUNT OF ESTATE (if known)	WHO BENEFITTED MOST
			Albany, New York His two sisters, Loretta Conolly and Margaret Burke—$25,000 each Estate taxes $134,330.90 His will stated: "Having provided during my lifetime for my children and grandchildren and having made other arrangements for my household help and employees, I intentionally omit to make any further provision for any of them." (He and his wife, Rose, had established a series of trusts in 1926, 1936, 1949, and 1959 both to avoid inheritance taxes and to keep the capital intact for future Kennedys.)
Charles F. Kettering, eighty-two (Dayton) automotive inventor and executive of General Motors	November 25, 1958 cerebral stroke	$200+ million	Charles F. Kettering Foundation and another philanthropic trust—bulk of estate His only son, Eugene Williams Kettering —unspecific amount of cash, his home, and all other real estate Seven relatives—cash bequests totaling $175,000

DECEASED	DATE AND MANNER OF DEATH	AGGREGATE AMOUNT OF ESTATE (if known)	WHO BENEFITTED MOST
Eli Lilly, ninety-one (Indianapolis) inheritance; grandson of founder and executive of Eli Lilly & Co. (pharmaceuticals)	January 24, 1977	$185 million	98 percent of estate went to charities Save the Children Federation—$3 million.
Henry R. Luce, sixty-eight (New York City and Phoenix) founder, Time Inc.	February 28, 1967 heart attack	$103 million	His second wife, Claire Boothe Luce—principal beneficiary Henry Luce Foundation—enough Time Inc. stock to give it controlling interest.
Mary Pickford (Mrs. Charles "Buddy" Rogers), eighty-six (Beverly Hills) actress	May 29, 1979 stroke	preliminary estimates placed the value at $10.3 million but the true value —which won't be known until her property is sold or distributed—is believed much greater. Her wealth during her life-	Mary Pickford Foundation—bulk of her estate and her home, "Pickfair." Her third husband, the bandleader Buddy Rogers who was eleven years her junior —$25,000 in cash, much of her personal property, real estate in California and Arizona, and $48,000 annually from a trust.

DECEASED	DATE AND MANNER OF DEATH	AGGREGATE AMOUNT OF ESTATE (if known)	WHO BENEFITTED MOST
		time was estimated at $50 million.	Her niece, Gwynne Pickford Ornstein—$200,000 trust for her and a $150,000 trust for her children Her stepson, Douglas Fairbanks, Jr.—$5,000 Her two adopted children, Roxanne and Ronald—$50,000 each plus an educational trust for their six children Fifteen friends and former employees—gifts ranging from $1,000 to $25,000 Smithsonian Institution—star sapphire and semiprecious stones; costumes from her films; weapons that once belonged to matinee idol Rudolph Valentino; and a set of Japanese swords.
Marjorie Merriweather Post (Washington, D.C., and Palm Beach) inheritance; Postum Cereal Co. later General Foods	September 12, 1973 long illness	$117 million	Three daughters, Mrs. Adelaide Riggs, Mrs. Eleanor Barzin, and Mrs. Nedenia (Dina Merrill) Robertson—about $30–40 million each including her personal property Federal government—her twenty-six-acre Washington, D.C., estate "Hillwood"

DECEASED	DATE AND MANNER OF DEATH	AGGREGATE AMOUNT OF ESTATE (if known)	WHO BENEFITTED MOST
			and her seventeen-acre Palm Beach estate "Mar-A-Largo" plus multimillion-dollar endowments to maintain them. Grandchildren—varying amounts with all sharing in their respective mothers' share of the estate upon their mothers' deaths (Exempted was one grandson, Antol Post De Bekessy, because he is already in line to receive "a very large trust fund I created many years ago"; and one granddaughter, Marjorie Durant Dye, because "it has been my pleasure to adequately provide for her during her lifetime.") Thirteen retainers "who have served me so efficiently and loyally over many years"—$5,000–$50,000 each Seventeen other employees or their relatives—lifetime monthly incomes of from $125 to $220

DECEASED	DATE AND MANNER OF DEATH	AGGREGATE AMOUNT OF ESTATE (if known)	WHO BENEFITTED MOST
John D. Rockefeller, Jr., eighty-six (New York City and Pocantico Hills, New York) inheritance; son of Standard Oil founder	May 11, 1960 pneumonia and heart strain	$160.5 million; gave away almost $475 million during his lifetime, which still didn't compare to the $600 million the original John D. gave away.	His second wife, Martha Baird Rockefeller—about $56 million in trust with full power to dispose of the principal during her lifetime or in her will Rockefeller Brothers Fund—about $75 million Individual bequests to various charities and Republican Party groups—about $23 million Lincoln Center for the Performing Arts —$5 million His five sons, David, John 3d, Laurance, Nelson, and Winthrop—Pocantico Hills, New York, real estate Federal government—real estate on Mt. Desert Island, Maine, to add to the Arcadia National Park Federal taxes—$10.4 million New York State taxes—$3 million

DECEASED	DATE AND MANNER OF DEATH	AGGREGATE AMOUNT OF ESTATE (if known)	WHO BENEFITTED MOST
John D. Rockefeller 3d, seventy-two (New York City and Pocantico Hills, New York) inheritance; grandson of founder, Standard Oil	July 10, 1978 car accident near Tarrytown, New York	$100 million; his lifetime giving tallied $94 million	His widow, Blanchette Hooker Rockefeller—real estate, some artworks, household furnishings, and other personal effects plus a trust fund of an undisclosed amount His son, John D. IV; and his three daughters, Hope Aldrich, Sandra Ferry, and Alida Dayton—portions of his art collection to share with their mother. The will indicated that they were receiving relatively small gifts because they had already been amply provided for by John D., Jr. A park planned for Pocantico Hills—his 25 percent interest in the 3,000 acres there Asia Society—300 Asian art objects appraised at $10–15 million Fine Arts Museums of San Francisco—American art collection valued at $10 million

DECEASED	DATE AND MANNER OF DEATH	AGGREGATE AMOUNT OF ESTATE (if known)	WHO BENEFITTED MOST
Nelson A. Rockefeller, seventy (New York City and Pocantico Hills, New York) inheritance; grandson of founder, Standard Oil; politician	January 26, 1979 heart attack	$66.5 million ($30 million of it in art)	Nine bequests to charitable and educational institutions including his alma maters, Loomis Inst. and Princeton—totaling $2.25 million J.D.R. 3d Fund—remainder of estate His second wife, Margaretta Fitler Rockefeller—substantial real estate, his personal property, and the residuary estate—all amounting to one-half of total estate His two sons by his second wife, Nelson, Jr., and Mark—trust funds of an undisclosed amount to try to bring their personal worth into parity with his four older children (Rodman C., Ann Roberts, Steven C., and Mary Morgan) by his first marriage His six children and one stepdaughter—articles of his personal property to be

411

DECEASED	DATE AND MANNER OF DEATH	AGGREGATE AMOUNT OF ESTATE (if known)	WHO BENEFITTED MOST
			selected by them up to a value of $25,000 for each
			Museum of Modern Art—art worth an estimated $8.5 million
			Metropolitan Museum of Art—1,610 works of primitive art valued in excess of $5 million
			Forgave three outstanding personal loans to aide Megan R. Marshack ($45,000), his press spokesman Hugh Morrow ($30,000), and Washington staff chief during his vice presidency Susan Cable Herter ($20,000)
			National Trust for Historic Preservation —his undivided one-fourth interest in the family-owned grounds at Pocantico Hills to use for a park

DECEASED	DATE AND MANNER OF DEATH	AGGREGATE AMOUNT OF ESTATE (if known)	WHO BENEFITTED MOST
Winthrop P. Rockefeller, sixty (Little Rock, Arkansas) inheritance; grandson of founder, Standard Oil	February 22, 1973 cancer	$175 million	His son, Winthrop Paul—beneficiary of his father's $125-million trust from John D. Rockefeller, Sr., set up in 1934; and the ranch house at "Winrock Farms" in Arkansas Charitable trust—the livestock and real-estate assets of "Winrock Farms" worth an estimated $50 million
Sarah Mellon Scaife (Mrs. Alan M. Scaife), sixty-two (Pittsburgh) inheritance, Mellon family	December 28, 1965	not available; fortune during her lifetime set at $400–700 million	University of Pittsburgh—$5 million Children's Hospital—$1 million Other nonprofit institutions—bequests totaling $1.9 million Rolling Rock Club, Ligonier, Pennsylvania—$1 million Sarah Mellon Scaife Foundation—four fifths of remaining estate Her son, Richard Mellon Scaife, and daughter, Cordelia Scaife May Duggan—remaining one fifth of estate plus her real estate and personal property

DECEASED	DATE AND MANNER OF DEATH	AGGREGATE AMOUNT OF ESTATE (if known)	WHO BENEFITTED MOST
Alfred P. Sloan, Jr. ninety (New York City) executive, General Motors	February 17, 1966 heart attack	$90+ million; by the time he died, he had already funneled $305 million into his own foundation	MIT (his alma mater)—$10 million Sloan-Kettering Institute for Cancer Research—$10 million Memorial Hospital for Cancer and Allied Diseases (New York City)—$10 million Alfred P. Sloan Foundation—$60 million Six household employees—bequests ranging from $500 to $17,500
Thomas J. Watson, eighty-two (New Canaan, Connecticut, and New York City) founder, IBM Corp.	June 19, 1956	$5 million	His widow, Jeanette Kittredge Watson—one-half the residuary estate in trust His direct descendants (i.e., two sons, Thomas, Jr., and Arthur; two daughters, Mrs. John N. Irwin II and Mrs. Walker G. Buckner; and eighteen grandchildren)—one-half of the residuary estate in trust Two of his New Canaan neighbors—$5,000 each

DECEASED	DATE AND MANNER OF DEATH	AGGREGATE AMOUNT OF ESTATE (if known)	WHO BENEFITTED MOST
			WHO BENEFITTED MOST
John Wayne, seventy-two (Los Angeles) actor	June 11, 1979 cancer	$6.9 million	Brick Presbyterian Church, Boy Scouts, Salvation Army, and Roosevelt Hospital—$200,000 each
			Forty-two past and present employees—tax-free bequests of $1,000 to $5,000 each
			Seven children—$5,000 multiplied by the difference between age twenty-one and the child's age at his death. This formula gave his eldest son, Michael, age forty-four, $115,000, for example.
			His ex-secretary, Mary St. John—$10,000
			His current secretary, Pat Stacy—$30,000
			Various nonprofit organizations—his artworks
			Various trust accounts, one of which will provide for his first wife, Josephine—remainder of estate

DECEASED	DATE AND MANNER OF DEATH	AGGREGATE AMOUNT OF ESTATE (if known)	WHO BENEFITTED MOST
			His third wife, Pilar, and a son-in-law were specifically excluded from the estate.
Sandra Ilene West (Mrs. Ike West, Jr.) thirty-seven (Beverly Hills) inheritance; oil	March 10, 1977	$2.5 million	Her brother-in-law, Sol West III—bulk of her estate *provided* he sees to it that she is buried according to instructions: ". . . next to my husband in my lace nightgown . . . in my 1964 baby-blue Ferrari with the seat slanted comfortably. . . . If a coffin is used other than for shipping he is disinherited except for $10,000." He carried out her instructions and had her driven to rest in a San Antonio Masonic cemetery. However, whether or not he inherits depends on the outcome of a court case to decide which of two wills is valid.

BIBLIOGRAPHY

This book is the product of 500 personal interviews with wealthy individuals and those in close contact with the rich. It is also the result of a cross-country research effort which took the author to more than fifty cities.

The author would like to thank the librarians of sixty local newspaper morgues which opened their files to her; and the personnel who so graciously assisted her when she visited the following libraries: Boston Public Library; Springfield (Mass.) City Library; Providence Public Library; Bridgeport Public Library; Rochester Public Library; Corning Public Library; New York Public Library; General Society of Mechanics and Tradesmen Library (N.Y.C.); Morristown (N.J.) Public Library; Somerset County (N.J.) Library; Wilmington Institute Libraries; Enoch Pratt Free Library (Baltimore, Md.); Martin Luther King Memorial Library (Washington, D.C.); Osterhout Free Library (Wilkes-Barre, Pa.); Philadelphia Free Library; Carnegie Library (Pittsburgh); Forsyth County Public Library (Winston-Salem, N.C.); Atlanta Public Library; Jacksonville Public Library; West Palm Beach City Library; Miami Public Library; Cleveland Public Library; Detroit Public Library; Indianapolis-Marion County Public Libraries; Chicago Public Library; Winnetka (Ill.) Public Library; Milwaukee Public Library; Minneapolis Public Library; St. Louis Public Library; Kansas City (Mo.) Public Library; New Orleans Public Library; Denver Public Library; Dallas Public Library; Fort Worth Public Library; Houston Public Library; Los Angeles Public Library; Palm Springs Public Library; San Francisco Public Library; and the Oakland Public Library.

The following books and periodicals were consulted either as source material or for their ideas and theories:

Books

Alix, Ernest Kahlar. *Ransom Kidnapping in America 1874–1974: The Creation of a Capital Crime.* Carbondale, Ill.: Southern Illinois University Press, 1978.

Alvarez, A. *The Savage God: A Study of Suicide.* New York: Random House, 1970.

Amory, Cleveland. *The Last Resorts.* New York: Harper & Bros., 1948.

———. *The Proper Bostonians.* New York: E. P. Dutton, 1947.

———. *Who Killed Society?* New York: Harper, 1960.

Armour, Lawrence A. *The Young Millionaires.* Chicago: Playboy Press, 1973.

Bainbridge, John. *The Super-Americans.* New York: Doubleday, 1961.

Baltzell, E. Digby. *Philadelphia Gentlemen, the Making of a National Upper Class.* Glencoe, Ill.: The Free Press, 1958.

———. *The Protestant Establishment: Aristocracy and Caste in America.* New York: Random House, 1964.

Barmash, Isadore. *The Self-Made Man: Success and Stress—American Style.* London: Collier-Macmillan, 1969.

Baruch, Bernard M. *Baruch: My Own Story.* New York: Henry Holt, 1957.

Bender, Marilyn. *The Beautiful People.* New York: Coward-McCann, 1967.

Bergler, Dr. Edmund. "Are You a Money Neurotic?" *Harper's Bazaar,* May 1958.

Birmingham, Stephen. *Our Crowd: The Great Jewish Families of New York.* New York: Harper & Row, 1967.

———. *The Right People: A Portrait of the American Social Establishment.* Boston: Little, Brown, 1958.

———. *The Right Places (for the Right People).* Boston: Little, Brown, 1973.

———. *Real Lace: America's Irish Rich.* New York: Harper & Row, 1973.

Blackwell, Earl (ed.). *The Celebrity Register.* New York: Simon & Schuster, 1973.

Bloom, Murray Teigh. *Rogues to Riches: The Trouble with Wall Street.* New York: G. P. Putnam's Sons, 1971.

Brady, Frank. *Hefner.* New York: Macmillan, 1974.

Brooks, John. *The Games Players: Tales of Men and Money.* New York: Times Books, 1979.

———. *The Go-Go Years.* New York: Weybright and Talley, 1973.

Brough, James. *The Ford Dynasty: An American Story.* New York: Doubleday, 1977.

Brown, Stanley H. *H. L. Hunt.* Chicago: Playboy Press, 1976.

Buckle, Richard (ed.). *Debrett's U & Non-U Revisited.* New York: Viking, 1978.

Burt, Nathaniel. *The Perennial Philadelphians: The Anatomy of an American Aristocracy.* Boston: Little, Brown, 1963.

Carr, Albert Z. *Business As a Game.* New York: New American Library, 1968.

———. *John D. Rockefeller's Secret Weapon.* New York: McGraw-Hill, 1962.

Carr, William H. A. *The Du Ponts of Delaware.* New York: Dodd, Mead, 1964.

Churchill, Allen. *The Splendor Seekers: An Informal Glimpse of America's Multimillionaire Spenders—Members of the $50,000,000 Club.* New York: Grosset & Dunlap, 1974.

———. *The Upper Crust: An Informal History of New York's Highest Society.* Englewood Cliffs, N.J.: Prentice-Hall, 1970.

Collier, Peter, and David Horowitz. *The Rockefellers: An American Dynasty.* New York: Holt, Rinehart and Winston, 1976.

Considine, Millie. *Wills: A Dead Giveaway.* New York: Doubleday, 1974.

Cowles, Virginia. *The Astors.* New York: Knopf, 1979.

Cuber, Dr. John F. "Sex in the Upper Middle Class," *Medical Aspects of Human Sexuality,* July 1974.

Dietrich, Noah, and Bob Thomas. *Howard: The Amazing Mr. Hughes.* New York: Fawcett, 1977.

Domhoff, G. William. *The Bohemian Grove and Other Retreats: A Study in Ruling-Class Consciousness.* New York: Harper & Row, 1974.

———. *Fat Cats and Democrats: The Role of the Big Rich in the Party of the Common Man.* Englewood Cliffs, N.J.: Prentice-Hall, 1972.

———. *The Higher Circles: The Governing Class in America.* New York: Random House, 1970.

———. *The Powers That Be: Processes of Ruling Class Domination in America.* New York: Random House, 1978.

Domhoff, G. William, and Hoyt B. Ballard. *C. Wright Mills and The Power Elite.* Boston: Beacon Press, 1968.

Dorian, Max. *The Du Ponts: From Gunpowder to Nylon*. Boston: Little, Brown, 1961.

Eidelberg, Ludwig, M.D. *Encyclopedia of Psychoanalysis*. New York: The Free Press, 1968.

Elliott, Osborne. *Men at the Top*. New York: Harper & Bros., 1959.

Esterow, Milton. *The Art Stealers*. New York: Macmillan, 1973.

Fenichel, Dr. Otto. "The Drive to Amass Wealth" (1935) *Psychoanalytic Quarterly*, Vol. VII, 1938.

Ferenczi, Sandor. "The Origin of the Interest in Money" (1914) *Contributions to Psychoanalysis*. Boston: R. J. Badger, 1916.

Fonzi, Gaeton. *Annenberg: A Biography of Power*. New York: Weybright and Talley, 1969.

Forster, Arnold, and Benjamin R. Epstein. *Danger on the Right*. New York: Random House, 1964.

Fosdick, Raymond B. *John D. Rockefeller, Jr.: A Portrait*. New York: Harper, 1953.

————. *The Story of the Rockefeller Foundation*. New York: Harper, 1952.

Freud, Sigmund. "Character and Anal Erotism" (1908), *Collected Papers*, Vol. II. Hogarth Press and Institute of Psychoanalysis.

Galbraith, John Kenneth. *The New Industrial State*. Boston: Houghton Mifflin, 1967.

Garrison, Omar. *Howard Hughes in Las Vegas*. New York: Lyle Stuart, 1970.

Gerber, Albert B. *Bashful Billionaire: The Story of Howard Hughes*. New York: Lyle Stuart, 1967.

Getty, J. Paul. *As I See It*. Englewood Cliffs, N.J.: Prentice-Hall, 1976.

————. *The Golden Age*. New York: Trident Press, 1968.

Gill, Brendan, and Jerome Zerbe. *Happy Times*. New York: Harcourt Brace Jovanovich, 1973.

Goldenson, Robert M., Ph.D. *The Encyclopedia of Human Behavior: Psychology, Psychiatry, and Mental Health*. New York: Doubleday, 1970.

Gould, Dr. Robert. "Measuring Masculinity by the Size of a Paycheck," *Ms. Magazine*, June 1973.

Goulden, Joseph C. *The Money Givers*. New York: Random House, 1971.

Graham, Sheila. *How to Marry Super Rich or Love, Money and the Morning After*. New York: Grosset & Dunlap, 1974.

Greene, Bert, with Phillip Stephen Schulz. *Pity the Poor Rich: It's a Losing Battle to Stay on Top but See How They Try*. Chicago: Contemporary Books, 1978.

Gunther, Max. *The Very, Very Rich and How They Got That Way.* Chicago: Playboy Press, 1972.

Halberstam, David. *The Best and the Brightest.* New York: Random House, 1969.

————. *The Powers That Be.* New York: Knopf, 1979.

The Handbook of Private Schools. Annual. Boston: Porter Sargent, 1979.

Heilbroner, Robert L. *The Limits of American Capitalism.* New York: Harper & Row, 1965.

Herndon, Booton. *Ford: An Unconventional Biography of the Men and Their Times.* New York: Weybright and Talley, 1969.

Hersh, Burton. *The Mellon Family: A Fortune in History.* New York: Morrow, 1978.

Hilton, Conrad. *Be My Guest.* Englewood Cliffs, N.J.: Prentice-Hall, 1957.

Hoffman, William. *David.* New York: Lyle Stuart, 1971.

————. *The Stock Holder.* New York: Lyle Stuart, 1969.

Holbrook, Stewart H. *The Age of the Moguls.* New York: Doubleday, 1953.

Hougan, Jim. *Spooks: The Haunting of America—the Private Use of Secret Agents.* New York: Morrow, 1978.

Howatch, Susan. *The Rich Are Different.* New York: Simon & Schuster, 1977.

Hoyt, Edwin P. *The Vanderbilts and Their Fortunes.* New York: Doubleday, 1962.

————. *The Whitneys: An Informal Portrait 1635–1975.* New York: Weybright and Talley, 1976.

Huber, Joan, and William H. Form. *Income and Ideology: An Analysis of the American Political Formula.* New York: The Free Press, 1973.

Huber, Richard M. *The American Idea of Success.* New York: Mc-Graw-Hill, 1971.

Huck, Virginia. *Brand of the Tartan: The 3M Story.* New York: Appleton-Century-Crofts, 1955.

Hunter, Floyd. *The Big Rich and the Little Rich.* New York: Doubleday, 1965.

Hutschnecker, Arnold A., M.D. *The Drive for Power.* New York: M. Evans, 1974.

Hyams, Barry. *Hirshhorn: Medici from Brooklyn.* New York: E. P. Dutton, 1979.

Hyman, Sidney. *The Lives of William Benton.* Chicago: University of Chicago, 1969.

Jenkins, Alan. *The Rich Rich: The Story of the Big Spenders*. New York: G. P. Putnam's Sons, 1978.

Johnson, Harry J. *Executive Life Styles: A Life Extension Institute Report on Alcohol, Sex and Health*. New York: T. Y. Crowell, 1974.

Josephson, Matthew. *The Money Lords*. New York: Weybright and Talley, 1972.

Kaschewski, Marjorie. *The Quiet Millionaires*. Morristown, N.J.: Morris County's Daily Record, 1970.

Kaufman, William. "Some Emotional Uses of Money" (1953), *Acta Psychotherapeutica, Psychosomatica et Orthopaedagogica*, Vol. IV (1956).

Kavaler, Lucy. *The Private World of High Society: Its Rules and Rituals*. New York: David McKay, 1960.

Keats, John. *Howard Hughes*. New York: Random House, 1966.

Kephart, William M. "Status After Death," *American Sociological Review*, October 1950.

Kirstein, George G. *The Rich: Are They Different?* Boston: Houghton Mifflin, 1968.

Klein, Melanie. "Early Development of Conscience in the Child," *Contributions to Psycho-Analysis, 1921–1945*. Hogarth Press and Institute of Psychoanalysis.

Konolige, Kit and Frederica. *The Power of Their Glory*. New York: Wyden, 1978.

Koskoff, David. *Joseph P. Kennedy: A Life and Times*. Englewood Cliffs, N.J.: Prentice-Hall, 1974.

———. *The Mellons: The Chronicles of America's Richest Family*. New York: T. Y. Crowell, 1978.

Kowet, Don. *The Rich Who Own Sports*. New York: Random House, 1977.

Kroc, Ray, with Robert Anderson. *Grinding It Out: The Making of McDonald's*. Chicago: Regnery, 1977.

Kutz, Myer. *Rockefeller Power: America's Chosen Family*. New York: Simon & Schuster, 1974.

Lea, Tom. *The King Ranch*. Boston: Little, Brown, 1957.

Leipold, L. E., Ph.D. *Jeno F. Paulucci: Merchant Philanthropist*. Minneapolis: T. S. Denison, 1968.

Lipset, Seymour Martin. *Political Man*. New York: Doubleday, 1960.

Livingston, Bernard. *Their Turf: America's Horsey Set and Its Princely Dynasties*. New York: Arbor House, 1973.

Lundberg, Ferdinand. *America's Sixty Families*. New York: Vanguard Press, 1937.

————. *The Rich and the Super-Rich: A Study in the Power of Money Today.* New York: Lyle Stuart, 1968.

MacKenzie, Norman (ed.). *Secret Societies.* New York: Crescent, 1967.

Manchester, William. *A Rockefeller Family Portrait: From John D. to Nelson.* Boston: Little, Brown, 1959.

Marts, Arnold. *The Generosity of Americans.* Englewood Cliffs, N.J.: Prentice-Hall, 1966.

Mason, Raymond K., and Virginia Harrison. *Confusion to the Enemy: A Biography of Ed Ball.* New York: Dodd, Mead, 1976.

Mayer, Martin, *The Bankers.* New York: Weybright and Talley, 1974.

Middlemas, Keith. *The Double Market: Art Theft and Art Thieves.* New York: Atheneum, 1975.

Mills, C. Wright. *The Power Elite.* New York: Oxford University Press, 1956.

Mintz, Morton, and Jerry S. Cohen. *America, Inc.: Who Owns and Operates the United States.* New York: Dial, 1971.

Morris, Joe Alex. *Those Rockefeller Brothers.* New York: Harper and Bros., 1953.

Morris, Lloyd. *Incredible New York.* New York: Random House, 1951.

Menshikov, S. *Millionaires and Managers.* Moscow. U.S.S.R.: Progress Publishers, 1969.

Moscow, Alvin. *The Rockefeller Inheritance.* New York: Doubleday, 1977.

Nevins, Allan. *Ford: The Times, The Man, The Company.* New York: Charles Scribner's Sons, 1954.

O'Connor, Harvey. *The Empire of Oil.* New York: Monthly Review Press, 1955.

————. *Mellon's Millions.* New York: John Day, 1933.

O'Connor, Richard. *The Golden Summers: An Antic History of Newport.* New York: G. P. Putnam's Sons, 1974.

————. *The Oil Barons: Men of Greed and Grandeur.* Boston: Little, Brown, 1971.

Odier, Charles. "L'Argent et les Névroses," *Revue Française de Psychanalyse,* Vol. II (1928) and Vol. III (1929).

O'Hara, John. *The Lockwood Concern.* New York: Random House, 1965.

Olshaker, Mark. *The Instant Image: Edwin Land and the Polaroid Experience.* New York: Stein & Day, 1978.

Orth, Penelope. *An Enviable Position: The American Mistress from Slightly Kept to Practically Married.* New York: Berkley Medallion, 1972.

Packard, Vance. *The Status Seekers.* New York: David McKay, 1959.

Paulucci, Jeno. *How It Was to Make $100,000,000 in a Hurry.* New York: Grosset & Dunlap, 1969.

Presley, James. *A Saga of Wealth: The Rise of the Texas Oilmen.* New York: G. P. Putnam's Sons, 1978.

Rasmussen, Anne-Marie. *There Was Once a Time.* New York: Harcourt Brace Jovanovich, 1975.

Rasponi, Lanfranco. *The Golden Oases.* New York: G. P. Putnam's Sons, 1968.

Rockefeller, John D. 3d. *The Second American Revolution: Some Personal Observations.* New York: Harper & Row, 1973.

Rodgers, William H. *Rockefeller's Follies: An Unauthorized View of Nelson A. Rockefeller.* New York: Stein & Day, 1966.

Róheim, Géza. "Heiliges Geld in Melanesien" (1923), *Int. Ztschr. f. Psa.,* Vol. IX.

Roosevelt, Felicia Warburg. *Doers & Dowagers.* New York: Doubleday, 1975.

Rubin, Dr. Theodore I. "Wraparound" section on money, *Harper's Magazine,* November 1973.

Saarinen, Aline B. *The Proud Possessors: The Lives, Times and Tastes of Some Adventurous American Art Collectors.* New York: Random House, 1958.

Sagarin, Dr. Edward. Question-answer section, *Medical Aspects of Human Sexuality,* August 1970.

Schrag, Peter. *The Decline of the Wasp.* New York: Simon & Schuster, 1970.

Shadegg, Stephen. *Clare Boothe Luce.* New York: Simon & Schuster, 1970.

Sheehy, Gail. *Passages.* New York: E. P. Dutton, 1976.

Sheppard, Harold L. (ed.). *Poverty and Wealth in America.* New York: Quadrangle, 1970.

Sloan, Alfred P. *My Years with General Motors.* New York: Doubleday, 1964.

Smith, Adam. *The Money Game.* New York: Random House, 1968.

Sopkin, Charles. *Money Talks!* New York: Random House, 1964.

Stern, Philip M. *The Rape of the Taxpayer.* New York: Random House. 1972.

Talese, Gay. *The Kingdom and the Power.* New York: World, 1969.

Tebbel, John. *The Inheritors: A Study of America's Great Fortunes and What Happened to Them.* New York: G. P. Putnam's Sons, 1962.

Thayer, George. *Who Shakes the Money Tree? American Campaign Financing Practices From 1789 to the Present.* New York: Simon & Schuster, 1974.

Thorndike, Joseph J., Jr. *The Very Rich: A History of Wealth.* New York: American Heritage, 1976.

Torgerson, Dial. *Kerkorian: An American Success Story.* Dial, 1974.

Vanderbilt, Cornelius, Jr. *Farewell to Fifth Avenue.* New York: Simon & Schuster, 1935.

————. *Man of the World: My Life on Five Continents.* New York: Crown, 1959.

————. *Palm Beach.* New York: Macaulay, 1931.

————. *Reno.* New York: Macaulay, 1929.

van der Zee, John. *The Greatest Men's Party on Earth: Inside the Bohemian Grove.* New York: Harcourt Brace Jovanovich, 1974.

van Rensselaer, Philip. *Million Dollar Baby: An Intimate Portrait of Barbara Hutton.* New York: G. P. Putnam's Sons, 1979.

Vaughan, Roger. *Ted Turner: The Man Behind the Mouth.* New York: W. W. Norton, 1978.

Veblen, Thorstein. *The Theory of the Leisure Class: An Economic Study of Institutions.* New York: New American Library, 1953.

Wagner, Walter. *Money Talks.* New York: Bobbs-Merrill, 1978.

Walker, John. *Self-Portrait with Donors: Confessions of an Art Collector.* Boston: Little, Brown, 1974.

Ward, John. *The Arkansas Rockefeller.* Baton Rouge: Louisiana State University, 1978.

Warner, Irving R. *The Art of Fund Raising.* New York: Harper & Row, 1975.

Werner, M. R. *Julius Rosenwald.* New York: Harper & Bros., 1939.

Whalen, Richard J. *The Founding Father: The Story of Joseph P. Kennedy.* New York: New American Library, 1964.

Wharton, Edith. *The Age of Innocence.* New York: Charles Scribner's Sons, 1968.

————. *A Backward Glance.* New York: D. Appleton-Century Co., 1934.

Whitaker, Ben. *The Philanthropoids: Foundations and Society.* New York: Morrow, 1974.

Whitney, C. V. *High Peaks.* New York: Mason/Charter, 1977.

Whyte, William H., Jr. *The Organization Man.* New York: Doubleday Anchor, 1957.

Widener, Peter Arrell Brown. *Without Drums.* New York: G. P. Putnam's Sons, 1940.

Wiseman, Thomas. *The Money Motive.* New York: Random House, 1974.

Wixen, Burton N., M.D. *Children of the Rich.* New York: Crown, 1973.

Wright, William. *Ball: A Year in the Life of the April in Paris Extravaganza.* New York: Saturday Review Press, 1972.

———. *Heiress: The Rich Life of Marjorie Merriweather Post.* New York: New Republic Books, 1978.

Zilg, Gerard Calby. *Du Pont: Behind the Nylon Curtain.* Englewood Cliffs, N.J.: Prentice-Hall, 1974.

Newspapers

Atlanta Constitution
Beacon Journal (Akron, Ohio)
Benton County Democrat
  (Bentonville, Ark.)
Boston Globe
Bridgeport Post-Telegram
Chicago Sun Times
Chicago Tribune
Daily Advance (Dover, N.J.)
Daily Oklahoman (Oklahoma
  City, Okla.)
Daily Record (Morristown, N.J.)
Dallas Morning News
Dallas Times Herald
Democrat & Chronicle
  (Rochester, N.Y.)
The Denver Post
Desert Sun (Palm Springs, Calif.)
Detroit Free Press
Detroit News
Evening Journal/Morning News
  (Wilmington, Del.)
Figaro (New Orleans, La.)
Fort Lauderdale News
Fort Worth Star-Telegram
Houston Chronicle
Houston Post
Indianapolis Star-News
Jacksonville Journal
Kansas City Star
Long Island Press
L.A. Free Press

Los Angeles Herald-Examiner
Los Angeles Times
Miami Herald
Milwaukee Journal
Minneapolis Star & Tribune
Newark News
The News American (Baltimore,
  Md.)
New York Herald Tribune
New York Journal American
New York Post
New York Daily News
New York Times
Oakland Tribune
Palm Beach Daily News
Palm Beach Post-Times
Philadelphia Daily News/
  Inquirer
Philadelphia Evening & Sunday
  Bulletin
Pittsburgh Post Gazette
Pittsburgh Press
The Plain Dealer (Cleveland,
  Ohio)
Plainfield Courier-News
  (Plainfield, N.J.)
Providence Journal
Rogers Daily News (Rogers,
  Ark.)
Rocky Mountain News
St. Louis Post-Dispatch
St. Petersburg Times-Independent

Newspapers (continued)

San Francisco Bay Guardian

San Francisco Examiner & Chronicle

The Society Section (Dallas, Texas)

Springfield Daily News/Republican/Union (Springfield, Mass.)

Star-Gazette (Elmira, N.Y.)

The Sunpapers (Baltimore, Md.)

Times Leader/Evening News (Wilkes-Barre, Pa.)

Times-Picayune/States-Item (New Orleans, La.)

Tulsa World/Tribune

The Wall Street Journal

The Washington Post

Washington Star-News

Westchester Rockland Newspapers (White Plains, N.Y.)

Wichita Eagle/Beacon

Wilmington Star (Wilmington, N.C.)

Magazines

America
American Heritage
Antiques
Art in America
Art News
Atlanta Magazine
Atlantic Monthly
Aviation Week
Boston Magazine
Business Week
Chicagoan
Christian Century
Clearing House
Collier's
Duns Review
Financial World
Forbes
FORTUNE
Good Housekeeping
Harper's Bazaar
Holiday
House & Garden
Ladies' Home Journal
Life
Look
Los Angeles Magazine

Mademoiselle
McCall's
The Nation
Nation's Business
National Review
New Jersey Monthly
New Republic
New West Magazine
New York Magazine
New Yorker
Newsweek
Palm Beach Life
Palm Springs Life
Parade
Philadelphia Magazine
Presbyterian Life
Ramparts
Reader's Digest
San Diego Magazine
San Francisco Magazine
Saturday Evening Post
Saturday Review
Science
Society
Sports Illustrated

Magazines (continued)

Texas Monthly
Time
Town & Country
Travel

U.S. News & World Report
Vogue
Washingtonian Magazine
Yachting